THE LETTERS OF

LAFAYETTE TO WASHINGTON

1777-1799

Memoirs of the
AMERICAN PHILOSOPHICAL SOCIETY
Held at Philadelphia
For Promoting Useful Knowledge
Volume 115

THE LETTERS OF

Lafayette

TO

Washington

1777-1799

Edited by
LOUIS GOTTSCHALK

Second Printing, edited and revised by
Louis Gottschalk and Shirley A. Bill

THE AMERICAN PHILOSOPHICAL SOCIETY
Independence Square · Philadelphia
1976

Copyright 1944 by Helen Fahnstock Hubbard
Renewed 1971 by Louis Gottschalk

Reprinted 1976 by permission of Mrs. Louis Gottschalk

Library of Congress Catalog Card Number 76-8599
International Standard Book Number 0-87169-115-9
US ISSN 0065-9738

Preface

Historians frequently abuse the concept of personal influence. The assumption that an older and more illustrious individual affected the conduct of a susceptible young contemporary is easy to make and hard to refute when there is an apparent similarity of conduct on the part of the two men.

Seldom, however, does the biographer have as much evidence for such a belief as in the case of Washington and Lafayette. Not only did other contemporaries insist that Lafayette's imitation of the American general was obvious, but Lafayette himself freely admitted that he regarded his friend as a model. The Prince de Talleyrand, after having observed Lafayette for about half a century stated that "he always acts as though he follows someone else's advice,"[1] and the Italo-American Philip Mazzei, who knew both Washington and Lafayette personally, expressed the more explicit opinion that Lafayette "made it a law to imitate General Washington in everything."[2]

The reader of the letters that are presented in this volume will find Lafayette himself time and again frankly avowing his spiritual indebtedness to his "father and friend." One such avowal will suffice here to illustrate them all. "I hope you will approuve [*sic*] my conduct," he wrote in his letter of June 29, 1782, "and in every thing I do I first consider what your opinion would be had I an opportunity to consult it." These avowals, taken together with Lafayette's conduct and his frequent declarations of devotion, leave no doubt about the genuineness of Washington's influence upon him. "It is an extraordinary phenomenon," said Mme de Staël, who well knew the social milieu from which Lafayette came, "that a character like M. de Lafayette should have developed among the highest ranks of the French nobility."[3] At least a partial explanation of that phenomenon

---

[1] Duc de Broglie (ed.), *Memoirs of the Prince de Talleyrond* (tr. R. Ledos de Beaufort; 5 vols.; New York, 1891-92), I, 52-53.

[2] *Recherches historiques et politiques sur les États-Unis de l'Amérique septenrionale* (4 vols.; Paris, 1788), IV, 117 and n.

[3] Duc de Broglie and Baron de Staël (eds.), *Considérations sur les principaux événemens de la Révolution française* (3 vols.; Paris, 1818), I, 271.

—as Mme de Staël herself recognized—is to be found in the high regard of the young French aristocrat for the austere Virginia planter and soldier.

The friendliness of Lafayette for Washington developed rather quickly. That of Washington for Lafayette was not only slower to mature but even at its highest point was circumspect and restrained. That was not only because of the Gallic ebullience of the one and the Anglo-Saxon sternness of the other; it was also because Lafayette, always ready to go to great pains to oblige his friends, seldom felt any inhibitions about asking favors, though Washington sometimes found it embarrassing to grant them. No matter how prominent Lafayette became, Washington always remained in a position of greater prestige; and politics frequently imposed restraints upon friendly considerations.

The old story that Lafayette came to America because he had heard the Duke of Gloucester speak with admiration of the Americans must now be discarded.[4] He came for several reasons but prominent among them was the instigation of the Comte de Broglie, who—probably without Lafayette's suspecting it—was hopeful of becoming commander-in-chief of the American army. Nevertheless, when the Marquis de Lafayette, an inexperienced stripling still in his teens, applied to Congress for a major-general's commission in the Continental Army, he said that one of his principal motives in coming to America had been to see service under General Washington.

Lafayette did not meet Washington until shortly after receiving his major-general's commission. The occasion of their first meeting was a dinner at the City Tavern in Philadelphia on July 31, 1777. Washington invited the young soldier to become a member of his military "family" for the ensuing campaign. Lafayette was struck by the majesty of Washington's face and figure; and Washington felt that the short young Frenchman with sparkling hazel eyes, long pointed nose, receding brow and reddish hair who had just been made a volunteer major-general by Congress was worthy of "esteem and attachment."[5]

[4]Louis Gottschalk, *Lafayette comes to America* (Chicago, 1935), pp. 50-51 and *passim*.
[5]Louis Gottschalk, *Lafayette joins the American Army* (Chicago, 1937), pp. 27-29. Hereafter quotations that are not otherwise accredited will be borrowed either from this work or its sequel, *Lafayette and the close of the American Revolution* (Chicago, 1942).

Lafayette, assuming that Congress intended the actual command of a division to accompany the rank of major-general, expected that the division would be given to him whenever Washington saw fit to do so. He therefore importuned the commander-in-chief, who had begun to resent foreign soldiers of fortune who expected high rank in the American army, for the actual command of a division. Upon inquiry Washington found that Lafayette's appointment had been purely honorary. It might have gone hard with the impatient volunteer if, at the same time, Washington had not received a request from Franklin, then in France, to take special care of the marquis, who had influential connections in his own country.

Washington took an early occasion to speak to the marquis. While informing Lafayette that certain objections to his being given a command existed in Congress, he attempted to soften that information. He assured the boy, at some length, of his own friendly and paternal regard. In doing so he acted partly from policy, partly from genuine liking. Lafayette, who had lost his own father when he was two and had developed no intimacy with the older men of his acquaintance, responded immediately. From the time of that conversation at Germantown in August, 1777, he gave to his "dear general" the most ardent devotion—part friendship, part hero-worship. Still little more than a boy, he took with complete absence of restraint the mature Washington's invitation to regard him as both friend and father.

Lafayette did not, however, abandon his plea for a command— to the annoyance of the commander-in-chief. The assignment of a division to Baron Dekalb, whose commission bore the same date as Lafayette's though his professional experience was at that time clearly greater, was a particularly embarrassing circumstance. Fortunately for both Lafayette and Washington, who continued to feel the weight of the marquis' French connections, the young volunteer had been acquiring an enviable military record. Washington himself had cited him for bravery in the battle of Brandywine on September 11, 1777, where he received a leg wound that put him in the hospital for several weeks; and at the battle of Gloucester, on November 25, he had distinguished himself for both skill and gallantry. Washington therefore felt that he could fairly recommend that Congress give

Lafayette the command he solicited. The youthful Frenchman had, Washington said, much of the military ardor which distinguished the nobility of his country as a class, and besides, if he were to fail in his desire, he would probably return in disgust to France—a contingency which might have "unfavorable consequences." So Lafayette, who had recently passed his twentieth birthday, obtained his division.

The marquis was solicitous not only for himself but for the French officers who had come with him to America. His persistent requests that they be given commissions—requests which Washington felt that he could not support without unfairness to American officers who usually, unlike the Frenchmen, had already rendered service to the cause—sometimes put a severe strain upon the commander-in-chief. Fortunately Washington also realized that Lafayette compensated for his solicitude for Frenchmen in America by his efforts to present the American viewpoint as favorably as possible to his compatriots. "I do most devoutly wish," the commander-in-chief confessed, "that we had not a single foreigner among us, except the Marquis de Lafayette, who acts upon very different principles from those which govern the rest."[6]

The growing friendliness between the two soldiers reached a critical point shortly after Lafayette obtained his division. In the fairly intimate circle of French officers in the Continental Army, among the most cordial was the French-Irish soldier Thomas Conway, brigadier-general. Conway had become one of the several persons in prominent positions in the American army and Congress who doubted Washington's ability as a commander-in-chief and hoped for other leaders. The activity of this group—never closely or formally organized—became sufficiently well known to induce Washington and his "family" to believe that there was a veritable cabal to oust him. The opponents of Washington secured conspicuous honors for Conway, though Washington was known to distrust him. Consequently historians have frequently referred to this episode as the "Conway cabal," although the "cabal" seems never to have been any more than a confidential understanding among some opponents of

[6] Washington to Gouverneur Morris, July 24, 1778, J. C. Fitzpatrick (ed.), *The writings of George Washington from the original manuscript sources, 1745-1799* (37 vols.; Washington, 1931-40), XII, 227-28.

Washington and Conway was not the most important of them.[7]

The existence of a group that sought to replace Washington, as well as Conway's association with it, was not at first realized by Lafayette. Conway had won the marquis' good will because the older man was an excellent officer and a genial companion, because they had some mutual friends in France, and because they had planned together certain grandiose schemes that would enable both of them to play more brilliant rôles in the war. Their boldest plan involved an attack upon India.

When Lafayette received his division, the prospect of winning his meed of glory in America seemed brighter than any that a remote India might hold forth. And at the same time he began to believe that there existed a faction hostile to Washington and that Conway was a member of it. He did not hesitate in his choice of allegiance between the two men. "I am now fixed to your fate," he informed the commander-in-chief on December 30, 1777, "and I shall follow it and sustain it as well by my sword as by all means in my power."

Conway's partisans, not at first realizing what Lafayette's attitude toward Washington actually was and knowing only his passion for "glory," persisted in trying to exploit the marquis' prestige against the interest of Washington. They secured Lafayette's appointment by Congress to the independent command of an expedition against Canada, whose success was bound to cast Washington's military reputation in the shade. Conway was appointed second in command. Lafayette saw in this maneuver an opportunity to reconcile his own glory with his loyalty to Washington. He demanded and obtained another second. Dekalb superseded Conway, who now found himself third in authority. At the same time Lafayette made clear his devotion to Washington, taking an especially keen delight in having obliged the Board of War, whose members he suspected of ill-will toward his hero, to drink a toast to the commander-in-chief. He also protested against the independence of his expedition from Washington's command, though not hard enough to secure an alteration of the status that had been conferred upon him. Washington remained carefully aloof from the whole affair, except to write

[7]Cf. Bernhard Knollenberg, *Washington and the Revolution. A Reappraisal. Gates, Conway, and the Continental Congress* (New York, 1940), pp. 37-92, and Gottschalk, *Lafayette joins the American Army*, pp. 65-165. See also the latter's review of the former's book in *Journal of Modern History*, XIII (1941), 97-98.

to his "dear Marquis" consoling letters as the bungling of the expedition increased the young man's despair. Through no fault of Lafayette's, the proposed invasion proved abortive, and the discredit of its failure fell upon Conway and the Board of War. Lafayette returned to Valley Forge (having missed the worst part of the winter's suffering of the Continental Army) and soon added to his military reputation by his skillful tactics at Barren Hill (May 20, 1778).

The battle of Monmouth Court House (June 28, 1778), in which General Charles Lee's conduct laid him open to the charges both of disobedience to the orders of Washington and of incompetence, revealed to Lafayette another enemy of his adored leader. Lafayette, who had been on good terms with Lee, had not known before of Lee's sympathy with the opponents of Washington. Although Lafayette's conduct in this battle won him no military citations, the result of the engagement, so far as Lafayette and Washington were personally concerned, was to bring them closer together. On the night of the battle they rested on the same military cloak together and spoke of Lee.

Meanwhile, France had formally entered the war. Lafayette now assumed the rôle of principal liaison officer between the American and French forces. Washington, who had often been annoyed when Lafayette had exercised his talents on behalf of the French soldiers of fortune, now set considerable store by the young man's efforts. He sent him to Rhode Island, where a naval expedition under Count d'Estaing had arrived and was expected to help the American army to recapture Newport. A bad storm wrought havoc with Estaing's fleet, and the French admiral insisted that he must withdraw to Boston and refit his vessels. Feeling ran high on both sides. French sailors were attacked and killed in the streets of Boston. Lafayette's sensibilities as a Frenchman were outraged by the manner in which the American generals in New England spoke of Estaing. But Washington knew how to soothe his young friend's resentment. He appealed to Lafayette's love of publicity, as well as his genuine devotion to France, America, and his general. "America esteems your virtues and your services, and admires the principles upon which you act," wrote Washington.[8] "Your countrymen in our army look up to you as their patron. The Count and his officers con-

[8]September 1, 1778, Fitzpatrick, *Writings of Washington*, XII, 382-83.

sider you as a man high in rank, and high in estimation, here and in France; and I, your friend, have no doubt but that you will use your utmost endeavours to restore harmony, that the honour, glory, and mutual interest of the two nation's [*sic*] may be promoted and cemented in the firmest manner."

While Washington upon occasion thus appealed to the young man's ambition to play a notable rôle in affairs, while he also from the first encouraged in him an independent spirit by inviting criticism and suggestions with regard to military matters—an invitation of which Lafayette made frequent use—Washington never permitted himself to indulge his friend's love of glory when the marquis' projects seemed to him inimical to the best interests of the United States. Toward the close of the year 1778 Lafayette was again deeply involved with members of the Congress in another proposal for a Canadian expedition. This plan was defeated only by the most strenuous exertions of the two men who were his best friends among Americans in high office—Henry Laurens, president of Congress, and Washington himself. Washington afterward let Lafayette know what his opinion in the matter was, but he took care to conceal from his young friend the degree to which his influence had been responsible for thwarting the cherished plan.

About this time Lafayette went back to France on furlough. The parting of the two men was "touching and painful indeed." When Lafayette recalled it in later years,[9] he could not help remarking that, though Washington was frequently brusque, he had himself never experienced anything but kindness from his past commander. And as for Lafayette's attitude toward Washington? "How could he have been anything but cherished by his disciple—he who, uniting all that is good with all that is great, was even more sublime in his virtues than in his talents? As a simple soldier, he would have been the bravest; as an obscure citizen, all his neighbors would have respected him; with a heart as upright as his spirit, he judged himself as he did other matters. In creating him expressly for this revolution, Nature did herself honor, and the better to exhibit her handiwork, she put him in a position where no one of his qualities would have sufficed if it had not been enforced by all the others." Before

[9] *Mémoires, correspondance et manuscrits du général Lafayette publiés par sa famille* (6 vols.; Paris, 1837-38), I, 62.

Lafayette sailed, Washington sent him a letter affirming that "there is no need of fresh proofs to convince you either of my affection for you personally, or of the high opinion I entertain of your military talents and merit."[10] This letter contained another addressed to Franklin, still in Paris, in which Washington declared his "very particular friendship" for Lafayette and bespoke for him "whatever services you may have it in your power to render him."[11]

During Lafayette's sojourn in France (1779-80), his son was born. The baby was named George Washington Lafayette "as a tribute of respect and love for my dear friend." Washington's letters at this period reveal a marked increase in the warmth of his feeling for Lafayette. "Your ardent and persevering efforts," he wrote, "not only in America, but since your return to France, to serve the United States; your polite attention to Americans, and your strict and uniform friendship for *me*, has ripened the first impressions of the esteem and attachment, which I imbibed for you, into such perfect love and gratitude, that neither time nor absence can impair." Washington went on to say that he would welcome Lafayette "in all the warmth of friendship to Columbia's shores" whether as an officer in the French army or as a major-general in the American army again, "or whether, after our swords and spears have given place to the plowshare and pruning-hook, I see you as a private gentleman, a friend and companion."[12] And one day when the French ambassador and his secretary came to visit the American commander, Washington asked about Lafayette with unconcealed tenderness, declaring that he knew no nobler or finer soul and that he loved him as his own son.

When Lafayette returned to America (April, 1780) bearing the military recommendations of his government, he became more than ever the liaison officer between the Americans and the French, and especially between Washington and Rochambeau, commander of the French expeditionary force whose sailing the marquis had helped to arrange. Upon the arrival of Rochambeau in America, Washington, who was unable at the time to leave his post, sent Lafayette to represent him at a joint conference in Rhode Island. He assured Rochambeau that he had the greatest confidence in Lafayette. In agreement with Rochambeau, who somewhat resented his youthful

[10] December 29, 1778, Fitzpatrick, *Writings of Washington*, XIII, 460-61.
[11] December 28 [29?], 1778, *ibid.*, p. 459.
[12] September 30, 1779, *ibid.*, XVI, 369-70.

countryman's aggressiveness, Washington was soon called upon to overrule Lafayette's desire for an immediate combined attack upon New York. Yet he gave testimony of his confidence in Lafayette's abilities by appointing him, on his return from Rhode Island, to the command of a picked infantry corps known as the Light Division, which was to form the vanguard of the Continental Army in the event of an attack on New York, and he continued to encourage Lafayette to make schemes and feints towards that end.

Lafayette also served as interpreter and secretary in the meeting between Rochambeau and Washington which occurred in Hartford, Connecticut, in September, 1780. It was on the return from this meeting that both generals nearly fell victims to the treachery of Benedict Arnold. Only the chance arrest of the British major John André just at the time that they were visiting the Arnolds saved West Point from falling into British hands. As a result of the meeting at Hartford Lafayette became convinced that the command of American operations should be unified under Washington more explicitly than it then was or than Rochambeau seemed willing to permit, and in January, 1781, he so wrote to the French ministers, Castries and Vergennes.

To Lafayette's disappointment, the Light Division was disbanded before it had seen action. As the winter of 1780-81 promised to be a very dull one from the military standpoint, he thought up a plan for a Spanish diversion in which he would participate; but, like the proposed Canadian expeditions and the attack on New York, this did not appear to Washington to be feasible. Instead, Washington gave Lafayette, in February 1781, the command of another body, made up largely of light infantry. It was intended to check Arnold's depredations in Virginia, and it nearly captured the renegade. Arnold was relieved by reinforcements sent from New York, however.

Lafayette's expedition started back to headquarters, but it was soon ordered to Virginia again. General Nathanael Greene, who was operating farther south, seemed in danger of being crushed between the British forces in Virginia and in North Carolina, where Lord Cornwallis was then commanding. Repeatedly Lafayette urged Washington to permit him to return north to participate in the attack that he momentarily expected would be made on New York, but Washington preferred that he remain in Virginia.

As events turned out, Lafayette won his greatest military glory because of Washington's advice, which never quite took the form of orders. For his own skill in keeping safely out of the way of Cornwallis, who had come to Virginia, and Clinton's orders to Cornwallis to take a position on the coast at Yorktown from which his troops could easily be transported elsewhere made it appear as if Lafayette had forced Cornwallis to retreat before him. And in fact, Cornwallis's position now became so difficult that when Admiral de Grasse, commander of the French West Indies fleet, sailed into the waters around Yorktown, Lafayette with the aid of De Grasse's men and boats was able to bottle up the British. Cornwallis was obliged to surrender when the French-American army under Washington and Rochambeau came up and laid siege to the town. In general orders following the victory, Washington cited Lafayette along with Generals Lincoln and Steuben for his part in the siege and in a subsequent letter to Lafayette spoke warmly of his "military conduct and other important services in the course of the last campaign."[13]

Lafayette shortly returned to France. As his boat left its anchorage in Boston harbor the young devotee bade his paragon farewell (December 23, 1781): "We are going to sail, and my last adieu I must dedicate to my Beloved General. Adieu, my dear General, I know your heart so well that I am sure no distance can alter your attachement [sic] to me. With the same candor, I assure you that my love, my respect, my gratitude for you are above expressions, that on the moment of leaving you I more than ever feel the strength of those friendly ties that for ever bind me to you, and that I anticipate the pleasure, the most wished for pleasure to be again with you, and by my zeal and services to gratify the feelings of my respect and affection." To Washington's nephew George Augustine Washington, he wrote (December 22, 1781) to ask for copies "by some sergeant that writes a fair hand" of his letters to the general. "When I grow old," he said, "I will find great satisfaction in reading over our correspondence during last campaign."[14] It is very likely that the letterbook now in the Hubbard Collection is the one that was prepared in answer to this request.

[13] November 15, 1781, *ibid.*, XXIII, 340-42.
[14] Gottschalk, *Lafayette and the close of the American Revolution*, p. 345.

Lafayette played a considerable role in the peace negotiations of 1782-83. The signing of the peace preliminaries found him at Cadiz, second in command of a combined Spanish-French expedition that was intended to carry the war to the West Indies and Canada. Hoping to be the first to convey the news of peace to America, he sent his personal servant on the corvette "Triomphe" with letters to Washington and others. "Were you but such a man as Julius Cæsar or the King of Prussia," he wrote Washington (February 5, 1783), "I should almost be sorry for you at the end of the great tragedy where you are acting such a part. But with my dear General I rejoice at the blessings of a peace where our noble ends have been secured. Remember our Valley Forge times, and from a recollection of past dangers and labours, we still will be more pleased at our present comfortable situation. What a sense of pride and satisfaction I feel when I think of the times that have determined my engaging in the American cause! As for you, my dear General, who truly can say you have done all this, what must your virtuous and good heart feel on the happy instant where the Revolution you have made is now firmly established. I cannot but envy the happiness of my grand children when they will be about celebrating and worshipping your name. To have had one of their ancestors among your soldiers, to know he had the good fortune to be the friend of your heart, will be the eternal honour in which they shall glory."

The end of Lafayette's career in the American Revolution was the beginning of his career in French politics. In the many progressive schemes that he now devised, Washington was somehow always involved—whether it was a plan to emancipate the Negro, to promote commerce between France and the United States, to grant religious toleration to the Protestants, or to spread the gospel of Mesmerism. The friendship of Lafayette and Washington became so well-known in France that his enemies were soon to call him *le Washington français* in derision. Conscientiously the French aristocrat studied his republican model. The imitation consisted not only in minor rules of conduct such as the refusal to accept pay for public services and to avoid hereditary distinctions, but also in Lafayette's conception of his own rôle in French politics. He thought of himself as both his country's liberator from royal tyranny and her defender against "anarchy," and at the same time cherished the ambition to be, like Washington, a great military leader. The imitation was not purely egocentric, for Lafayette by this time had really acquired liberal ideals that were a consequence of his American experience in general and his devotion to Washington in particular.

Lafayette had hoped to persuade his general to visit Europe, but repeated hints and invitations did not induce Washington to accept. To one invitation, more explicit than the others, the "beloved general" replied: "At length, my dear Marquis, I am become a private citizen on the banks of the Potomac, and under the shadow of my own vine and my own fig-tree, free from the bustle of a camp and the busy scenes of public life, I am solacing myself with those tranquil enjoyments, of which the soldier who is ever in pursuit of fame, the statesman whose wakeful days and sleepless nights are spent in devising schemes to promote the welfare of his own, perhaps the ruin of other countries, as if this globe were insufficient for us all, and the courtier who is always watching the countenance of his prince, in hopes of catching a gracious smile, can have very little conception. I am not only retired from all public employments, but I am retiring within myself; and shall be able to view the solitary walk, and tread the paths of private life with heartfelt satisfaction. Envious of none, I am determined to be pleased with all; and this my dear friend, being the order for my march, I will move gently down the stream of life, until I sleep with my fathers. . . . I thank you most sincerely, my dear Marqs., for your kind invitation to your house, if I should come to Paris. At present I see but little prospect of such a voyage, the deranged situation of my private concerns, occasioned by an absence of almost nine years, and an entire disregard of all private business during that period, will not only suspend, but put it forever out of my power to gratify this wish. This not being the case with you, come with Madame la Fayette and view me in my domestic walks. I have often told you, and repeat it again, that no man could receive you in them with more friendship and affection than I should do."[15]

From the moment of his return to France, Lafayette had contemplated another visit to America. He had finally made up his mind to go probably before Washington's invitation reached him. On March 9, 1784, he wrote, "I want to tell you that Mde de Lafayette and my three children are well, and that all of us in the family

[15] February 1, 1784, Fitzpatrick, *Writings of Washington*, XXVII, 317-20.

heartly [*sic*] join to present their dutiful affectionate compliments to Mrs. Washington and yourself. Tell her that I hope soon to thank her for a dish of tea at Mount Vernon. Yes, my dear General, before the month of June is over you will see a vessel coming up Pottowmack, and out of that vessel will your friend jump with a panting heart and all the feelings of perfect happiness."

But it was not until August 4, 1784, that Lafayette reached New York. Two weeks elapsed before he got to Mount Vernon, where he spent eleven days, learning to know his general's family and household better and establishing himself in the affection of all of them. Other interests and duties then took him elsewhere, and he did not return to Mount Vernon again until November. Washington went to meet him at Richmond, where the towns was kept agog for several days with balls and civic receptions in honor of its two illustrious guests. Traveling together, on November 24 they reached Mount Vernon, where Lafayette stayed only four days. Washington accompanied him as far as Annapolis and put him on the road to Baltimore before he returned home. They parted on December 1, 1784, never to meet again.[16] Washington had guessed that this would be their last meeting. Shortly after he reached Mount Vernon he wrote Lafayette: "In the moment of our separation upon the road as I travelled, and every hour since, I felt all that love, respect and attachment for you, with which length of years, close connexion and your merits have inspired me. I often asked myself, as our carriages distended, whether that was the last sight I ever should have of you? And tho' I wished to say no, my fears answered yes. I called to mind the days of my youth, and found they had long since fled to return no more; that I was now descending the hill I had been 52 years climbing, and that tho' I was blessed with a good constitution, I was of a short lived family and might soon expect to be entombed in the dreary mansions of my fathers. These things darkened the shades and gave a gloom to the picture, consequently to my prospects of seeing you again; but I will not repine, I have had my day."[17]

When Lafayette received this letter he was on board the "Nymphe" in New York harbor, ready to return to France. His

[16] J. Bennett Nolan, *Lafayette in America day by day* (Baltimore, 1934), pp. 217-39; Washington to Knox, December 5, 1784, Fitzpatrick, *Writings of Washington*, XXVIII, 5.

[17] December 8, 1784, Fitzpatrick, *Writings of Washington*, XXVIII, 7.

whole soul, he replied (December 21, 1784), rebelled at the idea that he might not see his "beloved general" again. "Could I harbour it an instant, indeed, my dear general, it would make [me] miserable. I well see you never will go to France. The unexpressible pleasure of embracing you in my house, of well coming [he meant *welcoming*] you in a family where your name is adored, I do not much expect to experience. But to you I shall return, and in the walls of Mount Vernon we shall yet often speack of old times. My firm plan is to visit now and then my friends on this side of the Atlantick, and the most beloved of all friends I ever had, or ever will have any where, is too strong an inducement for me to return to him, not to think that, when ever it is possible, I will renew my so pleasing visits to Mount Vernon.... Adieu, adieu, my dear General. It is with an unexpressible pain that I feel I am going to be severed from you by the Atlantick. Every thing that admiration, respect, gratitude, friendship, and filial love can inspire is combined in my affectionate heart to devote me most tenderly to you. In your friendship I find a delight which words cannot express. Adieu, my dear General. It is not without emotion that I write this word—altho' I know I shall soon visit you again.... Adieu, adieu."

But, as had so often happened in the past, Washington was right and Lafayette was mistaken. They never saw each other again. The events of the French Revolution soon swallowed up *le Washington français*. His letters became fewer, though sometimes lengthier, because of the tremendous events that Lafayette now had to tell about; and some of those he wrote never were delivered to their destination. No letters have been found for the period from May 25, 1788 to January 12, 1790, though Lafayette assured Washington in his letter of March 17, 1790, that he had written some and they must have been lost. His first letter after that gap gives testimony of his awareness of Washington's influence upon him. "How often, my beloved General, have I wanted your wise advices and friendly support!" When the Bastille was demolished, Lafayette sent one of its keys to Washington. "Give me leave, my dear General," he wrote on March 17, 1790, "to present you with a picture of the Bastille just as it looked a few days after I had ordered its demolition, with the main kea [*sic*] of that fortress of despotism. It is a tribute which I owe as a son to my adoptive father, as an aid de camp to my General, as a

Missionary of Liberty to its Patriarch." It seemed somehow appropriate that the English liberal Thomas Paine was the one to whom the *Washington français* entrusted the delivery to the American patriarch of that "token of victory gained by Liberty over Despotism."[18] Nor did it seem incongruous that Washington should send in return a pair of shoe buckles—"not for the value of the thing, my dear Marquis, but as a memorial and because they are the manufacture of the City [of New York]."[19]

The revolution in France proved harder for Lafayette to manage than Washington had found the American Revolution to be—perhaps because Lafayette was only an imitation of Washington or perhaps because the problems of France were less solvable than those of the United States. Lafayette soon found himself in opposition to the anti-monarchical Jacobins, who eventually became the dominant party in France. When they attacked the Tuileries Palace and deposed Louis XVI, Lafayette determined to flee to America. He did not succeed. He and his party were arrested by the Austrians, with whom France was now at war, and spent the next five years (1792-97) in several prisons in Prussia and Austria.

During that time Washington aided Lafayette generously though with caution. He sent 2310 guilders out of his own pocket to help Mme de Lafayette. He requested Thomas Jefferson as secretary of state to instruct American representatives abroad to make "all prudent efforts" to aid his friend.[20] But Washington could not forget that he was president of the United States as well as the friend of Lafayette, that the United States government was trying to preserve a strict neutrality in the war between the new French Republic and its numerous enemies, and that there was rapidly developing an acute conflict between pro-French and anti-French factions of the American people which he must do nothing to inflame. And so when Mme de Lafayette requested an American mission to demand her husband's release, he felt obliged to reply that such measures were "perhaps not exactly those" which he could adopt nor perhaps the

[18] Washington to Lafayette, August 11, 1790, Fitzpatrick, *Writings of Washington*, XXXI, 85.
[19] *Ibid.*, p. 88.
[20] Jefferson to Gouverneur Morris *et al.*, March 15, 1793, quoted in S. F. Bemis, "The United States and Lafayette," *Daughters of the American Revolution Magazine*, LVIII (1924), 408.

ones "most likely under actual circumstances to obtain our object."[21] But he assured her that he was not resting content with "inactive wishes" for Lafayette's liberation. "My affection to his nation and to himself are unabated, and notwithstanding the line of separation which has been unfortunately drawn between them I am confident that both have been led on by a pure love of liberty, and a desire to secure public happiness; and I shall deem that among the most consoling moments of my life which shall see them reunited in the end, as they were in the beginning, of their virtuous enterprise." Probably what Washington meant by implying efforts beyond "inactive wishes" was his part in urging Congress to appropriate a sum of money large enough to provide Lafayette with relief as compensation for his hitherto unaccepted salary as a general officer. Congress did appropriate nearly $25,000 for this purpose.

At about the same time, Washington planned to make a private appeal to King Frederick William II of Prussia for the release of Lafayette on parole. Washington proposed to be careful to stress that he separated himself from his official position in this instance, and acted on an "impulse of friendship" and out of "personal and affectionate anxiety."[22] A cabinet meeting on the subject led to the decision to send such a letter to Berlin by James Marshall, but Marshall was to be instructed not to deliver it unless it seemed likely to meet with a favorable response. Marshall visited Prince Henry, the king's uncle, who was an old acquaintance of Lafayette, but nothing came of his good offices since by that time Emperor Francis II had asked for the transfer of Lafayette to an Austrian jail. Lafayette and his fellow-prisoners were soon on their way to the dungeon at Olmütz.

Shortly afterward, the president's namesake, George Washington Lafayette, succeeded in making his way with a tutor to the United States. Their arrival could not have been more awkwardly timed, for public opinion in the United States was torn by the commercial treaty with England which John Jay had negotiated and which was considered by the pro-French elements of the population as too friendly to England. Washington could not afford to offend France and its American partisans, he felt, by befriending the son of

[21] *Ibid.*, p. 409; Fitzpatrick, *Writings of Washington*, XXXII, p. 390.
[22] Bemis, *loc. cit.*, p. 411; Fitzpatrick, *Writings of Washington*, XXXIII, 242-43, n. 77.

one who had been proscribed by the existing French government. He preferred therefore — perhaps too cautiously — that his namesake should not come to live with him and arranged for him to live in New York incognito under the family name of Motier. Only in April, 1796 (George had arrived in America in August, 1795) did the boy come to Philadelphia to make his home temporarily with his father's beloved friend.

George's pleas[23] and the representations of Dr. Justus Erich Bollmann, who had himself until recently been shut up in an Austrian prison because he had tried to help Lafayette escape from Olmütz, induced Washington to try again to make a personal attempt to obtain his friend's freedom. This time he addressed to the Emperor Francis "a *private* letter," entreating that Lafayette "be permitted to come to this country on such conditions and under such restrictions as your Majesty may think it expedient to prescribe."[24] Whether the letter ever reached the emperor is not clear. It would have made small difference in any case. The negotiations of peace between France and Austria, made possible by the victories of General Napoleon Bonaparte, resulted in the release of Lafayette as well as of his wife and two daughters, who had voluntarily joined him in his prison. The Austrian chancellor took pains to make it clear that the emperor had consented to the release of the prisoners largely because of "the particular interest which the United States appears to attach to it."[25]

For the Lafayettes there followed two years of exile, first in Hamburg, then in Holstein, then in Holland. George returned from Mount Vernon while they still lived in Holstein, and plans were soon afoot for the whole family to go to America and Mount Vernon. Mme de Lafayette's health, ruined by her voluntary imprisonment at Olmütz, did not, however, permit her to travel, and so the family stayed in Europe. It was probably just as well that they did, for to the scruples that had caused Washington to keep aloof from George Washington Lafayette for nearly a year after his arrival in America were now added the complications that resulted from the

[23] George W. Lafayette to Washington, December 25, 1795, Bemis, *loc. cit.* (sequel), p. 485.
[24] May 15, 1796, Fitzpatrick, *Writings of Washington*, XXXV, 45-46; cf. Bemis, *loc. cit.*, p. 487.
[25] Thugut to Buol-Schauenstein, September 13, 1797, Bemis, *loc. cit.*, p. 488.

undeclared war that the United States was then engaged in fighting on the high seas with France. Washington, though no longer president, was nevertheless vitally concerned with public policy. He stated his position frankly to Lafayette in order to impress upon him "the true cause" of his infrequent letters while assuring him that his friendship "had undergone no diminution or change." No one in the United States, he said, would receive Lafayette "with more ardent affection than I should after the differences between this country and France are adjusted and harmony between the nations is again restored. But it would be uncandid and incompatible with that friendship I have always professed for you to say (and on your own account) that I wish it before. For you may be assured, my dear Sir [no longer "my dear Marquis," for the French Revolution had abolished titles], that the scenes you wou'd meet with and the part you wou'd be stimulated to act in case of an open rupture or even if matters should remain in Statu quo, would be such as to place you in a situation in which no address or human prudence could free you from embarrassment. In a word you would lose the confidence of one party or the other, perhaps both, were you here under these circumstances." Washington went on rather testily to explain the conflicts among the American people, announcing that he had again assumed command of the American army to resist the pretensions of France.[26]

Washington never wrote to Lafayette again. Within a year he was dead, and Lafayette had meanwhile returned to a France dominated by Napoleon Bonaparte. Washington's will left to Lafayette "a pair of finely wrought steel pistols, taken from the enemy in the Revolutionary War."[27] The executors of Washington's estate sent them to Lafayette.

Eventually the letters that Lafayette had written to his "beloved general" also found their way into the archives of his château of Lagrange-Bléneau.[28] These letters remained in the Lafayette family until, following the First World War, they were offered privately for sale to Mrs. John Hubbard of New York City. Mrs. Hubbard was kind enough to put them in my care either in the original or in

[26] December 25, 1798, Fitzpatrick, *Writings of Washington*, XXXVII, 64-70.
[27] *Ibid.*, p. 286-87.
[28] Bushrod Washington to Lafayette, January 9, 1817, Hubbard Collection; Lafayette to Sparks, July 25, 1827, Harvard College Library.

microfilm copies for editorial purposes. More recently, Mrs. Hubbard presented the collection to Lafayette College, and Mr. Theodore Norton, librarian of the Van Wickle Library there, has also been most cooperative.

In order to diminish the editorial paraphernalia several procedures have here been used that may appear unorthodox. Proper names, for example, are seldom identified by footnotes. They fall into three categories: those too illustrious to need identification, those too obscure to be identifiable, and those neither too illustrious nor too obscure. Since the third category, for which alone footnotes would be more than ostentatious pedantry, are relatively few, the policy has been adopted of identifying in the "Index" all those identifiable. Frequent reminders to that effect have been scattered throughout the book for any who may overlook this apology.

References have seldom been made to the addresses and outside messages that are on the envelopes of some of these letters, nor to the crossings-out and corrections, sometimes in another hand—possibly that of Jared Sparks, who used and "edited" these manuscripts at the Château Lagrange-Bléneau. Fortunately such "editing" can usually be detected because Lafayette had the habit of crossing out with several strokes or a wavy line whereas the "editor" used a single stroke, leaving the words crossed out quite legible. In every such instance an effort has been made to arrive at Lafayette's original text.

We have tried also to present the errors of punctuation, orthography, grammar and idiom of the original, feeling that the constant improvement of Lafayette's English was not without interest and biographical importance. How easily that information can be lost will readily be obvious to the reader from the few letters (duly noted) that we have been obliged to copy from other printed collections whose editors have "Englished" Lafayette's style.

To have used the usual editorial *sic* for every error by Lafayette would have resulted in more trouble and confusion than helpfulness, and so it has been employed only sparingly. Nor have we tried to reproduce Lafayette's capitalization. In the first place it is not always clear when he meant a letter to be a capital; in the second place there were no rules that he followed about capitalization and the whole question seems to have been meaningless to him. We have on the other hand been careful to reproduce Lafayette's punctuation, because in that regard, except for the frequent use of dashes for periods, which he, and therefore we, have used interchangeably, he was more careful and regular.

We have also thought it desirable to give Lafayette's signature wherever it appeared, because it changed from time to time—not, as has so often been said, from *La Fayette* to *Lafayette*, for it was always either Lafayette or LaFayette (with no space between *La* and *Fayette*), but from *Marquis de Lafayette* to *Lafayette*. Often, indeed, in the early letters he used his title but it is now to be found crossed out—whether by himself or some later editor is not clear. In such cases we have not given the title.

Although the majority of the letters in this compilation have been published elsewhere, we have thought it wise to reproduce those that were published along with those that were unpublished, largely for the sake of completeness. It will be found, however, that the earlier publications are in remarkably few instances either complete or accurate. Most of them were based on the copies made by Jared Sparks and now in the Harvard College Library. Sparks's penchant for "improving" the text and for leaving out the parts that seemed to him, for one reason or another, objectionable, affected his own texts as well as those of others who depended upon him. In addition, most of the published letters for the period after 1781 are available only in French translation in Lafayette's *Mémoires*. In every instance that a letter was, so far as our researches could determine, hitherto entirely or largely unpublished, we have indicated that fact in a footnote—usually only by the single word *unpublished*. In every instance that the text was taken from some source other than the Hubbard Collection we have also indicated its source in a footnote. In every instance that the document existed in other than the original form in the Hubbard Collection and the original was available to us, we have borrowed our version from the original, indicating the source of the original likewise in a footnote. Where no indication to the contrary exists, the original forms part of the Hubbard Collection.

A great deal of care has been taken to verify the dates of each of the letters. We have found that Washington, though he may never have told a lie, was rather careless with datings. The dates in his endorsements often differ from those of Lafayette—sometimes because of the lack of clarity of Lafayette's handwriting, but often for no apparent reason whatsoever. Sometimes, too, Washington in his replies to Lafayette misdated the letters to which he was replying. Other editors of Lafayette's letters have also misdated them occasionally. In all such instances we have taken special pains to verify our datings. The reader who finds a reference elsewhere to a letter of a date not given in this collection will probably find that letter under another date which we considered the correct one.

It remains only to thank those who have helped me with this editorial task. To Mrs. Hubbard my thanks are especially due, for without her generosity this work could never have been prepared or published. To Mr. Edward Larocque Tinker, who first proposed to Mrs. Hubbard that I be permitted to edit her collection and has acted as adviser and advocate in many ways, I am also grateful. To Mr. Tinker, likewise, and to the Marchbanks Press this book owes most of its quality in format and design.

The staffs of the Lafayette College Library, the Library of Congress, the Harvard College Library, the Cornell University Library, the Historical Society of Pennsylvania, the Huntington Library, and the Morgan Library have been most cooperative. The Social Science Research Committee of the University of Chicago has supported my studies of Lafayette for many years. The investigations required to complete a compilation of this kind would have been impossible without that support. I wish to acknowledge my indebtedness to all of these institutions and their staffs.

Mr. Howard A. Vernon, Jr., prepared the manuscript copies of most of the letters and helped to discover which were the unpublished ones. Dr. Frances Acomb prepared the manuscript of many of the letters and likewise helped to discover the unpublished ones; she also helped to check all of them against the originals, microfilms or photostats, prepare the "Table of Contents," and write this "Preface." Miss Margaret Maddox and Mr. Roger Thompson also aided in preparing some of the manuscript. Miss Maddox, Mrs. Marie Rapoport, and my wife, Fruma Gottschalk, have aided me in the arduous tasks of proofreading and preparing the index. Without the loyal assistance of all these people, this work could not have been done in the time it took, and might not have been done at all.

Louis Gottschalk

Chicago, May 20, 1944.

Preface to The Second Printing

This book was first published in 1944. A privately printed, de luxe, limited edition of four hundred numbered copies, it was not easily accessible to libraries and scholars. The need for a more accessible reprint quickly became apparent, and since 1972, when copyright regulations permitted republication, this reissue has been in preparation.

In the intervening decades more authentic versions of eight letters of Lafayette to Washington have been placed at our disposal. A sizable collection of Lafayette papers (originally at his Château de Chavaniac) which Professor Gottschalk had sporadically examined when it was in the possession of the late Emmanuel Fabius, autograph dealer of Paris, has become readily available as the gift of Arthur H. Dean to the Cornell University Libraries. It contains complete contemporary copies, corrected in Lafayette's handwriting, of the two letters (Nos. 224 and 225, dated respectively April 19 and May 9, 1799) which appear below (pp. 381-385) in the incomplete French translation produced by the filiopietistic editors of the *Mémoires, correspondance et manuscrits du Général Lafayette* (Paris, 1837-1838). The complete English text of those two letters is now given in Appendix I (pp. 390-394). Appendix I also gives (pp. 389-390) hitherto unpublished passages (based upon the originals in the archives of the Society of the Cincinnati, Washington, D.C.) from two other letters (Nos. 165 and 167, dated December 25, 1783, and March 9, 1784, respectively, pp. 272-273, 276-277) which were not available in their entirety in 1944. In addition, the original text of No. 29, dated July 28, 1778 (p. 54), has been made available by the American Antiquarian Society, those of No. 108, dated April 18, 1781 (pp. 184-186), and of No. 131, dated August 24, 1781 (pp. 221-223), by the Library of Congress and that of No. 173, dated August 10, 1784, by the Hanzel Galleries, Chicago, Illinois.

A comparison of the versions of Lafayette's letters as reprinted here with those given in the first printing reveal many alterations of spelling and wording. Although Lafayette's English steadily improved, it never was as wholly free from error and Gallicisms as some of those who transcribed or edited his letters (and on whom reliance had to be placed in 1944) made it appear. Whenever, upon re-examining the manuscripts (or the reproductions thereof) used in 1944, we have detected misreadings, we have tried to make corrections that a decent respect for the authenticity of historical documents requires. Sometimes, indeed, the reader will find that the new version is less grammatical or orthographical than that of the 1944 edition. To ease the reader's task, we have placed the word AMENDED before the number of the twenty-one letters of which either text or the footnotes have been corrected or supplemented.[1] Amendments of the texts, index, or footnotes of the 1944 edition appear in Appendix II, Corrigenda and Addenda, and we have identified the change by page and line number. A supplementary index has also been provided for new materials not included in the 1944 Index.

That Lafayette wrote letters which so far remain unknown to us seems probable from his remark in his letter of May 9, 1799 (p. 391): "I find a greater proportion of my scribling has reached you than I had thought," thus implying that Washington had not received all of his "scribling." We have never found the letter of April 19, 1783, mentioned on p.263n. or that of September 5, 1788, mentioned on p.245n. or that written between June 6, 1791, and January 22, 1792, mentioned on p.358n. Furthermore, a letter written between June and August, 1789, has been lost, but we know a portion of its content. Busy as Lafayette was, he expressed his delight that Washington had been elected president of the United States, and in that letter (as he afterward recorded) he wrote "that this choice gave him all the more pleasure because his paternal friend could, with more disinterestedness and moderation than any other, test in that post what degree of executive power was needed for the maintenance of liberty in a republic."[2] Possibly also, Washington never received a letter dated either

---

[1]The numbers of the letters so affected are: 29, 33, 38, 50, 56, 108, 110, 121, 131, 165, 167, 169, 173, 208, 209, 210, 222, 224, and 225. The numbers of the letters whose footnotes are affected are: 152 and 211.

[2]Lafayette, *Mémoires, correspondance et manuscrits*, III, 200. Cf. Louis Gottschalk and Margaret Maddox, *Lafayette in the French Revolution: Through the October Days* (Chicago, 1969), pp. 252–253.

December 20 or December 27, 1797, and it is lost. Our reason for concluding (but not being certain) that this letter was never received is that, when Washington on December 25, 1798, enumerated the letters he had received from Lafayette dated between October 6, 1797, and September 5, 1798, he listed one of December 20, 1797.[3] If we assume that neither Lafayette nor his copyist Jared Sparks made an error in the date and that Lafayette wrote to Washington only once in December, 1797, then Washington must have been mistaken in dating that one letter December 20, and the correct date is December 27. Or if we assume that Washington was not mistaken and the other two men were, then the correct date for that one letter was December 20. But if Lafayette wrote twice in December, 1797, then obviously a letter was written on December 20 but has escaped our search.

The passages published for the first time in this reissue underline Lafayette's confidence in Washington's friendly understanding and discreet judgment. The now complete letters from the files of the Society of the Cincinnati add details to his frank opinion of some of his French comrades-in-arms in the War of American Independence. And the English versions of the letters of 1799 shed more light both upon the family affairs of the Lafayettes during their exile and upon Franco-American relations during the "quasi war" of 1797-1801. They also demonstrate the degree of fluency in English that Lafayette had attained by 1799.

The editors of Lafayette's *Mémoires* have frequently omitted family details and informal messages from the Lafayettes to the Washingtons and thus have deprived us of some pointed testimony upon the certainty with which Lafayette counted upon Washington's affection and approbation. A proper eighteenth-century aristocrat would hardly have confided to another aristocratic gentleman such matters as his dire financial distress or the illness of his wife and daughters or a family disagreement over a son's army enlistment, nor would he have sent "tender regard" to grandchildren, were the families of both not on very intimate terms.

The omissions from the French versions of the 1799 letters of Lafayette's comments on the "quasi war" between France and

[3] John C. Fitzpatrick (ed.), *The Writings of George Washington*, XXXVII (Washington, 1940), 64.

the United States are particularly striking. The care exercised by the editors in making such excisions is partly explained by the desire to avoid embarrassment of respected personalities. Lafayette himself had given instructions to that effect to Jared Sparks:

> Such extracts of my official letters as you think fit to introduce in your work are much at your service. I will say the same of extracts from private letters saving reflections on private characters which might wound individuals or their friends if such passages were to occur to you, as personalities may be writen on the spur of the occasion which should be afterward omitted.[4]

The excisions from the French translations of the 1799 letters may be accounted for also by the state of Franco-American international relations at the time the *Mémoires* appeared. President Andrew Jackson had just completed a difficult passage with the French government over payments for French spoliations of American shipping in previous Franco-American conflicts. Lafayette's frank disapproval forty years earlier of the French Directory's policy, his unhesitating readiness to accept the American view, could not have seemed appropriate material for his heirs to reveal to compatriots in 1837-1838.

The hitherto omitted material gives us a new insight into the "quasi war." That Lafayette yearned to help the United States and France to come to terms can be presumed. But that, probably innocently and meaning only the best for his two beloved countries, he spoke to the French chargé d'affaires in Hamburg on behalf of a self-appointed diplomat, Dr. George Logan, does not seem to have been known to students of that period. Logan, in consequence, promptly received a hard-to-get French passport—which he would perhaps have succeeded in getting in some other way, but Lafayette appears to have expedited matters. That Washington was displeased with Logan must surely have come to Lafayette's notice—if not through the press, then certainly through William Vans Murray.[5] In any event, in Lafayette's final (and long) letter to Washington he not only set forth his own sorrow over the state of American politics but also went to some pains to explain his role in the Logan matter. This letter doubtless reached

[4] Lafayette to Jared Sparks, November 15, 1829, Harvard College Library.
[5] *Cf.* Washington to Murray, December 26, 1798, Fitzpatrick (ed.), XXXVII, 71-72.

the general before his death in December, 1799, for in November he wrote with some consternation that he expected Lafayette in America at any time and feared that he would become embroiled in American politics.[6] Thus, when Washington died, he was persuaded that it was more a probable than an "improbable case" that Lafayette "would suddenly pop upon" him,[7] for he felt: "Poor fellow! . . . there is no asylum for him in Europe."[8]

Washington was wrong. Through the energy and good fortune of Mme de Lafayette the Château de Lagrange-Blénau proved a welcome asylum for the rest of his "filial friend's" life. There, the 1944 printing stated (p. xxiv), "the letters that Lafayette had written to his 'beloved general' . . . found their way." We no longer dare make such an unqualified statement. The full English texts of the 1799 letters are derived from the copies obviously retained for Lafayette's own record, and their provenance is the Château de Chavaniac. Hence we must conclude that some of Lafayette's letters to his "beloved general" (and perhaps even the ones that were sent by Bushrod Washington to Lafayette in 1817)[9] at one time were available at Chavaniac (and are now in the Arthur H. and Mary Marden Dean Lafayette Collection in the Cornell University Libraries).

In the preparation of this reissue we have been afforded most gracious and patient cooperation by the library staffs of Cornell University, Lafayette College, and the University of Chicago. We wish especially to acknowledge indebtedness to Mary F. Daniels, of the Cornell Rare Book Room, Phyllis S. Pestieau, Linda Pike, and Nancy Koltes, of the Lafayette Papers Project at Cornell, and Robert G. Gennett, of the David Bishop Skillman Library of Lafayette College.

Chicago, Illinois
July, 1974

Louis Gottschalk
Shirley A. Bill

[6]*Cf.* Washington to Secretary of State, November 3, 1799, *ibid.*, pp. 418–419.
[7]Lafayette to Washington, May 9, 1799, p. 392 below.
[8]Washington to Secretary of State, November 3, 1799, Fitzpatrick (ed.), XXXVII, 419.
[9]Bushrod Washington to Lafayette, January 9, 1817, Lafayette College Library, Hubbard Collection.

Contents

	Page
Preface	vii

1777

1.	October 14	3
2.	Ca. November 1	5
3.	Haddonfield, November 26	6
4.	December 1	8
5.	December 3	10
6.	Camp, December 30	13
7.	Valley Forge, December 31	16

1778

8.	January 5	18
9.	Ca. January 13	21
10.	January 20	24
11.	Flemington, February 9	24
12.	Albany, February 19	26
13.	February 23	29
14.	Albany, February 27	31
15.	March 13	33
16.	March 22	36
17.	Albany, March 25	36
18.	Valley Forge Camp, April 25	42
19.	Valley Forge Camp, May 15	43
20.	Valley Forge Camp, June 17	44
21.	Hopewell, June 24	46
22.	Cranberry, June 25	48

		Page
23.	Cranberry, June 26	49
24.	Hightstown, June 26	49
25.	Robin's Tavern, June 26	50
26.	June 26 (ten-thirty p.m.)	52
27.	Brunswick Camp, July 2	52
28.	Stratford, July 25	53
29.	Lyme over Saybrook Ferry, July 28	54
30.	Providence, August 6	55
31.	Camp before Newport, August 25	56
32.	Tiverton, September 1	61
33.	Camp near Bristol, September 3	64
34.	Warren, September 21	65
35.	Camp near Warren, September 24	67
36.	Boston, September 28	68
37.	Philadelphia, October 24	69

1779

38.	Boston, January 5; On board the "Alliance," January 10	71
39.	On board the "Alliance," January 7	73
40.	On board the "Alliance" off Boston, January 11	73
41.	St. Jean d'Angély near Rochefort harbor, June 12	74
42.	St. Jean d'Angély, June 13	78
43.	Havre, October 7	78

1780

44.	At the entrance of Boston harbor, April 27	82
45.	Camp at Preakness, July 4	82
46.	Preakness Camp, July 16	85
47.	Peekskill, July 20	88
48.	Danbury, July 21	89
49.	Hartford, July 22	90
50.	Lebanon, July 23	92
51.	Newport, July 26	93
52.	Newport, July 26 (seven p.m.)	95
53.	Newport, July 29	97

		Page
54.	Newport, July 31	100
55.	Newport, August 1	104
56.	Light Camp, August 10	105
57.	Light Infantry Camp, August 14	108
58.	Light Camp, August 28	109
59.	Light Camp, September 2	110
60.	New Bridge, October 7	111
61.	Light Camp near Totowa, October 12	112
62.	Elizabethtown, October 27	113
63.	Light Camp, October 27	115
64.	Light Camp, October 28	117
65.	Light Camp, October 30	118
66.	Light Camp, November 1	120
67.	Light Camp, November 8	123
68.	Light Camp, November 11	124
69.	Light Camp, November 13	124
70.	Light Camp, November 13	126
71.	Light Camp, November 14	127
72.	Light Camp, November 18	128
73.	Light Camp, November 19	129
74.	Paramus, November 28	130
75.	Philadelphia, December 4	131
76.	Philadelphia, December 5	133
77.	December 5 in the evening	136
78.	Philadelphia, December 9	136
79.	Philadelphia, December 13	139
80.	Philadelphia, December 16	139
81.	Philadelphia, December 19	141
82.	Philadelphia, December 26	142

1781

83.	Morristown, January 7	143
84.	Pompton, February 23	144
85.	Pompton, February 23	146
86.	Morristown, February 24	147
87.	Morristown, February 25	149
88.	Philadelphia, March 2	150

		Page
89.	Elk (Head of Elk), March 3	153
90.	Head of Elk, March 7	154
91.	Elk (Head of Elk), March 8	156
92.	On board the "Dolphin," March 9	157
93.	Off Turkey Point, March 9	158
94.	York (Yorktown), March 15	159
95.	Williamsburg, March 23	161
96.	Williamsburg, March 25	164
97.	Williamsburg, March 26	165
98.	Williamsburg, March 26	167
99.	Elk (Head of Elk), April 8	168
100.	Elk (Head of Elk), April 10	172
101.	Elk (Head of Elk), April 10	175
102.	Elk (Head of Elk), April 11	176
103.	Elk (Head of Elk), April 12	176
104.	Susquehanna Ferry, April 13	178
105.	Susquehanna Ferry, April 13	179
106.	Susquehanna Ferry, April 14	180
107.	Susquehanna Ferry, April 15	183
108.	Baltimore, April 18	184
109.	Baltimore, April 18	187
110.	Alexandria, April 23	187
111.	Camp near Bottom's Creek, May 4	188
112.	Richmond, May 8	191
113.	Camp Wilton at James River, May 17	192
114.	Wilton, north side of the James River, May 18	193
115.	Richmond, May 24	196
116.	Richmond, May 24	197
117.	Camp between the Rappahannock and North Anna, June 3	199
118.	Brock's Bridge, June 10	200
119.	Allen's Creek twenty-two miles from Richmond, June 18	201
120.	Camp, June 28	203
121.	Ambler's Plantation, July 8	204
122.	Malvern Hill, July 20 (private)	205
123.	Malvern Hill, July 20	207
124.	Malvern Hill, July 26	210
125.	Malvern Hill, July 30	211

	Page
126. Malvern Hill, July 31	213
127. Malvern Hill, August 1	214
128. Camp on the Pamunkey, August 6	215
129. New Kent Mountain, August 11	216
130. Forks of York River, August 21	218
131. Mattapony River, August 24	221
132. Mr. Ruffin's, August 25	223
133. Holt's Forge, September 1	225
134. Holt's Forge, September 1	225
135. Williamsburg, September 8	228
136. Camp Williamsburg, September 8	231
137. Williamsburg, September 10	232
138. Camp before York (Yorktown), September 30	233
139. Camp before York (Yorktown), September 30	234
140. Camp before York (Yorktown), October 16	235
141. October 23	236
142. November 29	237
143. "Alliance" off Boston, December 21; December 23	238

1782

144. Lorient, January 18	241
145. Versailles, January 30	242
146. Antony, March 30	244
147. Antony, March 31	248
148. Paris, April 12	248
149. Paris, April 12	250
150. St. Germain, June 25	250
151. Paris, June 29	252
152. Paris, September 1	254
153. Paris, October 14	254
154. Paris, October 24	256
155. Brest, December 4	257

1783

156. Cadiz, February 5	259
157. Bordeaux, March 2	262

		Page
158.	Paris, May 18	263
159.	Paris, June 10	264
160.	Paris, June 12	265
161.	Chavaniac in the Province of Auvergne, July 22	265
162.	Nancy, September 8	267
163.	Paris, November 11	270
164.	Paris, November 29	272
165.	Paris, December 25	272

1784

166.	Paris, January 10	274
167.	Paris, March 9	276
168.	Paris, March 9 (private)	278
169.	Paris, March 9	278
170.	Paris, March 9	281
171.	Paris, April 9	282
172.	Paris, May 14	283
173.	Philadelphia, August 10	284
174.	New York, September 14	285
175.	Albany, October 8	285
176.	Boston, October 22	287
177.	New York, December 17	288
178.	On board the "Nymphe," New York harbor, December 21	288

1785

179.	Versailles, February 9	291
180.	Paris, March 19	292
181.	St. Germain near Paris, April 16	294
182.	Paris, May 11	296
183.	Paris, May 11	298
184.	Paris, May 13	298
185.	Paris, July 9	300
186.	Sarreguemines on the French frontier, July 14	300
187.	Vienna, September 3	302

1786

		Page
188. Paris, February 6		303
189. Paris, February 10		310
190. Paris, May 24		311
191. Paris, October 8		313
192. Paris, October 26		313

1787

193. Paris, January 13	317
194. Paris, February 7	320
195. Versailles, May 1	321
196. Paris, May 5	322
197. Paris, August 3	324
198. Paris, October 9	326
199. Paris, October 15	332
200. Paris, October 15	332

1788

201. Paris, January 1	334
202. Paris, January 2	336
203. Paris, February 4	337
204. Paris, March 6	339
205. Paris, March 18	339
206. Paris, May 4	341
207. Paris, May 20	342
208. Paris, May 25	342

1790

209. Paris, January 12	346
210. Paris, March 17	347
211. Paris, August 23	348

1791

212. Paris, January 25	351
213. Paris, March 7	352
214. Paris, May 3	353
215. Paris, June 6	355

	1792	Page
216.	Headquarters, Metz, January 22	358
217.	Paris, March 15	360

	1797	
218.	Hamburg, October 6	363
219.	Lehmkuhlen, December 27	365

	1798	
220.	Wittmoldt, Holstein, April 26	368
221.	Wittmoldt, Holstein, May 20	369
222.	Wittmoldt near Plön, Holstein, August 20; August 21	373
223.	Wittmoldt, Holstein, September 5	378

	1799	
224.	Vianen, April 19	381
225.	Vianen, May 9	382

Appendix I	387
Appendix II	395
Index	403
Supplementary Index	435

THE LETTERS OF
LAFAYETTE TO WASHINGTON
1777-1799

1777

[1]

The 14 October 1777*

My Dear General

I do not do myself the honor of writing to you as many times as I would choose, because I fear to disturb your important occupations. But I indulge now that pleasure to me on the occasion of the two nominations of Congress. General Conuay is a so brave, intelligent and active officer that he schall, I am sure, justify more and more the esteem of the army and your approbation. For the Baron de Kalb who is unknown to your Excellency I ca'nt tell any particularity of his arrangements since his new convention with Congress, because I am not well acquainted with them. He was employed with succès in the last war in the line of ammunition and forages. I wrote to Canuay to congratulate him and I believe indeed that he will acquitt himself as well as possible. For Baron de Kalb I do not know where he is. I do'nt take the liberty of asking the sentiments of your Excellency about those promotions because I do not think that Congress could have done such a things in the army without your application and approbation.

I can't express to you, dear General, with what pleasure I heard General Gates's advantages over the queen's light dragoons's colonel. Without speaking of my very sincere love for our cause; without speaking of Congress, every thing important to your own succès, agreement, and glory procures me the greatest happinness.

Give me leave, dear General, to speack to you about my own affairs with all the confidence of a son, of a friend, as you favoured

*Pierpont Morgan Library, Lafayette correspondence, vol. I.

me with those two so precious titles. My respect, my affection for you, answered to my own heart that I deserve them on that side as well as possible. Since our last great conversation I would not tell any thing to your Excellency, for my taking a division of the army. You were in too important occupations to be disturbed. For the Congress he was in a great hurry, and in such a time I take my only right of fighting, I forget the others. Now that the ho^rable Congress is settled quiete, and making promotions, that some changements are ready to happen in the divisions, and that I endeavoured myself the 11 September to be acquainted with a part of the army and known by them, advise me, dear General, for what I am to do. It is not in my character to examine if they have had, if they can have never some obligations to me, I am not usued to tell what I am, I wo'nt make no more any petition to Congress because I can now refuse, but not ask from them, therefore, dear General, I'l conduct myself by your advices. Consider, if you please, that Europe and particularly France is looking upon me. That I want to do some thing by myself, and justify that love of glory which I left be known to the world in making those sacrifices which have appeared so surprising, some say so foolich. Do you not think that this want is right?—In the beginning I refused a division because I was diffident of my being able to conduct it without knowing the character of the men who would be under me. Now that I am better acquainted no difficulty comes from me. Therefore I am ready to do all what your Excellency will think proper. You know I hope, with what pleasure and satisfaction I live in your family. Be certain that I schall be very happy if you judge that I can stay in America without any particular employement when strangers come to take divisions of the army, and when myself by the only right of my birth should get in my country without any difficulty a body of troops as numerous as is here a division. We have there different ways of advancement as the different ranks of men. I know it is not right. But I would deserve the reproachs of my friends and family it I would leave the advantages of mine to stay in a country where I could not find the occasions of distinguishing myself. I do not tell all that to my general, but to my father and friend. For Congress I'l tell never nothing to them because tho' I like very much some as Mr. Lee, Mr. Lawrence, etc, some others did not behave with me with that frankness which is the proof of an honest mind. All what I have the honor to wraït to your Excellency in this letter is, if you please, under the most intimate secret, and confidence. I schall conduct myself entirely by your advices, and if you say that some thing is proper I'l do it directly. I desire only to know your opinion.

Among the officers who came on board of my ship, this whom Congress did pay the less regard to, is the very same whom I reccommended as the most able and respectable man and my best friend. He was coming only for me. If I was to be at the head of a division and your Excellency would be master of it, (as I am told that Stephens gives his dismission) I can not help to tell you that a division of Virginians as they are, principally with General Woodfort would be the most agreable for me.

I hope that I'l be in camp in three or four days where I'l be able to speack to your Excellency about all my businesses. I beg your pardon for being so tedious. It is for you a very disagreable and troublesome proof of my confidence. But that confidence is equal to the affection and respect which I have the honor to be with

Your Excellency's
The most obedient servant
The Mquis. de Lafayette

[2]

[*ca.* November 1, 1777]*

Mr de Vrigny who has now the commission of Major in the french service began by being in the rgt *of the family* de noaïlles, cavalry, from the year 1754 till 1758. He made in that intervall two campaigns of war near the person of my uncle the Marechal duc de mouchy then lieutenant general who gave him an honorable certificate of good conduct and behaviour

He was received after it in the corps of *horse rangers* under the famous partisan ficher as lieutenant; which corps was granted (ficher being dead) to the Mquis de Conflans officer of the greatest reputation in our service. That general who is a friend of mine gave me the best accounts of Mr de Vrigny who is yet Captain in the same rḡt

---

*This is apparently the letter mentioned by Washington to Congress, November 1, 1777: see Fitzpatrick, *Writings of Washington*, IX, 480. Unpublished.

called now *houzards de Conflans* with commission of Major as I mentionned above.

As I think that the military knowledge and experience of this gentileman, principally in the kind of war used till this moment by our light dragoons, could be useful to his excellency's gāl Washington army, I wishoud that he could be employed in it with the rank of lieutenant colonel.

[3]

Haddenfield the 26 November 1777

Dear General

I went down to this place since the day before yesterday in order to be acquainted of all the roads and grounds arround the ennemy. I heard at my arrival that theyr main body was betwen great and little timber creek since the same evening. Yesterday morning in recconnoitring about I have been told that they were very busy in crossing the deleware. I saw them myself in theyr boats and send that intelligence to general Greene as soon as possible as every other thing I heard of—but I want to acquaint your excellency of a little event of last evening which tho' not very considerable in itself will certainly please you on account of the bravery and alacrity a small party of ours showed in that occasion. After having spent the most part of the day to make myself vell acquainted with the certainty of theyr motions I came pretty late into the Glocester road betwen the two creeks. I had ten light horse with Mr Lindsey, almost hundred an fifty riflemen under colonel buttler, and two picquets of the militia commanded by colonel hite and ellis. My whole body was not three hundred—colonel armand, colonel laumoy, the chevaliers du plessis and gimat were the frenchmen who went with me—a scout of my men with whom was M^r du plessis to see how near were the first piquets from Glouster found at two miles and a half of it a strong post of three hundred and fifty hessians with field pieces (what number I did know by the unanimous deposition of theyr prisoners) and engaged immediately—as my little recconnoitring party was all in fine spirits I supported them—we pushed the hessians more than an half mile from the place were was theyr main body, and we made them run very fast—british reinforcements came twice to them but very far from recovering theyr ground they went alwais back—the darkness of the night prevented us then to push that advantage, and after standing upon the ground we had got I ordered them to return very slow to haddonfield—the ennemy knowing perhaps by our drums that we were not so near, came again to fire at us—but the brave major moriss with a part of his riflemen sent them back and pushed them very fast. I understand that they have had betwen twenty five and thirty wounded, at least that number killed amongst whom I am certain is an officer some say more, and the prisoners told me that the have lost the commandant of that body. We got yet this day fourteen prisoners. I send you the most moderate account I had from themselves. We left one single man killed a lieutenant of militia and only five of ours were wounded. Colonel Armand's, Chevalier du plessis's and major brice's horses have been wounded. Such is the account of our little entertainement, which is indeed much too long for the matter, but I take the greatest pleasure to let you know that the conduct of our soldiers is above all praises. I never saw men so merry, so spirited, so desirous to go on to the ennemy what ever forces they could have as that small party was in this little fight. I found the riflemen above even theyr reputation and the militia above all expectations I could have. I returned to them my very sincere thanks this morning. I wish that *this little succès of ours* may please you—tho' a trifling one I find it very interesting on account of the behaviour of our soldiers.

Some time after I came back Gāl Varnum arrived here. General Greene is too in this place since this morning. He engaged me to give you myself the account of the little advantage of that small part of the troops under his command. I have nothing more to say to your excellency about our businesses on this side because he is writing himself. I should have been very glad if circumstances had permitted me to be useful to him upon a greater scale. As he is obliged to march slow in order to attend his troops, and as I am here only a volonteer, I'l have the honor to wait on your excellency as soon as possible, and I'l set out today. It will be a great pleasure for me to find myself again with you.

With the most tender affection and highest respect I have the honor to be dear general,

Your excellency's the most obedient humble servant
Lafayette

[Dec. 1, 1777]*

Your excellency ordered me to give my opinion about those three places for winter quarters 1° the chain from about the Sculchill till Betheleem—2° this from Reading to Lancaster 3° building hutts about and quartering in Willmington.

I must confess my being prevented of fixing my sentiments in a decicise manner by my want of knowledge about very interesting points amongs them as

1° how far we should distress and perhaps disaffect those persons who schould be turned out from the diferents places they are in

2° how far we may expect to collect and keep with the army all the officers who perhaps will think themselves intitled to go home to occupate themselves with theyr businesses or pleasures if we are not in a kind of warlike quarters, and then we will loose the same advantages of theyr being instructed and disciplined we schould endeavour to gain in going into peaceful places

3° what effect can it make upon the people our leaving the country entirely oppened to the excursions, cruelties and also to the seductions of the ennemy, when we schall give them all the opportunities they can wish to draw all the provisions from every where and in the same time to inlist provincial soldiers

4° if our giving a greater idea of the army in covering the country and laying near the ennemy will more facilitate our making recruits than if we were in good confortables towns and not in a place and in a manner, which will seem to the eyes of people a kind of winter campaigne

5° till what point those different measures will please or distress the officers and (what is generally in the militar world the less attended to, and deserves the greater attention) our private soldiers

6° till what point we may depend upon our intelligences and light troops to avoid equally and being surprised and tiring the troops by false alarms.

7° if we can hope that the soldiers will now receive cloathes etc. in order to be fit for some winter marches and operations, if in

*Library of Congress, Washington papers. Unpublished.

case where they schould be defeated we may hope to meet them again.

Such are the points of knowledge which I am deprived of by my being stranger in this country, and my being stranger in the army, if I can speak so, for I have no officers no soldiers under my particular direction whom I could consult and know theyr temper, theyr inclinations, and all what it is possible to expect from them.

However I'l tell to your excellency my very imperfect sentiments about the matter

1st the first proposition seems to me the less eligible, and my reason for it is the scarcity of villages and principally the report of the commissaires and other gentlemen who know the country

2° the second seems to me the most prudent. There we schall be quiete, there we can discipline and instruct our troops, we can be able to begin a early campaign, and we shall not fear to be carried into a winter campaign if it pleases general Howe. Therefore in consulting only prudence, and as far as my little knowledge can go, I am at less certain that I'l have nothing to reproach to me in giving my choice to this second proposition.

However (and in making excuses to your excellency for such an indecision and refering myself to your knowledge about the suppositions I will make) if it was not distressing neither for officers neither for soldiers, if going to Lancaster etc. will disaffect and make a bad impression as far as to prevent our recruiting, if we can keep better our officers when we schall be in a kind of encampement near the ennemy, if principally you think that we schould be fit for some winter march's we should be able to support some disadventages then I am fully and with a great chearfulness of opinion that we must go to Willmington. My reasons would be then

1° this position enable us to do in the course of the winter what we shall think proper to annoy, to deprive of ressources of every kind, to attack if possible the ennemy

2° this position has some thing shining and military like which will make the best effect and upon the continent and even in Europe

3° the doctors, and American ones who know the manners and phisik constitution of our soldiers say that nothing is so confortable as well made hutts.

Prudence orders me to choose Lancaster but if the inconveniences I fear (without being able to know them) if those inconveniences I explain to your excellency are not as strong as they can be, if principally our present civil situation ask from us some thing shining and perhaps bold then I give all my wishes and all my choice to Willmington.

The Mquis de Lafayette, M. G.

[5]

[December 3, 1777]*

The project of calling a large body of militia for such a day, in order to attack the ennemy in Philadelphia, seems to me attended with so many difficulties, inconveniences, and bad chances, that if it is not looked upon as a necessary and almost desesperate enterprize, tho' it is a very shining and highly pleasing idea, however I cannot think it is a prudent and reasonable one. The reasons for my rejecting it are as follows.

1st I do not think that any body could advise your Excellency to attack only the redoubts in front, whatever could be our force; such an attack vould be attended with a greater loss but not a greater succès than if we had only continental troops.

2° We must therefore expect the moment where the ice upon the Schullchill will oppen to us all the left side of the ennemy's line and encampements. But or the climate makes a great difference betwen this country and the European ones, or one single fine day may frustrate all our hopes and preparations in putting a way all the ice. Then we schould expect one other moment before dismissing the troops, and in my actual supposition they are to be kept a very schort time

3° In Europe ice is brocken every night when it can facilitate the projects of the ennemy; if all is not cleaned, at least a ditch can be formed in the river. I know that we schould annoy theyr workmen, I know that such an operation would be very hard an troublesome for them. But in the first case I'l answer that every where military works are performed with the same inconveniences, in the second the people of Philadelphia can be employed there. When I say that we could trouble theyr operation, I suppose that our winter quarters are not in the back country.

*Library of Congress, Washington papers. Unpublished.

4° We ca'nt expect any secrecy in our collecting those forces, we ca'nt deceive the ennemy for theyr destination. Therefore (unless we could have a respectable body in the jersay) he can go of before fighting and then we must not entertain the hope of oppressing and destroying all that army, but only of recovering Philadelphia.

5° Supposing that we could go upon the ice we have one only way of attaking. For if we put the militia in first line, they will fall back upon the continental troops, and we can not depend enough upon our men to believe that we could maintain order and resolution amongs them. If the militia is in rear, and the regulars were repulsed certainly they will not advance where continentals troops do'nt succeed. If amongs us, I do'nt believe it would do better. Therefore our only way should be to make false attacks of militia, and true ones of continental troops, to have a curtain—what we call in French un rideau—of troops in the whole lenght of the Schulchill and on this side, of the redoubts, in order to cover the heads of our columns, and our points of attack, and to put the disorder amongs the ennemy by an easy fire. I wichoud too a body should be in the Jersay *in case it would be possible for the ennemy to retreat by the Delaware*. And does your Excellency think that such a quantity of troops could be raised?

6° When I consider all the difficulties of turning out some militia in interesting occasions I c'ant flatterer myself that all that people could be sent to your army for such a day, without the utmost difficulties. Each state will have an excuse for not sending as many men as they'l be desired. The cold, the rivers, the want of cloathes of every thing will seem sufficient reasons, if not to stay at home at least to arrive after the time of the rendezvous. Every one will trust upon the another and if we do not succeed all will be against us.

7° Have we in the continent all the cloathes, arms, ammunition etc. etc. which would be necessary for so many soldiers. Would it be possible to find subsistances, enough in cattle, forage etc. All things which I ca'nt know, but however I think worthy of being mentionned and that principally because the want of exactitude, the necessity of giving to them a light idea of what they are to do will engage us to keep them longer than we think.

8 I know that all those inconveniences can not be together;

because if we keep them some time, then we schall find an opportunity of going over the Schulchill in case that we can prevent theyr broking the ice; on the other hand if we have them only for few days, difficulties of subsistence will be much lesser; and if is impossible for the ennemy to pass the Delaware, certainly a body in jersay is quite useless. I can add that in case we could not go over the ice, it is possible to throw bridges upon the river. But, Sir, I have mentionned all the difficulties which strike me, because my opinion is not to begin such an enterprize unless we schall be certain of succeeding. A great schame for our arms, a great michief of our cause would attend our being repulsed when we schould attack a part of the British forces with all the united forces of America. Europe has a great idea of our being able to raise when we please an immense army of militia, and it is looked upon as our last but certain ressource. If we fall this phantom will fall also and you know that the American interest has alwaïs been since the begining of this war to let the world believe that we are stronger than we ever expect to be. If we destroy the English army, *our generous effort* will be admired every where, if we are repulsted it will be called *a rash and and laughable expedition*. Therefore we must not let a shining appearance and the pleasing charms of a bold fine enterprise, deceive us upon the inconveniences and dangers of the gigantesque and in the same time decisive expedition

However perhaps the interest of America, the wish of all the States, the instructions of Congress, the necessity of finishing soon the war, all these circonstances which are unknown to me, make it necessary for your Excellency to hazard some thing in this occasion. Perhaps the difficulties in the phisick and moral ressources of this country are not so great as I am affraid to find them. Perhaps it is possible to raise, to arm, to cloath, to subsist, to keep together and give some instructions to that so considerable army which according to my opinion is necessary; perhaps the weather is not so changeable in this country as it is in Europe; or some other means than going upon the ice could seem eligible to your Excellency. But if the difficulties which I fear are indeed true (what you can judge, and I can not know myself) then I am not for that expedition in considering it as only a militar one

If however I was deceived, or if politic cicumstance schould make it necessary to try such an enterprize, the following precautions seem me to be taken.

1° I do not ascertain the number of militia to be raised because it must be as large as we can arm, cloath, and subsist.

2° All possible exertions are to be taken for having them at the appointed time which time must be now as soon as it is possible.

3° Some instructions should take place before the operation only for some days, because if they were marched to the ennemy without the less idea of marching together such a disorder would prevent the succès of the less difficult enterprize.

4° The continental troops schould be sent in theyr inter quarters as soon as possible, to take a good rest, to recomfort themselves, to be reinforced by theyr men now scattered every where, by some recruits, and the whole to be managed and exerced by theyr genl. offficers. Under that point of vüe, and principally cloathes should be delivered to them, and theyr arms put in a good order. It seems to me that this prospect could engage us to be nearer from the ennemy than Lancaster is.

5° The soldiers and pricipally the officers of our army schould not be permitted to go home till it would be over

6° Proper means for recruiting the army schould be taken as soon as possible—one of the best according to my opinion would be (after having suppressed the substitutes) to annex a part of the militia of each state to theyr continental divisions in order to serve there for twelve months. I think that such a regulation is eligible in all cases. For a strong continental army well managed and disciplined, and ready to begin an early campaign, and to make use of all the unforeseen and soudain occasions, would do much greater service than all the militia in the world. And then militia should be made use of only in a less great number or in particular circomstances

The Mquis de Lafayette M. G.

[6]

Camp 30ᵗ december 1777

My dear General

I went yesterday morning to head quarters with an intention of speaking to your excellency but you were too buzy and I shall lay down in this letter what I wished to say.

I don't need telling you how I am sorry for all what happens since some time. It is a necessary dependence of my most tender and respectful friendship for you, which affection is as true and candid as the other sentiments of my heart and much stronger than a so new acquaintance seems to admit. But an other reason to be concerned in the present circumstances is my ardent, and perhaps enthusiastic wishes for the happiness and liberty of this country. I see plainly that America can defend herself if proper measures are taken and now I begin to fear that she could be lost by herself and her own sons.

When I was in Europe I thought that here almost every man was a lover of liberty and would rather die free than live slave. You can conceive my astonishment when I saw that toryism was as openly professed as wighism itself. However at that time I believed that all good Americans were united together, that the confidence of Congress in you was unbounded. Then I entertained the certitude that America would be independant in case she would not loose you. Take a way for an instant that modest diffidence of yourself (which, pardon my freedom, my dear general, is sometimes too great, and I wish you could know as well as myself, what difference there is betwen you and any other man upon the continent) You shall see very plainly that if you were lost for America, there is nobody who could keep the army and the revolution for six months. There are oppen dissensions in Congress, parties who hate one another as much as the common ennemy, stupid men who without knowing a single word about war undertake to judge you, to make ridiculous comparisons; they are infatuated with Gates without thinking of the different circumstances, and believe that attacking is the only thing necessary to conquer. Those ideas are entertained in their minds by some jealous men and perhaps secret friends to the British government who want to push you in a moment of ill humour to some rash enterprise upon the lines or against a much stronger army. I should not take the liberty of mentionning these particularities to you if I did not receive a letter about this matter from a young good natured gentleman at York whom Connway has ruined by his cunning bad advice but who entertains the greatest respect for you.*

I have been surprised at first to see the niew establishement of

*Probably Thomas Mullens, Conway's aide.

this board of war, to see the difference betwen northern and southern departements, to see resolves from Congress about military operations—but the promotion of Canway is beyhond all my expectations. I should be glad to see niew major generals after me, because as I know that you take some interest to my happiness and reputation, it is perhaps an occasion for your excellency to give me more agreable commands in some interesting instances. On the other hand Gal Connway says he is entirely a man to be disposed of by me, he calls himself my soldier, and the reason of such behaviour for me is that he wishes to be well spoken of at the French court, and his protector the M^{quis} de Castries is an intimate acquaintance of mine—but since the letter of Lord Stirling I inquired in his caracter. I found that he was an ambitious and dangerous man. He has done all in his power by cunning maneuvres to take off my confidence and affection for you. His desire was to engage me to leave this country. Now I see all the general officers of the army against Congress, such disputes if known by the ennemy, can be attended with horrid consequences. I am very sorry when ever I perceive troubles raised amongs the defenders of the same cause, but my concern is much greater when I find officers coming from France, officers of some character in my country to whom any fault of that kind may be imputed. The reason of my fondness for Connway was is being by all means a very brave and very good officer. However that part of maneuvres which seems so extraordinary to Congress, is not so very difficult for any man of common sense who applies himself to it. I must pay to Gal Portail and some French officers who came to speack to me the justice to say that I found them as I could wish upon this occasion. For it has made a great noise amongs many in the army. I wish indeed those matters could be soon pacified. I wish your excellency could let them know how necessary you are to them and engage them in the same time to keep peace and simulate love among themselves till the moment where those little disputes schall not be attended with such inconveniences. It would be a too great pity that slavery, dishonor, ruin, and unhappiness of a whole world schould issue from trifling differences betwixt some fiew men.

    You will find perhaps this letter very useless and even very importune—but I was desirous of having a pretty long conversation with your excellency upon the present circumstances to explain you what I think of this matter. As the proper opportunity for it is not to be found, I took the liberty of laying down some of my ideas in this letter, because it is interesting for my satisfaction to be convinced that you, my dear general, who have been indulgent enough as to permit me to look on you as upon a friend, could know the confession of my sentiment in a matter which I consider as a very important one. I have the warmest love for my country and for every good frenchman. Theyr succès feels my heart with joy—but, sir, besides Connway is an irishman I want country men who deserve in every point to do honor to theyr country. That gentleman had engaged me by entertaining my head with ideas of glory and shining projects, and I must confess to my shame that it is a too certain way of deceiving me.

I wish'd to join to the fiew theories about war I can have, and the fiew dispositions nature gave perhaps to me, the experience of thirty campaigns, in hope that I schould be able to be more useful in the present circumstance. My desire of deserving your satisfaction is stronger than ever, and every where you'l employ me you can be certain of my trying every exertion in my power to succeed. I am now fixed to your fate and I shall follow it and sustain it as well by my sword as by all means in my power. You will pardon my importunity in favor of the sentiment which dictate it. Youth and frienship make perhaps myself too warm, but I feel the greatest concern at all what happens since some time.

With the most tenderest and profound respect I have the honor to be,

              dear general,
                  Your most obedient humble servant
                          Lafayette.

[7]

Walley forge dec^r 31 1777

Dear General

I schould have much more reproached myself the liberty I took of writing to your excellency, if I had believed it could engage you in the trouble of answering that letter. But, now, as you have writen it, I must tell you that I received this favor with the greatest satisfaction and pleasure. Every assurance and proof of your affection fills my heart with joy, because that sentiment of yours is extremely dear and precious to me. A tender and respectfull attachement for you, and an invariable frankness will be found in my mind the more as you will know me better; but after those merits, I must tell you that very few others are to be found. I never wish'd as heartily to be intrusted by nature with an immensity of talents than on this occasion where I could be then of some use to your glory and happiness, as well as to mine own.

What man do not join the pure ambition of glory with this other ambitions of advancement, rank, and fortune[?] As an ardent lover of laurels, I cannot bear the idea that so noble a sentiment should be mixed with any low one. In your preaching moderation to the brigadiers upon such an occasion, I am not surprised to recognize your virtous character. As I hope my warm interest is known to your excellency, I dare entertain the idea that you will be so indulgent as to let me know every thing concerning you when ever you will not be under the law of secrecy or particular circumstancès.

With the most tender and affectionate friendship with the most profound respect

Your most humble and obedient servant
Lafayette.

1778

[8]

The 5 January 1778.*

Dear General,

As your excellency's opinion seems to agree with my ideas for taking in our service those non commissioned officers who came with Mr. du Coudray, I schall take the liberty of telling you what I know about it—how useful they would be in this army is a thing obvious to every body—those men join to a pretty great theory the greatest practice of theyr art—and not only they would be useful by themselves, but they could form our gunners, and sergeants of artillery —their pretentions would not be so extensive tho' theyr service could be greater than if you were to take officers of theyr corps—however pretty great advantages schould be proposed to them, because they enjoy in their own country both a good state and a flattering consideration—they have been, I believe, disatisfied with Congress when sent back—if your excellency would speack to the committee who is to come here, if General Knox was to receive orders of making to them good propositions should it be only for a campaign, if Mr. Du Plessis (I suppose this gentleman's affair will be soon settled) was to engage them, and promise them in my name that I schould take care of 'em, perhaps they could be induced to stay with us, and it would be a good acquisition.

I did not hear any thing about Mr. Connway's business since three days, but that he has proposed to Congress an expedition against St. Augustin, with troops raised in Europe—as my cloth will

*Unpublished. (Proper names are identified in the "Index" below.)

be here I schall make out a waist coat and every other part of the dress, to show it to your Excellency.

I think your Excellency will be obliged to make a general order, about every thing which is to be done since the moment where a guard arrive upon the parade till this where they go off from duty.*

Give me leave to mention to you a thing which I have thought of and could be perhaps attended with advantages—they are in the army some scattered Frenchmen who tho' they fight very well in the moment of an action are however troublesome to theyr officers and undisciplined beyond all expression—they excuse their disobedience by telling that they don't understand what is told to them—they will never be kept by theyr officers and perhaps they will spoil the others—but if they were collected in a body, and under some officer who could speack to them they would be quieter and disciplined and I thing (sic) some advantage schould arise from that arrangement—when the fight is over theyr officers do not know what to do with them—I propose to give them to the little French officer who was in the Northern army and whom I can answer for, as an honest man and a good officer—they schould have whatever denomination you would think proper, corps, regiment, compagny, but connected with a division or rather to Morgan's Corps and not independant, for a military independance would ruin the civil one—as that officer is neither an imprudent neither a young man I could answer for the discipline and good order of that corps *if not independant* I would take care myself of theyr conduct—my reason in speacking so is that I do not like to see any mischief done in this country by French men, and I am sure if that measure is not taken that I schall have alwaïs the disagreement to hear from every where many instances of un-

---

*At this point the following passage has been crossed out (probably by a later owner or editor):

in many different ways. Attending punctually the parade with men as clean as they can be, filing off in a good order before the general officer, relieving the other guards in a proper manner, sending an orderly man from the picquet to know where they are, laying around one or at most two fires without pulling down theyr cloathes, neither allowing any fire to theyr centrys, recconnoitring those who come in camp principally when numerous by a corporal and four men, and for the centrys challenging in the night, and in daytime schouldering theyr arms for any officer or troop who pass by, and [one word crossed out] them to general officers, are things which I take the liberty of mentionning to your excellency, because I have seen myself several faults in all those points, and it has been answered to me by officers and soldiers that they did not know what they were to do.

discipline and libertinage by those scattered men—I do not inclose the Canadian's Companies of Colonel Hazen in my project, I am alwaïs affraïd that our reinforcements will not arrive soon enough —collecting, inoculating, marching them, and the whole attended with many deliberations of Congress of the several States, etc. etc. will all that thing be done for begining an early campaign? for not our only interest but even the want of provisions will expel us very early from this place.

Don't you think, Sir, that if we have a very large army as I hope we schall, and I think we must absolutely, that a Quarter Master General with the rank of General officer with a considerable departement as in the European armys schould not be very useful?

Is it not very importunate and even very impertinent to lay before you my young and unexperienced ideas? but if they are unjudicious and unacceptable, I hope at least that you will not miss the sentiment which dictates them. I am very far from thinking myself able to give any advice in this army, but I dare hope that my warmest wishes for the good and right could inspire me some times with some tolerable ideas, and as I have no pretentions in it I'l see myself deceived by false ones without being surprised at all.

I am just now coming from the parade, where a French officer who has been those past days in Lancaster, told me that there are to be heard the most extraordinary and indecent things about the present businesses—they speack of Conway as a man sent by heaven for the liberty and happiness of America—he told so to them and they are fools enough as to believe it—he has desired Congress to send him as Ambassador to France or as Commander in Chief in Georgia in case he could not stay in this army to superintend it.

I am very glad to hear that Colonel Pickering is in the board of war because he is an honest man. I wish he may have strength enough as to oppose himself to the factions.

With the warmest affection and greatest respect I have the honor to be,

    Dear General,
     Your Excellency's the most obedient servant.
      Lafayette.

[9]

[ca. January 13, 1778]*

Dear General,

I schall make use in this particular instance of the liberty you gave me of telling freely every idea of mine which could strike me as not being useless to a better order of things.

There were two gentlemen, same rank, same duty to perform, and same neglect of it who have been arrested the same day by me —as I went in the night around the piquets, I found them in fault, and I gave an account of it the next day to your excellency—you answered that I was much in wrong not to have had them relieved and arrested immediately—I objected that it was then very late for such a changement, and that I did not know which was the rule in this army, but that the gentlemen should be arrested in that very moment, the last answer of your Excellency has been, "they are to have a court martial, and you must give notice of it to the adjudant general." Therefore Major Nevill made two letters in order to arrest them, one *for having been surprised in his post* and the other, for the same cause and *allowing his centrys to have fires which he could see in standing before the picquet.*

I give you my word of honor that there was not any exageration.

Now I see in the orders the less guilty punished in a manner, much too severe indeed, and dismissed from the service (it is among all the delicate minds deprived of his honor) when he was only to be severely reprimanded, and kept for some time under arrest—but it can be attributed to a very severe discipline.

What must I think of the same Court when they unanimously acquit (it is to say that my accusation is not true) the officer who joins to the same fault, entirely the same, this of allowing his centrys to have fire in his own sight—for in every service *being surprised* or being found in the middle of his picquet without any challenging or stopping centry, as Mjor Nevil riding before me found him, is entirely the same thing—and Mjor Nevil riding before me when I was busy to make a centry pull off his fire, can swear that such was the case with that officer—he can do more than swearing, for he can give his word of honor—and I think that idea *honor* is the same in

*This letter was occasioned by Washington's "General Orders" of January 13, 1778. See Fitzpatrick, *Writings of Washington*, X, 298.

every country. But the *prejugées* are not the same thing—for giving publickly the best of such a dispute (for here it becomes a trial for both parties) to an officer of the last military stage against one of the first, schould be looked on as an affront to the rank, and acquitting a man whom one other man accuses, looked upon as an affront to the person—it is the same in Poland for Count De Pulaski was much affronted of the decision of a court martial entirely acquitting Colonel Molens—however as I know the English customs I am nothing else but surprised to see such a partiality in a court martial.

Your excellency will certainly approuve my not arresting any officer for being brought before a court martial for any neglect of duty, but when they will be robbers, or cowards, or when they will assassinate, in all when the will deserve being cashiered or put to death.

Give me leave to tell your excellency how I am adverse to Court Martials—I know it is the English custom, and I believe it is a very bad one—it comes from theyr love of lawers [*sic*], speakers, and of that black apparate of sentences, and judgements—but such is not the American temper, and I think this new army must pick up the good institutions, and leave the bad ones where ever they may be—in France an officer is arrested by his superior, who gives notice of it to the commanding officer, and then he is punished enough in being deprived of going out of his room in time of peace, of doing his duty in time of war— no body knows of it but his comrades—when the fault is greater he is confined in a common room for prisonner officers and this is much more shamefull—notice of it is immediately given to the general officer who commands there—that goes too to the King's Minister who is to be reimplaced here by the commander in chief—in time of war it goes to the general in chief.

Soldiers are punished the same or next day by order of proper officers, and the right of punishing is proportionate to the ranks.

But when both officers and soldiers have done some thing which deserves a more severe punishement, when theyr honor, or theyr life, or theyr liberty for more than a very short time is concerned, then a Court Martial meets, and the sentence is known—How will you let an unhappy soldier be confined several weeks, with men who are to be hanged, with spies, with the most horrid sort of people, and in the same time be lost for the duty, when they deserve only some lashes—then almost no proportion in the punishements.

How is it possible to carry a gentleman before a parcel of dreadful judges at the same place where an officer of the same rank has been just now cashiered, for a trifling neglect of his duty; for, I suppose, speaking to his next neighbour in a maneuvre, for going into a house to speack to a pretty girl, when the army is on his march and thousand other things—how is it possible to bring to the certainty of being cashiered, or dishonored, a young lad, who has made a considerable fault because he had a light head, a too great vivacity, when that young man would be perhaps in some years the best officer of the army, if he had been friendly reprimanded and arrested for some time, without any dishonor.

The law is alwaïs severe, and bring with it an eternal shame full mark—when the judges are partial as in this occasion, it is much worse, because they have the same inconveniences as law itself.

In court martials men are tryed by theyr inferiors—how [two words obliterated here] to discipline I do'nt want to say—the publication exposes men to [be] despised by the least soldier—when men have been before a Court martial they schould be or acquitted or dismissed—what do you think can be produced by the half condemnation of a Gāl officer—what necessity for all the soldiers, all the officers, to know that *general Maxwell has been prevented from doing is* [sic] *duty by his being drunk*. Where is the man who will not laugh at him if he is told by him *you are a drunkard* and is it right to ridicule a man respectable by his rank, because he drank two or three gills of rum.

There are my reasons against Court Martials, when there is not some considerable fault to punish—according to my affair I am sorry in seeing the less guilty being the *only one punished*. However, I shall send to Court Martials, but for such a crime, that there will be for the judges no way of indulgence and partiality.

With the most tender respect I am,
    Your excellency's
      the most obedient servant,
        The M^{qis} de Lafayette.

[10]

The twenty [January 1778] a half past one.*

Dear General,

I have received just now a letter from Gāl Connway who is gone on to York town, and Mullens his aid de Camp who is not a wit, lets me know that his going there is in consequence of two repeated letters from Gāl Gates, and Miflin—that same man thinks that there are some projects to send Connway to Canada—they will laugh in France when they'l hear that he is choosen upon such a commission out of the same army where I am, principally as he is an Irishman, and when the project schould be to show to the frenchmen of that country a man of theyr nation who by his rank in France could inspire them with some confidence—but I mention that only as a remark I do not entertain myself any idea of leaving your army neither my Virginian division, but I would not loose a moment to inform your excellency of that journey towards Congress which means perhaps some much worse scheme against yourself or your army.

Our making fashines goes very slow—we are obliged to take alwaïs the same men—we want axes and when I ask some, five or six are sent for the whole wing—no spirits to be issued to the men—there have been too complaints for provisions, principally in general Waine's division, I am about to inquire if they are right, and in that case who is guilty for those fatigue partys being not supplied—however we'l do as fast as circumstances may permit.

With the tenderest affection and highest respect, I have the honor to be,

Your excellency's
the most obedient servant
Lafayette.

[11]

At Flemming town, the nineth february [1778]

Dear General,

I can not let go back my guide without taking this opportunity of wraitting to your excellency tho' I have not yet public business to speak of—I go on very slowly some times pierced by rain, some

*Unpublished.

times covered with snow, and not enterprising many handsome thoughts about the projected *incursion* into Canada—if success were to be had it would surprise me in a more agreable manner, by that very reason that I don't expect very shining ones—Lake Champlain is too cold for producing the least bit of laurels, and if I am neither drowned or starv'd, I'll be as proud as if I had gained two battles.

Mr. Duer had given to me a rendès vous at a tavern, but no body was to be found there—I went by Coriel ferry in compliance to the directions of Lord Stirling, and the advices of Mr. Tillmongh* and Gibs—I fancy Mr. Duer will be with Mr. Connway sooner than he had told me—they'l perhaps conquer Canada before my arrival, and I expect to meet them at the Governor's house in Quebec.

I have been told by the people in going along, that on the other side of the Delaware, there was a great plenty of scheep which the ennemy could take of very easely and which ought to be secured—that I can't give any particular intelligence about but I thought it proper to mention that report to your excellency—I have heard too that the ennemy keeps a great correspondance with the Jersays by Coopers ferry.

Could I believe one single instant that this *pompous command of a northern army* will let your excellency forget a little an absent friend, then I would send the project to the place it comes from—but I dare hope that you will remember me some times—I wish you very heartily the greatest public or private happiness and succès—it is a very melancholy idea for me that I can't follow your fortune as near your person as I could wish—but my heart will take very sincerely his part of every thing which can happen to you, and I am already thinking of the agreable moment were Il come down to assure myself your excellency of the most tender affection and highest respect I have the honor to be with

Dear general,
Your most obedient servant
the Mis de LaFayette

Will you give me leave to inclose here my most affectionate respects to your lady and my best compliments to your excellency's family.

*Probably Tench Tilghman, who, like Caleb Gibbs, was one of Washington's "family."

[12]

dear general   Albany the 19th February 1778

Why I am so far from you, and what business had the board of war to hurry me through the ice and snow without knowing what I schould do, neither what they were doing themselves? You have thought perhaps that theyr project could be attended with some difficulty, that some means had been neglected, that I could not obtain all the succès and the immensity of laurels which they had promised to me—but I defy your excellency to conceive any idea of what I have seen since I left the place where I was quiet and near my friend, to run myself through all the blunders of madness or treachery (God knows what). Let me begin the journal of my fine and glorious campaign.

According to Lord Sterling's advices I went by Coriels ferry to Ringo's tavern were Mr Düer had given me a rendes vous—but there no Düer to be found, and they did never hear from him—from thence I proceded by the state of Newyork and had the pleasure of seeing the friends of America as warm in theyr love for the commander in chief as his best friend could wish. I spoke to governor Clinton and was much satisfied with that gentleman. At lenght I got Albany the 17th tho' I was not expected before the 25th. G$\bar{a}$l Connway had been here only three days before me and I must confess I found him very active, and looking as if he had good intentions —but we know great deal upon that subject— —His first word has been that the expedition is quite impossible. I was at first very diffident of this report, but have found that he was right. Such is at least the idea I can form of this ill concerted operation in these two days.

G$\bar{a}$l Schuïller, G$\bar{a}$l Lincoln, G$\bar{a}$l Arnold had writen before my arrival to G$\bar{a}$l Connway in the most expressive terms that in our present circumstances there was no possibility to begin an enterprize into Canada. Hay dep. quarter master g$\bar{a}$l Cuyler dep. commissary g$\bar{a}$l, meassin* dep. clothier g$\bar{a}$l in what they call the northern departement are entirely of the same opinion. Colonel Hazen who has been appointed to a place which interferes with the three others above mentionned was the most desirous of going there. The reasons of such an ardor I think I may attribute to other motives than a mere love of the American cause. However (tho' he says he is himself

*I.e. Measam. (Proper names are identified in the "Index" below.)

ready in every thing concerning his duty what I can't be certain of) the same Hazen confesses we are not strong enough to think of the expedition in this moment. As to the troops they are disgusted, and (if you except some Hazen's canadians) affraid to the utmost degree to begin a winter incursion in a so cold country. I have consulted every body, and every body answers me that it would be mad to untertake this operation.

I have been shamefully deceived by the board of war. They have by the strongest expressions promised to me, three thousand, and (what is more to be depended upon, they have assured to me in wraiting *two thousand and five hundred combattans at a low estimate*. Now, sir, I do not believe I can find *in all* twelve hundred fit for duty, and most part of those very men are naked even for a summer campaign. I was to find Gāl Stark with a large body, and indeed Gāl Gates had told to me *Gāl Stark will have burnt the fleet before your arrival*. Well, the first letter I receive in Albany is from Gāl Stark who wishes to know *what number of men, from where, for which time, for which rendez vous I desire him to raise*. Colonel Bedels who was to rise too would have done some thing *had he received monney* one asks what encouragement his people will have, the other has no cloathes, not one of 'em has received a dollar of what was due to them. I have applied to every body, I have begged at every door I could since two days, and I see that I could do some thing was the expedition to be begun in five weeks. But you know we have not an hour to looze and indeed it is now rather too late, had we every thing in readiness.

There is a spirit of disatisfaction prevaling amongs the soldiers and even the officers which is due to theyr not being pay'd since an immense time. This departement is much indebted, and as near as I can ascertan for a so little time, I have already discovered near eight hundred thousand dollars due to the continental troops, some militia, the quartermasters's departement, etc. etc. etc. It was with four hundred thousand dollars whose only the half part is arrived to day that I was to undertake the operation, and statisfy the men under my commands. I send to Congress the account of those debts.

Some cloathes by Colonel Hazen's activity are arrived from Boston, but not enough by far, and the greatest part of it is not cut of.

We have had an intelligence from a deserter who makes the

ennemy stronger than I thought. There is no such thing as straw *on board of the vessels to burn them*. I have sent to Congress a full account of the matter. I hope it will oppen theyr eyes. What they will resolve upon I do not know, but I think I must wait here for theyr answer. I have inclosed to the president copys of the most important letters I had received. It would be tedious for your excellency, was I to undertake the minutest detail of every thing. It will be sufficient to say that the want of men, cloathes, money, and the want of time deprive me of all hopes about this expedition. If it may begin again in the month of june by the last, I can't venture to assure. But for the present moment such is the idea I conceive of the famous incursion as far as I may be informed in a schort time.

You excellency may judge that I am very distressed by that disapointement. My being appointed to the command of the expedition is known through the continent, it will soon be known in Europe as I have been desired by members of Congress to write to my friends my being at the head of an army. The people will be in great expectations, and what schall I answer?

I am affraid it will reflect on my reputation and I schall be laughed at. My fears upon that subject are so strong that I would choose to come again only a volonteer unless Congress offers me means of mending this ogly business by some glorious operation. But I am very far from giving to 'em the least notice upon that matter. Gāl Arnold seems very fond of a diversion against New York and he is too sick to take the field before four or five months. I schould be happy if some thing was proposed to me in that way, but I will never ask or even seem desirous of any thing directly from Congress. For you, dear general, I know very well that you will do every think to procure me the only thing I am ambitious of—glory.

I think your excellency will approve of my staying here till further orders and of my taking the liberty of sending my dispatches to Congress by a very quick occasion without going through the hands of my general. But I was desirous to acquaint them soon of my disagreable and ridiculous situation.

With the greatest affection and respect I have the honor to be
Your most obedient servant

The M^quis de Lafayette.

Will you be so good as to present my respects to your lady

[13]

The 23ᵈ february 1778

Dear General

I meet an occasion of wraiting to your excellency which I w'ont miss by any means, even schould I be affraid of becoming tedious and troublesome but if they have sent me far from you for I don't know what purpose, at least I must make some little use of my pen to prevent all communication be cut of betwen your excellency and me. I have written lately to you my distressing, ridiculous, foolish, and indeed nameless situation. I am sent with a great noise at the head of an army for doing great things, the whole continent, France and Europe herself by in by, and what is the worse, the british army are in expectations. How far they will be deceived, how far we schall be ridiculized, you may judge very well by the candid account you have got of the state of our affairs.

There are things, I dare say, in which I am deceived—Colonel [illegible]* is not here for nothing—one other gentleman became very popular before I went in this place. Arnold himself is very found of him. Every part I mean to look at, I am sure a cloud is drawn before my eyes. However there are points I can not be deceived upon. The want of monney the disatisfaction among the soldiers, the disinclination of every one (except the canadians who mean to stay at home) for this expedition, are conspicuous and as clear as possible. However I am sure I will become very ridiculous and laughed at. My *expedition* will be as famous as the *secret expedition* against rhode island. I confess, my dear general, that I find myself of very quick feelings whenever my reputation and glory are concerned in any thing. It is very hard indeed that such a part of my happiness without which I can't live, would depend upon the schemes which I never knew of but when there was no more time of putting them in execution. I assure you, my most dear and respected friend, that I am more unhappy than I ever was.

My desire of doing some thing was such that I have thought of doing it by surprise with a detachement. But it seems to me rash and quite impossible. I schould be very happy if you was here to give me some advices—but I have not any body to consult with. They have sent to me more than twenty french officers. I do'nt know

*The name has been scratched out but apparently is Troop. (Proper names are identified in the "Index" below.)

what to do with them. I beg you would give me the line of conduct you advise me to follow on every point. I am at a loss how to act, and indeed I do'nt know what I am here myself.

However as being the eldest officer (after Gāl Arnold has desired me to take the command) I think it is my duty to mind the business of this part of America as well as I can. Gāl Gates holds yet the title and power of commander in chief of the northern department. But as 200 000 dollars are arrived I have taken upon myself to pay the most necessary part of the debts we are involved in. I am about sending provisions to fort Schuïller. I'l go to see the fort. I try to get some cloathes for the troops, to buy some articles for the next campaign. I have directed some monney to be borrowed upon my credit to satisfy the troops who are much discontented. In all I endeavour to do for the best tho' I have no particular authority or instruction and I'l come as near as I can of Gāl Gates's intentions. But I want much to get an answer to my letter.

I fancy (betwen us) that the actual scheme is to having me out of this part of the continent, and Gāl Connway in chief under the immediate direction of Gāl Gates. How they will bring it up I do not know—but be certain some thing of that kind will appear. You are nearer than myself, and every honest man in Congress is your friend, therefore you may foresee and prevent if possible the evil hundred times better than I can. I would only give that idea to your excellency.

After having written in Europe (by the desire of the members of Congress) so many fine things about my commanding an army, I'l be ashamed if nothing can be done by me in that way. I am told Gal Putnam is recalled, and Goodell is expected on that part. But your excellency knows better than I do what could be convenient; therefore I do'nt want to mind those things myself.

The young british officer I came with do not seem a very good fellow. After he left me, he was met by Mr du Plessis in a tavern where he got drunk and made such a noise, and told so many indecent things, that du plessis arrested him till he could hear from me. I have writen to him that he could go to Boston. That little fellow is the greatest lyar I ever saw.

I have heard of a robbery from my late landlord which if it is true deserves he schould be hanged.

Will you be so good as to present my respects to your lady; with the most tenderest affection and highest respect I have the honor to be

Your excellency's

the most obedient servant
Lafayette

[14]

Albany the 27 February, 1778.

Dear General,

I hope your excellency will have received two letters from me, one by major Brice, and the other by a doctor who was going to head quarters—you will have seen very sorry accounts of our disappointement—that such an expedition they were so sanguine upon has not been prepared before hand, that or themselves or at least myself has been deceived so much, are things very surprising for every one who will inquire into the matter—however those very blunders will make the expedition, the troops intended for it, and myself ridiculous to the world, unless some means are given to me to mind our business and prevent people from laughing at us. I assure you, my dear General, that I find myself much concerned and unhappy in that affair.

You could perhaps think that the means of succès have been afterwards taken [?] out from me for particular reasons you know of—but I do'nt believe they had time to do it, and had been the expedition conducted for all points in theyr own way, we should have been prevented from proceeding by want of men, cloathes, pay, forage, and by the general disinclination for the enterprize.

I expect with the greatest impatience letters from your excellency and Congress, I hope you will excuse the impropriety of my sending immediately my despatches from here, about that very business of the expedition, but you will easely conceive my reasons for acting so—now tho' I do not know yet what I am neither what I schall be, my being considered (by Gal Arnold's desire), as the commander officer here gives me the right to do what I think best for the good of the service—I should very happy had I by a greater proximity, the opportunity of asking oftener your excellency's orders and advices.

My first care has been to pay the most necessary debts out of the 200,000 dollars which came in my hands—I have thought very necessary to send six month's provisions to Fort Schuyller—I have hurried the sending for the canon at Tyconderoga which will be mended if possible as fast as we'l be able to work—most part of 'em are desired for the defense of North river—I will give every assistance in my power for that so important defense, and indeed I am affraid it wo'nt be finish'd in time—I wish'd that point was not so far of to be able of giving an account of it to your excellency—our cloathier's stores are very poor—they keep immense quantities of 'em in and about Boston—it is very wrong.

I have found the departement of artillery stores in a very good order but much weakened by the last envoy you certainly know of —the hospitals are amazingly well—the soldiers in this town have a pretty good appearance—as I have been desired by Gal Schuyller to meet along with him the Indians at a grand treaty, I'l go to-morrow by Sconnectedy to John's town, and if possible to Fort Schuyller, there I'l be able to give your excellency an account of the troops in those quarters.

I have received some applications for arms, but I wo'nt dispose of any before knowing very certainly your intentions—the Baron de Kalb is arrived, and chooses to stay in this town during my little travel. Albany is full of French Officers who came to join me and I do not know how I will have them employed schould I stay in some particular command—I hope to receive in a few days orders from your excellency and when I'll be back I'l be able to send you a more particular account of everything.

General Gates, they say, is yet *Commander in chief of the Northern Department* but accounts will come by the nighest way from me to you, till the moment he will signify his holding the Northern command, and then I schall see what to answer.

I understood that John Adams spoke very disrespectfully of your Excellency in Boston—I do not know if it is true, but in that case I schould very sorry to have given to him letters for France—give me leave to say my opinion, my dear General; those ennemy's of yours are so low so far under your feet, that it is not of your dignity to take much notice of 'em—I don't speack however of the honorable the Continental Congress—for if I was General Washington I schould wrait very plain to them.

With the greatest respect and most tender affection I have the honor to be

      Your Excellency's
       the most obedient servant,
         The Marquis de Lafayette.

[15]

[March 13, 1778?]*

Dear General,

Alwaïs new instances where I find myself obliged to send to Congress was I not so sensible of your excellency's goodness for his officers and particular frienship for me, I schould be afraid you'd not forgive misses so many tho' unvolontary ones— but such is the case in this particular instance—we have in this place a British hospital, British Doctor, British Officers, tho' the situation of Albany do'nt seem fit for all this britannic train. The Doctor has leave from Gal Gates to go down to Niew York with his disabled men (on condition of theyr being exchang'd) as soon as he will have settl'd his accounts—upon those accounts a dispute arises—he wants to pay not what things cost to us but what they are allowed for in the rations of our people—or he will go himself with his men into New York, and from thence send pound for pound of equal quality. This second point I ca'nt grant because his superiors would not acknowledge the authority he had of making the bargain—The first I dare not take upon myself to settle, and therefore I send for an immediate answer from Congress because I am very desirous of seeing those people going home as soon as possible,—they already are, and can become much more, inconvenient to us in this place. I have writen to governor Clinton for knowing his opinion about sending to Newyork two or three British women, a British officer whose life depends says the surgeon on his going home, and a tory gentleman. I like better to have those people without than within, but however am not of opinion of giving them unlimited passes as a general my precursor has done several times.

General Schuyller and other commissioners of Indian affairs having applied to me for granting a small fort to the Onoyeda

*Unpublished. This is probably the hitherto lost letter mentioned in Gottschalk, *Lafayette joins the American army*, p. 137, n. 44.

indians, I send there C^lel Gouvion who will in the same time inspect the fortifications of Fort Schuyller as I have been prevented from going there myself. The Indians have cut theyr wood themselves, some tools, some picquets, and some militia from Tryon county will do the business.

Colonel bedel of the Militia and Gal [illegible] who say they have thousand men, and perhaps have not two hundred, want too have a fort where they furnish wood, workmen, garrison, and Engeneer, I have desired him to send me a geometrical plan of his projected fort with its profiles and dimensions.

Gāl Stark has desired me to mention to Congress, that he looks upon it as not only an useful but even a necessary thing, that two picquets—forts be built in the month of april one in the neigbourhood of Ognon river, the other in this of Skinburry. I have received another application from the people of Cherywalley who cry for a fort in theyr country as they are expos'd to the incursions of indians and torys coming up on their rear. This is a long list of forts, but we have the consolation to think that all those fortifications are reduced to some picquets—this of the Onoyeds seems me the most important and so I did not differ giving proper orders for it—the others I hope your Excellency will take in consideration, and after mentionning to Congress those of Gāl Stark and the one I have granted give me farther directions.

For the arrangement of the British hospital I think I'l do better to wrait not only to Congress but also to governor Clinton—and in case the governor schould advise me to let them go in giving proper securities, then I could take upon myself granting theyr going down.

General Stark has been two days in this town, and seems me very sanguine about a diversion towards Niew York—he says an immense number of militia who would never turn out but for this expedition would join the officer commanding there.

I must confess you, my dear General, that I have been too hasty upon a hint given to me of Congress recalling me without knowing my sentiments about it—you will have found some resentment in the letters and copys I have sent to your Excellency some days ago—but now I am told that Congress far from meaning any disagrement for me, have been kind enough as to expect knowing my sentiments before making any disposition of general officers. I assure you, my dear general, that I will do very chearfully every thing they will propose to me in such a manner—you know too well my heart to be in any doubt but I schall consider myself very happy to serve with you, when this recalling me will not be attended with the circumstances I was warranted to suspect. I say more—the command at Albany I do'nt look upon as fit for my desire of honorable opportunity, unless it would be extended below and that I have not any right to request—in all, my dear general, my mind will be alwaïs super satisfied to be as near you as possible, and I schall look upon any thing you will believe fit for me, as the very best thing I can wish for.

Inclosed I send to your excellency the letter of the British doctor and also my answer.

I have received a resolve of Congress concerning the defense of Hudson's river—it is very extraordinary indeed those precautions come so late, such works schould have been done two months ago—many canons are desired from me and Gāl Gates finds an immense part of artillery in his inkstand, as he had lately found three thousand men, provisions, cloathes, etc. you will see in my answer and this of Major Stephens what we can do in this moment.

Inclosed I send to your Excellency some petitions and resignations—besides that there is a Lt. Blakley of Colonel Lewingston rgt who wo'nt give up his commission till the resignation will be accepted, what I beg your leave for.

Farewell, my most dear and beloved general, do'nt forget your northern friend, and be certain that his sentiments for you will only end with his life—I beg you would present my respects to your lady and thousand compliments to the gentlemen of your family.

With the greatest respect I have the honor to be,
    Your Excellency's
        the most obedient servant,
       Lafayette.

The Canadian prisoners from Gāl Burgoigne's army apply every day to me to get leave to return to theyr familys—I send you the copys of my letter to Congress and that of Major Stephens—I have not heard from your excellency since the first letter.

[16]

[March 22, 1778]*

Dear General

I can never miss an opportunity of rembembering to your Excellency *the mighty commander in chief of the irruption into Canada*, and I seize with the greatest pleasure the first occasion of telling you how happy I have been to see in your last favor a new assurance of those sentiments of yours so dear to my heart. As soon as I have got intelligence by Gal Schuyller, that your were desirous of having some indians, I have dispatch'd three French men with black belts and yellow guineas to bring down as many as possible. I dare hope theyr love for theyr fathers schall engage some to come with me and I'l bring them to your Excellency, for my only actual scheme is to join you and get clear of many people. I have promis'd to those indians they schould have with 'em French officers if they would and I am bold enough to believe your Excellency will not disapprouve any engagement of mine. I schall be very happy to forward the execution of a business you seem desire, very happy also to see you again, and present myself to your Excellency the assurances of the most profond respect. I have the honor to be with

Your Excellency's
the most obedient humble
servant

The Mis de Lafayette

I am told my division will be six thousand strong—God may grant it!

[17]

Albany the 25th March, 1778.

Dear General,

How happy I have been in receiving your Excellency's favor of the tenth present I hope you'l be convinc'd by the knowledge of my tender affection for you—I am very sensible of that goodness which trys to dissipate my fears about that ridiculous Canadian expedition—at the present time we know which was the aim of the honorable board, and for which project three or four men have rush'd the country into a great expense, and risked the reputa-

*Library of Congress, Washington papers.

tion of our arms, and the life of many hundred men, had the General your deceived friend been as rash and foolish as they seem to have expected—oh American freedom what schall become of you, if you are in such hands!

I have the pleasure to inform you that a scouting party of twenty men gone from Bennington to Shelbon on Lake Champlain, having taken post there, was attacked in an house by a British officer at the head of forty five men British and Indians sent on purpose of taking our party who after a brave defense sallied out, and routed the ennemy—they kill'd five men and took six prisoners and fourteen stand of arms—among the prisoners two are wounded but four are in condition of being exchang'd for the same number made lately prisoner—General Stark and Lietn Colonel Safford who gave me that intelligence desire me both to obtain from your Excellency that exchange which they seem to have much at heart.

I have receiv'd a letter from the board and a resolve of Congress by which you are direct'd to recall me and the Baron de Kalb whose presence is deem'd absolutely necessary to your army. I believe this of General Connway is absolutely necessary in Albany and he has receiv'd orders to stay there, what I have no objection to as nothing perhaps will be done in this quarter but some disputes of Indians and torys—however you know I have wrote to Congress and as soon as theyr leave of staying here will come, I schall let Connway have the command of these few regiments and I shall immediately join my respectable friend—but till I will have received instructions for leaving that place from yourself I schall stay, as powerful commander in chief as if never Congress had resolv'd my presence absolutely necessary for the grand Army.

If you mean to recall Hazen's regiment I advise you take in exchange that of GanzeWort of Fort Schuyller, or that of Wanschoys[?] of Sconectady because they are much better on every respect—I think your Excellency schould order down the arms and ammunition of this quarter without loss of time for *reasons obvious*.

Since your last letter I have given up the idea of NewYork and my only desire is to join you—the only request I have made in coming here, and the only favor I have asked from your Commissioners in France, has been not to be under any orders but those of General Washington. I seem to have had an anticipation of our future friendship, and what I have done out of esteem and respect for your excellency's name and reputation, I schould do now out of mere love for General Washington himself.

I am glad to hear Gāl Green is Quarter Master General—it is very interesting to have there an honest man and a friend of yours—but I feel the greatest pain not to hear any thing about reinforcements—what can you do with an hand full of men? and my poor division whom I was so desirous of instructing, cloathing, managing myself in the winter, whom I was told I schould find six thousand strong for the opening of the campaign?—do'nt your excellency think that I could recruit a little in General Greene's division now that he is Quarter Master General—by that promotion I find myself very proud to be the *third* officer of your Army.

Inclos'd I have the honor to send a resignation of an officer who *dislikes* the service.

With the greatest respect and affection I have the honor to be
Your Excellency's
The most obedient humble servant,
Lafayette.

[18]

Sir*

The present questions are the most difficult to resolve upon that have been proposed since I have been in this army. There must be as much civil policy as generalship in the operations of the next campaign. On the other hand our forces, stores, magazines, ressources of every kind (I mean those which we schall get in the camp) are far from being ascertained. We do'nt know how many men we may depend upon, and had we as many as we could wish, I question if we could easely clothe and aliment them (at least as things seem now to stand)

Your excellency wants my opinion upon these three points—attacking New york—attacking Philadelphia—or staying in a fortified camp till the ennemy will go out and laying a plan of conduct for this case

1st An expedition against New york I am very improper to speack upon as I do not know that part of America—but I have been

*Library of Congress, Washington papers. Unpublished.

told those difficulties were not insuperable. You have seen in some of my letters that I was inclined to think of an undertaking upon that part. I schould before know what is King's bridge, and the other fortification behind that point—if Fort *Washington* can be left aside, or easely reduced—if a surprise can be effectuated—if false attacks may have all theyr effect—if we can get a sufficient quantity of boats—pontons etc. etc.—how far the schipping may help theyr land forces—all those things I made myself acquainted with only by way of conversation and it is not sufficient to fix upon an operation. However I understand that with the necessary preparations (and I question if they will be schortly made), twenty thousand men, could succeed in the operation and take the town for a time.

In that case fifteen thousand men, eight of 'em continental troops schould be left in our present camp strongly fortified under an officer who schould have orders to intercept as much as possible the communication of the enemy with the country. That force schould be absolutely necessary to the security of our stores. But let them be on the other side of the *Susquehana* which is very far, an army is yet indispensable for covering two disaffected states, and we must remember that the intention of the english ministry is to treat not only with Congress but with each state separately.

As we cannot hold *Newyork* the principal aim would be to destroy such stores as the ennemy schould not have yet on board of theyr vessels. It seems also very important to ruin as much as possible the islands belonging to the ennemy. Would not it be possible to fortify King's bridge on our side?—However if there was any propability of taking Philadelphia as there is no comparaison between the two conquests, even in the case of an offensive war from us, those parts seem to be considered in the secondary point of wiew. Then some continental troop, with such militia as could not conveniently come down may try to surprise posts by a *coup de main*, or make expeditions in the islands agreable to circumstances.

The expedition of Rhode Island I have nothing to say upon as I am stranger to our actual situation and projects in those quarters. But I believe jealousy must be given to the ennemy every where, but in our very points of attak.

I confess the taking of Philadelphia is the most agreable idea I can form. We send the ennemy out of two very disaffected states.

We begin the campaign in the most schining way. We make the best possible effect both in Europe and in America. But that enterprise is a very dangerous one. We must have at least twenty thousand good continental troops and about the same number of militia volonteers etc. We must be very depending upon our troops, for in every case, or we must storm strong fortifications or we must separate our forces two very dangerous steps.

The taking of *those redoubts and pallissades by regular approches* do not seem to me eligible, then or we must storm the place or we must shut[?] the communications of the ennemy.

For the latter enterprize I understand there is one single place where large vessels can be prevented from coming up. *Billinsport.* Then the fort schould be taken, batterys erected into it, and ten thousand good troops left in the Jerseys to support those batterys. Some thing could be sunk in the chanal as chevaux de frize.

But we prevent only the men of war from reaching Philadelphia. Transports may be sent by the other side of Long Island unless batterys be erected on *Tynicum Island* which is not an easy work and a large body left there to support them. One other army schould be betwen the Schuillchyll and the Delaware which would keep in echec the present forces of the ennemy. How far that project may prouve useful I am very far from ascertaining in my own mind, and speack only of it as the only way I know to embarass the communications of the ennemy. But let us speack of storms.

Storming such redoudts is the most hazardous enterprize the best and oldest troops can form. My wound had prevented me from assisting to the *recconnoissance* which has been made of 'em. They are I understand very strong.* But one commands all the others and there certainly we schould direct the true attak. Perhaps we can carry them. After that hard work schall be done Philadelphia is not ours. If the English fight well what certainly they will, the houses and the streets wo'nt be easely given up. I wish'd the best retreat could be left to them and known by theyr soldiers before the action, then they would not fight with the same obstinacy.

Certainly every soldierlike principle will forbidd to attak with new troops a chain of strong redoubts defended by old and dis-

*This intelligence of one commanding all the other I have heard from many officers among whom the Baron de Stueben [comment in margin by Lafayette].

ciplined men, with all the difficulties we schould meet after those redoubts be carried. But we have two reasons for risking some steps; the expectations of theyr reinforcements, and three dreadfull commissioners whom I fear more than ten thousand men. Your Excellency knows better than me what effect those propositions of peace may have, you know better than me what your soldiers fired with the hope of ending the war, of plundering the city etc. etc. may undertake of superior to the common military rules. The only thing I can say is that had we the certainty of storming the city, and cutting the British army to pieces what certainly would be the case, then reducing Philadelphia in ashes, and lossing the third part of the army would be a good bargain for America if it was attended with so happy consequences.

I beg leave to say what I think is to be done in the third case.

3d The idea of attacking, storming, with large well provided armies, in considering our past and present situation, seems a very romantic one. If by want of forces, of provisions etc. etc. and by the danger of the enterprizes, we are reduced to the old defensive plan this very plan who has been the salvation of America then my opinion is as follows.

Besides the troops of Fishkill, Providence etc. who are to keep *in echec* the forces of the ennemy, prevent his excursions, and undertake some thing themselves our grand army must alwaïs be the double of this of the ennemy. As the cause of America is not a trifling one we must not play an uncertain game. I wish'd the third of the army would alwaïs be in motion upon the flanks of the ennemy, to intercept his convoys, give frequent alerts to him, prevent him from taking any rest, and take all the opportunities offered to them. The other two thirds would be alwaïs compact, alwaïs upon the defensive. I mean *a defensive of marches and planed operations*. For with the double of the forces of the ennemy we schould be able to attak him were proper opportunities offered to us.

I think it would be useful to throw the war in some other provinces, but can not foresee how it could be done in the best manner. I wish the fighting spirit of Sir Henry Clinton may engage him to accept the fields of battle offered by *detachements* of our army in the Jersays where you have also the advantage of being supported by a good militia.

I must confess that tho' a little concerned by the idea that we schall not have such a numerous army as we want, my greatest fears are directed towards the need of provisions and supplies.

Such are, sir, some of the ideas I take the liberty of offering to your Excellency. I beg you would excuse theyr bad order as I write in a great hurry because I have past the time appointed by you, and you know that I was prevented from writing those two past days.

Could I know our present and future means of succeeding in those three different projects, it would not become a young stranger to point out a decisive one in an occasion where the knowledge of the civil and military interests of the nation, of the tempers of the people and soldiers, of the internal and external ressources of America is absolutely necessary. All what I can say is 1st that Newyork is more stranger to me than any other part of America but has this inconvenience that we can not hold it, (so at least I understand), 2d that the propriety of laying still in a fortified camp depends much on the reinforcements expected from England, and the effect those propositions of peace may have upon the people.

3d For Philadelphia it is by far the best scheme if it can be carried with succés. I don't believe we may be enabled to take that town by storm. But if it was the case, I think we are not to consider either burning houses, expending treasures, loosing men, in comparaison of the immense advantages we schould certainly get on every respect.

If we were to take an offensive party, then no time is to be lost for getting men, and the most profound secrecy must be kept.

I am however convinced that not so much on account of the *novelty* of our soldiers who are not fit for storms, than by a want of provisions, or arms, or men, we wo'nt be enabled to obtain in proper time a so happy succès. Then if there were no other reasons necessity will compell us to take the third party proposed by your Excellency I heartely wish I may be mistaken.

With the greatest respect I have the honor to be
Your Excellency's
The most obedient servant
The Mis de Lafayette

Valley Forge Camp 25th April 1778

[19]

Valley Forge Camp the 15th May 1778

My dear General

Agreable to your excellency's orders I have taken the oath of the gentlemen officers in Gāl Woodfort's brigade and theyr certificates have been sent to the adjudant-general's office. Give me leave now to present you with some observations delivered to me by many officers in that brigade who desire I may submit them to your perusal.* I know, Sir, (besides I am not of theyr opinion in the fact itself) that I schould not accept for you the objections those gentlemen could have as a body to any order from Congress—but I confess the desire of being agreable to them, of giving them any mark of friendship and affection which is in my power, and aknowledging the kind sentiments they honor me with have been my first and dearest considerations—besides that, be pleased to consider that they began by obeying to orders, and want only to let theyr beloved general know, which were the reasons of theyr being rather reluctant as far as reluctance may comply with theyr duty and honor) to an oath whose meanings and spirit was I believe misunderstood by them. I may add, sir, with a perfect conviction, that there is not one among them but who would be thrice happy were occasions offered to them of distinguishing yet by new exertions theyr love for theyr country, theyr zeal for theyr duty as officers, theyr consideration for the civil superior power and theyr love for your excellency.

With the greatest respect and most tender affection I have the honor to be

Your excellency's
The most obedient humble
servant
the Mis de Lafayette

---

*The "observations" of the officers is included in the Hubbard Collection, having evidently been enclosed in this letter. Fitzpatrick, XI, 411, n. 78, gives this document in part. (Proper names are identified in the "Index" below.)

[20]

Valley Forge Camp 17 June 1778*

The situation we are in renders it extremely difficult to have a settled notion of what is the best to be done, as the motions of the ennemy depend no so much of theyr circumstances in this country as of foreign events, Negotiations, or ministerial orders which are in this time entirely unknown to us—however the prevailing idea is that they will go to New york through the Jersays. How far that may be a just one I do'nt pretend to say, but if theyr intention was to be in New york as soon as possible, I see many good reasons for choosing to go by land.

1st An enterprize against Philadelphia, if succesfull, would be of an infinite and glorious advantage, and certainly if we could depend upon arriving to the redoubts undiscovered, by a night's march, I would be for moving this evening and attaking the few troops who I understand are left in the town. But I question much if we could be at half way, before they will get notice of it—and unless the certainty of being undiscovered till the moment of the attak was demonstrated to me, I would find the experiment too dangerous.

2d Remaining in this ground till the ennemy have begun an operation what so ever, is certainly the most effectual manner of avoiding an action; however if the enemy had a so very great desire of bringing us to it, I ask if it would not be possible to engage us out of this ground by some other means. I am of opinion that theyr army is as precious to them as ours is to us, and that they will not be found of fighting us, but upon equal grounds—what I understand may be avoided in the Jersays.

That country is unknown to me in almost all its parts, but I am told it is full of advantageous posts, and certainly by what is reported I would prefer to meet there the ennemy, than to oppose any operation of theyrs in north River by a battle, when theyr schipping gives them the opportunity of flying to and from us with the greatest ease.

Therefore in case it would be thought they are rather retreating through that state, I schould propose to remove the army towards the Delaware, at a little march from this place. It would perhaps

*Library of Congress, Washington papers. Unpublished.

44

hurry theyr operations, or alter them or let us know what they mean, three great advantages in war.

3ᵈ I am not found of sending any large detachements from the line, unless it would be some thing like the future light infantry, who being *choosen troops and more lightly* equipped may be join'd to the Jersay militia. But the body of the army must I think act together as much as possible—if any great advantage may be taken of attaking theyr rear guard it is vorth the while bringing the whole army, if not, it is not vorth the while risking a large part of it. I alwaïs except *the light infantry* for the reasons above mentionn'd.

4ᵗʰ How far it is practicable to stop the ennemy in theyr way to Amboy I do not know, on account of my ignorance of the country, and of the obstructions already made—but I think nothing schould be neglected in all cases to make theyr road as difficult as possible, and I think also the ennemy who retreats and who is obliged to embark gives a great advantage to this who pursues them.

5ᵗʰ The fifth question is difficult to be answered even by a man who would very well know the country, and the place where they could be overtaken, but if some other attak than small skirmisches was offered to us, I then would like it a general one.

6ᵗʰ I think that in all cases the sick schould be immediately removed—it seems that the quarter master general do'nt find great difficulties in doing it. Those sick will embarass our motions at all events—for that article an such stores as ought to be remov'd waggons, I think, are to be press'd and every thing done to get clear of them as soon as possible. If we quit this ground, a brigade may be left for guarding them, compos'd of such men as would be the least fitt for a quick march.

If by any motion whatsoever we may hurry theyr going through the Jersay and prevent theyr pillaging or stopping in it we gain an advantage even when it would oblige us to arrive a day latter, towards the Delaware state, where we schall not prevent theyr taking a post if they please at any rate. This reflexion of mine is on account of what has been said yesterday of theyr intention to go that way.

I know the sentiment of almost every body is to stay in our present ground till they ennemy will have taken theyr party—if it is the case we must entirely give up the idea of taking any material advantage of theyr retreat, what I confess I do with reluctance. However as I am almost the* of the general officers who knows less the country I rather refer to theyr sentiments than to this which promises a more agreable prospect—but every day, every hour in bringing new intelligences may give us a greater light. Then the instant schould be little use of without the long apparate of a council of war—where as in almost all the councils since men began to make war, nothing will be decided but to remain in the same place where the council has been met

The Mis de Lafayette

[21]

[Hopewell, New Jersey,]
[June 24, 1778.]†

Dear General

I have sign'd the paper because I have been told I schould sign it and because almost all the others who were of the same opinion as I am have also sign'd—for, Sir, I will easely schow you that there were six gentlemen *for more than fifteen hundred* and only six *for fifteen hundred*. They are as follows.

Gal. Lee	Baron de Stueben	Some of the second column
Lord Stirling	Gal. Portaïl	were for 2500, but would
Gal. Woodfort	Gal. Waïne	like much better 2000 than
Gal. Scot	Gal. Patterson	1500, as they have a notion of
Gal. Knox	Gal. Greene	attaking, and the others only
Gal. Poor	Gal. Lafayette	a notion of scouting.

Now, my dear General, I beg leave to tell some few words about my opinion. It is that Morgan be directed towards the rear of the right flank, and in a word the militia be directed to act about as it has been told and as I will not repeat for indeed I did not like theyr motions to be so minutely dictated by the council.

But for what regards the detachement from this army I am clearly of the opinion, that a choosen corps of two thousand five hundred or at least two thousand selected men ought to have been sent or are to be compleated towards the ennemy's left flank or rear —not to scout as some say, but to attak any part of the English army

---

*In another hand the word "yongest" [*sic*] has been added. But Lafayette was not the junior general present. See Gottschalk, *Lafayette joins the American army,* pp. 201-02.

†Library of Congress, Washington papers. Unpublished.

or of theyr baggage as will furnish a proper opportunity. Some certainly may be depend upon for many reasons too long to mention and very obvious for any body who knows how an army marches.

I would want the column of the main army to be at a proper distance along the left flank of the ennemy—I wish'd however our army would be rather towards the rear, that it would never run risk to be turn'd by the right, which may be easely avoided. If by a chance the corps would put such confusion among the ennemy, that a general attak might be advantageous, then I would not think *that with ten thousand men it is not proper to attak ten thousand English*—but let us only speack of what is likely to happen.

I do'nt doubt but a detachement of 2000 or 2500 selected men will find an occasion of attaking some part of the ennemy with advantage—of even beating those tremendous grenadiers if they fight with them—in a word I would lay my fortune, all what I possess in the world that if such a detachement is sent in proper time, some good effect, and no harm schall arise of it.

The other five gentlemen are of my opinion but principally G$^{al.}$ Portaïl and Baron de Stueben have begg'd me if the matter was yet spoken off to explain you an English how sorry, how distressed they are to see that we were going to loose an occasion which may be reputed as one of the finest ever offered.

In a word I think the measure consistent with prudence, military principles, with the honor of the American army and every one in it, and I am very far from entertaining the same opinion of this we are going to take. I have perceived my dear General, that you were rather inclin'd to follow the same way I so ardently wish for, and I would a council of war would never have been called.

Such a council is a school of logic, it may come an occasion of disputes for these gentlemen may come personal, it will never be a mean of doing what is consistent with the good of the service, the advantage of the occasion, and indeed the authority of the commander in chief.

But I forget that I write to the General, and I was ready to speack freely to my friend. I will finish in begging leave to add a word of protestation to my signature if you think that signature of mine may engage to believe that I did approuve of the project.

The Mis de Lafayette

[22]

Cranburry Half past nine o'clock.
[endorsed in another hand: June 25, 1778]

Dear General
Inclosed I have the honor to send you a letter which C^{lel} Hamilton was going to send me from this place when I arriv'd with the detachement, and which may give you an idea of the position of the ennemy—I will try to meet and collect as soon as possible our forces, tho' I am sorry to find the ennemy so far down that way—we'll be obliged to march pretty fast if we want to attak them—it is for that I am particularly concern'd about provisions—I send back immediately for that purpose and beg you would give orders to have them forwarded as speedily as possible and directed to march fast, for I believe we must set out early tomorrow morning—the detachement is in a wood, covered by *Cranberry* creek and I believe extremely safe—we want to be very well furnish'd with spirits as a long and quick march may be found necessary, and if Gal Scott's detachement is not provided it schould be furnish'd also with liquor—but the provisions of this detachement are the most necessary to be sent as soon as possible, as we expect them to march.

If any thing new comes to my knowledge I will immediately write to your excellency, and I will send an express in the morning.
I have the honor to be dear General,
Your most obedient Servant
Lafayette.

I wish also we could get some axes but it schould not stop the so important affair of provisions*—

[23]

Dear General,
I have receiv'd your orders for marching as fast as I could and I have march'd without waiting for the provisions tho' we want them extremely—Gal Forman and C^{lel} Hamilton sat out last night

---
*An endorsement in another hand follows:
An order was given today to the Commissary General of Issues to provide a Commissary for the detachment, and to send on with him immediately two days provisions for six thousand men, the reason of this number will be obvious—but lest he should be dilatory it will be well to spur him on.

to meet the other troops and we schall be together at *Hidestown**
or *some what lower*—Gal Forman is firmly of opinion that we
may overtake the ennemy—for my part I am not so quick upon the
subject as he is, but his sentiment is of a great weight on account of
his knowledge of the country—it is highly pleasant for me to be followed and countenanced by the army that if we stop the ennemy
and meet with some advantage they may push it with vigour—I have
no doubt but if we overtake them we possess a very happy chance.
However I would not have the army quite so near as not to be quite
masters of its motions, but a very little distance may do it—I have
heard nothing of the ennemy this morning—an officer of militia says
that after they had pitch'd theyr tents yesterday night they struk
them again—but I am inclined to believe they did not go farther and
that the man who brought the intelligence was mistaken. I expect
some at Hides town which I will immediately forward to you—I beg
when your excellency will write to me that you would let me know
the place you have reach'd that I might govern myself accordingly.

With the highest respect I have the honor to be,
Dear General,
Your most obedient servant,
de Lafayette.

at Cranburry 26 June [1778] at five o'clock [a.m.]

[24]

Hice town at a quarter after seven [a.m.]
[endorsed in another hand: June 26, 1778]

Dear General

I hope you have receiv'd my letter from Cramberry, where I
aquaint you that I am going to Hice town, tho' we are schort of
provisions. When I got there, I was very sorry to hear that Mr. Hamilton, who had been riding all the night, had not been able to find
any body who could give him certain intelligences, but by a party
who comes back, I hear the ennemy are in motion, and theyr rear
about one mile of the place that rear had occupied last night which
is 7 or eight miles from here. I immediately put G^als Maxwell's and
Wayne's brigades in motion, and I will fall lower down, with G^al
Scot's, with Jackson's rg^t, and some militia. I would be very happy

*I.e. Hightstown. (Proper names are identified in the "Index" below.)

if we could attak them before they halt, for I have no notion of taking one other moment but this off the March. If I can not overtake them, we could lay at some distance, and attak tomorrow morning, provided they don't escape in the night which I much fear, as our intelligences are not the best ones. I have sent some partys out, and I will get some more light by them.

I fancy your excellency will move down with the army, and if we are at a convenient distance from you, I have nothing to fear in striking a blow if opportunity is offered, I believe that in our present strength *provided they do'nt escape*, we may do some thing.

Gal Formon says that on account of the nature of the country, it is impossible for me to be turn'd by the right or left, but that I schall not quite depend upon.

An officer just from the lines confirms me the account of the ennemy moving. An intelligence from Gal Dikenson says that they hear a very heavy fire in the front of the ennemy's column. I aprehend it is Morgan, who had not receiv'd my letter, but it will have the good effect of stopping them, and if we attak, he may begin again.

Sir, I want to repeat you in writing what I have told to you, which is that if you believe it, or if it is believed necessary or useful to the good of the service and the honor of General Lee to send him down with a couple of thousand men or any force more, I will chearfully obey and serve him not only out of duty but out of what I owe to that gentleman's character.

I hope to receive soon your orders for what I am to do this day or tomorrow, to know where you are, and what you intend, and would be very happy to furnish you with the opportunity of compleating some little advantage of ours. I have the honor to be your most obedient servant,

de Lafayette

The road I understand the ennemy are moving by is the straight road to Montmouth.

[25]

At Robins's tavern half past four [p.m.]
[Endorsed in Washington's hand: June 26, 1778]

Dear General,

I have receiv'd your excellency's favor notifying your arrival at Cramberry and am glad to have anticipated your orders in not going too far—I have felt the unhappy effects of the want of provisions for I dare say if we had not been stopp'd by it, as we were already within three miles of the ennemy's rear, we would very easely have overtaken them and fought with advantage.

I have consulted the gal officers of the detachement, and the general opinion seems to be that I schould march in the night near them so as to attak the rear guard when on the march—we have also spoken of a night's attak—the latter seems dangerous—the former will perhaps give them time of escaping as it is impossible I would move quite close by them, at least nearer than three miles—C^lel Morgan is towards the right flank, Gal Dikenson is a little upon the left, G^als Scot and Maxwel have insisted upon going farther down than we are now. For Wayne's and Jackson's corps they have not had provisions at all but will be able to march in the night. I beg you would let me know your intention and your opinion of the matter, my motions depend much upon what the army will do for countenancing them—I beg you would be very particular upon what you think proper to be done and what your excellency will do. I wish indeed you would be so good as to anticipate the different cases which may happen according to the place where the ennemy lays—Gal Wayne, C^lel Hamilton and several officers have gone to recconnoitre it—I fancy they will lay about seven or eight miles from here—Your Excellency knows that by the direct road you are only three miles farther from Montmouth than we are in this place.

The ennemy is said to march since this morning with a great confusion and fright. Some prisonners have been made, and desertors come amasingly fast—I believe an happy blow would have the happiest effect, and I'll alwaïs regret the time we have lost by want of provisions.

I beg you would answer to me immediately and with the highest respect, I have the honor to be,
   Dear General,
      Your most obedient servant,
      Lafayette.

[26]

At half past ten [p.m.]*

Dear General,

Your orders have reach'd me so late, and found me in such a situation that it will be impossible to follow them as soon as I could wish,—it is not an account of any other motive than the impossibility of moving the troops and making such a march immediately for in receiving your letter I have given up the project of attaking the ennemy, and I only wish to join General Lee. I was even going to set out but all the brigadiers, officers, etc. have represented that there was a material impossibility of moving troops in the situation where ours find themselves. I do not believe Gal Lee is to make any attak tomorrow for then I would have been directed to fall immediately upon them without making 11 miles entirely out of the way. I am here as near as I will be at english town—to morrow at two o'clock I will set of for that place.

I do not know if Morgan's corps, the Militia etc., must be brought along with the other part of the detachement. Gal Forman who do'nt approve much of that notion, says that our right flank must be secur'd, unless to incur the most fatal consequences for the whole army.

I beg your pardon, Sir, if my letter is so badly writen, but I want to send it soon, and to rest one or two hours.

I have the honor to be,
Your Excellency's
Most obedient servant.
de Lafayette.

Be so good as to send a speedy answer of what you thingk proper to order me.

[27]

Brunswik Camp 2d July, 1778.

My dear General,

I have receiv'd one other letter from C^{lel} Armand where he aquaints me of his arrival at Congress, and where he says that his corps amounts already to about two hundred men provided it may

*This letter is endorsed in Washington's hand: 28 June 1778. It is, however, of June 26, 1778: see Gottschalk, *Lafayette joins the American army*, pp. 216-17.

be accepted by Congress and the expense of raising it approuv'd by them—the C^lel adds that a letter from you on the subject will much advance the expedition of his affair, as the gentlemen in Congress will certainly know whether the matter is agreable to your Excellency—for my part besides the esteem I have for that gentleman's character, and affection I entertain for his person, I believe the corps may prove very useful to the service first by its own exertions and merit, secondly by giving room to many stranger officers who cannot be employ'd in the line of the several States.

With the highest respect I have the honor to be
Dear General,
Your most obedient servant,
deLafayette.

[28]

Stratfort, 25 July [1778] at seven o'clock in the morning.*

Dear General,

Enclos'd I have the honor to send you a letter from Gal Sullivan which I took the liberty to oppen—if the suppos'd expedition against Providence has taken place we cannot come up time enough as to prevent it—but I am rather inclined to believe we will find the ennemy fortifying themselves, and therefore the sooner we may begin our visit the better it will be.

I have found Gal Varnum yesterday at this place, who says we could march much faster than we will do, was it not on account of provisions which ca'nt come up with us—there were no magazines prepar'd principally for the article of flour—the provisions must follow upon oxen-teams—however Gal Varnum has sent a head to take every precaution in his power, for facilitating our journey—if the baggage embarass us we'll leave it behind, we are much retard'd by the ferrys, and the best way will be to separate the brigades—

With the highest respect I have the honor to be,
Dear General,
Your most obedient servant,
Lafayette.

*Unpublished.

53

AMENDED [29]
Line [Lyme] over Saybrook Ferry
28th July 1778*

My dear General

I take the opportunity of an express going from Gen Sullivan to your excellency for to let you know how far we are advanced & in which situation is the detachement you have intrusted to my care. I am here with Gen. Glover's Brigade & we have all crossed the river. I hope we shall be at Coventry the 31st of the present. Gen. Varnum & his officers having represented to me that on account of the scarcity of flour, but principally on account of the ferrys which are very frequent & troublesome, it was much better to take the upper road, I have no objections to his going that way because he knows the roads & theyr advantages much better than I do in this part of the continent. It is true to say that had we been together we would have lost at least two days. Our men are in good spirits, not much tired for making such a march & will not want a long rest to be fit for action.

If the men were too much fatigued to-morrow I could halt one day at New London, because I dont believe Gen Varnum may be at Coventry before the 1st of next month. I have sent to day to Gen. Sullivan in order of knowing his directions when I arrive at Coventry which is 18 miles from Providence.

I am very uneasy on account of Col^{nl} Hamilton as I understand he was not yet arrived a few days ago. I hope some of the gentlemen of your family will be so kind as to let me know if they have heard from him. It seems to me that the British have a good mind to defend theyr ground & I hope we will have a very interesting work to perform. With the highest respect & most tender affection

I have the honor to be my dear general
Your most obt svt
Lafayette

I beg leave to present my compliments to your family.

---

*Early copy (ca. 1828-29) in the Harvard College Library, Sparks Mss LXXXVII. Unpublished. (Proper names are identified in the "Index" below.)

[30]

Providence 6th August 1778

Dear General

I have receiv'd your excellency's favor by Gal Greene, and have been much pleas'd with the arrival of a gentleman who not only on account of his merit, and the justness of his wiew, but also by his knowledge of the country and his popularity in this state may be very serviceable to the expedition. I willingly part with the half of my detachement tho' I had a great dependance upon them, as you find it convenient to the good of the service. Any thing, my dear general, you will order or even wish, schall alwaïs be infinitely agreable to me, and I will alwaïs feel happy in doing any thing which may please you or forward the public good. I am of the same opinion as your Excellency that dividing our continental troops among the militia will have a better effect than if we were to keep them together in one wing.

You will receive by Gal Sullivan an account of his dispositions, preparations, etc. I therefore have nothing to add but that I have been on board of the admiral the day before yesterday. I saw among the fleet an ardor, and a desire of doing some thing which would soon turn into impatience if we do'nt give them a speedy occasion of fighting. The officers ca'nt contain theyr soldiers and saylors, who are complaining that they are since four month running after the British without getting at them. But I hope they will be soon satisfied.

The Count d'Estaing was very glad of my arrival as he could oppen freely his mind to me. He express'd the greatest anxiety on account of his wants of every kind, provisions, water, etc. He hopes the taking of Rhode Island will enable him to get some of the two above mentionn'd articles. The admiral wants me to join the french troops to these I command as soon as possible. I confess I feel very happy to think of my cooperating with them, and had I contriv'd in my mind an agreable dream, I could not have wish'd a more pleasing event than my joining my countrymen with my brothers of America under my command and the same standards. When I left Europe I was very far from hoping such an agreable turn of our business in the American glorious revolution.

Tho' I have no account neither observations to give to your

excellency as I am here a *man of war of the third rate*, I will after the Expedition scribble some lines to you, and join to the account of Gal Sullivan the assurance that I have all my limbs and that I am with the most tender affection, entire confidence in yours, and high respect

Your excellency's most obedient humble servant,

Lafayette

I beg leave to present my compliments to the family and Mr de Chouïn.

[31]

Camp before Newport 25 August 1778

My dear General

I had expected for answering to your first letter that some thing interesting would have happened that I might communicate to your excellency. Every day was going to terminate our uncertainties. Nay, every day was going to bring the hope of a succès which I did promise myself to acquaint you off. Such was the reason of my differing what my duty and inclination did urge me to do much sooner. I am now indebted for two favors of yours which I beg leave to offer here my thanks for. The first letter reach'd me in the time we expected to hear again from the French fleet. The second I have just receiv'd. My reason for not writing the same day the French fleet went to Boston, was that I did not choose to trouble your friendship with the sentiments of an afflicted, injur'd heart, and injur'd by that very people I came from so far to love and support. Do'nt be surpris'd, my dear general; the generosity of your honest mind would be offended at the schoking sight I have under my eyes.

So far I am from a critical disposition that I will not give you the journal of our operations, neither of several instances during our staying here which however might occupy some room in this letter. I will not even say to you how contract'd was the French fleet when they wanted to come in at theyr arrival, which according to the rapport of the advertors would have had the greatest effect, how surpris'd was the admiral when after a made and agreed convention, one hour after the American general had given a new writen assurance, our troops made the landing a day before it was expected.

How mortified the French officers were to find out that there was not a gun left in these very forts to whose protection they were reccommanded. All those things and many others I would not take notice of, if they were not in this moment the suppos'd ground upon which it is said that the Count d'Estaing is gone on to Boston. Believe me, my dear sir, upon my honor. The admiral tho' a little astonish'd by some instances of conduct on our part, did consider them in the same light as you and myself would have done, and if he is gone off it is because he thought himself oblig'd by necessity.

Let us consider, my dear general, the motions of that fleet since it was propos'd by the Count d'Estaing himself and granted by the king in behalf of the United States. I wo'nt go so far up as to rembember other instances of the affection the French nation have for the Americans. The news of that fleet has occasion'd the evacuation of Philadelphia. Its arrival has oppened all the harbours, secur'd all the coasts, oblig'd the British navy to be together. Six of those frigattes, two of them I have seen sufficient for terrifying all the trading people of the two Carolinas, are or taken or burnt. The Count d'Estaing went to offer the battle and be a check to the British Navy for a long time at New York. It was agreed he schould go to Rhode Island an there he went. They prevented him from going in at first. Afterwards he was desired to come in, and so he did. The same day we land'd without his knowledge, an English fleet appears in sight. His being divided in three parts by *our directions* for tho' he is a *lieutenant general* he never avail'd himself of that title did make him uneasy about his situation. But finding the next morning that the wind was northerly, being also convinc'd that it was his duty to prevent any reenforcement at Newport, he goes out under the hottest fire of the british land batteries, he puts the british navy to flight, pursues them, and they were all in his hands when that horrid storm arrives to ruin all our hopes. Both fleets are divided, scattered. The Caesar a 74 guns schip is lost. The Marseïllois of the same size looses her masts, and after that accident is oblig'd to send back a ennemy's schip of 64. The Languedoc having lost her masts, unable to be govern'd, and make any motions, separated from the others, is attaqu'd by a schip of the line against which sche could only bring six guns.

When the storm was over, they met again in a schattered condition, and the Caesar was not to be found. All the captains represented to theyr general that after a so long navigation—in such a want of victuals, water, etc. which they had not been yet supplied with. After the intelligences given by Gal Sullivan that there was a British fleet coming they schould go to Boston. But the Count dEstaing had promis'd to come here again, and so he did at all events. The news of his arrival and situation came by the *Senegal* a frigatte taken from the ennemy. Gal Greene and myself went on board. The Count express'd to me not so much as to the envoy from Gal Sullivan, than as to his friend, the unhappy circumstances he was in. Bound by express orders from the king to go to Boston in case of an accident or a superior fleet, engag'd by the common sentiment of all the officers *even of some American pilots* that he would ruin all his squadron in differing his going to Boston, he call'd a new council of war, and finding every body of the same opinion, he did not think himself justifiable in staying here any more, and took leave of me with that true affliction of not being able to assist America for some days, which has been rewarded with the most horrid ungratefulness. But no matter. I am only speacking of facts. The Count said to me these last words—after so many months of sufferings, my men will rest some days, I will man my schips, and if I am assisted in getting masts, etc. three weeks after my arrival, I schall go out again, and then we schall fight for the glory of the French name and the interests of America.

The day *the Count* went off the general American officers drew a protestation, which as *I had been very strangely call'd there*, I refus'd to sign, but I wrote a letter to the admiral. The protestation and the letter did not arrive at time.

Now, my dear general, I am going to hurt your generous feelings by an imperfect picture of what I am forc'd to see. Forgive me for it. It is not to the commander in chief, it is to my most dearest friend General Washington that I am speacking. I want to lament with him the ungenerous sentiments I have been forc'd to see in many American breasts.

Could you believe that forgetting any national obligation, forgetting what they were owing to that same fleet, what they were yet to expect from them, and instead of resenting theyrs accidents as these of allies and brothers, the people turn'd mad at theyr departure, and wishing them all the evils in the world did treat them as a generous one would be asham'd to treat the most inveterate ennemys. You ca'nt have any idea of the horrors which were to be heard in that occasion. Many leaders themselves finding they were disapointed abandonn'd theyr minds to illiberality and ungratefulness. Frenchmen of the highest character have been expos'd to the most disagreable circumstances, and me, yes, myself the friend of America, the friend of General Washington, I am more upon a warlike footing in the American lines, than when I come near the British lines at Newport. Nay, many worthy characters, gentlemen to be entirely depended upon, assure me that the French hospital was abandonn'd as soon as the fleet went off, and that they could not find any body who would give them what they wanted. However they have been now sent to Boston, and by a French man who met them I am inclin'd to think they will be very unhappy all the rout.

Such is, my dear general, the true state of matters. I am sure it will infinitely displease and hurt your feelings. I am also sure you will approuve the part I have taken in it, which was to stay much at home with all the French gentlemen who are here, and declare in the same time that any thing thrown before me against my nation I would take as the most particular affront.

Inclos'd I send you the general orders of the 24th upon which I though I was oblig'd to pay a visit to General Sullivan who has agreed to alter them in the following manner. Remember, my dear general, that I do'nt speack to the commander in chief, but to my friend, that I am far from complaining of any body. I have no complaints at all to make you against any one. But I lament with you that I have had a occasion of seeing so ungenerous sentiments in American hearts.

I will tell you the true reason. The leaders of the expedition are most of them asham'd to return after having spoken of theyr Rhode Island succès in proud terms, before theyr family, theyr friends, theyr internal enemies. The others regardless of the expense France has been brought in by that fleet, of the tedious, tiresome voyage so many men have had for theyr service, tho' they are angry that the fleet takes three weeks upon the whole campaign to refitt themselves can not bear the idea of being brought to a small expense, to the loss of a little time, to the fatigue of staying some few days more in a camp, at some few miles from theyr houses. For I am very far to look upon the Expedition as miscarried, and there I see even a certainty of succès.

If as soon as the fleet will be repair'd which (in case they are treated as one is in a country one is not in war with) schall be done in three weeks from this time, the Count d'Estaing was to come arround, the expedition seems to offer a very good prospect. If the ennemy evacuates New york, we have the whole Continental army. If not we might perhaps have some more men, what however I ca'nt pretend to judge. All what I know is that I will be very happy to see the fleet cooperating with Gal Washington himself.

I think I will be forc'd by the board of general officers to go soon to Boston. That I will do as soon as requir'd tho' with reluctance for I don't believe that *our position on this part of the island is without danger.* But my principle is to do every thing which is thought good for the service. I very often have rode express to the fleet, to the frigattes, and that I assure you with the greatest pleasure. On the other hand I may perhaps be useful to the fleet. Perhaps too it will be in the power of the Count to do some thing which might satisfy them. I wish, my dear general, you would know as well as myself how desirous is the Count d'Estaing to forward the public good, to help to your succès, and to serve the cause of America.

I instantly beg you would reccommend to the several chief persons of Boston to do anything they can to put the French fleet in situation of sailing soon. Give me leave to add that I wish many people by the declaration of your sentiments in that affair, could learn how to regulate theyrs and blush at the sight of your generosity.

You will find my letter immense. I begun it one day and did finish the next as my time was swallow'd up, by those eternal councils of war. I schall have the pleasure of writing you from Boston. I am affraïd the Count d'Estaing will have felt to the quick the behaviour of the people on this occasion. You ca'nt conceive how distress'd he was to be prevented from serving this country for some time. I do assure you his circumstances were very narrow and distressing.

For my part my sentiments are known to the world. My tender affection for General Washington has yet added to them. Therefore

I do'nt want apologies for writing what has afflicted me as an american, and as a frenchman together.

I am much oblig'd to you for the care you are so kind as to take of that poor horse of mine. Had he not find such a good stable as this of head quarters he would have cut a pitifiul figure at the end of his travels, and I would have been very happy if there had remain'd so much of the horse as the bones, the skin, and the four schoes.

Farewell, my dear general; whenever I quit you I meet with some disappointement and misfortune. I did not want it to desire seeing you as much as possible. With the most tender affection, and high regard I have the honor dear general to be your excellency's
the most obedient servant
The Mis de Lafayette

I must add to my letter that I have receiv'd one from Gal Greene very different from the expressions I have right to complain of, and that he seems there very sensible of what I feel. I am very happy when in situation of doing justice to any body.

[32]

Tyver town 1st September 1778

My dear General

That there has been an action fought where I could have been and where I was not, is a thing which will seem as extraordinary to you as it seems so to myself. After a long journey and a longer stay from home (I mean from head quarters) the only satisfactory day I might have finds me in the middle of a town. There I had been sent, push'd, hurri'd by the board of general officers, and principally by G^{als} Sullivan and Greene, who thought I would be of a great use to the common cause, and to whom I foretold the disagreable event which would happen to me—I felt in that occasion the impression of that bad star which some days ago has influenced the French undertakings and which I hope will be soon removed. People say that I do'nt want an action more or less but if it is not necessary to my reputation of a tolerable private soldier, so at least it is to my satisfaction and pleasure. However I was happy enough as to arrive before the second retreat, it was not attended with such a trouble and danger as it ought to be, had not the ennemy been so sleepy, and then I was once more depriv'd of my fighting expectations.

By what I have heard from sensible and *candid* French gentlemen, the action does great honor to Gal Sullivan. He retreated in good order, he oppos'd very properly every effort of the ennemy, he never sent troops but well supported, and displayed a great coolness during the whole day. The evacuation I have seen extremely well perform'd, and *my private opinion* is that if both events are satisfactory to us, they are very schamefull for the British generals and troops. They had indeed so fine chances as to cut us to pieces, but they are very good people.

Now, my dear general, I must give you an account of that journey I have pay'd so dear. The Count d'Estaing arriv'd the day before in Boston. I found him much displeas'd at a protest you have heard off, and many other circumstances which I have reported to you. I did what I could in the occasion—but I must give the justice to the admiral that it has not disminish'd at all his warm desire of serving America. We waited together on the Council, General Heath, Gal Hancock and were very well satisfied with them—the last one did much distinguish himself by his zeal on the occasion. Some people in Boston were rather disatisfied—but when they see the behaviour of the Council, G^{als} Heath and Hancok, they I hope will do the same—I therefore, fear nothing but delays. The mâsts are very far off, provisions difficult to be provided. The Count d'Estaing was ready to come with his land forces and put himself under Gal Sullivan's orders, tho' disatisfied with the latter—but our new circumstances will alter that design.

I beg your pardon, once more, my dear general, for having troubl'd and afflicted you with the account of what I had seen after the departure of the French fleet. My confidence in you is such, that I could not feel so warmly upon any point, without communicating it to your excellency. I have now the pleasure to inform you that the discontent do'nt appear so much. The French hospital is arriv'd to Boston, tho' under difficulties which however I think I have diminish'd good deal by sending a part of my family with them, with order to some persons, and supplications to others to give them all assistance in theyr power. Now every thing will be right provided the Count d'Estaing is soon enabl'd to sail. Every exertion, I think, ought to be employ'd for that purpose in all the several parts of the continent—mâsts, bisket, water, and provisions are his wants. I long we have again the command, or at least an equal force upon the American seas.

By your letters to Gal Sullivan I aprehend that there is some general move in the British army and that your excellency is going to send us reinforcements. God grant you may send so many as with the militia will make a larger army that you might command them yourself. I long, my dear general, to be again with you, and the pleasure of cooperating with the French fleet under your immediate orders will be the greatest I may feel. Then I am sure every thing will be right. The Count d'Estaing (if Rhode Island is again to be taken what I warmly wish) would be extremely happy to take it in conjonction with General Washington, and it would remove the other inconveniences. I am now intrusted by Gal Sullivan with the care of Warren, Bristoll and the eastern schore. I am to defend a country with so few troops as are not able to defend more than a single point—I ca'nt answer that the ennemy wo'nt go where and do what they please, for I am not able to prevent any thing but from a part of theyr army, and this yet must not land far from me—but I answer that if they come with equal or not much superior forces to those I may collect, we schall flogg them pretty well. So at least I hope. My situation seems to be temporary for we expect much to hear soon from your excellency. You know Mr Touzard a gentleman of my family—he met with a terrible accident in the last action—for running before all the others, to take a piece of cannon in the middle of the ennemy with the greatest exces of bravery, he was immediately covered with theyr schots, had his horse killed, and his right arm put in pieces. He was happy enough not to fall into theyr hands and his life is not despaired of. Congress was going to send him a commission of major.

Give me joy, my dear general, I schall have your picture, and Mr Hancock has promis'd me a copy of that he has in Boston. He gave one to the Count d'Estaing, and I never saw a man so glad of possessing his sweet heart's picture, as the admiral was to receive yours.

In expecting with the greatest impatience to hear from your excellency which will be the general plans, and your private motions

I have the honor to be with the highest respect, the warmest and most endless affection dear general

Your excellency's the most obedient humble servant

Lafayette

AMENDED [33]

Camp Near Bristol
the 3d september 1778.

My dear General

I can't let Mons. de la Neuville go to head quarters without recalling to your Excellency's memory an inhabitant of the Eastern Rhode Island schore, who long much to be again reunited to you, and conceive now great hopes from Sir Henry Clinton's motion to Newport, that you will come to oppose him in person. I think if we mean to oppose the ennemy in this quarter that more troops are absolutely necessary, for we are not able to do any thing in our scattered situation—I confess I am myself very uneasy in this quarter, and fear that those people will put in theyr heads to take some of our batteries, etc—which if properly attak'd it will be difficult to prevent, and I am upon a little advance of land where in case of an alarm a long stay might be very dangerous—but we'll do for the best.

I am told that the ennemy is going to evacuate Newyork—my policy leads me to believe that some troops will be sent to Hallifax, to the West Indias, and Canada—that Canada I aprehend will be your occupation of next winter and spring—this idea, my dear General, alters a plan I had to make a voyage home, in some months, for as long as you fight I want to fight along with you, and I much desire to see your Excellency in Quebec next summer.

Mons. de la Neuville is going to head quarters—that gentleman I have a great regard for on account of his politeness, candour, and military merit. I am very happy that he deserves your Excellency's approbation—I will take his brother in my family, Mons. Touzard's arm is in a pretty good situation.

With the most tender affection and highest respect I have the honor to be

Dear General
Your Excellency's
the most obedient humble servant,
The Mis de La Fayette.

[34]

Warren 21st September 1778.

My dear General,

I am to aknowledge the reception of your late favor—your Excellency's sentiments were already known to me, and my heart had anticipated your answer I however confess it gave me a new pleasure when I receiv'd it—my love for you is such, my dear General, that I did enjoy it better (if possible) in a private sentimental light than in a political one—nothing makes me happier than to see a conformity of sentiments betwen you and me upon any matter whatsoever, and the opinion of your heart is so precious to me, that I will ever expect it to fix mine—I do'nt know how to make out a fine expression of my sentiments, my most respected friend, but you know I hope my heart, and I beg you would read in it—agreable to your advices and my own feelings I made all what I could for preventing any bad prejudice being taken on either side—that conduct I also closely kept in the late affair of Boston concerning Mr. de St Sauveur—I wish to have been of some use in both occasions, and I hope we have pretty well succeed'd—the Count d'Estaing is entirely ours—so at least I aprehend by his confidential letters to me, and it affords me a great pleasure—I have found by him an occasion of writing to France, and you'll better conceive than I may describe what part I have acted in the occasion—I thought the best way of speaking of these internal affairs, was not to speack of them at all, or at least very indifferently, so as to give any such report which might arrive as groundless and insignificant. I dare say my scheme will have the desired effect, and nothing will be thought of in France. I thought I would do well to let the Admiral know that you din't lay any blame upon him, and entertain'd the sentiments any honest Frenchman might wish upon this matter.

I am now going, my Dear General, to give you a piece of news—by two expresses sent from Boston in a great hurry I learn that a vessel is arriv'd from Nantz in Portmouth, who had left Europe the tenth of August and brings the following report

that after admiral Keppell had got those seven schips of the line he so much wanted, he went out again, and the French Fleet was ordered to meet him any where—the French had thirty one schips, and the English thirty-three—they met together the 26th

July—Keppell gain'd the wind ward and the battle begun—it was a very severe one—at lenght the British having lost Admiral Keppell who was kill'd, being very much schattered, and having besides the kill'd many wounded among whom was the second in command, gave way as fast as they could, and were warmly pursued in theyr flight by the French squadron. However the windy and foggy weather which came up prevented our taking more than one small man of war—but great many of the large ones were extremely damag'd—the English conceal'd themselves in theyr own harbours, and the French after having been three days at Brest went out again, and were at sea when the bearer left Nantz—the commanding officer of the first French division Mr. *Duchaffaut* had his nephew kill'd, and receiv'd in the same time a severe wound, while his son had the right arm taken off—the third division under the *Duke de Chartres* a prince of the blood was the most engag'd and contributed good deal to that very important victory.

There was, when the man sat out, a Spanish fleet ready to operate as bigg as the French one who had defeated Admiral Keppell—flatt bottom'd boats were preparing and troops encamping near the coasts—such are the intelligences I could get—they were sent first by M^{jor} *Brice* who is in Boston, and secondly by a French gentleman who incloses a note from Mr *de Borda* Major of the fleet directed to him—I expect at every moment a letter from the Count D'Estaing—However he can't but repeat the report of that French merchant man, as the dispatches from the Minister are directed to one Mr *Holker* Consul, in which these of the admiral must be inclos'd. I though your Excellency would be glad to get the above mentionn'd account as soon as possible. I am asham'd and indeed I am sorry for the famous navy of England, to see that she run away in every quarter of the world before the French flagg.

Agreable to a very useful article of a letter to Gal Sullivan, I have removed my most particular post of Bristol, and am in a safer place behind *Warren*. The few spies I have been able to get upon the Island seem rather think of an evacuation than of any enterprise—but you know NewYork is the fountain head.

I long much, my dear General, to be again with you—our separation has been long enough, and I am here as inactive as any where else—my wish and that you will easely conceive had been to cooperate with the French fleet. I do'nt know now what they will do—the Admiral has writen to me upon many ideas, and don't seem very fixed yet on any scheme—he wants to do—He burns with the desire of striking a blow and it is not fixed yet how to accomplish it. He wrote me that he wanted to see me, but I ca'nt leave my post lest some thing could happen—It has already costed dear enough to me. However if you give me leave, I'll ask this of Gal Sullivan and will do what I think best for both countries.

I have heard of a *pistolade* betwen two gentlemen which lasted very long without a great effect—it looks like our too much spoken off *cannonade* at Newport while the siege was continued. I have not yet been able to find out what your excellency desires me to inquire into on account of the French Queen—but the people of the Navy are too remoted from Versailles to have any knowledge of it and the Count D'estaing himself has not any intimacy with her—I'll get that intelligence from a better way, and *alwaïs agreable to your feelings on the matter* that you might do what you think fit to be done if the report is true.

I beg, my dear General, when you write to your lady that you would present my respects to her, and I beg also the liberty to make here thousand compliments to your family. With the highest respect, and most tender friendship I have the honor to be,

    Dear General
        Your Excellency's
            the most obedient servant
                Lafayette.

[35]

Camp near Warren 24 September [1778]

My dear General

I am going to consult your excellency upon a point in which I not only want your leave and opinion as the commander in chief, but also your candid advice as the man whose I have the happiness to be the friend—in an adress from the British commissaries to Congress, the first one after *jonhstone* was excluded, they speack in the most disrespectfull terms of my nation, and country—the whole is undersign'd by them and more particularly by the president Lord

Carlisle. I am the first french officer in rank of the American army, I am not unknown to the British, and if some body must take notice of such expressions, that advantage does, I believe, belong to me—do'nt you think, my dear general, that I schould do well to write a letter on the subject to Lord Carlisle, where I would notice his expressions in an unfriendly manner. I have mentionn'd some thing of that design to the Count D'estaing but want intirely to fix my opinion by yours which I instantly beg as soon as you will find it convenient. As every thing is perfectly quiet, and Gal Sullivan is persuad'd that I may with all safety go to Boston, I am going to undertake a schort journey towards that place. The admiral has several times express'd a desire of conversing with me. He has also thrown out some wishes that some thing might be done towards securing Boston, but it seems he alwaïs refers to a conversation for further explanation. My stay will be schort as I do'nt like towns in time of war when I may be about a camp. If your excellency answers me immediately I may soon receive your letter.

I want much to see you, my dear general, and consult you about many points, part of them are respecting myself. If you approuve of my writing to Lord Carlisle it would be a reason of coming near you for some instants in case the gentleman is displeas'd with my address.

With the most perfect respect, confidence, and affection I have the honor to be
My dear general
Your most obedient servant
The Mis de Lafayette

[36]

Boston 28th September 1778

Dear General

The news I have got from France, the reflexions I have made by myself, and these which have been suggested to me by many people, particularly by the admiral, increase more than ever the desire I had of seeing again your excellency. I want to communicate you my sentiments, and take your opinion upon my present circumstances—that I look upon as of an high moment to my private business and feelings. On the other hand I have some ideas, and have got some intelligences upon public interest, which I am very desirous of disclosing to your excellency. I am sure, my dear general, that your sentiments upon my private concerns are such, that you will have no objection to my spending some hours with you.

The moment at which the fleet will be ready is not very far, and I think it of importance to have settled my affair with you before that time. I am going to write to Gal Sullivan on the subject, and if he has no objections, I will go immediately to headquarters—but schould he make difficulties I beg you would send me that leave. I intend to ride as an express in changing horses on the road that I might have time enough. You may think, my dear general, that I do'nt ask what I never ask'd in my life, a leave of quitting the post I am sent to—without strong reasons for it—but the letters I have received from home make me very anxious of seeing you.

With the most tender affection and highest respect I have the honor to be

dear general
your excellency's
most obedient humble servant
Lafayette

[37]

Philadelphia the 24th october 1778

My dear General

You will be surpris'd to hear that I am yet in this city, and that I could never get out till this time. My own business was immediately done, and I receiv'd from Congress all possible marks of kindness and affection—but public affairs do'nt go quite so fast, and I am detain'd for the expedition of projects, instructions, and many papers which I am to carry with me. The zeal for the common cause prevents my leaving this place before I am dismissed. However I will certainly set out to morrow afternoon at farthest.

Congress have been pleas'd to grant me an undetermined furlough by the most polite and honorable resolves, to which they have added a letter for the king in my behalf. I will show the whole to your Excellency as soon as I'll have the pleasure to see you, and as I hope to arrive two days after this letter I think it is useless to trouble you with copies.

I have receiv'd an answer from Lord Carlisle, where he conceals himself behind his dignity, and by prudent foresight he objects to entering into any account in any change of situation.

There is a plan going on which I think you will approuve. The idea was not suggested by me, and I acted in the affair a passive part. I will speack to your excellency in longer terms, and with more freedom at the first interwiew. May I hope, my dear general, that you will order the enclos'd letters to be sent immediately to Boston, as some of them give orders for a frigatte to put herself in readiness.

With the highest respect and most tender affection I have the honour to be
>Your excellency's
>>most obedient humble servant
>>>Lafayette

⚜ 1779 ⚜

AMENDED   [38]

Boston 5th January 1779

Dear General

    In my difficult situation, at such a distance from you, I am obliged to take a determination by myself and this I hope will meet with your approbation. You remember that in making full allowances for deliberations the answer from Congress was to reach me before the 15th of last month, and I have long waited since without ever hearing from them. Nay, many gentlemen from Philadelphia, assure, Congress believe that I am gone long ago, and do'nt retain any idea of my being here. Tho' my affairs call me home, private interests would however induce me to wait for your Excellency's letters, for the decision of Congress about that exchange in case I was taken, and for the last determinations concerning the plans of the next campaign.

    But I think the importance of the distpatches I am the bearer off, the uncertainty and improbability of receiving any others here, the advantage my giving intelligences at Versailles may be for both nations, the inconvenience of detaining the fine frigatte on board of which I go, and the danger of loosing all the men who desert very fast are so important reasons, as oblige me not to delay any longer. I the more am of that opinion that Congress, having resolv'd to send about this time three fast sailing vessels to France, and the Marine Committee having promis'd me to give the despatches to such officers as I would reccommend, it is a very good way of forwarding theyr letters, and sending such ones as your excellency will be pleas'd to write me. I beg you would send copies of them by the several vessels.

To hear from you, my most respected friend, will be one the greatest happiness I may feel. The longer letters you'll write the more bless'd with satisfaction I schall think myself. I hope you will not refuse me that pleasure as often as you can. I hope you will ever preserve that affection which I do return by the most tenderest sentiments.

How happy, my dear general, I would be to come next spring, principally as it might get be propos'd, I need not to say. Your first letters will let me know what I am to depend upon on that head, and I flatter myself the first from me will confirm you that I am at liberty and that most certainly I intend to come next campaign.

My health is now in the best situation, and I would not rembember I ever was sick, was it not for the marks of friendship you gave me on that occasion. My good doctor* has attended me with his usual care and tenderness. He will see me on board and then return to h^d quarters, but the charge of your friend was intrusted to him till I was on the frigatte. I have met with the most kind hospitality in this city; and drinking water excepted the doctor has done everything he could to live happy. He dances and sings at the assemblies most charmingly.

The gentlemen who I hope will go to France have orders to go to head quarters, and I flatter myself, my dear general, that you will write me by them. I beg you would let the bearer of this C^{ptne} La Coloombe know that I do reccommend him to your excellency for the commission of major.

Be so kind, my dear general, as to present my best respects to your lady and the gentlemen of your family. I hope you will quietly enjoy the pleasure of being with Mrs Washington without any disturbance from the ennemy till I join you again. I also hope you will approuve of my sailing, which indeed was urg'd by necessity after waiting so long.

Farewell, my most beloved general, it is not without emotion I tell you this last adieu before so long a separation. Do'nt forget an absent friend and believe me for ever and ever with the highest respect and tenderest affection

Your most obed. serv. and affectionate friend

Lafayette

*Dr. John Cochran.

On board of the Alliance 10th january 1779

I oppen again my letter, my dear general, to let you know that I am not yet gone, but if the wind proves fair I schall sail to morrow. Nothing from Philadelphia—nothing from h^d quarters. So that every body as well as myself is of opinion that I would be wrong to wait any longer. I hope I am right and I hope to hear soon from you. Adieu, my dear and for ever belov'd friend, adieu.

[39]

On board of the Alliance 7th January 1779.*

Dear General,

This letter will be delivered to your excellency by Mr. Nevill my aid de Camp whom I beg you to favor with a leave of absence for joining me in France. Besides the affection I have for that gentleman, I also think his voyage may forward the public good as he will be intrusted with those distpatches Congress are going to send. May I beg you, my dear General, to hurry theyr expedition, and let us hear soon from you upon public business—the necessity of not loosing time is very obvious. I also intreat your friendship not to forget writing to me, and if you grant the leave I sollicit for Mr. Nevill his arrival with letters from you will make me extremely happy. That gentleman's father wanted him to cross over with me but there was no room in the fregatte and I engag'd those I could dispose off.

With the highest respect I have the honor to be
    Your Excellency's
      most obedient humble servant
        Lafayette.

[40]

on board of the Alliance off Boston
The 11th january 1779

The sails are just going to be hoisted, my dear general, and I have but the time of taking my last leave from you. I may now be certain that Congress did not intend to send any thing more by me.

*Unpublished. (Proper names are identified in the "Index" below.)

The Navy Board and Mr. Nevill write me this very morning from Boston that the North River is passable, that a gentleman from camp says he di'nt hear of any thing like an express for me—all agree to be certain that Congress think I am gone—and that the sooner I'll go will be the better.

Farewell, my dear general, I hope your french friend will ever be dear to you, I hope I schall soon see you again, and tell you myself with what emotion I now leave the coast you inhabit, and with what affection and respect I'll for ever be, my dear general

Your respectfull and sincere friend

Lafayette

Be so kind as to present my respects to Mrs. Washington and my compliments to all the family

[41]

St jean d'angely near Rochefort harbour 12th june 1779

My dear General

Here is at lenght a safe occasion of writing to you, here I may tell you what sincere concern I feel at our separation. There was never a friend, my dear general, so much, so tenderly belov'd, as I do love and respect you—Happy in our union, in the pleasure of living with you, in that so charming satisfaction of partaking any sentiment of your heart, any event of your life, I had taken such an habit of being inseparable from you, that I can't now get the use of absence and I am more and more afflicted of that distance which keeps me so far from my dearest friend. I am the more concern'd in this particular time, my dear general, as I think the campaign is oppen'd, you are in the field, and I ardently wish I might be there next by you, know any interesting event, and if possible contribute to your succès and glory. Forgive me for what I am going to say, but I ca'nt help reminding you that a commander in chief should never too much expose himself, that in case General Washington was kill'd, nay was seriously wounded, there is no officer in the army who might fill that place, that battle or action whatsoever should most certainly be lost, and the American army, the American cause itself, would perhaps be entirely ruin'd.

Inclos'd I send your excellency a copy of my letter to Congress, in which you will find such intelligences as I was to give them. The Chevalier de la Luzerne intends going to Congress through head quarters. I promis'd I would introduce him to y^r excellency, and I have requir'd him to let you know any piece of news he has been intrusted with. Such a conversation will better acquaint you than the longest letter. The Ministry told me they would let him know the true state of affairs before his departure. By what you will hear, my dear general, you'll see that our affairs take a good turn, and I hope England will get a good stroke before the end of the campaign. Besides the good dispositions of Spain, Ireland is good deal tir'd with English tiranny. I *in confidence* tell you that the scheme of my heart would be to make it as free and independent as America. Some private intelligences I have form'd there. God Grant they might succeed, and the era of freedom might at lenght arrive for the happinness of Mankind. I will know more about Ireland in some weeks and that I will immediately communicate to your excellency. For Congress, my dear general, there are so many people in it that one ca'nt safely unbosom himself as he does with his best friend.

In refering you to M^r le Ch^{er} de la Luzerne for what concerns the public news of this time, the present situation of affairs and the designs of our Ministry, I will only speak to your excellency about that great article money. It gave me much trouble, and I so much insisted upon it that the Director of Finances looks upon me as a devil. France has made great expenses lately, those Spaniards won't give easely theyr dollars. However Dr Franklin has got some monney for to pay the bills of Congress, and I hope I shall determine them to greater sacrifices. Serving America, my dear general, is to my heart an unexpressible happiness.

There is an other point for which you should employ all your influence and popularity. For God's sake prevent theyr loudly disputing together. Nothing hurts so much the interests and reputation of America as to hear of theyr intestine quarrels. On the other hand there are two partys in France. Mms Adams and Lee on one part, doctor Franklin and his friends on the other. So great is the concern which these divisions give me, that I can't wait on these gentlemen as much as I could wish, for fear of occasioning disputes, and bringing them to a greater light. That, my dear general, I entrust to your frienship, but I could not help touching that string in my letter to Congress.

Since I left America, my dear general, not a single line arriv'd from you. That I attribute to winds, accidents, and deficiency of opportunities for I dare flatter myself General Washington would not loose that of making his friend happy. In the name of that very friendship, my dear general, never miss any opportunity of letting me know how you do. I can't express you how uneasy I feel on account of your health, and the dangers you perhaps in this moment are exposing yourself to. Those you possibly may laugh at and call woman-like considerations, but so, my dear friend I feel, and any sentiment of my heart I never could, nay I never wanted to conceal.

I don't know what is become of C^lel Nevill and the Ch^er de la Colombe, I beg you would make some inquiries for them, and do any thing in your power for theyr speedy exchange in case they have been taken. Inclos'd I send you a small note for Mr Nevill. Give me leave to reccommend to y^r excellency the bearer thereof our new plenipotentiary minister, who seems to me extremely well calculated for deserving a general esteem and affection.

I know, my dear general, you want to hear some thing about my private affairs. Those I give an account off to Congress, and shall only add that I am here as happy as possible. My family, my friends, my countrymen made me such a reception, and show me every day such an affection, as I would not have durst to hope. I am since some days in this place where is the king's own Regiment of dragoons which I command, and some regiments of infantry which are for the present under my orders—but I hope to begin soon a more active life, and in consequence thereof my return to Paris is I believe very near. From there I'll get employ'd in whatever will be done against the common ennemy. What I want, my dear general, what would make me the happiest of men, is to join again American colours, or to put under your orders a division of four or five thousand country men of mine. In case any such cooperation or private expedition is wish'd for, I think (if peace is not settl'd this winter) that an *early* demand might be complie'd with for next campaign.

Our ministry are rather slow in theyr operations and have a great propension to peace, provided it is an honorable one, so that I think America must show herself in a great earnest for war till such conditions are obtain'd. American independance is a certain undoubtfull point, but I want that independence to be aknowledged with advantageous conditions—the whole, my dear general, betwen us. For what concerns the royal, ministerial, public good will towards America, I, an American citizen, am fully satisfied with it, and I am sure that alliance and friendship betwen both nations will be establish'd in such a way as will last for ever.

Be so kind, my dear general, as to present my best respects to your lady, and tell her how happy I would feel to present them myself to her, at her own house. I have a wife, my dear general, who is in love with you, and my affection for you seems to me so well justified that I can't oppose myself to that sentiment of her's. She begs you would receive her compliments, and make them acceptable to Mrs Washington. I hope, my dear general, you will come to see us in Europe, and most certainly I give you my word, that if I am not happy enough as to be sent to America before the peace, I shall by all means go there as soon as I may escape. I wo'nt forget telling you, my dear friend, that I have the hope of being soon once more a father.

All Europe wants so much to see you, my dear general, that you ca'nt refuse them that pleasure. I have boldly affirm'd that you would pay a visit to me after peace would be settled, so that if you deny it, you will hurt your friend's reputation through out the world.

I beg you would present my best compliments to your family and remind them of my tender affection for them all. Be so kind also to present my compliments to your general officers, to all the officers of the army, to all the friends I have there, to every one from the first major general till the last soldier.

I most instantly entreat you, my dear general, to let me hear from you. Write me how you do, how things are going. The minutest detail will be infinitly interesting for me. Do'nt forget any thing concerning yourself, and be certain that any little event or reflexion concerning you, whatever trifling you might believe it, will have my warmest attention and interest. Adieu, my dear general, I can't leave the pen, and I enjoy the greatest pleasure in scribling you this long letter. Don't forget me, my dear general, be ever as affectionate for me as you have been. Those sentiments I deserve

by the ardent ones which fill my heart. With the highest respect, with the most sincere and tender friendship that ever human heart has felt I have the honor to be
    Your excellency's most obedient humble servant
        Lafayette.

For God's sake write me frequent and long letters and speak most chiefly about yourself and your private circumstances.

[42]

St Jean d'Angely 13th june 1779

I just receive, my dear general, an express from Court, with orders to repair immediately to Versailles. There I am to meet M^r le comte de Vaux lieutenant general who is appointed to the command of the troops intended for an expedition. In that army I will be employd in the capacity of Aide Marechal General des logis, which is in our service a very important and agreable place—so that I'll serve in the most pleasing manner, and will be in situation of knowing every thing and rendering services. The obligation of setting off immediately prevents my writing to Gal Greene, to gentlemen of your family and other friends of mine in the army whom I beg to accept my excuses on account of that order I did not expect so soon. Every thing that will happen you shall most certainly be acquainted of by me and I will for the moment finish my letter, in assuring your excellency again of my profound respect and tenderest friendship. Farewell, my dear general, and let our mutual affection last forever and ever.

[43]

Havre 7th October 1779

My dear General

From those happy ties of friendship by which you were pleas'd to unite yourself with me, from the promises you so tenderly made me when we parted at Fishkill, I had such expectations of hearing often from you, that complaints ought to be permitted to my affectionate heart. Not a line from you, my dear general, is yet arriv'd into my hands, and tho' several ships from America, several dispatches from Congress or the French minister are safely brought to

France, my ardent hopes of getting at lenght a letter from General Washington have ever been unhappily disappointed. That bad luck I can't any way account for, and when I remember that in those little separations where I was but some days from you, the most friendly letters the most minuted account of your circumstances, were kindly writen to me, I am convinc'd you have not neglected, and almost forgotten me for so long a while. I am therefore to complain of fortune, of some mistake or neglect in acquainting you that there was an opportunity of any thing indeed, but what could injure the sense I have of your affection for me. Let me beseech you, my dear general, by that mutual, tender and experienced frienship, in which I have put an immense part of my happiness, to be very exact in inquiring for occasions, and never to miss these which may convey to me letters that I will be so much pleas'd to receive.

Inclos'd I send to your excellency the copy of my letters to Congress, which in concert with Mr Franklin's longer dispatches will give you a sketch of European intelligences. Contrary winds have much delay'd an expedition which, I think, should have been undertaken much sooner. The kings of France and Spain seem desirous of carrying it on before the winter. It may be however differed till next spring, and the siege of Gibraltar would be the only land expedition for the present campaign. In some week's time, when West India successes will be compar'd to these in Europe. My gazettes and predictions will have a greater degree of certainty, but one must not be a conjuror to see that England is in such a way that one may defy her to get up again, and that an happy peace bless'd with American independence will this or the ensuing campaign be the certain effect of the present war.

As my private circumstances are somewhat interesting to your frienship, I will tell you, my dear general, that since my last letter I have alwaïs been in this place, where head quarters had been fix'd. I was to disembark with the grenadiers forming the van guard, and am therefore one of the first who will land on the english shore. The king's own regiment of dragoons which he gave me on my return, was to embark at Brest, and join us a few days after the landing. From Count d'Estaing's Expedition on the American coasts the nation raises great expectations and very impatiently waits for intelligences. How unhappy I am to find myself so far from you on such an occasion, you will easily conceive. The impression of sorrow such a thought gives me cannot be alleviated but by the sense I have that the general opinion of the turn warlike operations would take this campaign. The ties of my duty towards my own country where my services had been employ'd for the expedition against England, and the hope I entertained of being here more usfeul to the United States, had not left me the choice in the party I should take for this campaign. I hope, my dear sir, you will agree in opinion with me.

Whatever may be Count d'Estaing's succès in America, it will bring on new projects and operations. My ideas I lay'd before your excellency at Fishkills. But permit me to tell you again how earnestly I wish to join you. Nothing could make me so delighted as the happiness of finishing the war under your orders. That I think if ask'd by you will be granted to Congress and your excellency. But be certain, my dear general, that in any situation, in any case, let me act as a French or as an American officer. My first wish, my first pleasure will be to serve again with you. However happy I am in France, however well treated by my country and king, I have taken such an habit of being with you, and am tied to you, to America, to my fellow soldiers by such an affection, that the moment where I will sail for your country, shall be one of the most wished for and the happiest in my life.

From an American newspaper I find that a certain english intelligence had been propagated through the United States—that at they head of fifteen hundred officers or non commissioned officers I was going to embark for America, and that with soldiers of your army embodied under them, I wanted to teach military discipline through the *American army*. However remoted I am from thinking of teaching my own masters, and however distant from such wiews was that command in France whose end you very well know, I could not help taking it as a reflexion on the *American army*. The English troops may remember that on some particular occasions I have not been to lament the want of discipline and spirit in the troops I had the honor to command. While we have but the same British army to fight with we need not looking out for any other improvement than the same qualities, which have often enabl'd my felow American soldier, to give, instead of receiving, pretty good leçons to an ennemy whose justly reputed courage added a new reputation to American bravery and military conduct.

The above article, my dear general, I beg you will have *printed in the several newspapers.*

As there is but a little time to write before the sailing of the vessel, I cannot remind of me the friends I have in the army, unless your excellency is pleas'd to make them thousand compliments from one who heartly loves them, and whose first wish is to be again in theyr compagny.

I congratulate you, my dear general, on the spirited expedition of Stoney point, and am glad it has added a new lustre to our arms.

Be so kind, my dear friend, as to present my best respects to your lady. Mine begs leave to be kindly remembered to you and to her. Thousand assurances of friendship wait from me on your family.

Oh, my dear general, how happy I would be to embrace you again!

With such an affection as is above all expresions any language may furnish I have the honor to be very respectfully.

        My good and beloved general
           Your affectionate
             friend
                  Lafayette.

1780

[44]
At the entrance of Boston harbour
27th April 1780

Here I am, my dear general, and in the mist of the joy I feel in finding myself again one of your loving soldiers. I take but the time of telling you that I came from France on board of a fregatt which the king gave me for my passage. I have affairs of the utmost importance that I should at first communicate to you alone. In case my letter finds you any where this side of Philadelphia, I beg you will wait for me, and I do assure you a great public good may derive from it—tomorrow we go up to the town, and the day after I'll set off in my usual way to join my belov'd and respected friend and general.

Adieu, my dear general, you will easely know the hand of your young soldier

Lafayette

My compliments to the family.

[45]
Camp at Precaness, July the 4th 1780

You know, my dear general, that I am very anxious of seeing the army well cloathed for this campaign. The importance of such a measure is on every account obvious, and from the knowledge I have of the auxiliary troops that are coming I can so well demonstrate its necessity, that I shall for the present but attend to the means of executing it.

In the space of six month (we know from experience) the coats of our soldiers begin to be worn out. So that there is no great inconvenience in giving some new cloathes to the drafts-men, and as, after they will be discharg'd, the number of the remaining soldiers will not much exceed six or seven thousand men, as those very men will have been compleately cloathed by the middle of july, I think I make full allowance for them by keeping in stores the seven thousand unmade suits that have been shipped by Mr Ross.

If more are wanted for the course of next summer, I engage to go over to France and bring back ten thousand compleat suits properly convey'd.

Excluding waggoners, servants, and all such people who don't want to be uniformly cloathed, we may calculate the Continental army to consist of fourteen thousand men in the field.

There may be found in the army four thousand coats and waïst coats which are not absolutely bad, four thousand stoks or cravatts, and one thousand pretty good hatts.

We may get from the stores fifteen thousand over alls, ten thousand pairs of shoes, three thousand round hatts, and some few shirts.

There are also six or seven hundred coats of every colour, to which may be added about three or four hundred of the same kind, and some indifferent hatts found in the army etc.

A small quantity of buff and red cloth to be bought for the facings of the Pensilvania and jersay lines.

The four thousand good hatts in the stores or in the army to be cut round, or cock'd in the form of cap, but to be in an uniform manner.

All the articles now in the possession of the clothier general to be immediately ordered to North River, and, if necessary, waggons should be press'd for theyr speedy transportation. I might write a letter to the Chevalier de Ternay, where he be desired to send to the most convenient place the cloathing which has been put under his convoy.

We shall then have ten thousand new coats and waïst coats, and four thousand old ones the whole of an uniform ground, ten thousand new hatts and stocks and four thousand old ones, five and twenty thousand over alls, more than twenty thousand shirts, and thirty thousand pairs of shoes.

Each soldier inlisted for the war let them be ten thousand shall have, if you choose, a new compleat suit, one hatt, one stock, two shirts, two pairs of over alls, and two pairs of shoes.

Each draft's man, if he has not the same, will at least receive an uniform decent coat, one stock, one hatt, one pair of over alls, and two pairs of shoes. He will not certainly come out but well provided with shirts.

By the above mentionn'd arrangement, there remain about thousand coats of every colour, thousand hatts which are not absolutely bad, and two thousand pairs of shoes. Those I propose to give to such men as will not appear under arms in the field, and, if necessary, some hunting shirts may be added to the said cloathing. The dragoons are generally better cloath'd than the infantry, and we might very easely compleat theyr coats or stable jackets as each different regiment could adopt a different colour.

As soon as the French cloathing comes, I wish the whole army might be cloath'd at once, in observing to give the round hatts to some particular brigades for the sake of uniformity, and to turn up the facings according to the agreed plan.

There will be then no excuse for the officers who out of neglect should suffer theyr men to loose a single article, and the most strict orders may be given for that purpose.

The French arms that are coming might be put in the hands of soldiers inlisted for the war.

I wish there was some distinction of one woollen epaulette for the corporal and two for the sergeant.

As the feathers became a distinction of ranks I wish such as have been pointed out might be forbidded to other officers, and for the Light division I will beg the leave of wearing a black and red feather which I have imported for the purpose.

Those ideas, my dear general, are not given to you as a great stroke of genius, but I heartly wish some thing of the kind may be thought proper.

Lafayette

[46]

[Preakness] Camp July the 16th 1780*

You have desired, my dear general, I would put in writing a summary of the ideas which I gave as my opinion in our conversation of last night. This I am the more inclin'd to do, that, tho' I feel for your delicacy on the occasion, I would think it very wrong not to go the same length with the French forces as you would do with those of the United States.

The idea of starving Newyork has been by me ever considered as a secondary one. I could not but think that twenty thousand very good troops, and ten thousand militia were equal to force the enemy from earth-works, the greater part of which are very little better than field momentary intrenchements. I thought that, we could at least take Brookline, and from there destroy the town, the shiping in the East River, and make the living on the island intolerable for the winter. To be candid, my dear general, I had not nor have I yet any material doubt, but that we were equal to reduce the whole by approaches or storms.

The possessing of the harbour, I confess, was considered by me as an immense advantage, and the arrival of Greaves I take to be a very unhappy circumstance. But in fixing the French points of defense to the entrance, or to the inside of the Hook, I had of course in great respect given up the conveniences of a free intercourse on North River. My meaning in gaining the harbour was then chiefly to obtain the two following advantages 1st to shorten our communications 2d to prevent succours coming in, or troops and ships sliping out.

In supposing that the French fleet amounting to twelve ships of the line may during one month cruize off the Hook, and during the whole siege put themselves in a commanding position, I clearly see that the first purpose will be entirely, and the second will be in any material measure answer'd according to our wishes.

1st Nothing in the world, my dear general, can persuade me that in the space of one month, while the French fleet will cruize off the harbour, there is any difficulty in sending from Philadelphia Chesepeak Bay etc. such quantities of flour forage etc. as will form along

*Library of Congress, Washington papers. Unpublished (Proper names are identified in the "Index" below.)

the Connecticut coasts any magazines we may want. And suppose they were insufficient, is it not ever in the power of a superior fleet to give such convoys as will safely conduct a number of merchant vessels from one part of the coast to the other? Nay, if we are in force out of the harbour we shall save even the transportation from Pensilvania to Staten Island, and our magazines may be form'd merely by water carriage.

2d The second article, my dear general, tho' not so positively ascertain'd may be however reduc'd to this. That for a while the harbour will be bloked up. That for ever we may establish the French fleet either by a cruize or by its laying on one anchor at Rhode island, in such a commanding position as will make it dangerous for a fleet of transport to go in or out of Newyork. So far at least, as will make it madly imprudent for them to think of sending for any reinforcement, and impossible to evacuate the city without loosing the best part of theyr troops and stores. While the French will lay at Rhode island, wont they at all time keep ships of the line and frigates off the Hook? Won't they be appris'd by us of any circumstance which may determine theyr whole fleet to the Hook in such occasions as may become ruinous for the ennemy.

For what relates to the possession of the Sound, it is agreed that from our batteries at Mauricinia, from the frigates at New London, we may (if superior at sea) depend upon a free navigation. And the less of our fleet will be confined in the harbour of Newyork, the more we shall insure our communication in those parts

In combining those ideas, my dear general, I conclude that with a good prospect of reducing the works on the three islands, with a more certain one of taking at least Brookline, and destroying the city of Newyork with the shiping in the East river, with such a superiority at sea as will reduce our communications almost to nothing, and block up for a while, endangering for ever any attempt of the ennemy to go in or out of the Hook, with that command of the Sound which in case of bad luck insures our retreat, we ought not (tho' lamenting Greaves's arrival) we ought not, say I, to relinquish our operation against Newyork.

To those considerations if I add that (in taking the half part of what I have been hitherto told about the advantages and chances of a British fleet without against a French fleet within) there is some possibility of forcing Admiral Greaves, if I add that we have some grounds to hope for a reinforcement from the West Indias, if I behold the sanguine wishes of France, the expectations of Europe, the efforts, the hopes, and particularly the situation of the United States, I will have more and more reasons to attempt this so glorious and decisive conquest.

But in confessing that if we don't attak Newyork we cannot attak any thing, that Canada is put by Congress out of the question, that Hallifax, Charlestown etc. are attended with greater difficulties and uncertainties and with a lesser safety, you so far decide with me in favor of Newyork, and I am so fully convinc'd some thing must be attempted, that (if the French fleet was inferior) I would then try to find out some warrantable way to answer, as far is might be possible, if not the whole at least some part of my scheme.

For what relates to the land operations, my dear general, my opinion is entirely agreable to yours. I wish only your mind to be more and more impressed with the many inconveniences of uniting (at least in the beggining) the French forces to our main army, which should not at any time give way but to a case of absolute necessity. From what I have heard, it seems that Oyster Bay would be the best place, but it may be easely ascertain'd. I shall therefore give you but a summary of my sense of that question, which perfectly coincides with your memorandum.

1st Establishing our communication as low down as possible on North River. 2d Uniting, exercising the army, forming an order of battle, cloathing and arming all our men at once. 3dly Forming in Delaware and Chesepeake Bay, flour, forage, vegetables magazines with transports ready to take them on board. 4thly Collecting cannon, mortars, ammunition, in a word any thing we are worth and freely pressing such waggons and horses as are necessary. 5thly Going down towards the 5th of August to Mauricinia, and establishing our batteries near Hell Gate, upon which the French will rendésvous at Oyster or Wistown Bay.

Then, my dear general, if by an evacuation of the upper posts, or by any disposition of the ennemy we think ourselves enabled to land on York island, there we must reintrench ourselves, and in operating that way send also a detachement to Long island upon which both will land at once and meet about *Wistown*.

But if we don't think proper to take possession of York island, then the same detachement to go in the same way to Long island from Mauricinia where the main army having reintrenc'd themselves will waït both for the reduction of Brookline, and for an opportunity, if offered, to land on York island without reinforcement.

In the third and worse case, if by an unforeseen bad luck you can't be safe without uniting the whole, then we must submit either to send for the French from or joining them at Oyster Bay.

Such are, my dear general, the ideas which I gave out in our last conversation, and which support my hopes for the intended and wish'd for operation.

Lafayette

[47]

Peeks Kill July the 20th 1780.

Dear General

Having heard of an express from Rhode Island being going through the Continental village I sent for him as it would not delay him more than an hour—Inclosed I have the honor to send you the letter from Gal Heath which I have oppen'd and also two letters from the French Generals to me—it seems, my dear General, that they have anticipated the desire you express'd yourself of settling our plans in a private conversation—that way indeed will do better than hundred letters, in case (what however I don't believe) they would wish to speak to yourself, I shall immediately send an express to inform you of it. But I dare say they will be satisfied with my coming.

I am glad to hear they are hunting after the Cork fleet, and those frigates being out will also apprize them of the ennemy's Naval Motions.

Adieu, my dear General, with a heart full of hopes and I think of well grounded expectations I have the honor to be very tenderly and respectfully

Your most obedient humble servant
Lafayette.

I beg my compliments may be presented to the family. It is much to be lamented that Paul Jones din't come in the first convoy—

in case there is nothing to fear from the ennemy I will send the cloathing to New London—Be certain, my dear General, that tho' by serious reflexions and calculations which I can prove to be right I have great hopes of succes, I shall however look upon, and speack of all the difficulties that may present themselves—I have on public and private accounts many reasons to feel the consequence of the plan in question, and to take the greatest care in considering by myself and explaining to others our circumstances—the delay of the small arms I don't consider as equally hurtfull to our affairs as will be the deficiency of powder—But as (even at the so much overrated calculations) we have enough of it for one month, I will try to get a supply from the fleet and then it will come to the same point. You'll hear from me as soon as possible after my arrival.

[48]

Danbury July the 21st 1780

My dear General

As I find an express going from Hartfort to General Greene, I send this letter to him, that you might hear some thing further about the recruits of Connecticut.

From the Colonel who, under Gal Parsons, is entrusted with the care of forwarding them I hear that by the first of August two thousand of them will be at West Point—but I had put in my head that they were to bring arms with them and I find it is not the case.

Gal Parson and myself will meet at Newtown where in mentionning again to him the necessity of hurrying the recruits to West Point, I will apprise him that you have been disappointed in the expectation of some powder and desire him to write to you how far in case of an emergency you might be provided for with that article from his state.

In case Gal Parson thought my waiting on the Governor and Council might answer any purpose, I would go three or four miles out of my way to preach to them some of my old sermons.

With the help of French horses whom I make free with on the road I hope I will arrive very soon at Rhode Island. Nothing about Greaves's fleet—but I am happy to think that they'll find our people ready to receive them at Newport.

When I wrote you, my dear General, that my heart was full of flattering expectations, it is understood that I suppose a sufficiency of arms and ammunition—which I thought so far useless to explain, as I hope you believe I have some common sense. But I had an idea that the recruits would be arm'd, and I yet think (tho' I had no reasons to be particular on that head) that you have many small arms in your stores—for what relates to the powder, I hope that what you will get from the states and what I flatter myself to borrow from the French Fleet will put you in a situation to wait for the Alliance—you may remember that the second division is to come before or very little after the beggining of our operations.

I however confess it is impossible not to be very angry at Captain Jones's delays: and much disappointed in our expectations—the only thing I want to know is if *you depend on a sufficiency of arms and ammunition for the first thirty days*. Be certain that before settling any thing my great bazis will be— *when, and how the second division come, and how far may we depend on the arms and ammunition coming with them.*

I have the honour to be respectfully
        Your most obedient humble svt
        Lafayette.

[49]

Hartfort July the 22d, 1780.

My dear General

I hasten to inform you that the missing transport is safely arriv'd on the 19th at Boston. She is said to be a two decker and to have on board a vast deal of powder with pieces of ordinnance, and also the baggage of the officers of *Bourbonnois*—the intelligence came this instant by an officer of our Army who saw the men encamp'd on the Commons from where they were to march to Providence—two American frigates were, I am told, ordered to convoy the ship arround to Rhode Island, but as theyr orders were to sail by to morrow, they will have time to receive contrary directions from the French Admiral—the inclos'd news-paper will acquaint you of Greaves's cruizing off Block island, and on theyr first appearance Chevalier de Ternay will certainly dispatch an express to Boston.

In a conversation which I had yesterday with General Parsons he told me that he thought the number of your arms in stores amounted to ten thousand exclusive of those which are now in the hands of the men—he seems to be of opinion, and so is C^lel Wadsworth that there is no inconvenience in theyr state's furnishing theyr drafts with arms, and giving even a larger proportion if thought necessary—they say those arms may be by the 5th of August at King's ferry—I was so particular as to make myself certain that this demand will not in the least impeach any other measure, and as it would be too distressing to fall short on that article, I will take on myself, tho' in a private capacity, to persuade the Governor and Council in the measure of arming every one of the men whom they send out, and forwarding the arms to King's ferry or West point as you may direct.

As to the matter of ammuntion, Gal Parsons thinks that (as far as he may guess) near fifty tons of powder might be collected—C^lel Wadsworth says he can't ascertain the quantity—they have three mills, and from what I can collect I am certain that if you attak New York this state will do every thing in theyr power—I will foretell the Governor that he will have a large demand of ammunition, and let you know how much we are to depend upon as far as I may guess from his answer—Mashushushet have say they a vast deal of powder.

I intend to breakfast at Newport the day after to morrow, and as soon as I can make out any thing worth the while from my conversations with them, I will let you know every matter that may be interesting.

With the highest respect and most tender friendship I have the honor to be,

    Dear General
      Your most obedient h^mble servant
        Lafayette.

I am told that the French are in a great want of vegetables—I think it will be agreable to them to forward theyr waggons and horses as much as possible.

AMENDED   [50]
                          Lebanon July the 23rd 1780.
My dear General
   I had this morning the honor to wait on his Excellency the Governor, and took the liberty, tho' in a private capacity, to inform him of our circumstances—the result of our conversation I will therein transmit to you and to be more certain of conveying the Governor's ideas, I am writing at his own house and will show him my letter before I fold it up.
   To begin by the article of powder which is so much wanted, and which from unforeseen circumstances may by its deficiency ruin all our expectations, I am by the Governor desir'd to tell you that you may depend upon 1^{stly} fifty tons for the present 2dly fifteen tons to be made up in the course of August by the three Connecticut Mills 3dly twenty tons which in case of an absolute necessity will be found out in this state—the whole amounting to eighty five tons which he would try to increase, if possible, to ninety—how far that may fulfill your expectations, I don't know, but his excellency will wait for a letter from you on this subject.
   As to the Balls, shells, etc. the Governor cannot as yet ascertain the quantity to be expected but thinks this state may go a great length.
   His ressources for arms have been, it seems, over rated by Gal Parsons and other gentlemen whose opinion I had communicated to your Excellency—the Governor thinks that it would be difficult to arm the whole of the recruits—he will however, if requested by you, do any thing in his power, and might have a good prospect of succeeding for the half part of them. Tho' I had no orders for this interwiew with Governor Trumbull; and from the knowledge of our circumstances took upon myself the freedom of disclosing them to him, I heard your Excellency's sentiments on one point so often, so strongly, and so repeatedly express'd that I could with all certainty assure him that you would not ask from the state more than is necessary to answer our great purposes, and in delivering the country from the danger of ruin, and the discrace of a shameful inability, to turn this decisive crisis to the honor and the safety of America.
   I took also the liberty of mentionning some thing about cloathing the officers, and assur'd the Governor that you thought the

measure to be highly necessary—he entirely agrees in opinion with me, and does not doubt but that at the first meeting of the council a sufficient sum in hard monney will be delivered for that purpose—the knowledge I have of C^lel Wadsworth zeal and activity, makes me desirous that he be intrusted with that business.

As to the cloathing from the fleet, it seems the Governor wishes it to be sent into Connecticut river, and I will engage the French Admiral into that measure—for I am very warm in this opinion, my dear General, and so I know you are, that as less trouble as possible must be given to the people whose exertions should be entirely thrown in such channels as are of absolute necessity. But if we can't send the cloathing arround without an eminent danger at its being taken, then his Excellency the Governor will send it with all possible dispatch and by press'd waggons from the boundaries of Rhode Island to any place on North River which is mentionn'd in Mr. Olney's instructions.

With the highest respect and most tender affection I have the honor to be Dear General

Your most obedient humble servant
Lafayette.

I have read my letter to the Governor and he agrees with the contents—he will immediately give orders about the mills and collect four hundred French arms he has in stock.

L. f.

[51]

My dear General   Newport July the 26th 1780

Every private intelligence from Long Island, and also the letters from Gal Howe and the officer on the lines do agree with the note I have receiv'd from C^lel Hamilton, and are all positive upon it that Gal Clinton with a great part of his Army is coming to attak the French troops.

In consequence of this Count de Rochambeau is fortifying both islands and making preparations of defense. He has requested our calling immediately a body of Militia which demand has been complied with by Gal Heath.

After many intelligences had been receiv'd I did yet persist in disbelieving the report, but they now come from so many quarters that I am oblig'd to yeld to the General idea and expect them in a little time.

I have no doubt but that in the course of the day we will receive some orders and some intelligences from head quarters—The French Generals have ask'd me if your army was in a situation to make a diversion or if a part of it would not be march'd immediately to our relief—My answer was that if you was able to do one or the other you would certainly not loose a minute, but that I could not tell them any thing positive, that however I thought you would come nearer to New york than you was when at Preakaness.

All the last day has been employ'd or in wiewing the camp with Count de Rochambeau or in helping Gal Heath in his arrangements—This morning the Count is gone to recconnoitre the grounds on the island—We dine together at the Admiral's and I will if possible begin our conversation on our affair exclusive of what we are now expecting from the ennemy.

In case you was to send some troops this way I wish I might get notice in such a time as to have some cloathing kept on the road but in all cases we should take some well looking and well drest men —that I only mention as a mere supposition.

If the ennemy mean regular approaches the French Generals say that they would give time for a succour to come—in all suppositions I don't think the French will be able to form a jonction before some time, as they can't leave the island before the fifteenth of next month (in supposing that they are not attak'd) they have many sick—but I will soon be able to tell you more about it, and had not those intelligences been so pressing I might have by this time fully spoken on our affairs with the French Generals.

For my part, my dear General, till orders from you fix any thing I am to do I will stay here under General Heath's orders and help him to the best of my skill—as soon as any thing important comes to us I will send you an express.

From private inquiries I hope the fleet will furnish us with some powder. As to the Militia who are call'd by Gal Heath the French army will spare to them such provisions as may be wanted.

I have the honor to be with the most perfect respect and tender affection

Your most obedient humble servant
Lafayette

[52]

Newport, July the 26th [1780] at seven o'clock p.m.

My dear General,

I had this morning the honor of writing to you by Gal Heath's express and inform'd you that we had from every official and private quarter minuted accounts of the ennemy's coming in great force to attak this island—for my part, I have been long time a disbeliever of the intelligence—But so many letters came to hand that at lenght I was forc'd to take the General opinion about theyr intended expedition—But tho' I wrote you in the morning I know you are anxious of hearing often from this quarter and will therefore desire Gal Heath to send an other express.

Nothing as yet (the ships of war excepted) has come in sight—But the French Generals who have not the smallest doubt about theyr coming are hurrying theyr preparations of defense.

General Heath and myself were invited to a meeting of the French general officers wherein to my great satisfaction the idea of holding both Kononikut and Rhode Island was abandonn'd, as it is assur'd that from the first one the ennemy cannot annoy our shipping, if in a certain position—Count de Rochambeau, Chevalier de Chattelux and myself went afterwards to dine with the admiral and the two French commanders have agreed to the following plan.

The transports to be put in the harbour of Newport—the shipping to Anchor along the shore from Brenton's point going North Wards where they are protected by batteries—a frigate and a cutter to be stationn'd in Sekonnet Passage—the army to encamp at its usual place, but upon the appearance of the ennemy to be in readiness to attak them at any point where they may disembark and if unsuccessfull to retire to the position which was once occupied by the ennemy—there they want also to place some militia—Count de Rochambeau can't hear of the idea of evacuating the island, and says he will defend this post to the last man—I could not help advising him very strongly and very often to erect works and keep a communication openn'd with the continent by Rowland's ferry or Bristol point—that matter will I hope be attended to in the course of the next day.

General Heath will inform you of the measures he has taken

95

in which as the second officer I am only to help him to the best of my power—the Count's urging request made it, I think, necessary to call for Militia.

The number of sick is such that by the return given before me to Count de Rochambeau it appears they will have but three thousand six hundred men fit for duty if they are attak'd within a few days—the fleet has a great proportion of sick men, and the ships are therefore poorly mann'd for the present.

Count de Rochambeau ask'd me so often if you would not send a body of Continental troops to theyr relief, if in the course of twelve days from this they could not be arriv'd etc. that I knew he wanted me to write to you about it, and at length he told me he did want it—but this must be *betwen us*—the Count says that he will stand a storm but if the enemy wanted to make a long work of it that a corps of Continental troops in theyr rear would have the best effects—that in this case the ennemy would be much expos'd on the island, and that the circumstances which would follow theyr reembarking would be so fatal to them as to facilitate our operations for the campaign—all this, my dear General, I was in a private manner desir'd to hint to you.

We could not speak of our grand operations and they are wholly taken in theyr expectations of the ennemy—but what might be an inducement to send a corps this way is that in any case the French will not be able to march before the fifteenth of August.

A return of the cloathing has been promis'd to me for this evening, but tho' I am sorry to be the news bearer of so many disappointements, I must tell you that from what they said to me nothing but a small part of the cloathing has been intrusted to them, and that not only nothing new has been done, but what I had settl'd has been undone by those arrangements of the Alliance which I can't conceive. Mr. Olney having appris'd Gal Heath that he was gone to his lady's near New Heaven and there waited for orders I have desir'd the General to order him here immediately and from here he will take such part of the cloathing as we have got—in case you was to send troops this way I think theyr rout to Providence should be known so that they might meet the cloathing on the way.

What you will do, my dear general, I don't know but it seems Count de Rochambeau is determin'd to defend Newport at all events.

With the most perfect respect and tender sentiments I have the honor to be, my dear General

Your most obedient humble servant
Lafayette.

[53]

Newport July the 29th 1780

My dear General

Your letter of the 22d came to hand last evening and I hasten to answer at least to a part of its contents—I shall begin by the disagreable disappointement I met with on account of our cloathing—inclos'd, my dear General, you will find the return of what has been put on board of the fleet which I have sent by a vessel to Providence, and which will be forwarded to head quarters as soon as Mr. Olney will appear at this place—By my last I informed you that he was at his Lady's and that I had requested Gal Heath to send for him—I can't tell you how much I feel for that shoking Arrangement of cloathing—but as it is not quite so essential as arms and powder, if we have no cloathing, I shall be the forwardest to advise our acting without it—I am apt to blush for neglecting improvements that are within my reach, but I readily do without those which are not in our power.

As to the affair of arms I spoke this morning to the Count, and am sorry to find that he has but the most necessary articles of exchange which are to answer to the dayly broken arms &c—his superfluous armament is coming in the second division, and for the present there is nothing to expect from that Quarter—the only way, my dear General, will be to request the States to pick up arms for theyr recruits—Governor Trumbull (as you may have seen by my letter from Lebanon) thinks there is a great deal of difficulty in this matter —but many other Gentlemen from that State assure that it can be done—I will desire C^{lel} Wadsworth to manage that affair with the Governor, and I will also write a private letter to Mr. Bowdouin and Governor Greene. As to the powder, my dear General, I hope the Navy will give us some—not however a great deal—You can't conceive how difficult it is for the present to speak with them on offensive plans—They expect Clinton at every minute, and say his succès will decide our operations—I had however this morning a conversation with the Land General and was to see in the evening the Admiral who, I am told, cannot come—so that I must delay it to be done tomorrow.

Connecticut will, I think, furnish you with a much greater quantity than you expected—how far it will fulfill your purpose, I hope to hear from you—But I can't flatter you to get so much from the fleet as two hundred, even as hundred tons.

I have fully considered, my dear General, the ideas of those French Generals, and made myself acquainted with every thing that has past since my departure from France—A great mismanagement in the affair of transports has prevented the whole coming here at once—But as the French and Spaniards have a superiority, there is no doubt but that if they join together as was intended the second division will be here in less than three or four weeks—The Fleet on this Continent will I hope be commanded by Mr Duchaffaut and will be very superior to that of the ennemy—if by an unlucky chance the junction was prevented, the second division would yet certainly come in the autumn and be in a situation to act during the winter—But I have all reasons to believe that they will be here in three weeks, and you may depend upon it that they will at all events be here for the winter—From what I have been intrusted with I have a pretty certain ground to hope that my letter will produce upon Count de Guichen the desir'd effect, and after an expedition which I can't trust to paper will be concluded, you may, I think, depend upon his coming this way with a good part of his fleet.

In a word, the French Ministry are determin'd to keep here during the war a Land and Naval force which will act on the Continent till a peace is concluded and to support it with all theyr power —they look upon Rhode island as a point to be kept for Receiving theyr Fleets and theyr Reinforcements of troops, and want the defence of it to be such an object as will insure the Bazis of our operations.

Before settling any thing the French Generals want to hear from theyr second division—*don't fear by any means* theyr acting *rashly* and be assur'd that you may very far depend on theyr *caution* —But our wants of arms and ammunition have made me also very cautious—if the States furnish us with a sufficiency of the first article, and almost a sufficiency of the second which we will make up with the Fleet, then I am most strongly of opinion that waiting for the second division is all together wrong and unwarantable.

I have however brought Count de Rochambeau to this—wiz.— that if the second division comes we must attak—that in all cases if we are masters of the water we may attak—and that we may do it if the Admiral thinks that we can secure the passage by Batteries, and if each part is equal to the whole of the ennemy.

We must now see what the Admiral has to say—What he wrote about the harbour of New york don't please me—if Duchaffaut comes, I answer for any thing you wish—tomorrow I will speack with the two gentlemen, so at least I hope, and will let you know theyr answers.

If the second division comes in time we shall certainly act and succeed—then we will have our arms, powder, cloathing &c.

I never thought, my dear General, that Clinton would come this way—nor do I think it now—but every body says he is coming —Governor Trumbull has it as a certainty, and upon his letter receiv'd this morning they have altered the arrangement I had settl'd to dismiss the extraordinary Militia—I hate troubling all those people and taking them from theyr harvest—General Heath is of my opinion, but the Intelligences are so particular so authentic that he dares not neglect to gather as many men as possible—Before you receive this, you will certainly know the truth of those reports

If you think, my dear General, that Clinton is coming, and if he disembarks upon Rhode island, I am clearly of opinion that three or four thousand Continental troops and the Militia landing on his rear while the Count would sally from Newport would ruin the British army and that the taking of New York would be but a trifle after such a stroke.

In case you adopt the measure I think that the communication with the main is very important—I went yesterday to the North end of the island, and had the works repair in such a way (at least they will be soon so) as to keep up a communication by Howland's Ferry for 8 or ten days after the ennemy will possess the island—I have also desir'd C^{lel} Greene, in case they appear, to run up the boats to Kedze [?] Ferry—signals have been establish'd from Watch point to Connanicut—all those arrangements I have made with the approbation and by the orders of Gal Heath.

You will by this express receive a letter from General Heath who applies for and most ardently wishes a leave of repairing to his command in the Grand Army.

For my part, my dear General, I will, I think wait your answer to this, and want to know if by the situation of your arms and ammunition there is a possibility of your acting before the second division comes—if from the answers of the States you think such a proportion of powder from the Fleet will be sufficient then I will be more positive—if however after my conversations I was to see that the second division must be waited for at all events, then I need not waiting for your answer to this. I will therefore, my dear General

1st or arrange with them a begining of operations before the second divisions comes, and then wait for your answer about arms and ammunition or the prospects I may have by myself to fix it entirely.

2d or fix our plans for the moment that the second division comes and then I will as soon as possible repair to head quarters.

They seem rather doubtfull of the possibility of landing safely and having a sufficiency of boats to carry them under the protection of our West Chester Batteries and I beg you will give me such a note about it as I might show to them.

With the highest respect and most tender friendship I have the honour to be dear General

Your most obedient humble servant
Lafayette.

All the officers and soldiers of the Army have a great desire to join the Grand Army, and hate the idea of staying at Rhode island. Lf.

[54]

My dear General   Newport July the 31st 1780

In consequence of a note from me the Admiral came to last evening, and defensive ideas gave way to offensive plans—our conversation was long and is not yet ended—but I hasten to write you a summary of what past between the Count, the Chevalier, and myself.

I first began in my own name to give them a pretty exact account of the situation we were in three months ago, of the super natural efforts which the country had made for the purpose of an immediate cooperation—I told them that by the first of January our Army would be dismiss'd, that the Militia was to serve only for three month—I added that for the defensive they were useless to us, nay they were hurtfull, and that I thought it necessary take New york before the winter—all that, my dear General, was said in my own name and therefore in a less delicate way than when I am your interpreter.

I then told them that I was going to speak from you and after many compliments, assurances of confidence &c I went on with your plan, beggining with the importance of possessing the harbour and going on about the three ways which you have directed me to point out as to be hereafter Regulated By Circumstances.

As to the possessing of the harbour the Chevalier told that he did not believe his ships might go in—but that if superior at sea, he would answer by cruizing off to protect the landing, the transportation, and prevent an evacuation—indeed to blockade the harbour.

The French General with the advice of the Naval Commander did not hezitate to prefer the going in transports to the point you know off—Both were of opinion that nothing could be undertaken unless we had a Naval Superiority, and as I know it is your opinion also (tho' it is not mine) I durst not insist on that article.

There was an other reason which made we wait for the reinforcement—I knew we had neither arms nor powder—I knew we would be at least a long time to get them—but as they did not think of making me the objection I put my assent to the others on the account of my private confidence in theyr superior abilities—told them that you also thought we should have a Naval Superiority—and added in my own name that however we must, any how, act before the winter, and get rid of a shamefull defensive.

The summary of the arrangement will, I presume, be this—that as soon as we hear of a Naval reinforcement we go where you know, and establish what you intend to fix—that if possible we get where I want you to be—that immediately the French will embark and go where you wish them to be or thereabout—that a number equal to the ennemy's whole force be stationn'd in that part—that they don't want there more than ten pieces of our heavy Cannon—that after every think will be disembark'd three weeks in theyr opinion will do the business on theyr side—that proper means will be taken by sea to keep up the communication and prevent an evacuation—that we must not give up that plan if we may begin in August or September—that fashines and other apparatus must be ready on the opposite shore—that they will take for us all the boats belonging to the Continent which will be at Providence—that as soon as our cloathing &c arrive it will without entering any harbour be sent to W.C. [Westchester?] or thereabout.

Theyr superiority at sea will I think take place in the course of this month—they have two ways to depend upon it. 1st Unless of an absolute impossibility the second division consisting of four other regiments and the remaining part of Lauzun's with the Alliance and all our stores, and with a strong convoy of ships of the line will be here very soon—when they will be heard off on the coast, Chevalier de Ternay will at all events go out and meet them—2dly The Gentleman I wrote to on my arrival* has full liberty to send here reinforcements—the Admiral has already applied to him, but I am going to make him write other letters *in my way*, and will send them tomorrow or the day after to C^her de la Luzerne whom I beg you will immediately desire to secure three fast sailing vessels for the West indias.

I am going this evening to fix places with pilots, and also to speak of the entrance of the harbour—Dobs and Shaw are here and I will have a full conversation with them and the Admiral both for the entrance of the harbour and the Navigation of the Sound—to morrow I call with as much secrecy as possible a number of pilots for the harbour of Hallifax and River St. Laurens.

Inclosed you will find a letter from Count de Rochambeau—he requests you will have the goodness of letting the Minister know what the French Army is about, as he had no time of writing to him —it is, I believe, very important 1st to send every where to meet the reinforcement and give them proper directions 2dly to have some vessels ready for the West indias.

The French set more value upon Rhode island than it is worth —I however got them to promise that in case of an operation they will not leave here a garrison, and that theyr magazines would be sent to Providence.

You know, my dear General, I did not expect Clinton, and tho'

*Comte de Guichen: see above p. 98.

I could not stand alone in my opinion, I ever lamented the calling out of the Militia—I am happy to inform you that they have been dismiss'd—Nothing can equal the spirit with which they turn'd out, and I din't neglect letting the French know that they have done more for theyr allies than they would have done for the security of theyr own Continental troops in a similar occasion.

As to the three month men, the French General wants them to establish the communication with the main—but I will soon request him to let them go to the Grand Army, and will in the same time get from this state as many arms and powder as possible—I have wrote to Mushashushet for the same purpose.

After I will have seen the pilots, and made calculations with the Commander of the Artillery and the first Engeneer whom the Count will consult, I shall draw a plan which I will get theyr answer to and repair with it to head quarters—in the mean time, I will receive answers from Boston and from Governor Greene.

The Admiral can't lend to us more than thirty thousands of powder—but you see that theyr demands as to heavy pieces are small—they indeed say that they don't want any on the island, and that theyr twenty ones will be sufficient—All that, my dear General, I will be more positive upon after the Commanders of Artillery and Engeneers will have made with us theyr calculations.

I hope, my dear General, that by the 5th or 6th of August I will have nothing more to do in this place.

The French army hate the idea of staying here, and want to join you—they swear at those that speack of waiting for the second division—they are enrag'd to be blockaded in this harbour—as to theyr dispositions towards the inhabitants and our troops, and the dispositions of the inhabitants and the Militia for them they are such as I may wish—you would have been glad the other day to see two hundred an fifty of our drafts that came on Kononikut without provisions and tents, and who were mix'd in such a way with the French troops that every French soldier and officer took an American with him and divided theyr bed and theyr supper in the most friendly manner.

The patience and sobriety of our militia is so much admir'd by the French officers, that two days ago a French Colonel call'd all his officers together to desire them to take the good examples which were given to the French soldiers by the American troops—so far are they gone in theyr admirations that they find a great deal to say in favor of Gal Varnum and his escort of Militia dragoons who fill up all the streets of Newport—on the other hand the French discipline is such that chiken and pigs walk betwen the tents without being disturb'd, and that there is in the camp a corn field from which not one leaf has been touch'd—the torys don't know what to say to it.

Adieu, my dear General, to morrow I hope having the pleasure of writing you an other letter and am with the highest respect with the Most tender friendship
Dear General
Your most obedient humble servant
Lafayette.

I beg, my dear General, you will present my compliments to the family.

[55]

Newport, August the 1st 1780.

My dear General,

Your letter to Count de Rochambeau mentionning the ennemy's embarkation, and your future movements against Newyork, a positive letter from Governor Trumbull, and a positive one from General Parsons, have once more altered the dispositions, and such of the Militia as had been dismiss'd have been again sent for.

In consequence of those expectations my offensive arrangements have been entirely cut short—they are wholy taken in theyr preparations—My letter of yesterday has been detain'd with the hope that some intelligence might be added to it—But I will send it this morning, and if it is possible to obtain from the Admiral some hours's conversation with Captains Dobs and Shaw, I shall to morrow morning dispatch an other express.

The dispositions of dèfence are, I believe, these—the French to occupy the English lines—General Heath to command a corps of militia on the Tivertown side—I to have his van guard on the island, and to watch the ennemy's motions almost all arround the island which is not a small affair—if the ennemy land I will try to oppose it, and the French will come in column to attak them with fix'd bayonnets—if this attak don't succeed they will retire behind the lines and take with them fifteen hundred militia, when with the few ones that may stay I will retire to Butt's hill and secure the communication with Gal Heath.

As you did not write to me, my dear General, I could not know what you want me to do—if you think seriously of entering on the island of New york, I am extremely sorry to stay here—if on the contrary you send troops this way, (which if the ennemy land would be fatal to them) I will not be to lament my being a way from the army. I shall feel very unhappy to be with some Militia when the Light infantry is acting under you, and had I been sent for I would have join'd you very fast, but if you can take Newyork I will heartly forget that I could have been there and feel nothing but joy—If, however there was time enough I'd beg you will send for me—if you send troops this way I believe they may strike a great blow.

The wind is against them, so that they won't be here before the day after to morrow. Adieu my dear General, with the highest respect I have the honor to be

      Your friend,

              Lafayette.

AMENDED   [56]

Dear General   Light Camp, August the 10th 1780*

After having stated the few facts that have taken place betwen this and the last meeting of general officers, and after having given to the Council a return of the ennemy's and our own force on this Continent, your Excellency wishes to know what plan in our present circumstances and in the suppositions we can make I would think better to pursue.

In case we have that naval superiority which we may in some measure depend upon, I am entirely of opinion that our attention must point towards the recovery of the Southern States. I would therefore from this moment prepare the provisions which it will be necessary to embark, and advise about the means immediately to procure transports when they will be call'd for.

As to send any Continental troops by land, unless I am strangely

*Library of Congress, Washington papers. Unpublished.

mistaken about the inconveniencies of such a journey, I think that the body of troops which would be sent there could not arrive but with great expense, great loss of men, and a greater loss of time. Those three evils combin'd together would only serve to lessen our force in this quarter without fulfilling there any timely or material purpose.

I would therefore wish that the general officer whosoever that has made the retreat of Gal Gates's army be directed to form as respectable a body of troops as will be in his power, and keep the ennemy in check without risquing a general action.

On our part I am entirely of a different opinion for the conduct we ought to have before the ennemy. The consequences of a defeat will alwaïs in this quarter be worse for them than for us. We ought, I think, to try every stratagem in our power for bringing the ennemy to an action on this side of the North River, and after our exertions will prouve fruitless, would advise (tho' not so strongly) to try the event of a battle on the other side. In case the ennemy were to make a detachement towards Virginia, I would fix all my ideas on a surprise against Newyork, and think the object too immense not to warrant a bold undertaking.

When the assurance of a naval superiority will warrant our preparations for the embarkation of troops, I would advise that six thousand men be ordered to a safe position about West Point, and four thousand be sent towards New London, while transports and provisions would be got in readiness and as soon as the superiority arrives would be sent to New London or Rhode island where the embarkation will take place.

I would then wish that every mean, every influence and even the presence of those who would have the greatest weight be employ'd in bringing the southern states to valuable exertions. It is to be hoped that the states will take some measures for to enlist a part of our recruits for the war. But in all cases three or four thousand men with the militia would for a month or two secure the posts at West Point—and such as would be in Carolina could not return till the expedition was over as the distance by land would be immense.

To that may be objected that we may be short of provisions etc. But if we have none of those ressources we are equally unfitt for any other operation.

If from probabilities it is possible to form by guess any idea I would think that by the month of December we might be in Carolina which is very near the time where a detachement if sent after the interwiew would arrive there by land.

In case on the contrary we have no naval superiority to expect, our prospects would then be very gloomy and I don't see any good chance in our favor, unless the frost was to admit of a *coup de main* against Newyork.

Without a naval superiority the expedition against Canada is the only one that has a probability in his favor. But from the want of cloathing, hard monney, and means of transportation, it has great inconveniences.

Nothing but time can unfold our future circumstances and decide if a naval superiority is to be depended upon in what case my opinion is positive, or if we are to be alwaïs inferior at sea when the circumstances of the time will fix our ideas, either to attak Canada, or to send to the Southern States which may then become necessary.

Indeed, sir, our ressources of every kind are so precarious that unless we depend on a more firm bazis it is impossible to fix on any operation. If we hope for a naval superiority in the space of one or two month, then the impropriety of sending troops by land, and the propriety of preparing an expedition by sea seem to be obvious. If on the contrary that hope of a superiority fails us, then our movements can only be regulated by the state of our ressources, the progress of the army under Lord Cornwallis, the dispositions of the Southern States, and such other events as cannot be presently fix'd upon.

Your Excellency asks if there is any point which we might for the present attak. In supposing that the ennemy do theyr duty I do not see the least prospect of that kind. Here we have only two chances before the winter—the first to draw them out of theyr works, the second if they were to detach any considerable force to try the event of a surprise which cannot be propos'd as a plan and merely depends upon the determination of the instant where it may be practicable.

Lafayette

[57]

Light Infantry Camp August the 14th 1780*

My dear General

You very well know that for many and many reasons both on account of the Country and on that of the French, I think it very important, Nay I might say politically necessary that some thing brillant be at this time perform'd by our troops—to those motives which are very strongly impress'd on my mind and which I might more fully explain in a conversation, I will add, my dear General, that I warmly wish to bring the Light infantry into an action which would put them in spirits for the Campaign.

There are two way of executing it which seem to offer a pretty good probability of succès, and the less they may be foreseen by the ennemy the more it is prudent to undertake them.

I have been this morning to Fort Lee, and from what I could discover it seems that the ennemy have two small Hessian Encampements one the North part of the Island—one of about four hundred men by Fort Washington—the other a little stronger at some distance from that Fort, which by the way is not so difficult of accès as I thought, and in which there appears to be but a small guard—from that place to Newyork, no troops are to be seen—all the ships are below Newyork excepting a small vessel who lays above Fort Lee and does not carry more than four or at most six pounders—so at least we have judg'd.

I can't help thinking that if no other troops are within supporting distance, it would be very easy to bring down boats along the shore with the tide, and when the tide would begin to come up to cross over York island a body of fifteen hundred men—the Right Column to march to the larger Encampement—the left one to the little Camp and to the fort—a night surprise would cause a great confusion in the two camps—on entering in Fort Washington we would burn the Magazine, destroy the provisions or stores and spike up the cannon, and after having kill'd a number and dispers'd the rest of the Soldiers in the Camps we might set fire to the tents—the distance of the shipping below, and the force of the tide coming up would

---

*The envelope is endorsed by Lafayette: "Public Service. In case the General was in bed this is not to be given to him before to morrow morning." (Proper names are identified in the "Index" below.)

make it very safe to go over and retreat with the Greatest ease.

That plan, my dear General, ought to be Minutely examin'd and I will to morrow come to your quarters about diner time—but in all cases would beg leave most earnestly to request you would be pleas'd to send for intelligences on that head.

An other project, my dear General, would be this—supposing that the ennemy have advanced a Corps towards Philip's house, can't we cross over from Dob's Ferry and cut them off? For that article I would also beg you to send for speedy intelligences which will only enlighten our Measures, and do not for the present engage us to any thing.

My motive for being so hasty about getting intelligences is that Gal Clinton's present position seems to afford a very good opportunity of fulfilling my purposes.

With the highest Respect and Most tender Affection
I have the honour to be,
  My dear General,
    Your most obedient humble Servant
      Lafayette.

[58]

    Light Camp August 28th 1780.*

My dear General

I alwais forgot mentioning to you what has past betwen Duke of Lauzun and Myself on account of the diminution that had been made in his horses—from what he told me I saw that it has been put upon this footing that you thought a greater number of horses than was necessary for carrying letters &c. would be quite useless—I explain'd the matter to him, told him you had decided that no less than hundred should be bought, and that in this case your determination had been an active and not a negative one—I even told him you had desir'd me to mention to him this matter very particularly.

The extreme desire which Duke de Lauzun had of serving in this expedition made him embark with the first part of his legion wiz three hundred hussars, hundred grenadiers, hundred chasseurs, and a compagny of artillery—The dress and accoutrements of the hussards make it almost impossible for them to serve a foot, and if

*Unpublished.

they are not mounted Duke de Lauzun had rather serve in the line, than to stay with the legion.

From what he told me, I know you will highly please him and his legion if you hint to Count de Rochambeau the propriety of compleating those horses—I would politically advise the measure and as our prospects are now confin'd to Charles town I will remark that If I am told Light Cavalry is there useful, and that we would be at loss to bring ours to that place.

May I, my dear General, without impropriety request that the *light division* excepting such of them as have fix'd feathers by the last regulations, be ordered to wear a *black and red feather*. I will untertake to furnish them, so that there will be no expense for the Continent, and unless you put that regulation in General orders, we will loose all our feathers, some of them have been already stolen a way.

No Pontgibault as yet, which added to our circumstances of provisions and our dull prospects of inaction, makes me feel very uneasy. Adieu, my dear General, most respectfully and affectionately I have the honor to be
Yours
Lafayette.

Inclos'd I send you the letters for Count de Rochambeau whereto I join a short one containing the daily intelligences but no political reflexion.

[59]

Light Camp Sept. the 2d 1780

Dear General

To my great disappointement M.Pxx* is return'd this morning and brings no details with him—I wanted him to go again, but you alone can induce him to do it—From what he says, the ennemy are going to undertake a great movement—he will himself wait on you and tell you what has been said to him about Rhode island, and what about improving the opportunity of theyr fleet's going to London—Tho' I do not believe they mean to go to Newport, thought however it was well to write a note to Count de Rochambeau which you will send or detain as your excellency thinks proper—Agreable

*Pontgibaud (Proper names are identified in the "Index" below).

to the arrangements of signals made by Mr P. . . . would it not be possible to hurry the movements of the ennemy without giving them time to ripen theyr measures?

With the most tender friendship and high regard I have the honor to be dear general

Your most obedient and affectionate servt
Lafayette.

[60]

New Bridge October the 7th 1780.

Dear General

Mr. Ward's corps being situated on the end of Bergen Neck, two and thirty miles from our army, Major Lee begun to move yesterday after noon and to execute the plan which he had propos'd. He march'd conceal'd through the woods so as to arrive on the ground by the breack of the day.

He had with him his own Corps, M^jor Parr's Riflemen, and a piquet of Light infantry under Captain Abbot.

Having arriv'd in due time, with a secrecy and dispatch, with does credit to himself and his troops—his object was much reduc'd by the unexpected absence of the greatest part of the Corps, and the plan precipitated by the accidental visit of an officer riding through the woods.

He then charg'd the ennemy who had an officer kill'd, a lieutenant, fifteen privates, and about the same number of horses taken—He retook seven farmers who had been stolen away by those people, and return'd to them the property which had been taken from them —The rest of the ennemy's Corps flew to theyr boats, from where they fir'd without effect—Lee did not loose a man, and had not one straggler.

Tho' by accident the object did not become important, the distance and peculiar position of that Corps, as well as the manner in which the plan was executed, are a new instance of M^jor Lee's talents and enterprising spirit.

To support M^jr Lee's movement the Light infantry took its line of march by the Liberty pole—C^lel Gimat's Regiment being stationn'd at Fort *Lee*, and the Militia of M^jor Gotchius at Bull's Ferry.

As the ennemy did not offer any disturbance, we cross'd over the New Bridge, having the river in our front—To morrow at the break of the day our quarter masters will go to Totawa Bridge, and I will march that way at sun rise unless I receive contrary orders.

I hear that we have lost a boat and four men, whom Lee will to morrow exchange for refugees.

With the most tender and respectfull attachement, I have the honor to be dear General

Your most obedient humble servant
Lafayette.

[61]

Light Camp near Totawa October the 12th 1780

My dear General

From Major Lee I just now hear that he has seen a man who has been in Newyork and told him that an embarkation has certainly taken place, said to be going to Virginia—that he got the intelligence in the City on Monday last, and that Dragoons were on board.

A young man that went into the City has lately sent word to his family that he had been press'd on board a Fleet which was going to sail.

Some days ago Major *Lee* communicated to me a private letter from Mr Simcoe who commands the Queen's Rangers wherein that officer seems politely wishing for a personal interview *as he will remain some days in New York*. From all those circumstances and what we have heard from other quarters, I am much inclin'd to believe that the embarkation has taken place and wish to know if any intelligence as to the fact itself, the destination, or the number is come to Head Quarters.

There is a plan, my dear General, which if successfull would be very brillant, and which at least is worth inquiring into its possibility.

The ennemy are far, I believe, from suspecting any enterprise from us against the Works on Staten Island—I think they may be surpris'd in that part, and can't help believing that a corps cross'd over at Elizabeth point, or what I would like better sent down the Passaïc on boats might attempt a stroke on the Works at the Watering place and Richmond, and I also think that with a sufficiency of boats and some other precautions we might make our retreat good—I don't give you, my dear General, any arrang'd plan about it, and confess that I want informations on that matter—the only thing I would request (if you don't dislike the idea) would be that the boats at *Kakeat* or any where else be sent for as soon as possible, and that people be procur'd who might give to us intelligences.

In the mean while, there is a way of getting boats which I beg the liberty to adopt—Major *Lee* having ask'd from me the permission of attempting the boats of the refugees as well as theyr galley in the night, and in the same time to strike at theyr troops on the Point, I have directed him to come to morrow morning that he may explain me his scheme and if I find it a prudent one, I beg leave to let him go on with it.

Unless we hunt for enterprises they will no more come in our way this Campaign—we can't any more build upon certain calculations—I go further, my dear General, and if the ennemy have made a considerable detachement, I would carry up my ideas to such a point as will perhaps have less difficulties than we believe when we will be upon the ground—we might at least make a diversion to give uneasiness to the ennemy—But the thing which I want now to submit to you is the Staten Island project, and the little enterprise propos'd by Major Lee.

With the most tender affection and high respect
            I have the honor to be my dear General
                Yours for ever
                    Lafayette.

[62]

Elisabeth Town October the 27th 1780.

My dear General

From what you have heard from Dr Hagen about the boats when on your way to headquarters, I don't believe that you may have kept any hope for our succès—The boats have been it seems reduc'd to five, and from the time when they were yet at the Little Falls you may see that they could not be here at the appointed hour.

I will not permit myself to reflect on this moment upon the many blunders committed on that affair by the quarter master general's departement—I was too certain of some brillant success, and military glory is too much idolised by me not to be rather severe on the occasion—I will content myself to say that from the report and common agrement of all the spies and guides collected together by Major Lee, from the negligence of the ennemy, the circumstances of the tide and a thik foggy weather, not one of those whom I led into the matter had the least doubt upon our success.

The only advantage I have got from it has been to convince myself that our troops are particularly fit for such an expedition on account of theyr patience and silence, and that if the other business could be supported upon a large scale, I would answer to carry it.

I have writen upon both Roads to the Commanding officer of the Brigade from the line that our expedition was relinquish'd and that I would advise him not to give to his men the trouble of going farther—I have also requested him to speack of this movement as if it had taken place on account of some intelligence that the ennemy meant to come out into the Jersays to attak us.

I have taken my position betwen Elizabeth town and Connecticut farms—Gal Clinton has not the time of making any disposition against us—To morrow at nine or ten I will march to our position of Crane's Town, and the day after to morrow to Totawa unless I receive contrary orders.

Newark Mountain was rather too far to march it this night and too near for to morrow because our men being in want of blankets will like better to join theyr tents again.

If your excellency approuves of this arrangement, I beg you will order our baggage to wait for us on our position of Crane's town—If you dislike the disposition your orders may reach us in the road.

I beg, my dear General, you will please to communicate our ill success and disgracefull disappointement to the Minister who said he would not leave Morris town untill he hears from me.

Had I any thing to reproach to myself on the occasion I would be inconsolable—I undertook the business because I thought myself equal to it, I wish the people in the quarter master departement had done the same for theyr plans.

I am my dear Gen

Yours Lafayette.

[63]

Light Camp October 27th 1780

My dear General

I am sorry to hear from Major Gibs that my letter of last night did not reach you before your departure from head quarters—it had been writen at one o'clock, as soon as I took my position for the night, and intrusted to C^{lel} Ogden who promised to send it by an officer acquainted with the roads.

Depending upon your communication of the sad intelligence to C^{her} de la Luzerne, I did not send to Morristown where he was to wait for the news of the succès.

Among the many blunders which have been committed in the Quarter Master's Departement, I shall extract from that compleat assortement some instances which (not for this glorious occasion that is for ever lost) but on any future one will show you how far you may depend upon their abilities.

You may remember that after a long time Mr Pickering assur'd to you that the boats were in compleat readiness, whilst they had no oars—He afterwards positively told that he had only three boats with him at camp, when two hours before I had seen five of them with my own eyes—The sending of those five boats two hours after that which you had appointed you have been early appriz'd of—But you don't perhaps know that instead of being at Dod's the night before last the boats from Suffrans arriv'd there last evening about sunset. To this report the man who receiv'd them eight miles this side of Sufferans adds, that they wanted then double trees and spread chains, so that he was obliged to loose about two hours in taking those things from Continental waggons and the inhabitants—when our affairs will be thus manag'd your best projects cannot fail of being defeated.

Had Mr Pickering follow'd the example of Gal Knox, every thing would have been here in proper time and proper order as was the artillery from the park—I confess, my dear General, that I cannot reconcile my feelings to the idea that by this neglect I have lost a most happy opportunity bless'd with all the little circumstances which may insure success—our expedition has taken the most foolish turn in the eyes of any one who is unaquainted with this circumstance of the boats.

When I was in hopes of seeing in time at least five of them, I gave up the Watering place, to think only of Richmont—But when I saw that we could not be there before the break of the day, I did not hezitate to relinquish an expedition which on that footing would have occasion'd a great profusion of blood for little or no purpose—But you will easely guess what I have felt on the occasion—I never have been so deeply wounded by any disappointement.

By Mercereau and C^lel Ogden I hear that the ennemy are collecting boats and intend a forrage into the Jersays—I would be very happy to know if you have got the like intelligence—Suppose they were to come out in force and at a distance from us, would not this be an opportunity for to execute your grand plan?

I beg you will let me know this evening if I am to march to morrow to our old ground at Totawa—if the ennemy were likely to come out, or if you thought of a certain plan, I would advise to keep Major *Lee* for some days as in both cases he will be a capital man—he is a most charming officer.

Arnold has issued a second proclamation wherein he invites the officers and soldiers of our army to join him, promising to them equal ranks to those they hold in the American Service.

I am told expresses were sent to me to acquaint me of the delay of the boats—but excepting Doctor Hagen I have not seen one of them—The boats have been sent to the two bridges by M^jor Gibs—I had brought them up with me, and in passing by them both conductors and waggoners have receiv'd the curses of every officer and soldier in the division—The men march'd last night very fast with such silence, good order, and desire of fighting as would have highly pleas'd you—The activity and ressources of Major *Lee* have been on that occasion display'd in such a way as entitles him to my eternal esteem and gratitude—I felt not only for me but for all the officers and men who had promis'd themselves so much glory on the occasion.

With the most tender affection and high respect
I have the honour to be my dear General
Yours
Lafayette

C^lel Ogden has remain'd behind to get intelligences—so that being uncertain if my first letter has reach'd you I would be happy to know in the course of the night if I am to march to morrow morning to the old ground.

[64]

Light Camp October 28th 1780.

My dear General

If I have properly understood your letter you had not an immediate occasion for me, and the matters you wanted to talk of with me are not to be so soon put in execution as to require my going this day to head quarters. I have therefore differed the moving of my troops and that of my person till to morrow. If on the contrary there was the least occasion for my going to head quarters I beg you will please to let me know it that I may immediately go there.

Inclos'd I have the honor to send you Arnold's second proclamation, which in point of impudence exceeds all his former works. If *Lee* goes from me I will apply for some dragoons from other Corps—the difference made by his presence in my security is equal to the doubling of piquets and patroles—I wish Congress would give him a corps of two hundred horse and three hundred foot. Was an other commission necessary I would give it to him because the poor fellow cannot help having abilities superior to his rank—he will, I think, be very useful to the Southward.

Inclos'd are two letters for Rhode island which I have receiv'd from Philadelphia. The Minister has told me that one of his letters to Count de Rochambeau had been an immense number of days along the road, and that he has found one of his letter to me from Rhode island in I don't know whose hands at Harfort. I think the best way is to keep those letters for the expresses or when pressing to send expresses for them—if an express goes to morrow I will send to Count de Rochambeau a project for a contract of flour which I will show to you before I seal my dispatch.

Adieu, my dear General, with the highest respect and tenderest affection I have the honor to be

Yours

Lafayette.

[65]

My dear General Light Camp October the 30th 1780

In our conversations upon military operations, you often have told me that since the beggining of the campaign your eyes were turn'd towards a project upon which I generally agree in opinion with you, and beg leave to offer some observations.

Far from lessening my desire of finishing the campaign by some brillant stroke, the project of Staten island, tho' miscarried, has strengtened my opinions as I have clearly seen by the details of this operation that we should in all human probability have succeeded and that our men were fully equal to any enterprise of this kind.

My reasons for wishing to undertake some thing are these 1st Any enterprise will please the people of this country, show them that when we have men we do not lay still, and even a defeat (provided it was not fatal) would have its good consequences 2dly The French Court have often complain'd to me of the inactivity of that American Army who before the Alliance had distinguish'd themselves by theyr spirit of enterprise. They often have told me, your friends leave us now to fight theyr battles and do no more risk themselves. It is moreover of the greatest political importance to let them know that on our side we were ready to cooperate. Be sure, my dear general, that many people's interest will be to let it believe that we *were not ready*, and if any thing may engage the Ministry to give us the ask'd for support it will be our proving to the nation that on our side *we had been ready*. So far was the Chevalier de la Luzerne convinc'd of this (and on this point the Minister's interest is the same with ours) that he was made happy by my mentionning to him the Staten island affair. I well know the Court of Versailles, and was I to go to them, I would think it very impolitical to go there unless we had done some thing. 3dly It is more than probable that mediators will interfere this winter into a negotiation. There England will say, how can we give up people whom we consider as half conquered—Theyr best fortified city has been taken by an army not much superior to the people that were to defend it—Theyr Southern Army was routed almost as soon as look'd at by the British troops —Newyork is so much ours that they dare not approach it, and Gal

Washington's army does not exceed five thousand men. What shall France answer principally now that from the letters I have receiv'd I find that the Charlestown affair has brought our arms into contempt. But what difference if France might say—The American army has taken sword in hand your best works—They have offered to you the battle upon your own island, and perhaps, may they add, (for news encrease in travelling) are they now in possession of Newyork.

Upon these considerations, my dear general, what I want is this—to find an expedition which may wear a brilliant aspect, which affords probable advantages, and an immense tho' very remoted one, which if unsuccessful does not turn fatal to us, for the loss of two or three hundred men half of them being inlisted for two months I don't consider as a ruinous adventure.

The bazis of the plan will be that Fort Washington being in our possession may with the Fort *Lee* batteries protect our crossing North River, and be a security for our retreat, principally if some works are added on the point of reimbarkation. The taking of Fort Washington we may demonstrate to be very probable, and upon that point you are of my opinion.

The ennemy have on the upper part of the island from fifteen hundred to two thousand men who would immediately occupy all the other upper posts. Theyr army on Long island would repair to Newyork, and there would also retire the troops posted at Harlem.

As soon as Fort Washington would be ours, the army should cross over to the island, and those of West Point arrive in the same time (which calculation may be easely done) so that we would effectually or possess all the upper posts or cutt them off from theyr main army. Some militia would come to our assistance and as those posts are not well furnish'd with provisions we should take them at least by famine.

The ennemy's army consist of nine thousand men. They must certainly leave one thousand in theyr several posts. Fifteen hundred of them at least will be either kill'd at Fort Washington or block'd up at Laurel Hill etc. They will then have between six or seven thousand men to attak ten. The two thousand militia (in supposing that they durst take them out) I don't mention because we may have four thousand militia for them. Under such circumstances is it probable that Sir Henry Clinton will venture a battle? If he does and by chance beats us we retire under Fort Washington. But if we beat him, his works will be at such a distance, that he will be ruin'd in the retreat. If on the contrary, principally if he knows that the French army is coming and if we spread the report of a second division or Count de Guichen being upon the coasts he will keep into his works, and we will some way or other carry the upper posts. When we are upon the spot we may recconnoitre Newyork and see if something is to be done. If Clinton was making a forrage into the Jersays I would be clear for pushing into the city.

If we undertake, the circumstances of the weather make it necessary that we undertake immediately. I would move the army as soon as possible to our position near the New Bridge. This movement may invite Clinton into the Jersays and bring us nearer to the point of execution.

Tho' my private glory, and yours, my dear general, both of which are very dear to my heart, are greatly interested not so much for the opinions of America but for those of Europe in our doing some thing this campaign, I hope you know me too well to think I would insist upon steps of this nature, unless I knew that they are politically necessary, and have a sufficient military probability.

I have the honor to be
Yours
Lafayette

The 600 men of Lauzun's legion might be got in twelve days. If our movements had no other effect but to make a diversion in favour of the southward it would on that footing meet with the approbation of the world, and perhaps impeach the operations of Gal Leslie.

[66]

Light Camp November the 1st 1780*

Dear General

In consequence of your Excellency's orders I am to give you my opinion upon these three point—1st When it will be proper to go into winter quarters 2^d where those winter quarters are to be

*Library of Congress, Washington papers. Unpublished.

taken 3dly if any thing further may be done to oppose the ennemy's operations in the south ward.

The month of November being generally good in America, I would not advise your Excellency to go into winter quarters untill the first of December. I would be sorry to leave to the ennemy any opportunity to say that we have permitted them to take the field during this campaign. I would remain in such a situation as to prevent theyr making any forrage with security. And so far am I convinc'd that doing some thing will be useful to our affairs in Europe, that I would stay in the way to improve any opportunity which chance or a bad disposition of theyrs may offer. Our remaining in the field will also retard any further detachement which they might intend. The only objection that may be found against this opinion of mine, is that our soldiers must have time for building barraks. But if the arrangement which I propose is adopted, a small addition to the garrison of West Point will be able to make all the hutts which may be wanted for the small remains of our army.

2dly West Point and North River being our most important point of defense, I would logde near that fort and posts thereto belonging. The whole of our troops (Pensilvanians excepted)—these I would send to the position of Morristown where hutts are ready to receive them. It should, I think, be very proper that the arrangements of the army be settl'd when we enter into winter quarters, so that each field officer, and each regiment be in its proper place. I would consider if upon the whole it was not better to order that the two forts at King's Ferry be defended to the last extremity, leaving into them a very small garrison. The great business of our winter quarters should, I think, be to attend to the instruction of the officers, and particularly to the forming of good non commissioned officers and putting them upon a more respectable footing.

3dly As to the last article, I will not so much *officially* as *confidentially* propose to you an idea which if executed may have the happiest effects towards checking the progress of the ennemy.

When the expedition against Charlestown was spoken off Count de Rochambeau offered to send Lauzun's Legion by land. Why should we not get them for a winter's campaign of so much consequence as that of the South ward where regular troops are so much wanted on our side, where the communications of the ennemy are so extensive as to admit of handsome strokes with a good corps of cavarly and light infantry, and where the extension of a British post will perhaps (if there is a mediation) determine the independency of one or two states. But this affair requires great deal of delicacy.

As I am too much your friend for to have any reserve with you, I will tell that I would not have you to make directly the proposal, but I want the proposal to be made and to be accepted.

Chevalier de La Lucerne who as well as myself hates to see the French troops idle, and who on a political point of wiew wishes the ennemy to hold as little ground as possible in America when peace will be talk'd off, will, I am sure, be please'd with this idea. Suppose you was to write me a confidential private letter on the subject, I would send it to him, and request him to make in his own name the proposals to Count de Rochambeau.

The second article would be to make it agreable to Duke de Lauzun—for people who are not us'd to our wars, such a long journey would appear tedious, but if you adopt the mode which I am going to propose, I am sure that the hope of a larger command and an active life would make him happy in the project. With Duke de Lauzun we must not act merely upon the scale of *what is the best*, but in the same time engage his wishes by some agreable hopes. I would propose that Duke the Lauzun's horse be march'd from Hartfort by the 15th of November. They will certainly be at Hillsborough by the first of January.

As to the infantry, those three hundred men might be embark'd at Rhode island on board of frigatts and by the first of December take a fresh wind to go to such a place as would be pointed out.

I would take out of our Light infantry four hundred men under the command of two colonels, who would be embark'd at Philadelphia on board some French fleetes that are in the river and convey'd by the confederacy. I would in my letter to Duke de Lauzun give him a confidential assurance that four hundred men of the Light infantry should be added to his command with a corps of Militia. The other wing of Gal Greene's van guard might be under Gal Morgan, and they would be commanded by a major general.

The manner of sending the troops to the south ward and other details of this plan might be alter'd for the best. The great thing is that a corps of thousand men, as good as ever were into the field three hundred of whom cavalry would by the first of January be at Hillsborough where they would serve during January, February, March, and April, and if next campaign we get the naval superiority they may in eight days be again at Rhode island.

  I have the honor to be
    Your Excellency's
      Most obedient humble
        Servant
          Lafayette

[67]

Light Camp November the 8th 1780*

Dear General

  Here is a letter from Mercereau† which says very little, and the little which is said in it I don't take to be true—But thought I had better send his scroll to head quarters. I have sent him word that there was no monney for such intelligences as these.

  Captain Ogden told me that one our Jersay spies had lately writen to you—I have directed him to go to head quarters and report of some thing relating to a letter from Arnold. The circumstance which Ogden mentions of Sir Henry going to Long island with his baggage seems to indicate a speedy embarkation under the Commander in chief.

  From what I have been able to ascertain, (whatever may be said by the ennemy) it seems that the surprise of Staten island would have been compleat.

  If a friendly fleet has really been seen to the South ward I am inclin'd to believe they are the Spaniards who had been directed to attak Pensacola.

  With the most respectfull and affectionate sentiments I have the honor to be, My dear General

         Yours
           Lafayette

P.S. The inclos'd came from Mercereau.†
          L.f.

*Unpublished.
†In the name Mercereau the last six letters have been scratched out but are still legible.

[68]

Light Camp November 11th 1780*

Dear General

From Doctor B....† I have receiv'd intelligence that there has been a very hott press in New york, and that Admiral Rodney is going to sail—If we believe the report, the Mayor himself was with the press gang and the cartmen were taken in the streets which shows that they are in hurry to set out—I am taking the best measures I can to hear from the islands, but nothing may be so certain as the accounts of the unknown gentleman who, I hope, will be prevail'd upon to return to the city. I am surpris'd we don't hear from Europe.

I have the honor to be most respectfully and affectionately dear General   Yours
                                    Lafayette.

[69]

Light Camp November the 13th 1780*

My dear General

On my return from your quarters, I found here one of my spies from Newyork, and after having taken down his information I have sent him again to the ennemy's lines from which he is to bring fresh intelligences on Wenesday morning—the fellow is sensible enough, but how far we may depend upon him I cannot tell.

He left Newyork Friday evening, and on Saturday was at Bergen point—The British Army lay on Long Island about White Stone and Jamaica where they are fitting up old hutts and will take theyr winter quarters—in New york 1st R^{gt} of Anspachers, 42d Regiment call'd Highlanders, one Compagny of Hessian Grenadiers, and Robertson's R^{gt} of New Levies—towards the North end of the island chiefly Hessians—at Staten Island, the same troops as before at the Watering place, detachements at the Flag Staff—Richmond reinforc'd by an Hessian Regiment, sixty men at Decker's Ferry—at Bergen the refugees. Gal Clinton is in Newyork, Knypausen on Long Island, Arnold quarters at Robertson's.

Rodney's ships are the Sandwich, Terrible, Intrepid, Alcide,

*Unpublished.
†Burnet. (Proper names are identified in the "Index" below.)

Ademant, Triumph—many frigats—The Rabauk, Rowley, and two other frigats have sail'd on Friday last—Twesday, Wenesday, and Thursday a very hott press—Rodney was to sail yesterday, his ships were in North River—some believe he means to intercept Paul Jones who is it said is coming with many vessels full of stores, and to prevent the communication betwen the Delaware and Rhode Island.

In the last embarkation under Leslie and (he believes) two Brigadier Generals they had betwen three and four thousand men with forty three transports—the number difficult to be so well ascertain'd as there were many detachements—the present embarkation which was said to sail with Rodney and to reinforce the Corps under Leslie, consist of Seventeen or Eighteen Hundred Men, and are chiefly detachements from regiments without Artillery—theyr Transports to the number of Sixteen were ready at the Watering place—the troops to embark from Long Island—the recruits arriv'd from England are said to amount to two thousand or thereabout—with this embarkation they take spare arms.

Since our last attempt they are much more careful on Staten island—they double the centries—the Militia patrole on horse back—the nearest post to us is Decker's Ferry—the boats are in or by the City.

None of the Cork Fleet arriv'd—they have certain accounts that this Fleet has been eleven weeks out—it is reported they have been taken by the French off Madeyra—no late arrival from England nor from the South ward—they are scanty for provisions—nothing but hard bread for the soldiers who complain about it—the allowance some what reduc'd.

My informant is a *London trader* is well acquainted in New york, and some times examin'd by them—they say he is a very honest man, but I don't think it impossible that my *Louis d'or* may some times meet with *English guineas* in the bottom of his purse—I gave him an instruction and some intelligences for the ennemy, which, if he betrays me, may answer an other purpose.

When last in the City Arnold enquir'd of him when Mrs Arnold (who, he knows, was sent over to Newyork) was expected in Elizabeth town.

An other intelligence I have receiv'd (but how far to be credited I don't know) says that we may depend upon Rodney's going to the West indias—that his Fleet consist of eight sails of the line—weather Arbuthnot goes with him or not the informant cannot tell—one hundred drafts chiefly from the 22d R^{gt} are gone on board the Men of War—Number of our officers taken in frigats and privateers are on board the Fleet, and from thence will it is said be sent to England there to be exchang'd.

I expect some other people's intelligences and will communicate every one of them to Your Excellency, so that we may compare them with such as you will, I hope, soon receive, and from them form a general idea of the ennemy's situation.

I have the honour to be with the highest respect and most tender affection dear General

Yours

Lafayette.

P.S. To morrow morning if nothing new occurs, I will send a party of eighty Light Infantry men towards the opposite side to Aquakanac, and Wanyer's [?] horse towards Schuyller's Ferry, where they say we may get some hay to feed them for a few days.

[70]

Light Camp November 13th 1780

My dear general

In revolving into my mind the chances of discovery by the moon light, and on the other hand the inconveniences of staying longer than you wish under our tents, I have thought if there was some position which might might enable us to take the advantage of the first hours in the night—How far the sending of the Pensilvanians towards Aquakanac, and going ourselves to the Hakinsac position may awaken the ennemy I cannot pretend to say—The most difficult affair in this would be the article of the boats—C^{lel} Smith will go tomorrow morning to West Point, unless any intelligence receiv'd at head quarters had made it useful that the enterprise be attempted soon, in which case he would go and reconnoitre the place —Suppose he was to bring from West Point C^{lel} Gouvion who has often examin'd the place with the eye of an engeneer—These ideas, my dear general, are rather started into my mind, but not fix'd, and I thought I should communicate them.

Most affectionately and respectfully yours

Lafayette.

The Marquis de Laval Montmorency one of the most illustrious families in France is on his way to camp—The Chevalier de Chattelux a relation and friend of mine, major general in the French army is also coming—I every day expect my brother in law, and his friend Count de Charlus only son to the Marquis de Castries who enjoys a great consideration in France and has won the battle of Closter Camp—Duke of Lauzun has also writen to me that he would come soon—These five gentlemen may by theyr existence at home be considered as the first people in the French army—This little history I give you before theyr arrival in consequence of what you have desir'd from me in the begining.

I write some letters to the commanding officers at Fishkills, West Point, and King's Ferry, so that the gentlemen may be directed to come by the best road to my quarters from which I will present them to you—I think the letters ought to be sent as soon as possible.
P.S. As Gal Heath commands in all those posts, I think upon recollection that I had better write to him alone—You might also send him a line on the subject.

[71]

Light Camp November the 14th 1780*

Dear General

A man is just arriv'd at my quarters who says that the Cork Fleet arriv'd in Newyork on Sunday last—his informant saw himself thirty six vessels coming up—the man adds that Gal Smith is gone to the city and suppos'd to embark with this late envoy of troops—But I don't put a perfect dependance on what he says nor on the inclos'd letter he has brought me from Merc. . . .†—I am sure that the ennemy's force on Staten island is not by far so large as he makes it.

My forraging party did not go this morning, and I am the more glad of it as the weather has been bad—I will do myself the honor of dining at head quarters.

Most affectionately and respectfully
                             Yours
                                    Lafayette.

*Unpublished.
†I.e. Mercereau. (Proper names are identified in the "Index" below.)

[72]

Light Camp November the 18th 1780*

My dear General

I have receiv'd three different accounts from New york, and tho' the authorities are not unquestionable I will lay them before you that we may compare them with other accounts.

A man sent in by Dr. Burnet says that part of the Cork Fleet is arriv'd, betwen twenty and forty sails—that the rest is given over for lost—the troops in Newyork about 1500—at Bergen 250—there was an alarm on the 15th at Staten island—Rodney had sail'd the same day—no troops went with him.

A letter from New york through *Hend* . . . says that the troops in the City consist of the 42^d, Gal Robertson's Corps, one Bataïllon of Hessians, some of Brown's Corps—Sir Henry Clinton's baggage return'd from Long Island—one Mr. A.B.H. had given intelligence that I was on the 15th going to attak Staten Island with three thousand men—the main part of the Army lays from Flushing to Domices Ferry—Rodney had not sail'd but was to set out immediately—all ships of the line fell down the Narrows except the Adament 74 who lays at the Battery and rides Commodore—Rodney has taken with him about seventy of Odel's New Corps and a draft of hundred and ninety soldiers from several regiments to serve as Marines—A number of invalids about 200 are embark'd in the Fleet for England which as well as the West India Fleet will sail with Rodney and on parting from him the first one will be convoy'd by the *Sandwich* and *Terrible*—the above letter is brought over by one *Wood ruff* whom you know, and whose account is pretty much the same—He only thinks from some questions which were ask'd that the ennemy will be out in eight days to forrage—the number of provisions carried in from Shrewsbury *is above conception*—on this account the price of beef much lowered—Bergen refugees about 200. An other man writes me—that at Paulus Hook they have the 54th and two compagnies of Hessians, in all about 428 men—at Fort Washington about 500 all most all Germans—at King's Bridge does not yet know—in Newyork one German regiment, some thing second British which I can't read and Robertson's New Levies—on Staten Island one regiment of Germans, Simcoe's Legion, two regi-

*Unpublished.

ments of New Levies—the main part of the Army on Long Island some at Flatt Bush, some at Newtown White Stone &c—theyr winter quarters will, he thinks, be to the North ward of Jamaïca where a large number of Hutts is built—they will soon go into winter quarters—then the man gives me an account of piquets an patroles at Paulus Hook and Staten Island—Rodney has not yet sail'd, but will soon—he has taken about 228 soldiers, and some invalids—the Fleet consists of Men of War and Merchant Men but no embarkation—about ten days ago about 4, or 5 frigats have sail'd—the fleet fell down to the Narrows.

From these accounts, my dear General, I find that Rodney has sail'd, or will soon set out—that the main body of the ennemy are upon Long Island—that they have few troops in Newyork—but what surprises me, is to hear that no embarkation takes place—after what you told me some days ago, I thought there was certainly a detachement going to the Southward, and can't help believing it still in some measure.

C^lel Smith return'd last night—I have sent him this morning to a man who if he chooses may give us intelligences—I expect also to hear in a few days from a Gentleman who takes no money—but would like better to have a letter from Tamage's friend.

Inclos'd you will find some news papers wherein the ennemy announce Gal Woodfort's death—you will find in one of the papers an impertinent performance of Mr. Revington's which however does not want humour.

With the most affectionate and respectfull Sentiments
I have the honour to be, my dear General
Yours
Lafayette.

[73]

My dear General   Light Camp November the 19th 1780*

C^lel Smith having rode all night return'd this morning at four o'clock from Elizabeth town and gave me the following account of his journey.

He first saw the doctor whom I wanted to employ, who told him that every one of the men arriv'd from England had been reim-

*Unpublished.

bark'd again a few days ago—that he saw himself many of them going on board—that he thinks Gal Philips will have the command—He went in again last night and from him I will get pretty accurate intelligences by the 21st or 22^d—

C^lel Smith has fix'd a new chain through a gentleman in Elizabeth town, who told him the same thing as the doctor, and added that Mr. Lenox a British D. Commissary of Prisoners had confidentially told a friend that there was an embarkation going on—Lenox's private opinion was that they were going to possess the Heights of Wilmington—I don't believe Mr. Lenox's plan of campaign, unless there is a treaty going on, and they want to have a footing every where—but it seems my informants of yesterday were mistaken, which I attribute to the precaution the ennemy take of embarking theyr troops from the points of Staten and Long Island.

The ennemy have not a mouth full of forage for theyr horses upon Staten island—they have been very particular in inquiring about the state of forage, hay, grain &c in the neighbourood of Elizabeth town and Newark—so that they are expected to come out.

Gal Smith is gone to England—Skinner commands on the Island.

This is, my dear General, what I could get since our conversation of yesterday, and these accounts seem more favorable than the last ones.

Lafayette.

P.S. C^lel Smith repeats in very strong terms what I wrote last morning concerning the provisions that were carried in to the ennemy.

[74]

My dear General   Paramus November the 28th 1780

We arriv'd last night at this place and were much favor'd by the weather in our recconnoitring of the Island where, I confess, my feelings were different from what I had experienc'd when looking at these forts with an hope full eye—I saw the fatal centry C^lel Gouvion alluded to on an upper battery of Jeffery's Hook—I also saw a small vessel playing off this Hook, but quite a trifling thing without guns and but two men on board—Nothing else on the river but the usual guards of Spiting devil.

As you have been pleas'd to consult me on the choice of an

adjudant general, I will repeat here, my dear general, that tho' I have alwaïs delt with Gal Hand on an other point of wiew his zeal, obedience, and love of discipline have given me a very good opinion of him.

C^lel Smith has been by me wholly employ'd in that line and I can assure you that he will perfectly answer your purpose.

Unless however you was to cast your eye on a man who, I think, would suit better than any other in the world—Hamilton is, I confess, the officer whom I would like to see in that station—At equal advantages his services deserve from you the preference on any other—but his knowledge of your opinions and intentions on military arrangements, his love of discipline the advantages he would have on all the others principally when both armies will operate together, and his uncommon abilities would render him perfectly agreable to you—The use of him would be increas'd by this perferrement, and on other points he would render the same services —An adjudant general ought allwaïs to be with the commander in chief—Hamilton should therefore remain in your family, and his great industry for business would render him perfectly serviceable in all circumstances—On every public or private account, my dear general, I would advise you to take him.

I shall on my arrival at Philadelphia write you how matters are going upon which I will build my private schemes—But I heartly wish that some account or other from Europe may enable you to act this winter on maritime operations—I hate the idea of being from you for so long a time—but I think I ought not to stay idle—At all events I must return when your immediate army takes the field.

I flatter myself with the hope of meeting Mrs Washington on the road—Adieu, my dear general, most affectionately and respectfully yours

Lafayette

[75]

My dear General   Philadelphia December the 4th 1780

I will for this time write a very short letter to you, and cannot be more particular either on public or private business, untill some few days stay in this City have enabl'd me to get further informations.

131

I have been greatly disappointed in my not meeting Mrs Washington—I have been very angry with my bad fate which led me into an other road at the only moment when I could miss her—This has been the more the case, as I knew you was uneasy about her, and I wanted both to send you an express and to advise her to the best way of meeting you as soon as possible.

The Southern News are expected this evening—Leslie has re-embark'd and will probably go to Charleston—the Southern Members are pleas'd to like my going towards theyr country—however, I cannot for the present be determin'd, as I don't yet know if the Campaign will be active, and if succours are to be expected from France.

By a vessel arriv'd from there who left L'orient before the middle of October we hear that nothing material had happen'd except the taking of the Merchant Fleet—Both Naval Armies were in port—there was an expedition of, I think, ten ships of the line and five thousand men ready to sail—this vessel came in compagny with Jones who is daily expected—but a very little part of our cloathing will be on board—some will come on board the Serapis—Jones who mounts the *Ariel* has dispatches from the French Court for us—he however might have been detain'd by a storm off the French Coast which separated the little convoy—in the vessel arriv'd was a Mr. Ross who, I hope, will give me some account of the cloathing, and Baron D'arent who got rid of his rupture, has a star with a cross and a ribbond, and is upon very good terms with the King of Prussia, too.

Congress have debated a motion about your being desir'd to go to the Southward, but have determin'd that you would better know than they if it was more useful to go or to stay—I am more than ever of this last opinion.

On my arrival, I found one of the salt meat vessels sold and the other to be sold today—I have spoken on the subject to almost every member of Congress who promis'd that they would take the best measures in theyr power to get these provisions.

Cher de La Luzerne has communicated to me in the *most confidential way* a Spanish plan against St. Augustine—upon which I am building a letter for the Generals of this Nation, and using the best arguments in my power to engage them either to send twelve ships of the line to take us and conduct us to Charleston, or to render theyr operation as useful as possible to Gal Greene—to morrow I will write you about it. If I have time before the departure of the Confederacy that is going to the West indias, I will send you the original if not, a copy of my letter. This is entirely *Confidential* as I have not the Chevalier's permission to mention it.

Adieu, my dear General, Most respectfully and affectionately Yours   Lafayette.

[76]

My dear General   Philadelphia December the 5th 1780

By my letter of yesterday I have mentionn'd to you that a Spanish expedition was intended against S^t· Augustine. They mean to set out at the end of december which will certainly delay them till the middle of january. It consists of twelve ships of the line, some frigats, bomb ketches, and a large number of troops. I have advis'd the Minister to communicate officialy to you this intelligence, and also to Count de Rochambeau, that proper means, if convenient, might be taken to improve it.

For my part, my dear general, I have conducted myself agreably to what you said to me in our last conversations. That if in the course of the winter a naval superiority was obtain'd our business was to push for the south ward, and that you would take for that purpose four thousand French and two thousand Americans. Nothing against Newyork may be undertaken before the end of May. Any thing therefore that could employ us during February, March, and April is worthy of our attention.

The Confederacy was going to sail for some cloathing which we have in the West Indias. No time was left to waït for an answer from you. I knew perfectly your sense of this affair. I therefore, with the advice of Chevalier de la Luzerne, wrote him a letter dated from camp, wherein I explain to him that some thing might be made in conjonction for the public good, and wherein I strengthten my opinion by your sentiments on this matter, without however bringing myself, and you still less in any formal application to the Spanish Generals.

Inclosed you will find a copy of this letter, the first part of which mentions that if after having landed theyr troops in Florida they would send theyr ships of the line for us, we might on three weeks notice before the departure of the squadron have in readiness six thousand men for a powerfull diversion in Carolina. Theyr own interest is the only thing I seem to consider this business, and I endeavour to invite Spanish caution into this measure. But unless a more particular application is made, I do not believe that this part of my letter will have any effect.

The second part will, I hope, be productive of some good for America. I urge the necessity immediately to oppen a correspondance with General Greene that he may by his maneuvres facilitate the operations of Spain. I tell them that unless they land a corps of troops on the boundaries of Georgia with a wiew at least to threaten Augusta and Savahna theyr expedition will run a great risk. I advise the measure of cruizing off Charlestown harbour, the whole under theyr idea of theyr own interest.

I have also writen to the Naval French Commander of the West Indies advising him to succour Chevalier de Ternay which I know he will not do. But I take this opportunity of damning theyr foolish neglect in not appearing on our coasts when they return to Europe —And I do also advise that in theyr cruizes from S^t. Domingo they may some times appear off Savahna and Charlestown harbour. Inclos'd you will find a copy of this letter.

Tho' I do alwaïs speack of the beggining of February, it is however certain that any time in February would be convenient to go to the south ward. March and April are more than sufficient to the taking of Charlestown—And in all cases, I know from our last conversations that you wish for a naval superiority this winter in order to succour the Southern States.

I had this morning, my dear general, a long conversation with the Chevalier de la Luzerne relating to a southern operation. He is as well as myself clearly of opinion that unless a formal application and a plan of campaign are propos'd to them, they will not send theyr ships to us—In this late case theyr coming ought still to be questionn'd. But if you thought it better to try, you might propose to the French Generals to send there a frigat and see with them what might be done in conjonction—Suppose they were to take four thousand men, leaving some and the militia at Rhode Island—we could on our part muster two thousand Americans—However the Spaniards are so positive and strict in following litteraly theyr instructions that I don't believe any thing will engage them to come—But my letter which I look upon as a mere cipher on the first proposition will, I hope, engage them to impart theyr projects to Gal Greene, and of course this diversion will become useful to us.

Suppose Count de Rochambeau and C^her de Ternay were to send to Havana a copy of your letter I think they ought to intrust it to Vicomte de Noaïlles who will soon return to Rhode Island and whose name is highly respected by the Court of Spain for many particular reasons too long to be here mentionn'd.

I have seen Mr Ross and find that very little cloathing is to be immediately expected—They have some arms on board the Alliance, and I think hundred bales of cloth on board a vessel under Jones's convoy. The remainder will come with the Serapis—Unless the storm has forc'd Jones to put in some French harbour, he may be expected every minute.

The Assembly of Pennsylvania have before them the affair of the recruits—But proper arrangements are not properly supported—They are fond of volontary inlistements. I have an appointement for to morrow with Gal Mifflin where I will debate this matter with him.

To morrow, my dear general, I will go to Brandiwine with C^her de Chattelux, and also to Red Bank, Fort Mifflin, etc. On my return, I hope to find news from France, and I will write you my determination about my going to the south ward.

Inclos'd you will find a news paper wherein Congress have printed a letter from Gal Gates relating to a new success of Sumpter.

Congress have lately receiv'd letters from Mr Jay and Mr Adams but nothing very particular—they have more fully writen by other opportunities that are expected—Portugal have entered into the Convention of Neutrality and with such conditions as to show theyr partiality to our side of the question.

Adieu, my dear general, most respectfully and affectionately
Yours
Lafayette

My respects to Mrs Washington and compliments to the family. Mr. Washington is gone to day.

[77]

December the 5th [1780] in the evening

My dear general

However acquainted I may be with your intentions, I thought upon the whole that I should better waït for your approbation before I present any opinion of yours to the Spanish or French generals in the West Indias. I will, I know, loose the opportunity of the Confederacy, but many vessels are going that way and if my letters meet with your approbation I shall send them by triplicates. I impatiently waït for your answer.

I will write to Gal Greene to let him know of this intended expedition which tho' uncertain as all human events are may be however in a great measure depended upon.

I confess that I don't hope to prevail upon the Spaniards to come here. But if you will you Count de Rochambeau and C^{her} de Ternay may try. In that case I wish you would write to both of them. My letter will at all events give some remoted chance of theyr doing what I wish and insure theyr communicating with Gal Greene. For political reasons I also wish to draw them into this correspondance.

C^{her} de la Luzerne wishes his paquet to Count de Rochambeau to be forwarded as speedily as possible.

Adieu, my dear general, yours most respectfully and affectionately

Lafayette

Inclos'd I send you something relating to the Southern Army.

[78]

Philadelphia December the 9th 1780*

My dear General

You will be surpris'd to hear that other vessels are arriv'd from France, and that we have not receiv'd by them any public nor private dispatches—all the paquets were on board the *Ariel* who was disma[s]ted in the storm and put back into L'orient—Mr de Vauban who was intrusted with these letters thought it not advisable for himself or his paquets to come on board of Merchant vessels and very foolishly rode back to Versailles—how disappointed and displeas'd

*Unpublished.

I have been with the account, you may easely guess—I have made myself certain that since the letter receiv'd in the same time as mine, no other public dispatch is arriv'd in the Minister's hands.

But I have receiv'd by these vessels an intelligence which both on private and public accounts makes me extremely happy—the Marquis de Castries whom I have some times mentionn'd to you as a man of great worth and my intimate friend has been made Minister of the Navy—I told you my opinion of Mr de Sartine, and you may see that we are greatly benefited by the alteration—Mr Sartine was an honest man, and good enough to other purposes but entirely unfitt for such a departement—M^{quis} de Castries is the very man I had often mentionn'd as the object of my wishes—I am going to write to him a confidential letter—relating to money, ships &c—The vessels left France about forty days ago, and as the appointement was recent, I hope M^{quis} de Castries will soon send us intelligences—the more so as his son* is the friend I some times spoke you of as being in this French Army—Mr de Castries is very intimate with the Minister of Finance.

By the Captains of those Vessels we hear that Count D'estaing has been made generallissimo of the Spanish Forces, and is gone to sea with a Combin'd Squadron of Sixteen ships—perhaps is he gone to the West indias where if you approuve of it I may write to him—perhaps S^t· Augustine will be the object of his enterprises—God grant we might combine some thing.

Mr Laurens has been confin'd into the Tower *under suspicion of High treason,* and Congress seem determin'd to retaliate.

They have after many debates decided that an envoy be sent to France and not a Secretary—that envoy is to give an account of our situation, ask succours, and return immediately—he will be nam'd the day after to morrow—[John] Laurens who refuses, Mr Henry who knows nothing of our affairs, and Hamilton are spoken of—I think they will choose this last—who ever goes must go soon—when it is decided I will write to you as the expresses of Congress don't ride very speedily.

I have found here L^t· C^{lel} Nevill my old aid de Camp—he came with Gal Woodford to Newyork—it is said that Gal Lincoln's aids have been exchang'd and that it is generally the case with aids de

*Comte de Charlus. (Proper names are identified in the "Index" below.)

camp to G^al officers actually in our service—I warmly desire to have him—I am told Cornwallis has no powers to treat those matters—Can you, my dear General, think of some method to get him out which it is proper for me to take?

I am more than ever puzzled, my dear General, to know what to do—this change of Minister may send us some intelligences—every body advises against my going to the South ward—there is alwaïs a possibility of an expedition where you will want me—I see that the people in whom you confide the most are in a great part for the present far from you—I also candidly confess that private affection for you makes me hate the idea of leaving the man I love the most in the world to seek for uncertainties at a period when he may want me—on the other hand the Southern Members want me to go—there is a possibility of being useful, and the love of glory spurs me on—I waït for your answer and your opinion to my 1st letter—in two or three days I shall write to you.

Adieu, my dear General

Most aff^ly and resp^ly yours
Lafayette.

My best respects wait on Mrs Washington and my compliments on the family—this new change of the Minister and the hope arising from it add to determine Count de Damas and Viscount de Noailles to return soon to Newport—I request, my dear General, you will please to order that the bearer have means to proceed on as he carries to Count de Charlus the intelligence.

*A letter dated Cadix September 25th mentions that Count d'estaing commands the combin'd fleet and is gone to sea—in this case his going with 16 ships could not be true—I will endeavour to ascertain this matter

Mr. Carmichall writes that Spain has lent hundred and thirty thousand dollars—it is not a great deal—the disposition of that court are very satisfactory—Portugal does every thing we want—letters are just arriv'd from St. Domingo but not deciphered.

L. f.

*The postscript that follows is found in the Hubbard Collection after the letter of November 28, 1780, but in the Sparks Manuscripts in the Harvard College Library (Vol. 87, fols. 259-61) it is affixed to this letter. It is also to be found as part of the letter of December 4, 1780 in *Memoirs, correspondence and manuscripts of General Lafayette published by his family* (New York, 1837), p. 487. It seems most logically to belong where the Sparks Manuscripts place it.

[79]

My dear General   Philadelphia December the 13th 1780

I have not yet receiv'd your answer to any of my letters—since my last no news have come to hand—I hope we shall soon some way or other hear from France.

After many debates Congress have elected C^lel Laurens as an envoy to France—but he still refuses to go and thinks Hamilton ought to be sent—how this will end I do not know—Doctor Franklin has a party against him—I think it would be very wrong to recall him.

The letter which I wrote to you from Paramus has been put into the hands of C^lel Gouvion who was then going to New Windsor—there was nothing material in it but what related to Hamilton.

Vicomte de Noailles and Count de Damas will take Albany in theyr way to Newport—C^her du Plessis is with them and has requested I would write to you on a particular business of his—he is gone to France on furlough and therefore hopes he may be entitl'd to the half pay—as Fleury and himself are the only ones in this same case, I think it would be well to decide it in theyr favor.

C^her du Buisson whose wounds do not seem so very dangerous as I expected is earnestly soliciting that I will send a letter of his to Gal Reidezel—Inclos'd you will find it as well as a line from me which I reluctantly wrote—if you find the least impropriety in it, I request, my dear General, you will please not to send it—at least to suppress mine—I hate to have the air of asking any favor from them, and drew as cold a letter as decency could permit.

Will you be pleas'd, my dear General, to present my respects to Mrs Washington and my best compliments to the family—

Most affectionately and respectfully
    I have the honour to be
        Your friend   Lafayette.

[80]

My dear General   Philadelphia December the 16th 1780

Your favor of the 8th inst. never came to hand Before last night—my former letters will have explain'd to you my sentiments relating to a journey southwards—I most heartly thank you, my dear General, for the kind and friendly letters you have been pleas'd to send to me—I am so happy in your friendship that every mark of your affection for me gives me a degree of pleasure which far surpasses all expressions.

As I have writen to you before, my dear General, there is an intelligence of some ships and troops having been put in readiness at Brest—there is a possibility of a Spanish officer waïting on you for the sake of a cooperation—we are also to expect news from my friend the New Minister of the French Navy, and before they arrive you would not like my departure.

Two other reasons have weight with me—the first that if the ennemy make this detachement without which nothing material will happen in the South ward, and if the intelligence is true about the fast recruiting of Six Month men, there is (not a probability) but a possibility of some thing to be done in this quarter—The second is that for reasons I will explain to you when we meet a visit from you to the French Army is to be much wish'd, and in this case you will be glad that I may accompagny you.

Under this circumstances, to which is added a natural reluctance to part from you and this Army, and some idea that upon the whole my staying will be more agreable to you, I think, my dear General, that unless new intelligence comes I will soon return.

C^lel Laurens persists in refusing to go and hopes Hamilton may be sent whom he thinks better calculated for the purpose—But I don't believe now that this plan may be effected, and in that case I should advise Laurens to accept of the Commission provided he is merely a *Messenger* and not an *envoy* that would supersede the old doctor [Franklin].

The Assembly of Pennsylvania have pass'd a Bill for theyr officers which seems satisfactory to them—Before I go, I will yet intrigue for the affair of filling up the Bataillons—Mifflin behaves perfectly well.

Adieu, my dear General, Most affectionately and respectfully
                Yours
                  Lafayette.

My best respects wait on Mrs. Washington and compliments to the family.

[81]

Philadelphia December the 19th 1780

My dear General

None of your answers to my several letters has yet come to hand. I am told that you have writen to Congress giving an account of a large embarkation under Knypausen—How far it will influence your projects, and of course your advices for my private conduct I hope to know by your next letter—A vessel is, it is said, arriv'd in Boston after a short passage from France—her dispatches have not yet been receiv'd.

By letters from the Southern States it is said that Tarleton met with a defeat—but these are mere reports, tho' accompagnied with some degree of probability.

A letter dated Edenton North Carolina mentions that a vessel was just arriv'd from Spain having on board an American Gentleman who says that Count de Guichen was arriv'd in Cadiz—that the Combin'd Fleet amounted then to 74 ships of the line, exclusive of Barcelo's squadron, of five ships cruizing off the Capes, five other gone on a secret expedition, and those which are in Brest—The combin'd fleet under Count D'estaing was going to sea—other intelligences say that the Affrican princes have excluded the British from theyr ports, and that the English Channel Fleet had been much shattered in a storm.

God grant that in this last motion of the combin'd fleet common sense may have dictated the necessity of increasing the Naval force on our Coast—I have again writen very pressing letters to Governement in General, and some Ministers in particular urging the necessity of furnishing us with ships, money, stores, cloathes, etc.

I think C^{lel} Laurens will go to France—but there will be many debates, I believe, before he sets out.

The Assembly of Pensilvania will this day pass the bill for recruiting theyr troops by classing property—Some members of Congress have mentionn'd to me the idea of sending the Pennsilvanians by land to Carolina which I made it a point to discourage.

Adieu, my dear General, Most affectionately and respectfully

Yours Lafayette.

My respects if you please to Mrs. Washington and compliments to the family.

[82]

Philadelphia December the 26th 1780

My dear General

C^lel Laurens having been appointed by Congress to go to France and sollicit succours for the next campaign he has also been directed to take your orders at head quarters—I am by order of Congress to have a conference with him, and intend giving him many letters for France—As in your instructions to Laurens the presence of one who knows these people may be agreable to you, I shall set out for head quarters Friday or Saturday morning.

Some officers who are arriv'd from Newyork report that an embarkation of eighteen hundred men has sail'd a few days ago.

A vessel from Havanna arriv'd yesterday by which we learn that the Pensacola expedition has much suffered in the storm—Sixteen hundred men are arriv'd at Campiche—The remainder of the transports has not yet been heard off—The ships of the line put back into Havanna but were neatly refitted and going to pursue the same operation—Nothing about St Augustine—The Governor writes only two lines to Francisco and promises a longer letter by the return of a dispatch boat—I have communicated these intelligences to Gal Greene by an express that was just going.

In expecting the pleasure of seeing you before long, I have the honor to be, My dear General

Your most affectionate friend and humble servant
Lafayette.

In the Virginia Gazette there is an extract of a letter from an officer at the Southern Camp, mentionning the defeat of Tarleton by Sumpter—each of them had *(it is said)* from six to seven hundred men—I beg, my dear general, you will present my respects to Mrs Washington and remember me to the family.

1781

[83]

Morristown January the 7th 1781

My dear General

As you will receive a letter from G^al S^t· Clair who had been desir'd by Congress to go with me to the Pensilvania line, I have nothing to add but that I am here with him, and that I impatiently wait for your arrival which has been announc'd by M^jor Fishburne on his going through this place.

This affair is the more serious as the men have appointed a Committee compos'd of theyr Ring Leaders through whom every thing goes to the Soldiers—they also have officers of theyr own making, and seem determined in theyr resolution. Nothing is to be hoped but from force or such a division among them as would produce a partial dissolution—the Militia don't seem very willing to fight them—Gal Waïne was in hopes that they could be divided—but how far he may succeed I do not know.

Your going there would be extremely imprudent, and the probability of success is not by far such as to justify your exposing yourself to any danger of the kind—the less so as the possessing of your person would be an inducement to theyr joining the ennemy.

We hear that there has been the night before last some commotion in C^lel Barber's detachement—but it has been stopped without any great difficulty.

G^al S^t· Clair will let you know how we came among them, and how we have been advis'd by theyr Committee to make *a short retreat*—Adieu, my dear General, in waiting for you or for your orders I have the honor to be Most respectfully and affectionately

Your most obedient humble servant

Lafayette.

[84]

Pompton February the 23d 1781*

My Dear General

Your letter of yesterday is just come to hand, and its contents shall be ponctually obei'd—The addition of a Pennsylvanian detachement would be very advantageous, and I will try to get it under the circumstances and in the way which you have pointed out—I had already writen to the commanding officer of the Jersay troops respecting the detachement, and to Colonel Dayton to request intelligences—Your letters to both will be sent either this evening or to morrow very early—In this late case I shall myself be the bearer as I intend to set off at sun rise for Morristown.

The detachement had a great trouble to cross the ferry and made afterwards a long march through bad roads—They halted last night within eight miles of the Yellow House, and came up to it this morning—But the rain was so hard, and the road was so bad that I have halted them at this place (the hutts being three miles out of the way) where they are getting provisions, and where the waggons are collected—To morrow they will sett off and the day after arrive at the hutts in Morristown—I have sent back an officer per Bataïllon with orders to get some more Baggage for the officers who came totally unprovided, and to have it carried in two impressed waggons to Morristown where I will leave them orders for theyr jonction with us—inclosed I send to your Excellency the return of the wanting cloathes which have been carefully examined by C^{lel} Smith (the jersay troops excepted) and which it would be very important to forward as soon as possible.

To morrow morning I will set off for Morristown, there make proper arrangements for the reception of the troops, the jonction of the jersay detachment and such precautions as will deceive as much as possible the ennemy—I will also write to C^{lel} Pickering, and when every thing will be settled set off myself for Philadelphia.

Mr de Castaing Aide de Camp to Gal du Portaïl is arrived here last night and brought me dispatches from France Arrived by the Ariel under command of Paul Jones—My letters are of an old date excepted one from Doctor Franklin which I have the honor to in-

*Library of Congress, Washington papers. There is a contemporary copy in the letterbook in the Hubbard Collection. Unpublished.

close—Chevalier de La Luzerne writes me word that his dispatches are also of an old date and say nothing—I am told there are some more for me at Philadelphia but they certainly are of a private nature—My only letter from Count de Vergennes is a quadruplicate of the 3d of June—Mr de Sartine writes an answer to my letter from Boston relating to some recommandations in favor of the officers of the frigat Hermione—Perhaps Mr de Rochambeau will be happier than the Chevalier and myself or will have letters for us—We cannot fail to receive soon answers to our letters by the Amazone.

How disappointed I have been in hearing that the Ariel brought no cloathing your Excellency will easely conceive—This circumstance would nevertheless be in favor of what Paul Jones gives as his opinion wiz that Mr de La Touche Treville is coming here with 11 ships of the line and 8000 men—He also thinks that Count D'estaing is gone with 22 ships of the line to the West Indias. Mr de Castaing will beg your permission to bring the dispatches to Count de Rochambeau.

Chance or a design of the ennemy has thrown in my way a man who gives a very bad account of himself. He left Newyork the day before yesterday and I was going to put him under guard. But I made him previously some questions that might mislead him respecting my projects. In the course of his examination he said that Colonel Robertson was going with 500 men to reinforce Arnold.

I then asked how many ships of the line the ennemy had in Newyork. He said five under Admiral Greaves. I asked if he heard of the gale of wind that had disabled the British ships. He answered—No. Upon my asking the name of these five ships he could only make out three. The *Iras* who he says had been upon a cruize towards Charleston but has already been *five weeks* in New york. The Bumont of 50, and the Ledrout French India man of 50 also. This last is not considered, I think, as a ship fit for any action, and must be out of the question—I ask'd if the hospital ship was there. He said yes but unfit for action.

My confidence in this man is but small, and he was not even consistent in what he said since he had so much exagerated his first accounts. I don't even like the history he gives of himself—But thought the matter too important not to have him sent to head quarters to which Mr de Castaing will conduct him immediately.

If my informations at Morristown corroborate this account, I shall be able to forward it to Philadelphia and from thence to the commander of the French ships with less uncertainty.

Supposing the account to be true it would make the British force about equal to ours, and the naval commanders at Chesapeak Bay and Rhode island ought to know it that they may govern themselves accordingly. The *Iras* whom (by the way) I did not hear of before this time, and the 50 if existant would be superior to the French 64 and the frigats. But having never heard of that ship, and as the *Iris frigat* may be mistaken for a ship of the line by that man, I do not credit an account which you would have got heretofore.

With every sentiment of respect and the most tender attachement I have the honor to be dear general

Your most humble servant and affectionate friend
Lafayette

Will your Excellency please to present my respects to Mrs. Washington, Mrs. Hamilton, and compliments to the family.

[85]

My Dear General   Pompton February the 23d 1781*

Since writing the inclosed, my fears are gone a way and the 64 has vanished into the frigat the Iris—the importance of the thing, and perhaps the mistrust of my first judgement in occasions upon which I am personally sanguine had been the reasons of my being so particular—They will still influence the precaution I take of sending you the man, but he is such a fool or such a knave that his intelligence amounts to nothing

My first letter was writen after a few slight questions which he answered as I have writen to your Excellency—Since this time I have examined him more carefully, and find that the history he gives of himself is the more improbable as it is said the man under whom he pretends to have inlisted at Newyork in 1776 never was with the ennemy before 1777 and never at Newyork before 1778

Among the five ships of the line he reckons two sloops of war who says he as well as every sloop of war are ships of the line—The

*Library of Congress, Washington papers. There is a contemporary copy in the letterbook in the Hubbard Collection. Unpublished.

sixty four at Newyork is which is called *the Iris frigat*—She had an engagement of the coast of Virginia with a French frigat—She brought to Newyork the account of the taking of Charlestown—He thinks she is commanded by a Captain Montaigu (who I was told has relieved Hawker) but tho' he cannot ascertain this circumstance he has never heard during the four years he was in Newyork of any other ship of this name than the *Iris frigat* whom he assures to be a ship of the line

Unless I was to hear some thing less inconsequent and stupid on the ennemy's force, I will not write to Chesepeak Bay untill I arrive at Philadelphia. But tho' I do not at all credit that foolish report, I send the man to you, so that your Excellency may not be troubled by the least doubt on that matter

With the most tender affection and highest respect I have the honor to be

    Your Excellency's
     Most humble servant
      and eternal friend
       Lafayette

[86]

My dear General Morristown February the 24th 1781*

The heavy rain we had and the extreme badness of the roads have much added to our difficulties—But the troops have marched with great chearfulness and order, and will be to morrow very early at Morristown—they will arrive at Trenton on the 28th, and as I set out to morrow for Philadelphia I will take care to have boats provided for them

I have spoken most particularly to Colonel Dayton respecting intelligences—his spies have been sent in to night—I will take every measure that may for some few days serve to deceive the ennemy

The detachement has been thus far well furnished with provisions, and will take enough at this place to last them untill they arrive at Trenton where I will have an other magazine ready for them—the troops have the greatest zeal, and preserve the most strict order in their march as well as their cantonnements

Colonel Dayton told me this evening that he had just received

*Library of Congress, Washington papers. There is a contemporary copy in the letterbook in the Hubbard Collection. Unpublished.

the following intelligence from good authority—that Arnold had given notice at Newyork of the arrival of a French ship of the line and two frigats in the Bay of Cheseapeake—Arnold it is said is strictly blockaded and cannot by any means get out—He begs for relief, but none can be given from Newyork as theyr largest ship is the *Iris frigat* of thirty two guns—people are very uneasy at Newyork, and I begin to hope that their fears are grounded—Dayton is positive upon their having no ship of force at Newyork.

It is also reported that a packet from Falmouth has brought to them disagreable intelligences but the other account respecting Arnold is so minuted and so well founded upon what we know that I thought it ought to be communicated to your excellency

Having found here axes I have added them to the tents which I was to take, as C^lel Gouvion finds a great insufficiency in the number that had been settled by the quarter master

The dispatch we make on our march the more exceed my expectations as the roads are shokingly bad but the men are not fatigued, and none stays behind. Whatever may be my desire to precipitate our movement I will take the greatest care not to do it to the detriment of the troops. This detachement is excellent.

Count de Ste Même and Mons. de St Victor are with me—they ask your permission to follow me and so will Count de Charlus etc— I told them that you would have no objection to it as far as may be consistent with their arrangements with Count de Rochambeau upon which you will not intrude, and that the American Army will be happy in all times to be honor'd with the visit of such *Volonteers*— But these expressions will still do better from you, and the word *Volonteer* must not be forgotten for reasons obvious in any thing you'll order me to answer to them

With the most tender affection and highest respect I have the honor to be, my dear general
     Your excellency's
      Most obedient humble
      servant and affectionate
      friend
       Lafayette

I request you will please to present my respects to M^rs. Washington and M^rs. Hamilton and my compliments to the family

[87]

Morris town February the 25th 1781*

My dear General

Inclosed I have the honor to send an intelligence that is just now come to hand—Whatever may be the object of this expedition, it will be highly important for Duke of Lauzun's Legion to hear of it as soon as possible—Lauzun may be at Rhode island—His lieutenant colonel is also a very good officer.

Mons. de Murnan will be the bearer of this and ride day and night—Having no men and believing the expedition would be a short one, he has joined me and upon my refusal goes for your excellency's leave—Independant of the importance of this letter, I like better to let him ride post, than to undeceive him as to our destination

You have not said to me, my dear general, when you intend going to Rhode island—In case it was postponed untill you hear of our succès or failure, nothing on my part would be wanting to join you speedily as soon as my presence with the troops would not be necessary, if your excellency directed me to do so.

With the most tender affection and highest respect
    I have the honor to be
        My dear general
            Your most obedient
                humble servant
                    Lafayette

I beg leave to request my respects to Mrs. Washington Mrs. Hamilton and compliments to the family.

---

*Library of Congress, Washington papers. There is a contemporary copy in the letterbook in the Hubbard Collection. Unpublished. (Proper names are identified in the "Index" below.)

[88]

Philadelphia March the Second 1781*

My dear General

Your letters of the 25th and 26th are both come yesterday to hand, which shows that the expresses have not made great dispatch —I would have done myself the honor of writing to your excellency, had I not every minute waïted for intelligences from the south ward

Your excellency remembers that our shortest calculation on the arrival of the troops at Head of Elk was for the 6th of March— I am happy to inform you that they will be there this day, or to morrow early, and notwistanding the depth of the mud, and the extreme badness of the roads, this march which I can call rapid (as for exemple they came in two days from Morristown to Prince town) has been performed with such an order and alacrity that, agreable to the report, two men only have been left behind, and yet these two men have embarked at Trenton with some remains of baggage—At every place where the detachement have halted they have found covering, and wood, etc ready for them and there has not been the least complaint made to me from any inhabitant—Every third day they have drawn their provisions,—the cloathing has been also distributed, and having embarked yesterday at Trenton they past the city about two o'clock by a wind which was extremely favorable

Congress have given to our troops the advance of one month pay which will be distributed at the Head of Elk in new emission

The artillery consisting of one 24 six 18 two brass one 8 inch howitz, two 8 inch mortars, in all twelve heavy pieces, four 6 pounders and two small howitzes, with a sufficient proportion of ammunition will be at the Head of Elk this day and to morrow, so that by the 4th I hope we shall be ready to sail

A quantity of medecines and instruments, and fifteen hundred pairs of shoes will be at the Head of Elk before we embark.

Vessels will be in readiness to receive us with thirty days provisions on board—I am also assured that we'll have a sufficient quantity of boats to land the detachement, and two heavy scows will be added for the artillery—The public and some of the private

*Library of Congress, Washington papers. There is a contemporary copy in the letterbook in the Hubbard Collection.

armed vessels in the Bay have been ordered to Head of Elk—Two dispatch boats are there and four more have been asked for—As a farther security for our subsistence, I have got the Minister's permission to dispose of the French flour and salt meat along the Bay in a case of necessity

On my arrival at this place, I heard that Mr de Tilly the French commander had conferred with the Virginians, but upon seeing that nothing could be done immediately he was undetermined wether to stay or return to Rhode island—Fearing that our letters might miscarry, and wishing to hurry the preparations of the militia, I complied with the earnest sollicitations of the Minister of France to send on C^lel Gouvion, and directed him to go either by land or water (as the state of the Bay would permit) on board the French squadron, and afterwards to Baron de Stubens's camp where he may apprise these gentlemen of our force, our intentions, and the time of our arrival

This minuted account I give to your excellency to show you that nothing on our part has been wanting for the succès of the expedition—our preparations have in every article fulfilled and in the most important one, time, have exceeded what had been expected.

Your letter was sent by express to G^al S^t. Clair who immediately came to town—But nothing having been done for the settling of the accounts, none of the promises having been complied with, and the men being much scattered, it has, (after much consideration) been thought impossible to embark any number with us, and G^al S^t. Clair promises to make every exertion for the sending of two or three hundred in a few days whom however I am not to depend upon

I am myself going to the Head of Elk, and shall arrive there this evening—it has not been possible for me to leave sooner the City, as the three days I have remained here have been fully emploïd in making and forwarding preparations.

Before I go I will waït on the Board of the Navy and propose the sending of the frigats—But the Trumbull having not her complement of men, and that of the Ariel having mutined at sea I am affraïd we will find difficulties

The preparations made at New york—the return of the America—the remasting of the Bedfort—the impossibility Mons. Destouches is under to give us any farther assistance—the uncertainty of what Mons. de Tilly may have determined before he had received your letter—such are, my dear general, the many reasons which from a pretty certain expedition have lately made a very precarious one —Under these circumstances, indeed, there must alwaïs be more or less danger in going down the Bay and venturing upon the low country about Porsmouth

Being unaquainted with the answer you have received from Count de Rochambeau and Mons. Destouche, I am not able to judge how far I may depend upon the same ship being ordered again to Chesapeak in case (before the reception of your letter) she had thought proper to sail—Her coming was not in consequence of your proposition, her going was relative to the difficulties of an expedition very different from ours, and I wish I might know if (tho' Mons. Destouches can't give farther assistance) this assistance at least may be depended upon so as to hope for the return of the ship should Mons. de Tilly have left the Bay

The bottom of the Bedfort is said to be damaged—the America was said to have been dismasted—Suppose those circumstances were trüe they would be in our favor—

If a detachement was to go from Newyork to Porsmouth, Westpoint would be less in danger—If Cornwallis continues advancing, perhaps our being in the neighborhood of Arnold may be of service

I will however confine myself litterally to my instructions, and if C^{lel} Gouvion writes me with certainty that Mons. de Tilly is gone, *If I am not led to suppose he will return*, I will march back the detachement—for the present I am going on because upon the increasing of the ennemy's force at Gardner's Bay, you recommend *dispatch* to me

I hope, however, that I will hear from your excellency. Now that the chain is established C^{lel} Pikering says that in six days I may receive your answer at the Head of Elk—The hope of seeing the French ship again or some other reason may detain me—But your answer will determine my motions, and I can receive it by the 8th which is about the time when it was thought we would arrive at the Head of Elk

My expectations are not great, and, I think we have but few

chances for us—I shall make all possible dispatch, and listen particularly to the voice of prudence—However some hazard must be ran, if we undertake in this circumstances

Gal Duportaïl having not left this place, I am led to hope that if we don't go I may return in time for the journey to Rhode island

I most instantly beg, my dear general, you will favor me with an immediate answer

With the highest respect and most tender affection I have the honor to be   Your most obedient
                                    humble servant
P. S.   Lafayette

One of our transports from Trenton had got a ground but the troops on board of her will still be in time at the Head of Elk—Some new difficulties have been made for the collecting of shoes, but I will try to get over them—From the extraordinary motions of Lord Cornwallis whom we have not heard of these many days, and from the movements in Newyork I am led to hope that I will hear from you respecting my future conduct, and that I may be at head quarters before you think it prudent to leave New Windsor

[89]

Elk March the 3d [1781]*

My dear General

Having been empowered by Congress, the Board of War, and the Virginia delegates to oppen any letter directed to them, I also took the liberty of reading that of Baron de Stubens to your Excellency wherein I found useful intelligences

My presence had been necessary to forward every article from Philadelphia—as soon as it could be spared I came here with all possible speed—but notwistanding promises the vessels were not ready—My exertions shall be such that I hope we may be embarked before we hear of the arrival of our friends

Most Respectfully and affectionately
    I Have the Honor to Be
        Your Excellency's
            Most obedient Humble
                Servant   Lafayette

*Library of Congress, Washington papers. There is a contemporary copy in the letterbook in the Hubbard Collection. Unpublished.

[90]

My dear General   Head of Elk March the 7th [1781]*

    Contrary winds, heavy rains, disappointements of vessels, and every inconvenience to which we had no remedy have been from the day of my arrival combined against our embarkation. I hope however we will be on board to morrow morning, and as nothing certain has been heard from the French ships, no time will be lost on our part for the celerity of the expedition

    The troops will embark five miles below this place and three miles higher up than the point where General *Howe* landed—There will be more room for the arrangement of our vessels, and the shallowness of water insures us against the enterprises of any vessel of force—In this situation we may waït for intelligences from our friends

    The State of Maryland have made to me every offer in their power—I will improve this opportunity of making up some deficiencies in the quarter master and engeneer departements, of insuring to us a good stock of provisions and upon the intelligence received that Baron de Stubens was gone with a large detachement to the south ward I had hinted the possibility of getting some militia from the lower counties and repairing some cannon at Baltimore—But having read the inclosed letter from the Baron, I will write again to Governor *Lee* (as my letter has been gone but two days) and save the State from any expense of that kind.

    To the obtaining of the vessels has been joined the difficulty of getting them up the river, as they were taking every opportunity to slip off—All the vessels, three excepted, are only bay crafts, and our admiral ship mounts twelve guns—I have prepared some kind of orders for that fleet, but hope to be relieved from my naval command by the arrival of a French frigat, and have at all events sent for Commodore Nicholson of Baltimore—Mr McHenry has been very active in accelerating the measures of his state

    By a letter from Clel Gouvion dated Wihecomoco River I find that after many adventures he had landed there on the 4th and was proceding by land to his destination—The wind is fair enough to come up the Bay and I hope soon to hear from our friends

*Library of Congress, Washington papers. There is a contemporary copy in the letterbook in the Hubbard Collection.

The inclosed letter from the Baron having first come into my hand, and being on public service as it was writen upon *to be forwarded with dispatch* I took the liberty to oppen it—but was very sorry to have done it after a letter of the same date had come also to hand—Both say the same thing (at least in every material point) and I am happy to find that the Baron's preparations are going on rapidly

Whatever may be the Baron's opinion upon the facility of taking sword in hand the fortifications at Porsmouth, I will not hazard any thing before I have considered the matter with my own eyes—Arnold had so much time to prepare, and plays so deep a game—Nature has made the position so respectable, and some of the troops under his orders have been in so many actions, that I don't flatter myself to succed so easily as it may be thought—The prospect of preserving naval superiority must, I think, decide if we are to save blood shed by regular approaches, or to risk our men into the dangers of an assault—But I would like to destroy the works in some measure, before we attempt to storm them—A conversation with the Baron, with C^{lel} Gouvion, and some other officers, joined to what I can see myself will better fix my mind on the matter than it can be at present

When I left Philadelphia General Waïne was not far from hoping he could soon collect thousand men but I am not so sanguine in my expectations—I am however trying to prepare matters for this number of men, but think that a sufficiency of vessels (unless ours are sent back) will not be obtained within a few days—Let Gal Waïne arrive in time or not, when he comes under my direction, I wish to know if in case we succeed he must be sent on to General Greene

Supposing he is to go there, would your excellency think of selecting some riflemen for the Grand Army? It seems to me that I heard you once mentionning this matter

The State of Virginia, I am told, finds difficulties to the keeping of prisoners—Suppose some thing of this kind was started to me, am I to alter any thing in what you said to me on the subject?

I am in a great hurry to go, my dear General, but, let us succeed or fall in the object we have in view, I sha'nt be less hurried to return with the detachement to head quarters, where I hope to be again as soon as you may possibly expect

With the highest respect and most tender affection I have the honor to be, my dear general
> Your most obedient servant and affectionate friend
> Lafayette

I beg you will present my respects to Mrs. Washington and Mrs. Hamilton and my compliments to the family—I have received Mr. Washington's answer. He is waïting for me at the Baron's quarters.

[91]

Elk March the 8th 1781*

My dear General

Your letter of the 1st inst did not come to hand untill last evening, and I hasten to answer to his contents, tho' I will in a few hours be better able to inform you of my movements

From what I hear of the difficulties to convey us down the Bay, I very much aprehend that *the winds* will not permit any frigate to come up—Comte de Rochambeau thinks his troops equal to the business, and wishes that they alone may display their zeal, and shed their blood for an expedition which all America has so much at heart—The measures He is taking may be influenced by laudable motives, but I suspect they are not entirely free from selfish considerations

God grant this may not be productive of bad consequences—Baron de Viomenil will also want to do every thing alone—as to the French troops their zeal is laudable, and I wish their chiefs would reserve it for the time when we may cooperate with an assurance of success

I heartly feel, my dear General, for the Honor of our Arms, and think it would be derogatory to it, had not this detachement some share in the enterprise—this consideration induces me to embark immediately, and our soldiers will gladly put up with the inconveniences that attend the scarcity of vessels—we will have those armed ones (tho' the largest has only twelve guns) and with this every body assures that we may go without any danger to Annapolis

For my part I am not yet determined what to do—But if I see no danger for our small fleet to go to Annapolis, and if can get Com-

*Library of Congress, Washington papers. There is a contemporary copy in the letterbook in the Hubbard Collection.

modore Nicholson to take the command of it, perhaps shall I proceed in a small Boat to Hampton where my presence can alone be able to procure a frigat and where I will try to cool the impetuosity or correct the political mistakes of Both Barons.

Whatever determination I take, Great deal must be personally risked—But I hope to manage things so as to commit no imprudence with the excellent detachement whose glory is as dear, and whose safety is much dearer to me than my own

I have wrote to General Greene, and will write to the Governors either to get intelligences or to prepare means to operate, But (General Greene excepted) I do not give them any hint of our intentions farther than the expedition against Porsmouth

Whan a man has delicate games to play, and when chance may influence so much his success or miscarriage, He must submit to general blame in case of misfortune—But your esteem, my dear general, and your affection will not depend upon *events*—With the Highest Respect and most tender friendship I have the Honor to be My dear General

Your Most obedient Humble Servant
Lafayette

[92]

On board the Dolphin March the 9th 1781

My dear General

Here I am at the mouth of Elk River and the fleet under my command will proceed to Annapolis where I am assured they can go without danger—They are protected by the Nesbitt of twelve guns, some field pieces on board the vessel that carries C^{lel} Stevens, and we are going to meet one eight guns, and one six guns vessel from Baltimore—With this escort we may go as far as Annapolis—No vessel of the ennemy ever ventured so far up, and if by chance they should—our force is superior to any cruizer they have in the Bay—At Annapolis we will meet Commodore Nicholson whom I have requested by a letter to take the general command of our fleet, and if there was the least danger to proceed farther down they are to remain at Annapolis untill I send them new orders.

As to myself, my dear general, I have taken a small boat armed with swivels and on board of whom I have put thirty soldiers. I will precede the fleet to Annapolis where I am to be met by intelligences, and agreable to the state of things below will determine my personal motions and those of the fleet.

With a full conviction that (unless you arrived in time at Rhode Island) no frigat will be sent to us, I think it my duty to the troops I command and the country I serve, to overlook some little personal danger that I may ask for a frigat myself, and in order to add weight to my application I have clapp'd on board my boat the only son of the Minister of the French Navy, whom I'll take out to speak if circumstances require it.

Our men were much crouded at first, but I unload the vessels as we go along and take possession of every boat that comes in my way.

These are, my dear general, the measures I thought proper to take—The detachement is, I hope, free from danger and my caution on this point has been so far as to be called timidity by every seaman I have consulted—Captain Martin of the Nesbitt who has been recommended by Gal Gist make himself answerable for the safe arrival of the fleet at Annapolis before to morrow evening.

With the highest respect and most tender affection I have the honor to be, my dear general

Your most obedient humble servant and friend
Lafayette.

Will you be pleased, my dear general, to present my respects to Mrs Washington, Mrs Hamilton and the family.

[93]

Off Turkey Point, March the 9th [1781].*

My Dear General,—Commodore Nicholson has joined us sooner than I expected; he answers to conduct the detachment to Annapolis without the least danger, there he will wait for intelligence from me, but says that if the French fleet are below he might go with safety (if not for the vessels at least for the troops) to the point of

---

Memoirs, correspondence and manuscripts of General Lafayette, pp. 496-97. (The editor has obviously corrected the grammar, spelling and punctuation of the original.) (Proper names are identified in the "Index" below.)

our destination. Nicholson will be very useful to the French fleet as he knows well the bay.

I will be at Hampton to-morrow night or the day after, and three days after my arrival, if the French (whose arrival has not been heard of) consent to send a frigate, the detachment may come in two days from Annapolis.

Most respectfully, my dear General, your's &c.

P.S.—I have written to the State of Maryland to tell them we don't want any of their Militia. I have left to the Navy Board to judge of the propriety to send out the Ariel adding that it was no more essential.

[94]

York March the 15th 1781*

My dear General

The number of small frigats and privateers that are in the Bay has made it impossible for me to carry the detachement farther down than Annapolis, and I have requested the Governor of Maryland as well as the principal officers of the detachement to give out that we were going to join Gal Greene. But the object of the expedition is so perfectly known every where that our sole dependance to keep Arnold must be upon the aprehension he has of a French fleet being cruizing off the Capes

For my part I came in a barge from Annapolis, and very luckly escaped the dangers that were in the way. C^{lel} Harrison will have given to your Excellency a minuted detail of the of the reasons which have prompted me to this measure. I have taken his advice on the matter, and have no doubt but that your Excellency (considering the probability that no frigat would have been sent) will approuve of the step I have taken to forward as much as possible both the advantage of the expedition and the honor of the American arms.

On my arrival (yesterday after noon) I have found that Baron de Stubens had been very active in making preparations, and agreable to what he tells me we shall have five thousand militia ready to operate. This with the Continental detachement is equal to the business, and we might very well do without any land force from Newport

*Library of Congress, Washington papers. There is a contemporary copy in the letterbook in the Hubbard Collection.

By papers found in the baggage of a British officer (taken in a boat) it seems that Gal Gregory had a correspondance with the ennemy. The Baron has suspended him, but he is still with the troops.

Arnold is so well acquainted with the coming of the detachement and his object is so well known that as I said before our only chance to keep him must be the idea of a French fleet being off the Capes. He is fortifying at Porsmouth and trying to get provisions. There has been some trifling scarmishes with the militia.

To my great disappointement the French fleet have not yet appear'd. If the project has not been given up, they must be expected every minute. They had double the time which they wanted, and such winds as ought to have brought them in four days.

I wanted to hold up the idea of my going to the south ward—but the Baron says that if the detachement is not announc'd he militia will desert. He wanted me to take the command immediately, but I thought it more polite not to do it untill the detachement arrives or operations are begun.

In your first letter to the Baron, I wish, my dear General, you will write to him that I have been much satisfied with his preparations. I want to please him, and harmony shall be my first object.

As in all cases (even this of my going to the south ward and coming here to make arrangements with the Baron) I would recconnoitre the ennemy's works I will take an opportunity of doing it as soon as possible. They have not been as yet reconnoitred by the Baron, and I think it therefore more necessary for me to see with my own eyes.

As I am just arrived, my dear General, I cannot give you a very exact account of matters. This letter I send by duplicata and have the honor to be with the highest respect and most tender affection
      Your Excellency's
        Most obedient Servant and friend
         Lafayette

I request that your Excellency will please to present my respects to Mrs. Washington Mrs. Hamilton and compliments to the family.

[95]

Williams Burg—March the 23d 1781*

My Dear General

By former letters your Excellency has been acquainted with my motions from my arrival at the Head of Elk to the time of my landing at this place. The march of the detachement to Elk had been very rapid and performed in the best order. Owing to the activity of Lt C^{lel} Stevens a train of artillery had been provided at Philadelphia, and notwistanding some disappointements, namely that relating to the want of vessels, no delay should have been imputed to us in this cooperation.

Having received your Excellency's letter by which the sailing of the French Fleet became a matter of certainty, I determined to transport the detachement to Annapolis, and did it for many essential reasons. The navigation of the Bay is such that the going in and going out of Elk River requires a different wind from those which are very fair to go up and down the Bay. Our stopping at Annapolis and making some preparations on the road to Carolina might be of use to deceive the ennemy. But above all I thought with your Excellency that it was important both to the succcess of the operation and the honor of our arms that the detachement might be down to cooperate, and from the time when the French were to sail and the winds that blew for some days, I had no doubt but that our Allies were in the Chesapeak before we could be arrived at Annapolis.

Owing to the good dispositions of Commodore Nicholson whom I requested to take charge of our small fleet, the detachement was safely lodg'd in the Harbour of Annapolis, and in the conviction that my presence here was necessary not so much for preparations to which Baron de Stueben provided as for settling our plans with the French and obtaining an immediate convoy for the detachement I thought it better to run some personal risk than to neglect any thing that could forward the success of the operation, and the glory of the troops under my command.

On my arrival at this place, I was surprised to hear that no French Fleet had appeared, but attributed it to delays and chances so frequent in naval matters. My first object was to request that

*Library of Congress, Washington papers. There is a contemporary copy in the letterbook in the Hubbard Collection.

nothing be taken for this expedition which could have been intended for or useful to the Southern Army whose well fare appeared to me more interesting than our success. My second object has been to examine what had been prepared, to gather and forward every requisite for a vigorous cooperation, and besides a number of militia that would have amounted to five thousand, I can assure your Excellency that nothing would have been wanting to insure a compleat success.

As the position of the ennemy had not yet been reconnoitred, I went to Gal Müllemberg's camp near Suffolk, and after he had taken a position nearer to Porsmouth, we marched down with some troops to view the ennemy's works. This brought on a trifling scarmish during which we were enabled to see some thing, but the insufficiency of ammunition which had been many days expected prevented my engaging too far to push the ennemy's out posts, and our reconnoitring was postponed to the 21st when on the 20th Major McPherson an officer for whom I have the highest confidence and esteem sent me word from York* where he was stationned that a fleet had come to anchor within the Capes.

So far was it probable that this fleet was that of Mr Destouches, that Arnold himself appeared to be in a great confusion, and his vessels notwistanding many signals durst not for a long time venture down. An officer of the French Navy bore down to them from York, and nothing could equal my surprise in hearing from M^jr McPherson that the fleet announced by a former letter was certainly belonging to the ennemy

Upon this intelligence the militia were removed to their former position and I requested Baron de Stubens (from whom out of delicacy I would not take the command untill the cooperation was begun or the Continental troops arrived) to take such measures as would put out of the enemy's reach the several articles that had been prepared

On my return to this place I could not hear more particular accounts of the fleet. Some people think they are coming from Europe. But I believe them to be the fleet from Gardner's Bay. They are said to be twelve sails in all frigats included. I have sent spies on board, and shall forward their report to head quarters

* *York* has been crossed out and *Hampton* written in by another hand.

Having certain accounts that the French have sailed on the eighth with a favorable wind, I must think that they are coming to this place, or were beaten in an engagement, or are gone some where else. In those three cases, I think it my duty to stay here untill I hear some thing more which must be in a little time. But as your excellency will certainly recall a detachement composed of the flower of each regiment, whose loss would be immense for the army under your immediate command, and as my instructions are to march them back as soon as we lose the naval superiority in this quarter, I have sent them orders to move at the first notice from me which I will send to morrow or the day after, or upon a letter from your excellency which my aid de camp is empowered to oppen

Had I not been here upon the spot, I am sure that I would have waited an immense time before I knew what to think of this fleet, and my presence at this place was the speediest means of forwarding the detachement either to Hampton, or back to your excellency's immediate army

By private letters we hear that General Greene had on the 15th an engagement with Lord Cornwallis. The honor of keeping the field was not on our side. The ennemy lost more men than we did. General Greene displayed his usual prudence and abilities both in making his dispositions and posting his troops at ten miles from the first field of battle where they bid defiance to the ennemy and are in a situation to check his progresses

With the highest respect I have the honor to be
    Dear General
        Your excellency's
            Most obedient humble
              servant
                Lafayette

Major McLeane who has already lost his baggage in going to search the French fleet will carry this by water to Head of Elk.

A copy of this letter, my dear general, is by me sent to Congress. It is for this reason that I insist on the necessity of sending back the detachement to head quarters. I hope, my dear general, that my conduct will meet with your approbation, and it is the thing I the most heartly wish for. I beg you will present my respects to Mrs. Washington and comp^{lis} to the family

[96]

Williams Burg March the 25th 1781*

My dear General

My letter of the 23d to your excellency will, I hope, be safely transmitted and the bearer of it Mjr Mc Leane assured me that in case he was obliged to loose the dispatch boats, he could find means to get a shore and forward the dispatches by land

In this letter I gave to your excellency an account of what had past since I left Annapolis, and communicated the intelligence of a British Fleet having anchored in Lyn Haven Bay. This account however, you will have sooner received from the Governor of Virginia, than you might possibly from me, as my position with the troops near Porsmouth being intended to reconnoitre the works and get on board of ships in Hampton Road, intelligences from the Capes were more speedily forwarded through Williamsburg than they might have been in going arround to Suffolk

My surprise at not hearing of the French Fleet was, I confess, very great, nor could I reconcile my mind to this uncertainty. But intelligences received yesterday have put it out of doubt that they have done their best endeavours towards the cooperation, and my accounts being gathered from many quarters, and from men who were at the first engagement your excellency may depend upon their veracity

On the sixteenth inst both fleets fell in near Capes with each other. They both consisted of 8 ships of the line fifties included with the difference of twenty guns in favor of the ennemy. Each ship of the line and each frigat singly engaged a partner, and the action lasted during three glasses. The ennemy had two 74 much worsted (one of them had 65 men killed) the London suffered in her rigging, and the British Fleet sheered off for Cheseapeak while the French stood in a line formed in good order. The ennemy have sent their wounded up to Porsmouth, taken all the sailors and marines at that place, and refitted their damaged ships. They were also reinforced from Porsmouth by the *Charon*, a 44 that can be made a fifty, and two large frigats

But it appears that our Allies are determined to carry the point,

*Library of Congress, Washington papers. There is a contemporary copy in the letterbook in the Hubbard Collection.

and that the addition to the British force has not prevented them from appearing near the Capes. Last morning the whole Birtish Fleet with the reinforcement went to sea, and about eleven o'clock we heard a furious canonade which lasted more than three hours

The action must have been bloody and obstinate. Upon its event depends the fate of our expedition. I wish it had been in my power not to make your excellency a partaker of our anxiety untill I might have known on what side victory has been. But the fresh winds that blew last night make it impossible to have any account this morning. I shall therefore send off these present intelligences which have come last night to hand, and as expresses with proper officers are stationned at Hampton, I shall speedily forward every account that appears to be certain and interesting

I have directed that Arnold be circumscribed within his works on both sides of the Dismal Swamp. The water is still oppened to him, but every armed vessel in the rivers is getting ready to do what little service can be expected from them. The detachement at Annapolis is also ordered to be in the most perfect readiness

With the highest respect I have the honor to be
Your excellency's
Most obedient humble servant
Lafayette

[97]

Williams Burg March the 26th 1781*

My dear General

As I hope my letters of the 23d and 25th have been safely transmitted, and this will be accompagnied by a letter of the same date forwarded through the hands of the President of Congress, I shall only add such parts of my information as I mean to be confidential.

From my late intelligences I am led to suppose that our Allies are gone to Cape Fear. The first engagement was in their favor and I am sorry they did not pursue their advantage. As to the canonade which every officer and myself among them is certain to have dis-

*Library of Congress, Washington papers. There is a contemporary copy in the letterbook in the Hubbard Collection. Unpublished except for an excerpt in Charlemagne Tower, *The Marquis de La Fayette in the American Revolution* (2 vols.; 3rd imp.; Philadelphia, 1926), II, 247-48.

tinctly heard, I begin to fear it has been a very uncommon effect of thunder. Tho' many people would think it madness in me not to stick to the opinion that it certainly was a cannonade.

My informant a gentleman taken by the *Charlestown* and lately escaped from that frigat assures me positively that the French have been seen at anchor at Cape Fear and that the British have declared war against Holland.

The return of the British Fleet with vessels that must be transports from New York is a circumstance which destroys every prospect of an operation against Arnold. The number of men is not what I am affraid off, and the French and Continental troops joined with the militia must be equal to a pretty serious siege—But since the British Fleet have returned and think themselves safe in this Bay, I entertain very little hopes of seeing the French flag in Hampton Road.

The expences of this expedition are very great, and the minds of the Virginians are so disposed as to make me more obstinate to pursue the expedition. Upon its success great deal depended, particularly for Gal Greene's army. Never has an operation be more ready (on our side) nor conquest more certain. But since we must give it up, I shall return to Annapolis where the troops may have received orders from you, or I may have some letters directed to me. If none are arrived, I shall return to Head quarters, and march the detachement as fast as possible.

Unless Baron de Viomenil strikes a great blow the Southern States are much endangered and these low parts of Virginia are at the disposal of the ennemy. As it is possible I may hear from Willmington I shall request C^{lel} Gouvion to stay some few days and oppen such letters as might be directed to me.

If the detachement from Newyork is strong that place must be weak, and it increases my desire to join your Excellency—as matters have turned out it would have been better I had not brought the troops to Annapolis. But the arrival of the French Fleet could not then be questioned, and this removal of our troops was the best means I could think off to level all difficulties of a convoy. As to my personal motions, they were necessary to get intelligences and decide matters

I request your Excellency will please to present my respects to

Mrs. Washington Mrs. Hamilton and compliments to the family—
Believe me, my dear general, most respectfully
                              Yours
                                    Lafayette

[98]

Williams Burg March the 26th 1781*

My dear General

By intelligences just received I hear that the British fleet have returned to Lyn Haven Bay, and that they were accompagnied by a number of vessels supposed to be transports from Newyork.

From a conversation with a gentleman who having been taken a few days before the engagement was during the action on board the Charleston frigat, I have got a particular account of what has past on that meeting of the two fleets. The intelligence he gives comes pretty near to what I have mentionned in my last. He says that the action was general, lasted five glasses, and that the ennemy had been worsted. Whatever may be our prospects in this part, I am still in hopes that our Allies will render some valuable service to the Southern States.

The same gentleman from whom I got these accounts gives me the most positive assurance that war has been declared between the Dutch and the English. As to the canonade mentionned in my last (tho' every man in this place, every officer on duty that sent a report, and almost every intelligence from below assure that there has been a noise of cannon heard for many hours) I begin to suspect it may have been produced by thunder, and your Excellency will remember that in the retreat of General Clinton through the jersays a similiar noise had obliged him to march his army seven miles to the support of General Knypausen whom he thought had been attaked by us.

Unless further orders are received from your Excellency I shall make it a point to follow your former instructions, and with the highest respect have the honor to be
                 Your Excellency's
                        Most obedient Humble Servant
                                          Lafayette

*Library of Congress, Washington papers. There is a contemporary copy in the letterbook in the Hubbard Collection. Unpublished.

[99]

Elk April the 8th 1781*

My dear General

Your excellency's letters of the 5th and 6th inst are just come to hand, and before I answer to their contents beg leave to give you a summary account of the measures I have lately taken. As to the part of my conduct you have been acquainted with, I am happy, my dear General, to find that it has met with your approbation

When the return of the British Fleet put it out of doubt that nothing could be undertaken for the present against Porsmouth, I sent pressing orders to Annapolis in order to have every thing in readiness and even to move the troops by land to the Head of Elk. I myself hastened back to Maryland, but I confess could not resist the ardent desire I had long ago of seeing your relations and above all your Mother at Frederick Burg. For that purpose I went some miles out of the way, and in order to conciliate my private happiness to duties of a public nature, I recovered by riding in the night those few hours which I had consecrated to my satisfaction. I had also the pleasure of seeing Mount Vernon, and was very unhappy that my duty and my anxiety for the execution of your orders prevented my paying a visit to Mr. Custis

On my arrival at Annapolis, I found that our preparations were far from promising a speedy departure. The difficulty of getting waggons and horses is immense—No boats sufficient to cross over the ferries—the State very desirous to keep us as long as possible, as they were scared by the apparition of the Hope 20 guns and the Monk 18 guns who blockaded the Harbour and who (as appeared from intercepted letters) were determined to oppose our movements

In the circumstances, I thought it better to continue my preparations for a journey by land, which, I am told, would have lasted ten days on account of ferries, and in the mean while had two eighteen pounders put on board a small sloop which appeared ridiculous to some, but proved to be of a great service

In the morning of the 6th Commodore Nicholson went out with the sloop and an other vessel full of men. Wether the sound of 18 pounders or the fear of being boarded operated upon the ennemy I am not able to say. But after some maneuvres they retreated so far

*Library of Congress, Washington papers. There is a contemporary copy in the letterbook in the Hubbard Collection.

as to render it prudent for us to sail for this place. Every vessel with troops and stores was sent in the night by the Commodore to whom I am vastly obliged, and having brought up the rear with the sloop and other vessel I arrived this morning at Elk. It is reported that the ships have returned to their station. If it is so, they must have been reinforced and their Commander had already applied for the augmenation of force.

Before I left Annapolis I received a letter from General Greene which being intended to be delivered by C^lel Moriss was very short, and refers [?] to propositions which C^lel Moriss was to make to Baron de Viomenil and myself. That officer came within twenty miles of Williams Burg, and hearing from Baron de Stubens that I was just gone he thought it useless to communicate propositions which related to a cooperation with the French forces

By this express and letters from the Baron I did not hear any thing further of the ennemy's arrival in the Chesapeak but what I have once mentionned, but hearing that General Greene was in want of ammunition I took the liberty of leaving for the Southern Army four 6 pounders with 300 rounds each, near hundred thousand cartridges and some small matters which I left to the care of the Governor and General Smallwood, requesting them to have waggons and horses impressed and to send them to a place of safety where they must be by this time. I also wrote to the Governor of Virginia, to General Greene and the Baron, and those stores will set off in a few days under the care of a detachement for the Maryland Line commanded by L^t. C^lel Stuart

On my passage from Annapolis two men came on board our vessels whom I suspected to be spies, and we therefore put on the appearance of British. They were at first cautious, but upon M^jor Mc Pherson's describing some acquaintances of theirs in the British Army, they were entirely satisfied, and told us that they had been on board the other vessels, that they used to furnish the army with flour and that a sloop was just waiting for an opportunity to slip off. They offered to guide us, and one of them is gone with Mc Pherson to secure the sloop least the rebels should order her up. As soon as he returns I will have both hanged as spies

In consequence of previous orders every thing was in readiness for our movement. The troops were ordered to march to morrow morning, and I expect a sufficiency of vessels is now at Willmington or Christiana Creek—so that I was in hopes to join your excellency in a very few days

Your letter of the 6th ordering me to the south ward is just come to hand. Had I been still at Annapolis, or upon the road by land (and of course with the same means to return which I had to advance) your commands would have been immediately obeïed. But necessity keeps us here for some days, and as your letter came in two days your answer to this must be here before we are in a situation to move

When your excellency wrote to me, I was supposed to be at Annapolis or very near that place with the means of returning, which makes a great difference. An other still more material is that instead of joining either Arnold or Philips (if Philips is there) Lord Cornwallis is so disabled as to be forced to a retreat as appears from General Greene's letter

To these considerations I have added this one which is desisive —that being only fitted to march twelve miles part of it in the State of Delaware, and a part of of [*sic*] our provisions being asked for from Philadelphia, it is impossible to have the necessary apparatus to march and subsist or to cross ferrys on our way towards the Southern Army so as to leave this place under four or five days. As to a transportation through the Bay, we cannot expect the same good luck of frightening an ennemy who must know how despicable our preparations were, and we must at least waït for the return of look out boats which if sent immediately will not probably return under five or six days

In these circumstances, my dear general, I am going to make every preparation to march to Virginia so as to be ready as soon as possible. I shall keep here the vessels, and will also keep those which have been ordered to Christiana Creek. This state of suspence will distract the ennemy's conjectures and put me in a situation to execute your excellency's orders which will be here before I can be able to move with any degree of advantage towards the south ward.

Had it been possible to obey to morrow morning I should have done it immediately. But since I am obliged to make preparations, I beg leave to make these observations which I I [*sic*] would have been allowed to present, had I been at the meeting of general officers

The troops I have with me being taken from every northern regiment, have often (tho' without mentionning it to me) been very uneasy at the idea of joining the Southern Army. They want cloathes, shöes particularly, they expect to receive cloathes and monney from their States. This would be a great disappointement for both officers and men. Both thought at first they were sent out for a few days and provided themselves accordingly. Both came chearfully to this expedition, but both have had already their fears on the idea of going to the south ward. They will certainly obey, but they will be unhappy and some will desert

Had this corps considered themselves as light infantry destined for the campaign to be separated from their regiments it would be attended with less inconveniences and such a corps in the course of the campaign might be brought there particularly by water without difficulty as they would be prepared accordingly

Supposing the Jersay line were to join the detachement of their troops at this place it would hardly make any difference as we have been but five days coming from Morristown to the Head of Elk

These considerations, my dear general, I beg you to be convince are not influenced by personal motives. I would most certainly like better to be in a situation to attak Newyork nor would I like in an operation against Newyork to see you deprived of the New England Light Infantry, but I think with you that these motives are not to influence our determination if this is the best way to help General Greene.

By the letters I have received from my two friends Marquis de Castries and Count de Vergennes I am assured that we shall soon get an answer to our propositions against Newyork, and strongly led to hope that having a naval superiority the army under your immediate command will not remain inactive

At all events, my dear general, I will use my best endeavours to be ready to move either way as soon as possible and have the honor to be with the highest respect and affection

Your most obedient humble
servant and friend
Lafayette

I beg you will present my respects to Mrs. Washington Mrs. Hamilton and the family.

[100]

Elk April the 10th 1781*

Dear General

By my letter of the 8th your Excellency will have known of my arrival at this place and the preparations I was making to proceed south ward. I took at the same time the liberty to inform you that the great want of monney, baggage, cloathing, under which both officers and men are suffering and the hope they had of being furnished with a part of these articles from their States would render it very inconvenient for the troops to proceed immediately by land. They begin to be sensible of the reason which detains them here, and are uneasy about it as they are so unprovided for the journey. I have however hurried on preparations and will be able to set off to morrow morning. The circumstance of my being ready sooner than I expected, and a letter from the Governor of Maryland informing that six ships whom I take to be plundering vessels were coming up the Potowmack induce me not to wait for your Excellency's answer. Not that I pretend to defend the towns of Alexandria Baltimore and Annapolis at a time, or to stop the depredations of the ennemy's parties, in a country where their naval superiority renders it impossible, but because I don't think any consideration must delay the execution of superior orders, and because if this Corps was not sent south ward they would with alacrity march back thirty or forty miles more to rejoin the Grand Army.

Having received no particulars of your Excellency's journey to Rhode island but by the news paper, a letter from you to Mr. Lund Washington, and some private letters of some friends, I cannot know what change has taken place in your plans, and am not able to account for the inactivity which you foresee for the Grand Army. Letters from Ministers, letters from my friends, intelligences from other quarters, every thing was combined to flatter me with the hope that our grand and desicive object would be in contemplation. I then was not displeased with the dispositions of the ennemy that weakened that place. It is probable your Excellency's plans have changed and you intend to prosecute the war to the south ward.

*Library of Congress, Washington papers. There is a contemporary copy in the letterbook in the Hubbard Collection.

I had yesterday the pleasure of dining on board the Hermione and left her under sails to go to Rhode island where she will probably be the day after to morrow. M^r de La Touche Treville uncle to Captain La Touche will, it is said, command the Squadron of the Second Division. I was conversing with his nephew in whom he has an entire confidence on an expedition against New york and he assured me that his uncle's plan would certainly be to take possession of the Harbour, and send a force up North River—which you know is entirely the thing that you wanted Mr de Ternay to do.

Monsieur de La Touche having confidentially told me that he had a great influence over Monsieur Destouches, I observed to him how important it was for the common cause that the French Fleet might have the greatest possible activity. We were also conversing of the difficulties we laboured under for transportation, and he told me that the next day after his arrival at Rhode island, unless such obstacles occurred as he could not foresee, Monsieur Destouches would make you an offer of the ship L'eveïllé and the four frigats to carry twelve hundred men to any port of the Continent you might think proper. Those ships are too strong to be affraid of frigats, and too fast sailors to be in the least concerned by the fear of a squadron. Thinking that (particularly as Lord Cornwallis has retreated) our march would take us forty days where desertion and sickness occasioned by want of shoes and every other necessary as well as by the heat of the sun would much reduce our numbers, and that these ships with the addition of the two frigats at Philadelphia armed *en flute* would in sailing only the 4th or 5th of May carry 1500 men to Willmington George town or any place in the rear of Lord Cornwallis or the neighbourood of General Greene I thought it my duty to encourage this idea which would bring us to the point of operations sooner than we could arrive by land. It would also give you the time of forming at Morristown or Trenton a detachement well provided agreably to the project you had in contemplation after the return of this Corps when the appointement of officers could be made without affecting the delicacy of the regimental officers nor the honor of those already emploïed. While we would be operating Mr Destouche might keep cruizers off Charleston

These ideas, my dear General, are only thrown out in consequence of the freedom which you have often ordered me to take.

What Mr Destouches may do is uncertain, and I did not think myself authorized to express to him the least wish on that head. It was my duty to relate our difficulties to you and the chances I foresaw to see them relieved in some measure. But unless the bad weather of which there is now a prospect makes it impossible, I will be to morrow at the ferry at the Susquehana.

You may have known from Mr de la Luzerne that two millions and a half had been given to Mr. Franklin and that Marquis de Castries and Count de Vergennes were trying to obtain a sum more adequate to our wants. That however the Minister of France has requested me not to mention as it was as yet an uncertainty, and would perhaps give ill grounded hopes destructive of the internal efforts we ought to make. I am told that just before the departure of Mr de la Peyrouse some dispatches were sent to Brest, but do not think they contain any thing relating to our operations as Marquis de Castries writes me that the determination of the Council upon our letters will be sent by the ship who is to convoy the expected vessels.

I am very sorry I have not seen the aid de camp who had a verbal message from General Greene. Inclosed I send to your Excellency the letters I have received on the occasion. Perhaps did he mean to propose an expedition towards Cape Fear or George town which might be made with the light squadron above mentionned. An additional circumstance is that the Eveïllé will now be commanded by Mr de Lombard Captain La Touche's uncle who is entirely under that gentleman's influence.

I write to the Board of War for to get some shoes and other parts of cloathing. I will this morning speack to the commanding officers of Bataïllons on our intended journey. But have not yet said any thing to C^lel Gimat and Major Galvan because it is possible that new circumstances may engage you to change your dispositions. Going by water, if possible would level most all difficulties. But if I don't hear from you I will alwaïs proceed on. Requesting your Excellency to present my best respects to Mrs. Washington and compliments to the family I have the honor to be with the highest respect your Excellency's

Most obedient and affectionate Servant
Lafayette

[101]

Elk April the 10th [1781]*

Dear General

Agreably to Your Excellency's permission Major Troop has my leave to return to the army. The commanding officers have represented that he was under indispensable necessity to go, and we can very well do without him untill the arrival of an other major

Colonel Vose is, I am told, very desirous to return to the Army. He has there a regiment, and before we join General Greene our bataïllons will be very small. But other business recall him, and I beg leave to represent to Your Excellency that C^{lel} Smith would be very well calculated for such a command

When appointed to the adjudant generalcy of this small corps, C^{lel} Smith had the hope that we would either operate against Arnold, or be a van guard to your army as they had been last year. But the corps being thrown into the line of the Southern Army C^{lel} Smith would act as an inspector under officers who are inferior to him in rank of commission. He is for the present unwell at this place where your letter would find him, and untill I receive your answer I will differ hearing the reasons of C^{lel} Vose

With the highest and most affectionate respect I have the honor to be

Your excellency's most obedient
humble servant
Lafayette

By a gentleman just from Philadelphia I am assured that the Pennsylvania line is ready to march to the southward, and that Congress have received the official intelligence of an embarcation having taken place at Newyork destined to New Castle. In that case we would be upon the spot. But unless I receive contrary orders from you, or I see the ennemy in the River I wil not delay the execution of your orders

---

*Library of Congress, Washington papers. There is a contemporary copy in the letterbook in the Hubbard Collection. Unpublished.

[102]

Elk April 11th 1781*

Dear General

This letter will be delivird to Your Excellency by Capt Rochefontaine who is joining the grand Army and will leave this Corps with the few Sapers and and Miners we had taken from West Point. I dont apprehend they may be useful to us, and it would have been very inconvenient for them to be seperated from their Corps where they are to receive every kind of supply—with the highest respect.
I have the honor to be
Your Excellencys
Most Obed^t Hum. Servt
Lafayette

[103]

Elk April the 12th 1781†

Dear General

Owing to a very heavy rain and a most stormy night I was yesterday obliged to counter mand the orders I had given to the troops, and upon the representation that the roads to the Susquehana would be impassable, I differed our departure to this morning. We shall encamp on a ground near the Ferry and be as expeditious as possible in crossing the river. In consequence of your Excellency's permission I have allowed some officers to return to the Army with orders to report themselves to head quarters.

The extreme wants of the officers have induced me to permit an officer per bataïllon and one of the Jersay line to return to the Army and get some cloathes for themselves and the rest of the Corps. This measure appeared to be necessary, and C^{lel} Barber is gone to Philadelphia with a letter to the Board of War exposing our wants and requesting some tents, over alls, shirts, shoes etc. While these will be preparing I thought I might indulge him to go to Morristown, as I think his presence will be necessary at Philadelphia by the time when our supplies will be forwarded.

Major Troop being gone we want a field officer to reimplace

*Contemporary copy in the letterbook in the Hubbard Collection. Unpublished.
†Library of Congress, Washington papers. There is a contemporary copy in the letterbook in the Hubbard Collection. Unpublished.

him. C^lel Barber and Major Reed are happy to remain with us and I am no less happy to keep these excellent officers. Colonel Vose is (I am told) desirous to return—The officers of his bataïllon knowing that it was his inclination have waïted on C^lel Smith to express to him the ardent desire they had, in case C^lel Vose allowed to go, that C^lel Smith be appointed to the command. This circumstance I thought worth communicating to Your Excellency. Smith is sick for the present, and a letter would find him either here or at Philadelphia. Was he to be attached to a light corps as he last last year I think he would be glad to act as inspector, but in the Southern Army would be under an officer to whom he is superior in rank of commission.

As to C^lel Gimat and Major Galvan, now that their fate is going to be decided in a way which cannot but affect their feelings and reputation, I think myself obliged to submit to Your Excellency an observation which for fear of appearing partial I had hitherto omitted. I will therefore *confidentially* impart to you that Major Galvan is very unpopular among the officers, while Colonel Gimat is particularly beloved. Complaints have often been made to me against the one, while the other has ever received from the officers under his command the most flattering testimonies of affection, and I may go so far as to say that the recalling of C^lel Gimat will be very disagreable to his bataïllon. This I mention to Your Excellency, not that I think the sentiments of the officers must induce you to recall Major Galvan, a measure which I would be far from advising, but because this opposition being perhaps owing to the partiality of the officers for or against private persons, and this circumstance being of a very serious nature for these two gentlemen, I thought it my duty not to withdraw any particulars from Your Excellency's knowledge.

With the highest and most affectionate respect I have the honor to be

                Your Excellency's
                Most obedient humble servant
                Lafayette

I beg leave to present my respects to Mrs. Washington and compliments to the family

[104]

Susquehana Ferry, April the 13th 1781*

Dear General

I have received Your Excellency's letter relating to C^{lel} Gouvion. It would have been very agreable to me to keep this officer. Your orders have been sent to Philadelphia where he is for the present. However distant I may be from the scene, I am happy to find that Your Excellency hopes to undertake the grand object we have had in contemplation

By a letter just received from the Board of War it seems that representations of wants have been made which they have mistaken for objections from me to our journey south ward. I have said to some officers that our proximity to the Southern States was the reason which had induced Your Excellency to send this detachement. But I hope I need not assuring you that never I thought of intimating the least idea of alteration to Your Excellency's projects, but such as you could think of making yourself after your own ideas and intelligences. Perhaps my letter to the Board will appear appear direspectfull or impolite. But nothing could stop me in an instance where it might be suspected I objected to your plans, or even differed in opinion. You know me too perfectly not to think an explanation useless

It is confidently *reported* that the Second Division is arrived to the Capes of Delaware consisting of nine ships of the line. This was the number mentionned to me by Marquis de Castries to be in harbour. Your Excellency would in that case have a brilliant campaign to the north ward

With the highest and most affectionate respect I have the honor to be

Your Excellency's
Most obedient humble servant
Lafayette

---

*Library of Congress, Washington papers. There is a contemporary copy in the letterbook in the Hubbard Collection.

[105]

Susquehana Ferry April the 13th 1781*

Dear General

Had Your Excellency's answer to my letter of the 8th been forwarded with an equal celerity with your favor of the 6th I would have received it before this time. But whatever change my new situation could made in Your Excellency's dispositions I thought it my duty in the mean while to obey the positive orders I had received. The troops are now crossing the ferry and will with all possible speed proceed to Richmond

By a letter just received from General Greene I find that he is strongly of opinion that I must go to the south ward. His intention is to carry the seat of war into South Carolina, there by preventing a jonction between Arnold and Cornwallis. He gives me many excellent reasons to justify the movement he requests me to make to Richmond, and they will if possible increase my zeal to execute Your Excellency's orders

General Greene's opinion is that Lord Cornwallis will fall down towards Willmington. His own project is to carry the war into South Carolina. Under these circumstances a corps of light infantry embarked at Philadelphia on board a light squadron might have been upon the seat of war in a very short passage

I cannot help fearing, my dear general, that our campaign will take a defensive turn which is far from answering to our first plans and expectations

Major Mc Pherson is with me as a volunteer. That officer has most zealously employed himself and has most dangerously been exposed in the discovery of a plot made to furnish the enemy with provisions. He has managed this matter with infinite adress, being for two days and one night with six soldiers who as well as himself put on the air of British and in compagny with a spy who thought them to be ennemy and by a most violent gale of wind crossed the Bay in a small boat by which means he was made sensible that a trade of flour is carried with the enemy from the Western Shore of Maryland and saved a magazine of 800 barrels of continental flour which would other wise have fallen into the hands of the ennemy

*Library of Congress, Washington papers. There is a contemporary copy in the letterbook in the Hubbard Collection.

In case we proceed southerly perhaps will it be possible for General Greene to give Major Mc Pherson a command in some detachement, and I would be happy if he was recommended to him by Your Excellency

My determination being to go on with rapidity unless I am recalled, Your Excellency may easely judge of my movements from the answer I will probably receive in a few hours

Was I to assure Your Excellency that this journey is perfectly agreable to the troops I would not use that candor which you have so many rights to expect. But their zeal and discipline insure their readiness to obey. I shall do my utmost to prevent desertion, and, unless I was recalled, shall proceed with celerity. But beg Your Excellency to remember that experience has often taught us how much reduced has ever been the number of our troops from the time of their departure to that of their arrival at the Southern Army

With the highest and most affectionate respect I have the honor to be

Your Excellency's
Most obedient humble servant
Lafayette

[106]

Susquehana Ferry April the 14th 1781*

My dear General

Your Excellency's letter of the 11th has overtaken me at this place, and having given to you an account of every measure I thought proper to take, I will only add that I am still at the ferry where the troops have crossed the river, but the wind blows so high that it has been impossible to take the waggons over, and I am obliged to have others impressed on the southern side of the Susquehana.

Your Excellency mentions the propriety of remaining at the Head of Elk untill shoes can be collected. But the prospects I have from the Board of War are not flattering enough to encourage this measure. On the other side General Greene is pressing in his advices, and will soon be so in his orders to me. I cannot obtain any good account of Philips's motions, nor oppose the schemes he may have

---

*Library of Congress, Washington papers. There is a contemporary copy in the letterbook in the Hubbard Collection.

formed untill I am much farther advanced. And disatisfaction and desertion being two greater evils than any other we have to fear, I am anxious to have rivers, other countries, and every kind of barrier to stop the inclination of the men to return home.

Many men have already deserted. Many more will I am affraïd take the same course. Whatever sense of duty, ties of affection, and severity of discipline may operate shall be emploïed most earnestly by me, and I wish we might soon come near the ennemy which is the only means of putting a stop to that spirit of desertion

I am sorry to inform your excellency that the uneasiness in C^lel Vose's bataïllon has increased to the highest pitch. Their hatred to Major Galvan is not without foundation as he does not treat them with that even temper which troops have right to expect. But should not prove so prejudiciable had the officers and men the least confidence in C^lel Vose, or Colonel Vose the least firmness to superintend the conduct of his Major and other officers. These last have complained to me, but I did not think it consistent with discipline to give them a redress when C^lel Vose is present and is to answer for the maintenance of good order and a proper conduct in his corps. In the mean while the men desert, the officers are disatisfied, Major Galvan goes on in the same way, which he thinks to be the best, and I cannot punish this officer who is active, zealous, but plagues the bataïllon with a peculiar line of conduct which cannot bring any charge upon him and is not cheked by his colonel

Many articles, and indeed every one which compose the apparatus of a soldier will be wanting for this detachement. But shoes, linnen over alls, hunting shirts, shirts and ammunition will be the necessary supplies for which I request Your Excellency's most pressing orders to people concerned and most warm entreaties to the Board of War. I wish it was possible to have the men equiped at once, and this would be a great saving of expense

While I am writing to Your Excellency the wind rises more and more which will much impede our passage for such stores as were to cross over with the waggons and the guard appointed to stay with them. At such a distance from the ennemy, I cannot give Your Excellency any account of their movements, but by the last intelligences General Philips was still at Porsmouth

Should the French get a naval superiority an expedition against

Porsmouth is very practicable. These compagnies filled up to their proper number, and some other troops to increase the corps to two thousand would with a detachement of artillery from Philadelphia be equal to the attak of that post. 3000 militia can with the greatest ease be collected. In case the remainder of Duke de Lauzun's Legion arrives that corps could come in the fleet. But should the French become superior at sea the British fleet in Chesepaeke would be in danger and in every case if Your Excellency thinks of sending any reinforcement this way (let it be the Jersay troops or recruits) their coming by water to James or York River may save an immense trouble and expense

My heart and every faculty of my mind have been these last years so much concerned in the plan of an expedition against———* that I am very desirous to hear by the first safe opportunity what reasons can have overthrown the project

Some disputes that have at first happened betwen the Jersay and New England troops make me think that these last must be as much as possible separated from the Pennsilvanians

While I was writing this, accounts have been brought to me that a great desertion had taken place last night—nine of the Rhode island compagny—and the best men they had who have made many campaigns and never were suspected. These men say that they like better hundred lashes than a journey to the south ward. As long as they had an expedition in view, they were very well satisfied. But the idea of remaining in the Southern States appear to them intolerable and they are amazingly averse to the people and climate. I shall do my best, but if this disposition lasts, I am affraïd we will be reduced lower than I dare express

With the highest and most affectionate respect I have the honor to be

    Dear General
      Your most obedient humble
       servant
        Lafayette M.G.

---

*I.e. New York. (Proper names are identified in the "Index" below.)

[107]

Susquehana Ferry April the 15th 1781*

Dear General

C^lel Gouvion by whom I have received letters and intelligences from Philadelphia is just going to Head Quarters. This opportunity being safer then common express I beg leave to adress a few lines to Your Excellency.

The Board of War can not supply our wants. Indeed they nor Congress did not think we would be ordered to the south ward and of course have not been so much in earnest for giving us supplies. But had their wishes been very sanguine, they were not able to afford us any great succour.

The Pennsylvanians consist of 1200 men and could be compleated but for want of monney. They are ready to march, but have declared they did not choose to move untill they had received three month's pay. Monney is consequently searched for every where. The Pennsylvanians being upon that footing and very well equiped, we can not wonder at the desertion of our soldiers circumstanced as they are.

Nothing can make me more unhappy that the incessant desertion of our best, finest and most experienced soldiers. This detachement will be reduced to an handfull of men, and they say that arriving at the end of operations, three month before the campaign oppens in Carolina they will be still more reduced by the disorders of that unwholesome climate.

A letter from you relating to the delays of the French makes a great noise at Philadelphia. Indeed it gives me pain on many political accounts. There are many confidential communications which you once had requested from me, and which my peculiar situation with both sides of the alliance would enable me to make. But having been ordered from you, and many things I had to say not being of a nature which would render it prudent to entrust them to paper, these personal services must be out of the question so long as the war continues in Carolina.

By Chevalier de La Luzerne I hear that the French Army have offered to come to North River and must be upon their move by this time. This does not coincide with what had been said at Hartfort—but in calculating a correspondance with France, proves that

*Library of Congress, Washington papers. Unpublished.

183

I was right in telling you that this Court truly wanted their troops to be active. As to the Second Division, the hope of acting against —— [i.e. New York] the sanguine wishes of France on the occasion, he is of the same opinion with me. I would have sent this letter, had it not been too expressive of his grief for my departure owing to a peculiar friendship for me, and the idea his Court may have of my services in a cooperation.

Considering the footing I am upon with Your Excellency, it would perhaps appear to you strange, that I never mentionned a circumstance lately happened in your family*. I was the first who knew of it, and from that moment exerted every means in my power to prevent a separation which I knew was not agreable to Your Excellency. To this measure I was prompted by affection for you, but thought it was improper to mention any thing about it, untill you was pleased to impart it to me.

Having been some what concerned in the project of sending the First Division, and wrote many letters about the Second, I am embarassed how to make any more dispatches to the French Governement untill I know more of our present circumstances. If any safe opportunity was to offer I would be very happy to hear some thing of our situation. Chevalier de La Luzerne writes me that you have now 8000 men under arms and before you attak Newyork will have 12000. He says that the ennemy have only 5000 regulars at that place. But certainly he must be mistaken.

With the highest respect I have the honor to be
Your Excellency's
Most obedient humble servant
Lafayette

AMENDED [108]

My dear general   Baltimore April 18th 1781†

Every one of my letters was writen upon so lamentable a tone that I am happy to give you a pleasanter prospect. The anxiety I feel to relieve your mind from a small part of those many solicitudes and cares which our circumstances conspire to gather upon you, is the reason of my sending this letter by the chain and with a particu-

*Washington's quarrel with Hamilton the preceding February.
†Contemporary copy in the letterbook in the Hubbard Collection. (The original is in the Library of Congress, Washington papers but war conditions did not permit consultation of it.)

lar recommendation. When I left Susquehana Ferry it was the general opinion that we could not have six hundred men by the time we would arrive at our destination. This and the shocking situation of the men offered the more gloomy prospects as the board of war have confessed their total inability to afford us relief. Under these circumstances I have employed every personal exertion and have the pleasure to inform you that desertion has I hope been put to an end.

On my arrival on this side of the Susquehana I made an order for the troops wherein I endeavourd to throw a kind of infamy upon desertion, and to improve every particular affection of theirs. Since that desertion has been lessen'd* Two deserters have been taken up one of whom is hanged to day and the other (being an excellent soldier) will be forgiven but dismissed from the corps as well as an other soldier who behaved amiss. To these measures I have added one which my feelings for the sufferings of the soldiers and the pecularity of their circumstances, have prompted me to adopt.

The merchants of Baltimore lend me a sum of about 2,000 pounds which will procure some shirts, linnen overalls, shoes, and a few hatts. The ladies will make up the shirts and the overalls will be made by the detachment so that our soldiers have a chance of being a little more comfortable. The money is lent upon my credit, and I become a security for the payment of it in two years time, when by the French laws, I may better dispose of my estate. But before that time, I am to use my influence with the French court in order to have this sum of money added to any loan congress will have been able to obtain from them.

In case you are told my dear general that my whole baggage has been taken in the bay I am sorry I cannot discountenance the report. But when the mention of papers and maps will be made, dont apprehend any thing bad for the papers nor maps you have put in my possession. Nothing has been lost but writing paper and printed maps. The fact is this. When at York I had some continental soldiers and my baggage to send up in a safe barge and an unsafe boat. I of course gave the barge to the soldiers who easily went to Anapolis. The baggage was put in the boat and has not been since heard of. But being aware of the danger I took by land with me every article

*The words *which is greatly owing to the difficulties of returning* follow, but have been crossed out in another kind of ink. Cf. the postscript and the note on p. 186 below. (Proper names are identified in the "Index" below.)

185

that was on public accounts in the least valuable. By a letter from Baron de Stuben, dated Chesterfield Court House the 10th of April, I find that General Philips has at Portsmouth 1500 or 2000 men ad'ed to the force under Arnold. Proper allowance being made for exagerations I apprehend that his whole army amounts to 2500 men which oblige me to hasten my march to Fredericksburg and Richmond where I expect to receive orders from General Greene.

The importance of celerity, the desire of lengthning the way home, and immense delays that would stop me for an age have detirmin'd me to leave our tents, artillery &c under a guard, and with orders to follow as fast as possible while the rest of the detachment by force marches and with impress'd waggons and horses will hasten to Fredericksburg or Richmond, and by this derange the calculations of the enemy. We set off tomorrow and this rapid mode of travelling added to my other precautions will I hope keep up our spirits and satisfaction.

I am my dr genl &c

*P.S. The word *lessened* does not convey a sufficient idea of what experience has proved to be true, to the honour of our excellent soldiers. It had been announced in general orders, that the detachment was intended to fight an enemy far superior in number, under difficulties of every sort. That the general was, for his part, determined to encounter them, but that such of the soldiers as had an inclination to abandon him, might dispense with the danger and crime of desertion, as every one of them who should apply to headquarters for a pass to join their corps in the north might be sure to obtain it immediately.†

*This postscript is not in the contemporary copy. It is taken from the version given in the *Memoirs, correspondence and manuscripts of General Lafayette*, pp. 405-06. As is regularly true of the letters published in that work, the grammar, spelling and punctuation of the original have been corrected there.

†The copy in the Sparks Mss LXXXIV contains an endorsement in Lafayette's handwriting, probably written at the time the copy was made:
"Note. Some details have been given elsewhere relative to the admirable conduct of the light infantry forming the corps sent to Virginia under circumstances the most defavorable. Since the day when they were officially apprised they had great difficulties and dangers to encounter and a superior ennemy to combat not one instance of desertion took place, and altho' a want of harmony betwen them and the Southern people had been anticipated they and the Virginia militia lived together in perfect mutual amity and confidence. They also lived on the best terms with the Pennsylvanians when they had joined the army."

[109]

My dear General   Baltimore April the 18th 1781*

The bearer of this Mr Lavaud came to me with a recommendation from Viscount de Choiseuïl in the West Indies, and an other from Major General Lincoln who by this time must be with the Army. He wishes to serve as a volonteer, but I told him that my family was full, and could not be increased with French aids de camp—that my detachement was small, and had no room for volonteers. He then asked me a letter for your Excellency which I chearfully give to him, but offered it as my advice that he ought to turn his projects some other way. General Lincoln who introduces him to me will be a better patron than myself who have no acquaintance with this gentleman.

    With the most affectionate respect I have the honor to be
        My dear General
            Your most obedient humble servant
                Lafayette

AMENDED   [110]

My Dear General   Alexandria April 23d 1781†

Great happiness is derived from friendship, and I do particularly experience it in the attachement which unites me to you. But friendship has its duties, and the man that likes you the best will be the forwardest in letting you know every thing where you can be concerned

When the ennemy came to your house many Negroes deserted to them. This piece of news did not affect me much as I little value those concerns but you cannot conceive how unhappy I have been to that hear Mr. Lund Washington went on board the ennemy's vessels and consented to give them provisions. This being done by the gentleman who in some measure represents you at your house will certainly have a bad effect, and contrasts with spirited answers from some neighbours that had their houses burnt accordingly.

You will do what you think proper about it, my dear General,

---

*Historical Society of Pennsylvania, Gratz Collection. There is a contemporary copy in the letterbook in the Hubbard Collection. Unpublished.
†Library of Congress, Washington papers. There is a contemporary copy in the letterbook in the Hubbard Collection.

but, as your friend, it was my duty *confidentially* to mention the circumstances

With the help of some waggons and horses we got in two days from the camp near Baltimore to this place. We halted yesterday, and having made a small bargain for a few shoes are marching to Frederis Burg. No official account from Philips, but I am told they are removing stores from Richmond and Petersburg. I am surprised no body writes to me, and hope soon to receive intelligences

Our men are in high spirits. Their honor having been interested in this affair, they have made it a point to come with us, and discontents as well as desertion are entirely out of fashion

Requesting my best respects to be presented to Mrs. Washington and compliments to the family I have the honor to be with those sentiments which you know

My dear General
Your most obe^{nt} ervant and friend
Lafayette

The Chevalier* writes me that Count de Rochambeau is going to join you—so that both armies will cooperate. I had rather remain in Virginia than go to Carolina. This I mention because orders are to come from General Greene. But if the detachement is to go more southerly I will get there as fast I can

[111]

My dear General   May the 4th Camp near Bottom's Creek 1781†

I request you will receive my affectionate aknowledgement for your kind letters. Every mark of friendship I receive from you adds to my happiness as I love you with all the sincerity and warmth of my heart, and the sentiment I feel for you goes to the very extent of my affections

Inclosed I send you, my dear general, two copies of letters to General Greene which I also have sent to Congress for their information. You will also find copies of the strange letters I have received from General Phillips and the answers which if he does not behave better will break off our correspondence

*Chevalier de La Luzerne.
†Library of Congress, Washington papers. There is a contemporary copy in the letterbook in the Hubbard Collection.

The leaving of my artillery appears a strange whim. But had I waited for it, Richmond was lost, and Major Galvan who has exerted himself to the utmost cannot be with us under two days as he never could obtain or seize horses for the artillery and ammunition waggons. It is not without trouble I have made this rapid march. General Phillips has expressed to an officer on flag the astonishement he felt at our celerity, and when on the 30th as he was going to give the signal to attak he recconnoitred our position Mr. Osburn who was with him says that he flew into a violent passion and swore vengeance against me and the corps I had brought with me

I am however, uneasy, my dear general, and do not know what the public will think of our conduct. The little dependance they put upon the militia I cannot expose in an official letter. I cannot say that no boats, no waggons, no intelligence not one spy could be obtained that if once I had been maneuvring with Phillips he had every advantage over me—that a defeat would have scattered the militia, lost the few arms we have, and knocked down this handfull of Continental troops. Great deal of michief had been already done. I did not know but what the ennemy meant to establish a post. Under the circumstances I thought it better to fight on none but my own grounds, and to defeat the main and most valuable object of the enemy. Had I gone on the other side, the ennemy would have given me the slip and taken Richmond, leaving nothing to me but the reputation of a rash unexperienced young man. Our stores could not be removed

No orders from General Greene have as yet come to me. I cannot conceive the reason of his delay in answering my letters. In the mean while Philips is my object, and if with a thousand men I can be opposed to three thousand in this State I think I am useful to General Greene. In a former letter he tells me that his object is to divide the ennemy, and having no orders I must be regulated by his opinion. I wish he will call for the Pennsylvanians and leave me here*

The ennemy are gone down the river. I have detached some

*In the original the following words have been crossed out, but they are to be found in the letterbook copy: "At all events I should be very averse to be joined by the Pennsylvanians as they would [another hand has crossed out *would* and inserted *might*] spoil the Jersey soldiers and fight first those or New England." (Proper names are identified in the "Index" below.)

189

militia to Hood's where I mean to make a fort. C^lel Ennis with an other corps of militia is going towards Williams Burg. His orders are, in case the enemy land there to annoy them and in case they mean to establish a post he is to disturb them untill I arrive. This position is 16 miles from Richmond, 42 from Williams Burg 60 from Frederis Burg. I have sent an officer at Point Comfort and established a chain of expresses to know if they appear to turn towards Potowmack. Should it be the case Frederis Burg will have my attention. Having missed Richmond Mr. Hunter's works at Frederis Burg must be their next object as they are the only support of our operations in the Southward.

Your first letters, my dear General, will perhaps tell me some thing more about your coming this way. How happy I would be to see you I hope I need not to express. As you are pleased to give me the choice, I frankly shall tell my wishes. If you cooperate with the French against the place you know, I wish to be at Head Quarters If some thing is cooperated in Virginia I will find myself very happily situated. For the present, in case my detachement remains in this State I wish not to leave it as I have a separate and active command tho' it does not promise great glory. But as you gave me leave to do it I shall in a few days write to you more particularly on my private concerns. It is not only on account of my own situation that I wish the French Fleet may come into the Bay. Should they come even without troops it is ten to one that they will block up Phillips in some rivers and then I answer he is ruined—Had I but ships my situation would be the most agreable in the world.

Adieu, my dear General, you will make me happy to write me some times—With the highest respect and most tender affection have the honor to be

Yours

Lafayette

My respects to Mrs. Washington and I beg leave to present compliments to the family
C^lel Vose is not determined to go untill the ennemy are more remote. I beg you will please only to know the willingness of other colonels without sending any untill I write more particularly to Your Excellency

[112]

Richmond May the 8th 1781*

My Dear General

There is no fighting here unless you have a naval superiority or an army mounted upon race horses. Phillip's plan against Richmond has been defeated, he was going towards Porsmouth, and I thought it should be enough for me to oppose him at some principal points in this State. But now it appears I will have business to transact with two armies and this is rather too much.

By letters from North Carolina I find that Lord Cornwallis who I had been assured had sailed for Charlestown is advancing towards Hallifax. In consequence of letters from the same quarter General Phillips has altered his plans and returned to a place called Brandon on the south side of James River where he landed the night before last. Our detachement is under march towards the Hallifax Road. His command of the water enabled him to land where I could not reach him. The bridge at Peters Burg is destroïed, and unless he acts with an uncommon degree of folly he will be at Halifax before me. Each of these armies is more than the double superior to me. We have no boats, few militia, and less arms. I will try to do for the best, and hope to deserve your approbation.

Nothing can attract my sight from the supplies and reinforcements destined to General Greene's army. While I am going to get beaten by both armies or each of them separately the Baron remains at Richmond where he hurries the collection of recruits and every other requisite. I have forbidded every departement to give me any thing that may be thought useful to General Greene, and should a battle be expected (an event which I will try to keep off) no consideration will prevent our sending to Carolina 800 recruits who, I hope, may be equipped in a fortnight. When Gal Greene becomes equal to offensive operations this quarter will be relieved. I have wrote to Waïne to hasten his march but unless I am very hard pushed shall request him to proceed south ward. The militia has been ordered out but are slow, unarmed, and not yet used to this business. General Greene from whom I had as yet no letters was on

*Library of Congress, Washington papers. There is a contemporary copy in the letterbook in the Hubbard Collection.

the 26 before Camden but did not think himself equal to the storming of the works.

    Most respectfully and affectionately, my dear General
Yours
Lafayette

    My respects, if you please, to Mrs. Washington and compliments to the family.

[113]

Camp James River at Wilton 17th May 1781*

Dear General

    My correspondance with one of the British Generals, and my denial of a correspondance with the other, may be perhaps misrepresented. I shall therefore give an account of what has passed, and hope your Excellency and General Greene will approve of my conduct.

    On the arrival of our Detachment at Richmond, these† letters were brought by a flag which I have the honor to inclose and which as Commander of the Troops in this State it became my duty to answer. The inclosed letters were successively sent in pursuit of General Phillips, who received them both with a degree of politeness that seemed to apologize for his unbecoming Stile.

    General Phillips's being dead of a fever, an Officer was sent with a passport and letters from General Arnold. I requested the gentleman to come to my Quarters and having asked *if General Phillips was dead* to which he answer'd in the negative, I made it a pretence not to receive a letter from General Arnold, which being dated *Head Quarters* and directed to the Commanding Officer of the American Troops, ought to come from the British General Chief in Command. I did however observe that should any other officer have written to me I would have been happy to receive their Letters

    The next day the Officer returned with the same passport and letter, and informed that he was now at liberty to declare that Gen-

---

*This version is based on a copy, corrected and signed but not written by Lafayette, that is in the Pierpont Morgan Library, Yorktown Collection, I, 67. Another copy (signed but not written by Lafayette) is in the Library of Congress, Washington papers. There is a third copy in the letterbook in the Hubbard Collection.

†The copy in the Library of Congress reads *three*.

eral Phillips was dead, and Gal Arnold was Commander in Chief of the British Army in Virginia. The high station of General Arnold having obliged me to an explanation, the inclosed Note was sent to the Officer of the Flag and the American Officer verbally assured him that was I requested to put in writing a minute account of my motives my regard for the British Army was such that I would chearfully comply with the Demand.

Last Evening a Flag of ours returned from Petersburg who had been sent by General Nelson from the advanced Corps he commands, and happened to be on his way while the British Officer was at our Piquets. Inclosed is the Note written by General Arnold in which he announces a determination of sending our Officers and men to the West Indies.

The British General cannot but perfectly know that I am not to treat of partial Exchanges and that the fate of the Continental Prisoners must be regulated by a superior authority to that with which I am invested.

With the highest respect I have he honor to be Your Excellency's

Most Obedient Humble Servant
Lafayette

[114]

Wilton North side of Jas. River*
May 18th 1781

Dear General

Having been directed by Genl Greene to take Command of the Troops in Virginia, I have also received orders from him, that every account from this Quarter be immediately transmitted to Congress and to your Excellency;—in obedience to which I shall have the honour to relate our Movements, and those of the combined Armies of the Enemy.—

When Genl. Phillips retreated from Richmond, his project was to stop at Williamsburg, there to collect Contributions which he had imposed;—This induced me to take a position between

*The original (signed but not written by Lafayette) is in the Library of Congress, Washington papers. There is a contemporary copy in the letterbook in the Hubbard Collection. (Proper names are identified in the "Index" below.)

Pamunky & Chickahomany Rivers, which equally covered Richmond & some other interesting parts of the State, and from where I detached Genl. Nelson with some Militia towards Wmsburg.

Having gott as low down as that place, General Phillips seemed to discover an intention to make a Landing, but upon advices received by a vessel from Portsmº the Enemy weighed Anchor, and with all the sail they cou'd crowd hastened up the River; this intelligence made me apprehensive that the enemy intended to manoeuvre me out of Richmond, where I returned immediately & again collected our small force.

Intelligence was the same day received that Lord Cornwallis (who I had been assured to have embarked at Wilmington) was marching thro' N. Carolina. This was confirmed by the landing of Genl Phillips at Brandon South Side of James River. Apprehending that both Armies would move to meet at a central point, I marched towards Petersburg and intended to have established a Communication over Appamattox & Jas. River, but on the 9th Genl Phillips took possession of Petersburg, a place where his right flank being covered by Jas. River, his front by Appamattox, on which the Bridges had been destroyed in the first of the invasion, and his left not being attackable but by a long Circuit through Fords that at this Season are very uncertain I cou'd not (even with an equal force) have gott any chance of fighting him, unless I had given up this side of Jas. River and the Country from which reinforcements are expected.—

It being at the Enemy's choice to force us to an action, while their own position insured them against our Enterprises I thought it proper to shift this situation, and marched the greater part of our troops to this place, about ten miles below Richmond. Letters from Govr. Nash, Genl. Sumner & Genl. Jones are possitive as to the arrival of Col. Tarleton, and announce that of Ld. Cornwallis at Hallifax. Having received a request from N. Carolina for amunition I made a detachment of 500 men under Genl Muhlenberg to escort 20,000 Cartridges over Appamattox, and to divert the Enemy's attention Colo. Gimat with his Batn. & 4 field pieces cannonaded their position from this side the River. I hope our Ammunition will arrive safe, as before Genl Muhlenberg returned he putt it in a safe road with proper directions. On the 13th Genl. Phillips died and the

Command devolved on General Arnold. General Wayne's Detachment has not yett been heard of, before he arrives it becomes very dangerous to risk any Engagement where (either of the British Armies being vastly superior to us) we shall certainly be beaten, and by the loss of Arms, the dispersion of Militia, and the difficulty of a junction with Genl. Wayne we may loose a less dangerous chance of resistance.

These considerations have induced me to think that with our so very great inferiority, and with the advantage the Enemy have by their Cavalry & naval superiority, there woud be much rashness in fighting them on any but our grounds, and this side of the river, and that an engagement which I fear will be soon necessary, ought if possible be deferred till the Pensylvanians arrive, whom I have by several letters requested to hasten to our assistance. No report has lately come from near Halifax tho' a very active officer has been sent for that purpose but every intelligence confirms that Ld. Cornwallis is hourly expected at Petersburg, it is true there never was such difficulty in getting tollerable intelligence as there is in this country, and the immense superiority of the enemy's horse render it very pracarious to hazard our small parties—Arnold has received a small reinforcement from Portsmouth

      Dr General

        Your most obedient Humble Servant

          Lafayette.

P.S.

In justice to Major Mitchell and Capt Muir who were taken at Petersburg, I have the honour to inform your Excellency that they had been sent to that place on public service. I have requested Genl. Lawson to collect and take comd. of the Militia south of Appamattox—local impediments was thrown in the road from Hallifax to Petersb^e and precautions taken to remove the horses from the Enemy's reach. Shou'd it be possible to get arms some more militia might be brought in to the field. But Genl Greene & myself labour under the same disadvantage. The few militia we can with great pains collect arrive unarmed and we have not a sufficiency of weapons to putt into their hands.

[115]

Richmond May 24th 1781*

Dear General

The jonction of Lord Cornwallis with the other army at Peters Burg was an event that from local circumstances and from their so great superiority it was impossible to prevent. It took place on the 20th and having lost every hope to operate a timely stroke in conjonction with the Pennsylvanians, my ideas were confined to defensive measures. I therefore moved up to Richmond where precautions were taken to remove every valuable property either public or private

By an officer that was in Hallifax after Lord Cornwallis I find he has not left any post at that place. It appears his sick and wounded remained at Willmington and were reimplaced by that garrison. Reports concerning his numbers are so different that I cannot trust any thing but my eyes. Untill such an opportunity offers, this is the order of march in which it is said his Lordship crossed Roanoke—C^{lel} Tarleton's Legion, C^{lel} Hamilton's Corps, 23d, 71st, 33d British Regiments, 200 Tories, an Hessian Regiment, the Light Infantry and Guards with six field pieces. I am told General Leslie and General O'Hara are with him. I have received successive and repeated accounts that a British fleet of transports was arrived at Hampton. They were said to consist of 14 large vessels, and 16 smaller ones under convoy of three frigats. Mr. Day d. q. m. at Williams Burg writes that on the 22d 12 sails of large ships a sloop and a schooner got under way opposite James town. Those ships full of men, and some horses on board the sloop. We have no accounts of any fleet having sailed from New york.

Yesterday after noon we had an heavy rain which Colonel Tarleton improved in surprising some militia in Chesterfield County thirty of whom fell into his hands

This morning at nine o'clock the ennemy moved from Peters Burg towards City Point and destroïed the bridge they had lately constructed over Appamatox. I have just received accounts that a body of them has landed at Westover. These are said to be the men who came up the river from Hampton, previous to which Gen-

*Library of Congress, Washington papers. There is a contemporary copy in the letterbook in the Hubbard Collection.

eral Arnold had received a small reinforcement from Porsmouth

To my great mortification I have heared this morning that the Pennsylvanians are not so near as I had been by every account positively assured. General Waïne writes me he will hasten to our support and I am confident he will not loose time at this critical moment. But before he arrives it is impossible that 900 Continentals and 40 horses with a body of militia by no means so considerable as they are reported to be and whom it is so difficult to arm, be with any advantage opposed to such a superiority of forces, such a number of cavalry, to which may be added their very prejudiciable command of the waters

Our handfull of men being the point to which militia may be collected, and the only check, however small it is, that the ennemy may have in this State, it ought I think to be managed with a great deal of prudence as its preservation is so very important to the fate of operations in Virginia

With the highest respect I have the honor to be
   Your Excellency's
      Most obedient humble servant
       Lafayette

[116]

Richmond May 24th 1781*

My dear General

My official letter a copy of which I send to Congress will let you know the situation of affairs in this quarter. I ardently wish my conduct may meet with your approbation. Had I followed the first impulsion of my temper, I would have risked some thing more. But I have been guarding against my own warmth, and this consideration that a general defeat which with such a proportion of militia must be expected would involve this State and our affairs into ruin, has rendered me extremely cautious in my movements. Indeed, I am more embarassed to move, more crippled in my projects than we have been in the Northern States

Had the Pennsylvanians arrived before Lord Cornwallis I was determined to attak the ennemy and have no doubt but what we

*Library of Congress, Washington papers. There is a contemporary copy in the letterbook in the Hubbard Collection.

would have been successfull. Their unaccountable delay cannot be too much lamented, and will made an immense difference to the fate of this compaign. Should they have arrived time enough to support me in the reception of Lord Cornwallis's first stroke, I would still have thought it well enough. But from an answer of General Waïne received this day and dated the 19th I am affraid that in this moment they have hardly left York town

Public stores and private property bring removed from Richmond this place is a less important object. I don't believe it would be prudent to expose the troops for the sake of a few houses most of which are empty. But I am wavering betwen two inconveniences. Was I to fight a battle I'll be cut to pieces, the militia dispersed, and the arms lost. Was I to decline fighting the country would think herself given up. I am therefore determined to scarmish, but not to engage too far, and particularly to take care against their immense and excellent body of horse whom the militia fears like they would so many wild beasts

A letter from General Greene to General Sumner is dated 5th May seven miles below Camden. The Baron is going to him with some recruits and will get some more in North Carolina. When the Pennsylvanians come I am only to keep them a few days which I will improve as well as I can. Cavalry is very necessary to us. I wish Lauzun's Legion could come. I am sure he will like to serve with me, and as General Greene gave me command of the troops in this State Lauzun might remain with me in Virginia. If not Sheldon's Dragoons might be sent. As to Moylan I do not believe he will be ready before a long time

Was I any ways equal to the ennemy, I would be extremely happy in my present command. But I am not strong enough even to get beaten. Governement in this state has no energy, and laws have no force. But I hope this assembly will put matters up on a better footing. I had great deal of trouble to put the departements in a tolerable train. Our expenses were enormous, and yet we can get nothing. Arrangements for the present seem to put on a better face but for this superiority of the ennemy which will chase us where they please. They can over run the country and untill the Pennsylvanians arrive we are next to nothing in point of opposition to so large a force. This country begins to be as familiar to me as Tappan and Bergen. Our soldiers are hitherto very healthy and I have turned doctor to regulate their diet.

Adieu, my dear General, let me hear some times from you. Your letters are a great happiness to your affectionate friend

Lafayette

My respects if you please to Mrs Washington and compliments to the family.

As I am for the present fixed in the command of the troops in this State, I beg it as a great favor that you will please to send me C^lel Gouvion. Should a jonction be made with General Greene he will act as my aid de camp.

[117]

Camp betwen Rappaahanock and
North Anna June 3d 1781*

My Dear General

Inclosed you will find the copy of a letter to General Greene. He at first had requested I would directly write to you, since which his orders have been different, but he directed me to forward you copies of my official accounts. So many letters are lost in this way that I do not care to avoid repetitions. I heartly wish, my dear General, my conduct may be approved of particularly by you. My circumstances have been peculiar, and in this state I have some times experienced strange disappointements. Two of them the shoes at Charlotte's ville, and the delay of the [Pennsylvania]† detachement have given me much uneasiness and may be attended with bad consequences. There is great slowness and great carelessness in this part of the world. But the intentions are good, and the people want to be awakened. Your presence, my dear General, would do a great deal. Should these detachements be increased to three or four thousand, and the French Army come this way, leaving one of our generals at Rhode island, and two or three about Newyork and in the Jersays you might be on the offensive in this quarter, and there could be a Southern Army in Carolina. Your presence would do immense good,

*Library of Congress, Washington papers. There is a contemporary copy in the letterbook in the Hubbard Collection.
†One word illegible but apparently an abbreviation of Pennsylvania.

but I would wish you to have a large force. General Washington before he personally appears must be strong enough to hope success

Adieu, my dear General, with the highest respect and most tender affection, I have the honor to be

Yours   Lafayette

If you persist in the idea to come this way you may depend upon about 3000 militia in the field relieved every two months. Your presence will induce them to turn out with great spirit

[118]

Dear General   Brock's Bridge 10th June 1781*

    The disapointement C^lel Tupper met with is so singular that I wish to give Your Excellency a full account of this affair

    When the detachement was at the Head of Elk C^lel Vose expressed a desire to return to the North ward founded upon the particular circumstanes he was under which nothing but fear of giving exemple to his officers and men prevented him officialy to signify. From what he often said the general opinion of every officer was that C^lel Vose would be happy to be relieved, and under this light I mentionned the matter to Your Excellency. My intention was either to make it a meritorious act in your opinion for C^lel Vose to remain, or if convenient to give you an opportunity to oblige this gentleman

    But however known has been C^lel Vose's opinion and desire on this matter I cannot say he ever made any application to me to be relieved

    C^lel Tupper is arrived and to our surprise C^lel Vose has expressed quite a different disposition from what he had mentionned at the Head of Elk. Indeed circumstances were not the same and in the midst of a campaign at a time when an action is expected C^lel Vose thinks it a disgrace to leave his command. He represented that his sentiments had not been officially expressed, and that for the present his honor and feelings could not be reconciled to the arrangement

    C^lel Tupper from a motive of delicacy for the feelings and

---

*Library of Congress, Washington papers. There is a contemporary copy in the letterbook in the Hubbard Collection. Unpublished.

respect for the reputation of his brother officer is willing to desist from his pretensions to the command and wishes to return to his regiment. But in case some more troops were sent this way I beg leave warmly to request that C^{lel} Tupper be appointed to the command of them. I have felt for his disappointement—more indeed than I can express and shall be happy in the opportunity to serve with this officer for whom I entertain a very high and affectionate regard

With the highest respect I have the honor to be

Y^r Exy's Most obedient humble servant

Lafayette

[119]

Allen's Creek 22 miles from Richmond
18th June 1781*

My dear General

Independent of public motives private attachement for you renders it very hard to me that our correspondence is so much interrupted. I heartly feel for the accident that has put some of your letters in the hands of the ennemy—the more so as the friendship that you are pleased to honor me with had induced you to confidential communications. Letters from the late governor of this State to me have also been taken and their contents improved by the ennemy. The inclosed copy will give you an official account of transactions in this quarter. So much I owe to my General, but with my friend I beg leave to be more confidential

The conduct of the Baron, my dear General, is to me unintelligible—every man woman and child in Virginia is roused against him. They dispute even on his courage but I cannot believe their assertions. I must however confess that he had 500 and odds new levies and some militia, that he was on the other side of a river which the freshet rendered very difficult to be crossed particularly by people that had no boats, that the greater part of the accounts make Simcoe 400 strong half of them dragoons, that our stores on the south side were destroïed by about 30 or 40 men—that the Baron went to Staunton River about 70 miles from the Point of Fork—

*Library of Congress, Washington papers. There is a contemporary copy in the letterbook in the Hubbard Collection. Unpublished except for an excerpt in Tower, II, 333-34. (Proper names are identified in the "Index" below.)

that the militia abandonned him and I am informed the new levies deserted from him, because they did not like his maneuvre. General Lawson and every officer and soldier both in the regulars and militia are so much exasperated again the Baron and cover him with so many ridicules that after I have obtained a jonction with him I do not know where to employ him without giving offense

Had not the Assembly at Charlotte ville and the State Board of War sent for arms which they intended to fight with and which upon the ennemy's approach were left in their way, had the twelve hours been improved that were given them by three repeated alarms, had not the Baron abandonned an unattakable position before so inferior a force, the reason of which no man of sense will be able to understand, I would have the pleasure to say that Lord Cornwallis's journey to Virginia has not produced him the smallest advantage. The delays of the Pennsylvania Line, the neglects in the several departements have all been combined to bring about what the Baron's retreat has effected. Our loss is not very considerable, but in our situation we cannot afford loosing. This affair has chagrined me but the enclosed copy will show you that I avoid reflecting on the man who ought to have better managed our affairs. Upon him was my entire dependance in that respect. The Baron wished for a journey to the South ward, the orders to stay in this State had been intercepted but all this cannot be an excuse. I request you, my dear General, to remember that this communication is not to the Commander in Chief*

I heartly wish, my dear General, our movements may meet with your approbation. In spite of every obstacle thrown in our way I shall collect our forces to a point—800 light infantry 700 Pennsylvanians, 50 dragoons, 900 riflemen 2000 militia and 400 new levies (the remainder having deserted) will be the utmost extent of forces we can expect. But the harvest time will soon deprive us of the greatest part of the militia. Governor Nelson will I hope be a supporter of spirited measures.

What little I have concerning N. Y. is in a chest with Mr. Charles

---

*A copy of this letter in the Sparks Mss LXXXIV is endorsed in Lafayette's handwriting: "We must be tender of the good Baron's fame; and if a publication takes place, give an extract rather than a full length letter, saying only that in a private letter I expressed dissatisfaction." This was written to Sparks in 1829. Tower, II, 333-34, gives the excerpt concerning Steuben.

Washington's papers near the mountains in Orange County. I shall try to get it, and will in my next be able better to explain the meaning of the new arrived fleet. Some say the vessels are empty which might look as if they came for a reinforcement to New york, or perhaps do they carry stores from that place to Portsmouth

Adieu, my dear General, with the highest respect and most tender affection I have the honor to be your h^bl servant and friend

Lafayette

Mr. [George A.] Washington had today some fever but only caused by fatigue and his assiduity in the business we have upon hand

[120]

Camp 28 June 1781*

My Dear General

Inclosed I have the honor to send you copy of my letter to General Greene. The ennemy have been so kind as to retire before us. Twice I gave them a chance of fighting (taking care not to engage farther than I pleased) but they continued their retrogade motions. Our numbers are I think exagerated to them, and our seeming boldness confirms the opinion

I thought at first Lord Cornwallis wanted to get me as low down as possible and use his cavalry to advantage. But it appears he does not as yet come out, and our position will admit of partial affairs. His Lordship had (exclusive of the reinforcement from Portsmouth said 600) 4000 men 800 of whom dragoons or mounted infantry. Our force is about equal to his but only 1500 regulars and 50 dragoons. Our little action more particularly marks the retreat of the ennemy. From the place he first began to retire to Williamsburg is upwards of 100 miles. The old arms at the Point of Fork have been taken out of the water. The cannon has been thrown in the river undamaged when they marched back to Richmond. So that His Lordship did us no harm of any consequence, lost an immense part of his former conquests and did not make any in this State. General Greene demanded of me only to hold my ground in Virginia. But the movements of Lord Cornwallis may answer better purposes than that in the political line

*Library of Congress, Washington papers. There is a contemporary copy in the letterbook in the Hubbard Collection.

Adieu, my dear General, I don't know but what we shall in our turn become the pursued ennemy and in the mean while have the honor to be most respectfully and affectionately
Yours
Lafayette

George is at a gentleman's house with a fever—but is much better now and I expect him every moment. Langborn's zeal and activity during this campaign have unfortunately put him in the ennemy's hands while he was reconnoitring

AMENDED [121]

Amblers plantation 8th July 1781*

The inclosed copy, my dear General will give you an account of our affairs in this quarter. Agreeably to your orders I have avoided a general action, and when Lord Cornwallis's movements indicated it was against his interest to fight, I have ventured partial engagements. His Lordship seems to have given up the conquest of Virginia.

It has been a great secret that our army was not superior and was most generally inferior to the enemy's numbers, our returns were swelled up as generally militia returns are but we had very few under arms particularly lately and to conceal the lesning of our numbers I was obliged to push on as one who had heartily wish'd a general engagement. Our regulars did not exceed 1500 the enemy had 4000 regulars 800 of whom mounted. They thought we had 8000 men I never encamped in a line and there was a greater difficulty to come at our numbers.

Should, as I presume it will, a detachment be sent to General Greene I shall move the Pensylvanians and Virginians first. The Pennsylvan's I know have great objections but common sense points out the expediency of this arrangement which had already been made by General Greene. I affraid Congress will be applied to on the occasion and request you will inforce my opinion. Adieu my dear General, I am going confidentially to write you by a safe hand and shall only add the expressions of my affection and respect
Lafayette

*Contemporary copy in the letterbook in the Hubbard Collection.

[122]

Malvan Hill July 20th 1781*

Private

My Dear General

This letter is not by any means directed to the Commander in chief, but to my most intimate and confidential friend. I will lay before you my circumstances and my wishes. Certain I am you will do whatever you can for me that is consistent with your public duty

When I went to the southward you know I had some private objections. But I became sensible of the necessity there was for the detachement to go, and I know that had I returned there was no body that could lead them on against their inclination. My entering this State was happily marked by a service to the Capital. Virginia became the grand object of the ennemy as it was the point to which the Ministry tended. I had the honor to command an army and oppose Lord Cornwallis when incomparably inferior to him, fortune was pleased to preserve us. When equal in numbers tho' not in the kind of troops, we have also been pretty lucky. Cornwallis had the disgrace of a retreat, and this State being recovered, governement properly reestablished, the ennemy are under protection of their works at Portsmouth

It appears an embarkation is taking place, probably destined to Newyork. The war in this State would then become a plundering one, and great maneuvres be out of the question. A prudent officer would do our business here, and the Baron is prudent to the utmost. Would it be possible, my dear General, that in case a part of the British troops go to Newyork I may be allowed to join the combined armies. I know the command of a separate army ought not to be quitted. But, besides the services I may render in the cooperation, some arrangements which I leave to your goodness for me to think of may put me in a very brilliant station

Mr de Choisy I am told is very unhappy to be left behind. Perhaps these French troops will be replaced by militia which requires a general officer. Perhaps a corps of observation in the Jersays will be given to an other. The militia requires a Major General as it will be very numerous. Does not General St. Clair take command of the

*Library of Congress, Washington papers. There is a contemporary copy in the letterbook in the Hubbard Collection.

Pennsylvania Line, and will not this line be forwarded to the southward rather than the New England Light infantry. So that, my dear General, I hope some thing may be found for me in the Continental part of the Army—the more so as it seems it will form one or two divisions of the combined army under your command.

I have calculated that nothing very material would happen before September. By that time your forces will be collected, cloathed, and arranged. A succour from the West Indias may arrive. You will then decide if the upper part of the island, Long island, Staten island or Newyork island is to be in our possession. This letter goes to day by a faithfull servant. Will arrive the 29th at Camp. Your answer may be with me so that I may set out the 10th and arrive at head quarters about the 20th. This matter I have not mentionned to any body and wish it may rest *between you and me*

Lord Cornwallis is every day inquiring about my going to the Grand Army—which, he says, must be soon the case. This induces me to think they believe you are in earnest in your preparations

The command of this army has been a great matter for me. You may end this campaign of mine in the most brillant manner by the command I may, with *some arrangements* get in the combined army. The services I may render with respect to the *cooperation* may be a very good reason, and my coming unexpectedly unless I have many senior officers in the way may entitle me to a great command. Should not a great part of the operating army in this quarter go to Newyork I would not trouble you with my wishes to return to hdqrs. But do not, I pray, believe I have the least notion of calculating upon commands (tho' in my personal circumstances they become peculiarly important to me). If I may be of the least good [?] to you, it will make me happy to serve as a volunteer aid de camp to you

Forgive a letter, my dear General, that is writen in the confidence of the most intimate and tender friendship

July 20th

Private

Since writing the inclosed, my dear General, an officer of Tarleton's Legion who has been taken was brought to my quarters. He had much conversation with my aids de camp, and being an unguarded young man spoke very freely. He says Lord Cornwallis and C^{lel}

Tarleton are certainly going to Newyork. He adds the Light Infantry and a regiment of horse do certainly embark for the same place. Preference is given to such troops as were the most fatigued in their maneuvres through Virginia. He thinks the Guards are to remain here—does not know the disposition of any other troops. I thought this was worth mentionning to you. Would to God this embarkation could be intercepted!

I have this day seen the order of battle. It appears to me *General St. Clair* is not comprehended in it. The Jersay troops not being there are I presume destined to a diversion with the New *Jersay militia*. *Newengland*, or the *whole body of the militia* will perhaps furnish some generals employement so that I hope I may be put in. At all events, I would be with you, and of course would be very happy

Should the ennemy remain quiet in this state the Baron might do very well. But if the siege of Newyork does not succeed and there is no peace I imagine you will march here in force

Adieu, my dear General, you will not forget this letter is entirely private and by no means directed to the Commander in Chief. With every sentiment of respect and the most tender affection I have the honor to be, my dear General

Yours
Lafayette

In case there is no appearance of a move of the ennemy and no propriety in our going towards Portsmouth, I intend reconnoitring the grounds about Frederiksburg where if I am made certain nothing will happen in my absence I may meet your letter

[123]

Malvan Hill July 20th 1781*

My dear General

No accounts from the Northward, no letters from Head Quarters. I am utterly a stranger to every thing that passes out of Virginia—and Virginian operations being for the present in a state of languor, I have more time to think of my solitude. In a word, my

*Library of Congress, Washington papers. There is a contemporary copy in the letterbook in the Hubbard Collection.

dear General, I am home sick and if I can't go to Head Quarters wish at least to hear from there

I am anxious to know your opinion concerning the Virginia campaign. That the subjugation of this State was the great object with the Ministry is an undisputable fact. I think your diversion has been of more use to this State than my maneuvres. But the later have been much directed by political views. So long as Mylord wished for an action, not one gun has been fired—the moment he declined it we have been scarmishing. But I took care never to commit the Army. His naval superiority—his superiority of horse, of regulars, his thousand advantages over us were such that I am lucky enough to have come off safe. I had an eye upon European negotiations and made it a point to give his Lordship the disgrace of a retreat

So soon as he had crossed he improved the opportunity to send Tarleton into Amelia—but was disapointed in the stores which he expected to find, and which had been previously removed. I thought at first the cavalry would join Rawdon, aand detached Waïne and Morgan either to maneuvre Tarleton down or to determine his course. Upon this he retired with precipitation towards Portsmouth where the British Army is for the present

From every account it appears a part of the army will embark—the Light Infantry—the Guards—the 80th Rgt—the Queen's Rangers are, it is said, destined to Newyork. Of this I have sent accounts by water to Rhode island but question if the boats will arrive. My opinion was the cavalry should push towards Carolina—but their late movements seem to indicate a different intention. Lord Cornwallis, I am told, is much disappointed in the hopes of command. I cannot find out what he does with himself. Should he go to England, we are, I think, to rejoice for it. He is a bold and active man, two dangerous qualities in this Southern war

General Waïne's Pennsylvanians never exceeded about 700—fighting and desertion have much reduced them. I have sent him to Goode's Bridge upon Appamattox. The three Pennsylvania bataïllons have been reduced to two—about 250 each fit for duty. To this I have added 300 Virginia New levies—General Morgan and 500 riflemen and some dragoons is also at Goode's Bridge to support Waïne. But the moment the embarkation sails Morgan will return and the others proceed to Carolina. I have obtained from the executive that 2000 militia be ordered to Boyd's Ferry upon Dan River. This force will give General Greene a decided superiority. I am determined to reinforce him at my own risks—it is important for the treaty that Carolina be reconquered.

The Light Infantry and whatever militia remains are encamped upon Malvan Hill—the most airy and healthy place this side of the mountains. I have a post at Sandy Point to examine the ennemy's movements. I shall have some militia in the vicinity of Williamsburg —the Glocester County militia in their own county. C^{lel} Parker has some on the south side of James River. The few boats that remain are collected at Four Miles Creek. Such is for the present our situation. I have endeavoured to attend to the health and refreshement of our men—while I had parties to gain intelligences and prevent plunders. I have directed Parker's detachement, about 300 militia to keep clear of danger from an attak. His men are from the adjacent counties to Suffolk. The executive have promised I should in a little time have 5000 militia—Let it be 4000 and the Light infantry, in case 2000 men go to Newyork, 600 must be kept as a garrison in Portsmouth, and the remainder tho' we cant prevent their plundering may be prevented from forming any establishment in the State— provided we can make up a body of cavalry—the most difficult of all works in this country. Nothing but a treaty of alliance with the negroes can find out dragoon horses, and it is by those means the ennemy have got a formidable cavalry.

Inclosed, my dear General you will find some plans relating to the islands of Newyork. I could not sooner get at them during the retreat, and during the pursuit our small army had as little baggage as is possible with militia and I endeavoured to give the example.

George has been very sick but has now recovered and is with me. In Mercer's volunteer dragons there was a young nephew of yours who is very promising and served as a dragoon with the utmost zeal and activity and gallantry.

Major Galvan having obtained leave to return to the Northward is now on his way to Philadelphia. The cloathing you have long ago sent to the Light Infantry is not yet arrived. I have been obliged to send for it and expect it in a few days. These three Bataillons are the best troops that ever took the field. My confidence in them is unbounded. They are far superior to any British troops, and none will ever venture to meet them at equal numbers. What a pity these men are not employed along with the French Grenadiers! They would do eternal honor to our arms. But their presence here, I must confess, has saved this State, and indeed the Southern part of the Continent.

Adieu, my dear General, with the highest respect and most tender affection I have the honor to be

Your most obedient humble servant
Lafayette

[124]

My dear General   Malvern Hill July 26th 1781*

I had some days ago the honor to write to Your Excellency and informed you that a detachement from the British Army would probably embark at Portsmouth. The two bataïllons of Light Infantry and the Queen's Rangers were certainly, and the Guards with one or two British regiments were likely to be, ordered upon that service. My conjectures have proved true and 49 sails fallen down in Hampton Road the departure of which I expect to hear every minute.

A prisoner British officer lately mentionned Lord Cornwallis himself was going. However I think General Leslie is the man who commands the embarked troops. Pottowmack and the Cheseapeak are the announced objects—but I think the true destination is New york.

I have directed men of observation to send me intelligences respecting the movements of the fleet. Horses will be ready upon the road and an officer sent the moment I hear of their sailing. Some days ago I communicated my conjectures to the French Admiral, but question if my letters could arrive safe.

It appears the ennemy have some cavalry on board. The conquest of Virginia and the establishement of British power in this State, having not succeeded to the expectations of the British court, a lesser number might be sufficient to the present purposes, and two thousand men easely spared. So that I do not believe the present embarkation is under that number.

*Library of Congress, Washington papers. There is a contemporary copy in the letterbook in the Hubbard Collection.

So far as a land force can oppose naval operations and naval superiority, I think the position now occupied by the main body of our small army, affords the best chance to support the several parts of Virginia.

On his precipitate return from Amelia County Colonel Tarleton suffered some loss from militia light parties.

With the highest respect I have the honor to be, my dear General

Your most affectionate servant
Lafayette

The Charon 44, and three frigats with two 20 guns ships form the convoy of the fleet

[125]

My dear General   Malbern Hill July 30th 1781*

Your letter of the 13th is just come to hand. The moment a perfect intelligence can be got, Major McPherson will be dispatched. But some expressions in your last favor will, if possible, augument my vigilance in keeping you well apprised of the ennemy's movements.

There are in Hampton Road thirty transport ships full of troops —most of them Red Coats. There are eight or ten brigs which have cavalry on board. They had excellent winds and yet they are not gone. Some say they have received advices from Newyork in a row boat. The escort, as I mentionned before, is the Charon and several frigats—the last account says seven.

The Light Infantry, Queen's Rangers, and two British regiments are, I think, on board. Two German regiments are it seems destined to the same service. I cannot be positive, and do not even think Lord Cornwallis has been fully determined. I have got in Portsmouth many people that watch his motions—but none has been able to slip out. His Lordship went to Old Point Comfort—had a survey taken of the properest place to build a fort—had the soundings examined— and returned to Portsmouth with General Leslie.

This State is so difficult to be defended that one false step involves the one that does not command the water into a series of inconveniences. His Lordship has taken pilots for the Bay and for

*Library of Congress, Washington papers. There is a contemporary copy in the letterbook in the Hubbard Collection.

Pottowmack. That, I suppose, is a feint, but a march south of James River throws me out of supporting distance for any thing that is north of it. A march to the north gives the ennemy command of every thing south of the river.

Two bataïllions of Light Infantry and the militia are at this place, the healthiest and best watered spot in the State. General Waïne at Goode's Bridge on Appomatox with the Pennsylvanians and Virginia Continentals—and looks towards Roenoke or Pottowmak. Müllenberg with a bataïllion of Light Infantry some riflemen and the horse has an intermediary position betwen me and Suffolk in the neighboorod of which moves a party of militia under C^{lel} Parker. General Weedon is in person at Frederiksburg and the moment a fleet appears will call out the militia. Gregory is on the other side of the Dismal Swamp. I cannot hear from him, but sent him orders by a safe hand to call out the militia, mount some cannon at the passes, and take out of the way every boat which might serve the ennemy to go to North Carolina.

You know, my dear General, that with a very trifling transportation, they may go by water from Portsmouth to Wilmington. The only way to shut up that passage is to have an army before Portsmouth and possess the head of these rivers—a movement which unless I was certain of a naval superiority might prove ruinous. But should a fleet come in Hampton Road and should I get some days notice our situation would be very agreable.

I am endeavouring to get a cavalry, and it is not without trouble. Transportation is a great objection to the formation of magazines. A naval superiority would also level that difficulty. It appears a pretty large body of troops have been sent to Kemp's Landing—some cannon removed from Portsmouth—But nothing that can make His Lordship's intentions perfectly understood. Any certainty of a naval superiority, I would wish to know instantly, as then I will give His Lordship every opportunity to go up the rivers.

With the highest respect and most tender affection, my dear General

            Yours

               Lafayette

There is a chain of expresses—but I shall see that it is more properly conducted

[126]

Private Malvern Hill, July 31st 1781*

My Dear General

A correspondant of mine servant to Lord Cornwallis writes on the 26th July at Portsmouth, and says his master, Tarleton, and Simcoe are still in town but expect to move. The greatest part of the army is embarked. There is in Hampton Road one 50 guns ship, and two six and thirty guns frigats etc. 18 sloops loaded with horses. There remain but nine vessels in Portsmouth who appear to be getting ready. Mylord's baggage is yet in town. His Lordship is so shy of his papers that my honest friend says he cannot get at them. There is a large quantity of Negroes. Very valuable indeed—but no vessels it seems to take them off. What garrison they leave I do not know. I shall take care, at least, to keep them within bounds. The troops I mentionned in my last to have crossed over in nineteen boats from Portsmouth to Norfolk were it is said going to Lowel's Point—a good embarking place. From what is said of the Negroes, tho' it is not very plain, I should rather think they are working on the water side. My accounts from Portsmouth are later than the fellow's epistle, but as a servant has opportunities to hear I thought it was worth communicating to Your Excellency.

General Müllemberg with a corps of Light infantry, riflemen and horse is moving towards Portsmouth. But altho' I do not think they are going up the rivers or the Bay, the less so as they have made a parade of taking pilots on board, I had rather act on the cautious scale, and by keeping a supporting position, leave no chance to His Lordship to out maneuvre us.

Should a French Fleet now come in Hampton Road the British Army would, I think, be ours.

I am litterally following Your Excellency's instructions, and shall continue to do so to the best of my power. I am impatiently waiting for the officer you have mentionned. Major Galvan having returned to the Grand Army, I would be happy to see him replaced by Major Trescot. Notwistanding the extreme fatigues of the cam-

*Library of Congress, Washington papers. There is a contemporary copy in the letterbook in the Hubbard Collection. Unpublished except for brief extracts in the *Memoirs, correspondence and manuscripts of General Lafayette*, p. 425, and Tower, II, 411.

paign, our light infantry is much improved in point of discipline and maneuvres.

No news from General Greene. He had hopes to maneuvre Rawdon down to Charlestown. Our army there has the advantage of the ennemy on one point wiz an excellent cavalry which in that country makes up for other disadvantages. By intelligences direct from Charlestown, I find that the reinforcement consisted of at least 1500 men who had been made to believe they were sent to a peacefull garrison. They had brought their wives and expected to live very comfortable. But on their being ordered out they revolted and were not quelled without difficulty. General Williamson the same who was at Savahana, and afterwards took protection has been taken within 6 miles of Charlestown.

I am going to send a flag to Lord Cornwallis. I owe him the justice to say that his conduct to me has been peculiarly polite, and many differences betwen commissaries very graciously adjusted by him to my satisfaction.

With the highest respect and most tender affection I have the honor to be

My dear General
Your most obedient humble servant
Lafayette

[127]

Malvern Hill 1st August 1781*

Sir

I have the honor to inclose your Excellency the report which has been made me this morning from Commodore Barron, of the fleets having sailed, and of its destination being Baltimore.

With the greatest respect I have the honor to be Sir
Your Excellency's
most ob sv^t
Lafayette

I beg leave to mention Maj^r Macpherson to your Excellency for his very distinguished zeal and services in this quarter.

*The original (signed but not written by Lafayette) is in the Library of Congress, Washington papers. There is a contemporary copy in the letterbook in the Hubbard Collection. Unpublished. An almost identical communication was sent to Governor Thomas Sims Lee of Maryland and is now in the Van Winkle Library of Lafayette College among the Essex County Country Club Collection. (Proper names are identified in the "Index" below.)

[128]

My dear General   Camp on Pamunkey August the 6th 1781*

    The embarkation which I thought and I do still think to have been destined to Newyork was reported to have sailed up the Bay, and to be bound to Baltimore—in consequence of which I wrote to Your Excellency, and as I had not indulged myself too near Portsmouth I was able to cut across towards Frederiksburg. But instead of continuing his voyage up the Bay My Lord entered York River and landed at York and Glocester. To the former vessels were added a number of flatt bottomed boats

    Our movements having not been precipitate, we were in time to take our course down Pamunkey River and will move to some position where the several parts of the Army will unite. I have some militia in Glocester County—some about York. We shall act agreably to circumstances but avoid drawing ourselves into a false movement which for want of cavalry and command of the rivers would give the ennemy the advantage of us. His Lordship plays so well that no blunder can be hoped from him to recover a bad step of ours

    The troops in York and Glocester are two bataïllons of Light Infantry, 2 large Anspach Regiments, the 80th and 76th which are said the two largest ones in the British Army the 43d the Queen's Rangers and some horse—Lord Cornwallis himself Commands. General O'Hara is in Portsmouth with the remainder of the troops. Leslie is, it is said, gone in a frigat to Charlestown

    You must not wonder, my dear General, that there has been a fluctuation in my intelligences. I am positive the British Councils have also been fluctuating. I am so earnest in my opinion that I would still not be surprised if the light infantry and Anspachers were detached to Newyork.

    York is surrounded by the river and a morass—the entrance is but narrow—there is however a commanding hill, at least I am so informed which if occupied by them would much extend their works. Glocester is a neck of land projected into the river and opposite to York. Their vessels the biggest of whom is a 44 are betwen the two towns. Should a fleet come in at this moment our affairs would take a very happy turn

*Library of Congress, Washington papers. There is a contemporary copy in the letterbook in the Hubbard Collection.

General Gregory and C^lel Parker have been directed to collect forces and press near Portsmouth. I have writen to North Carolina to be guarded against any movement by land. I have writen to Maryland for their new levies, and as agreably to your intentions His Lordship's remaining in the state keeps me with this army I am still more anxious, if possible, to receive the private communications that have been announced.

Had not your attention been turned to Newyork some thing with a fleet might be done in this quarter. But I see Newyork is the object and consequently I attend to your instructions by Captain Olney

It is the more important for me to know what Lord Cornwallis ought to do for fulfilling your Excellency's wishes, as we might try to influence His Lordship's maneuvres and endeavour to determine them towards a wrong point

Vessels are gone back to Portsmouth—it is thought to fetch troops and cannon. Perhaps His Lordship does not choose to keep two distant posts

I beg, my dear General, you will forgive the more than usual scribling of this hasty letter and have the honor to be with a respect equal to my affection

                      My dear General
                          Your obedient servant and friend
                                  Lafayette

[129]

New Kent Mountain 11th August 1781*

My Dear General

Your Excellency's public and private letters of the 30th July have safely come to hand for which I return you my warmest thanks. Be sure, my dear General, that the pleasure of being with you will make me happy in any command you will think proper to give. But for the present am with you of opinion I had better remain

*Library of Congress, Washington papers. There is a contemporary copy in the letterbook in the Hubbard Collection. Unpublished except for excerpt in the *Memoirs of General Lafayette*, pp. 426-27.

in Virginia. The more so as Lord Cornwallis does not chuse to live us, and circumstances may happen that will furnish me agreable opportunities in the command of the Virginia Army

I have pretty well understood you, my dear General, but would be happy in a more minuted detail which, I am sensible, cannot be intrusted to letters. Would not Gouvion be a very proper ambassador. Indeed at all events I would be happy to have him with me. But I think he could perfectly well answer your purpose. A gentleman in your family could with difficulty be spared. Should some thing be ascertained, Count Damas might come under pretence to serve with me. It is known he is very much my friend.

But to return to operations in Virginia I will tell you, my dear General, that Lord Cornwallis is entrenching at York and Gloucester. The sooner we disturb him the better. But unless our maritime friends give us help we cannot much venture below. I think his force may amount to four thousand six hundred including the garrison at Portsmouth which I think will be evacuated. It is I believe in contemplation to send a detachement of about 1500 men to Newyork. But I cannot yet be positive. The British Army are sickly. The greatest part of their wounded have died. Should they detach I will reinforce General Greene

There is a point, my dear General, upon which I want confidentially to speak to you *alone*. The Pennsylvanians and Virginians have never agreed but at the present time, it is worse than ever. I receive every day complaints. Some from the executive I have been obliged to take notice of. The Governor and Council have told me they would insist upon having justice by me from General Waïne's procedings. G^al. Waïne thinks he and his people have not been well used. In a word, I perceive the seeds of a future dispute betwen states. And every day the troops remain here adds to the danger. I will consequently make use of your name to reinforce Gal Greene with the Pennsylvanians and keep the bataïllon of 600 Marylanders that is coming on. I wish you will countenance me as General Greene must have a proportion of old soldiers. The mode of making war and procuring supplies in Carolina is better adapted than the management we must have with the Virginians. Upon them depend all southern operations. I therefore beg, my dear General, you will do as if I had been acting by superior orders and keep the matter secret. I do it for fear of worse consequences—and have maturely considered.

Adieu, my dear General, with the highest respect and most tender affection I have the honor to be
        Yours
          Lafayette

[130]

Forks of York River August 21st 1781*

My dear General

Your favor of the 15th has safely come to hand. I am going to give you an account of matters in this quarter

The greatest part of the ennemy are at York which they do not as yet fortify but are very busy upon Gloster Neck where they have a pretty large corps under C^{lel} Dundass. They have at York a 44 guns ship—frigats and vessels are scattered lower down. There is still a small garrison at Portsmouth. Should they intend to evacuate, at least they are proceeding with amazing slowness

From the ennemy's preparations I would infer that they are working for the protection of a fleet and for a defense against an other. That (in case they hold Portsmouth) the main body would be at York and a detached corps upon Gloster Neck to protect the water battery. Their fortifications are much contracted. From the ennemy's caution and partial movements I would conclude their intelligence is not very good, and they wish to come at an explanation of my intentions and prospects

We have hitherto occupied the forks of York River thereby looking both ways. Some militia have prevented the ennemy's parties from remaining any time at or near Williamsburg and false accounts have given them some alarms. An other body of militia under C^{lel} Ennis has kept them pretty close in Gloster town and foraged in their vicinity

Upon the receipt of your orders I wrote to the Governor that the intelligence of some plans of the ennemy rendered it proper to have 600 militia collected upon Black Water. I wrote to Gal Gregory near Portsmouth that I had an account the ennemy intended to

*Library of Congress, Washington papers. There is a contemporary copy in the letterbook in the Hubbard Collection.

push a detachement to Carolina which would greatly defeat a scheme we had there. I have requested Gal Waïne to move towards the southward and be ready to cross James River at Westover. A bataïllon of Light infantry and our only 100 dragoons being in Gloster County I call them my vanguard and will take my quarters there for one or two days while the troops are filing off towards James River. Our little army will consequently assemble again upon the waters of Chicaomeny, and should James town island be thought a good place for a jonction we will be in a situation to form it while we render it more difficult to the ennemy to attempt a journey to Carolina

I shall to day write to the Gentleman*. Nothing as yet has appeared. I will take measures that he may hear from me the moment he arrives.

Taking whatever is in the rivers, and taking position of the rivers themselves while the main body defends the Bay—forming a jonction of land forces at a convenient and safe point—checking the ennemy but giving nothing to chance untill properly reinforced—this is the plan I mean to propose

Some days ago I sent Washington† to contrive the Maryland new levies out of their state. These Marylanders will be 500 Virginians 400 Pennsylvanians 600—light infantry 850—dragoons 120. Such is the Continental force and in the course of 8 days the already called for militia will make 3000. Every thing I put at the lowest estimate but we may depend upon 2500 Continentals rank and file exclusive of artillery and three or if more wanted four thousand militia. Maryland would send 600 militia at least—I have 200 more dragoons and horses ready and am waïting for accoutrements

There is such a confusion in affairs in this part of the world that immense difficulties are found for a proper formation of magazines. I have however strongly urged the matter. The moment I received your first letter I sent Mr. McHenry to Richmond who had long conversations about it with the Governor and Council. I have recommended such places as might answer your purposes. This State has a large quantity of beef—of corn—some flour—very little rum. Maryland ought to be early called upon. Water transportation

---

*I.e. Comte de Grasse.
†George Augustine Washington.

will I hope ease our difficulties. Had we any thing like monney, matters would go on very well. The dry season has rendered most of the mills useless

We have no cloathing of any sort—No heavy artillery in order—some arms will be wanting—some horse accoutrements—and great deal of Ammunition. Nothing but your own entreaties may have a sufficient quantity of those articles transported to the head of the Bay

In the present state of affairs, my dear General, I hope you will come yourself to Virginia, and that if the French Army moves this way, I will have at least the satisfaction of beholding you myself at the head of the combined armies—In which case I beg leave to recommend you may be accompagnied by the heads of departements which will save you an immense deal of trouble. The men we have now here could not be equal to the task of a campaign upon so large a scale

In two days I will write again to your Excellency and keep you particularly and constantly informed. Unless some thing is done the very moment, and it will probably be difficult, Lord Cornwallis must be attaked with pretty great apparatus. But when a French Fleet takes possession of the Bay and Rivers, and we form a land force superior to his, that Army must soon or late be forced to surrender as we may get what reinforcements we please

Adieu, my dear General, I heartly thank you for having ordered me to remain in Virginia and to your goodness to me I am owing the most beautifull prospect that I may ever behold.

 With the Most Affectionate Respect I Have the Honor to be
  My dear General
   Your Excellency's
    Most obedient Humble
     Servant
      Lafayette

AMENDED [131]

My Dear General   Mattapony River 24 Augt 1781*

This letter will be handed by Col^o Morris who waits upon your Excellency with General Greene's sentiments upon the different ways to improve Count de Grasses assistance. I have been desired to add my accounts, but the last letter I had the honor to write has anticipated the informations which General Greene wanted me to give.

The Light Infantry are 850—the Pensylvanians about 600—Virginia exchanged soldiers and new levies 400 the Marylanders will be 600. We have 120 dragoons and a chance to obtain 60 more. Had we accoutrements we could have 200 more whom Col^o White has in readiness with 200 excellent horses 60 of which I hope to equip by dismounting volunteers. As to militia we may in a few days have 3000. A demand from you upon the State of Maryland will procure 1000 well armed militia. The conduct of some people in that State appears to me very injurious to public interests. The new levies have been every day detained, every petty pretence employed to prevent their joining either General Greene or this army. The danger of Baltimore upon which I was not very hasty to quiet them brought on a confession that the men were ready. I then demanded them in the most urging terms. At last I sent George† there who writes me they make a beautiful battalion but he could not obtain more than a promise to send them in three or four days. Portsmouth is evacuated with some precipitation I wait for a more particular account before I write officially. Yesterday Mr de Camus a French officer of the navy has reconnoitered the shipping in York River. There are 60 sail 10 of which armed vessels the largest a 50 gun ship, their situation very much exposed. The enemy are not yet fortifying at York. What is doing at Glocester is rather upon a contracted scale. They do not appear very much alarmed. Col^o Dundas was heard to say that an English and French fleet had saild in the same time. The intelligence respecting Count de Grasse has been kept a

---
*Letterbook in the Hubbard Collection. The version in Jared Sparks (ed.), *Correspondence of the American Revolution, being letters of eminent men to George Washington* (4 vols.; Boston, 1853), III, 342-45 is erroneously dated June 24, 1781. (Proper names are identified in the "Index" below.)

†George Augustine Washington.

profound secret. My coming in this country has attracted this side a large part of the enemys force. In the mean while General Wayne was filing of towards Westover and the remainder of the army to Ruffins Ferry. Should the enemy move southerly we shall be at Westover before Wayne has done crossing as the cavalry will be hurried on. The moment Count de Grasse arrives I will collect our force about Soans Bridge and wait for intelligences from him

Colo Gimat and the French officer I have mentioned are gone to Portsmouth under pretence to see the fortifications (which I have ordered to be leveled) and will proceed to Cape Henry in order to deliver my dispatches to the French Commanders, and give them every information in their power

Heavy artillery and every thing relative to a siege from the cannon to the tools are not to be found this side of Philadelphia. Cloathing and particularly shoes—arms, dragoons and horse equipments ammunition of every kind are articles which Your Excellency will be obliged to send from the Northward. I may add medicines and hospital stores. Could Lauzun's Legion be forwarded with dispatch they will be extremely useful. They might come with you and would in the mean time serve to the safety of your journey

As to provisions my dear General, want of sistem will render our subsistance difficult unless intelligent Commissaries are immediately sent on. If you intend as I hope, to come yourself you might send on the Heads of departments— Mr. Clayborne D. Q. M. Genl. is doing nothing but to write letters. An early application upon the State of Maryland may be productive of great good

My expectations have not as yet been communicated to any General Officer not even to the Executive. I will however to day write a private letter to the Governor. Count De Grasse will no doubt arrive before long. In case important operations are carried on in Virginia which I think cannot fail to succeed Mr. Morris ought to send some hard money. From the moment I took the command of this army their has not been a farthing sent from the Treasury and this State money is good for nothing. With the highest respect and affection

I have the honor to be
My dear General
Your affectionate friend
Lafayette

P. S.

Lord Cornwallis's force at Richmond was 4000. There were then at least 1000 in Portsmouth. Some have been killed and some are sick but if you add sailors he will have much upwards of 5000 men at the lowest estimate

[132]

Mr. Ruffin's August 25th 1781

My dear General

Independant of the answer to your letter of the 15th, I have been very particular in a second letter instrusted to C^lel Moriss—but at this moment wish to send you minuted and repeated accounts of every thing that passes in this quarter.

The ennemy have evacuated their forts at Ivy, Kemp's Landing, Great Bridge and Portsmouth—their vessels with troops and baggage went round to York—some cannon have been left spiked up at Portsmouth—But I have not yet received proper returns.

I have got some intelligences by the way of this servant I have once mentioned—a very sensible fellow was with him and from him as well as deserters I hear that they begin fortifying at York—They are now working by a windmill at which place I understand they will make a fort and a battery for the defense of the River—I have no doubt but that some thing will be done on the land side—The works at Gloster are finished—They consist of some redoubts across Gloster Neck and a battery of 18 pieces beating the River.

The ennemy have 60 sails of vessels into York River—the largest a 50 guns ship two 36 frigats—about seven other armed vessels—The remainder are transports some of them still loaded and a part of them very small vessels—It appears they have in that number merchant men some of whom Dutch prizes—The men of war are very thinly manned—On board the other vessels there are almost no sailors.

The British Army had been sickly at Portsmouth—The air of York begins to refitt them—the whole cavalry have crossed on the Gloster side yesterday evening a movement of which I gave repeated accounts to the militia there—But the light infantry and main body of the militia are at this place—Gal Wayne on the road to Westover and we may form our jonction in one day—I keep parties upon the ennemies lines. The works at Portsmouth are levelling—The moment

I can get returns and plans I will send them to Your Excellency—The evacuation of a post fortified with much care and great expense will convince the people abroad that the ennemy cannot hold two places at once—I have mentionned it in a letter to Congress wherein I send them copy of one I have received upon an other subject—The enlisting of our soldiers, and impressing them into British service—I thought you had rather the matter should be directly laid before Congress, and consequent measures entirely left with them—Inclosed you will find an other copy of that letter.

The Maryland troops were to have sat out on Monday last—but God knows if they will keep the engagement.

There is in this quarter an immense want of cloathing of every sort, arms, ammunition, hospital stores, and horse accoutrements. Should a maritime superiority be expected I would propose to have all those matters carried from Philadelphia to the Head of Elk. The numbers of the British Army fit for duty I *at least* would estimate at 4500 rank and file—Their sailors I cannot judge but by intelligences of the number of vessels—There is an amazing quantity of Negroes—But (except at Working) they may become an uncumberance*—In a word this part affords the greatest number of regulars and the only active Army to attak, which having had no plan of defense, must be less calculated for it than any garrison either at Newyork or in Carolina.

I have writen a private and confidential letter (but not quite so) to the Governor—I speak in pretty general terms, and just so much as was necessary—No news of any sort has come to hand.

With the highest respect and most sincere affection I have the honor to be

    My dear General
     Your most obedient h^{ble}
      servant
       Lafayette.

I am sorry to inform you that Gal Campdell of the Riflemen—the one of King's Mountain—lately died of a fever at New Castle.

---

*The version of this letter in the *Memoirs of General Lafayette*, pp. 527-28, which omits this sentence (among others), is erroneously dated August 29, 1781.

[133]

My dear General   Holt's Forge September the 1st 1781

I am happy to inform Your Excellency that Count de Grasse's Fleet is safely arrived in this Bay—it consists of 28 ships of the line with several frigats, and convoys a considerable body of troops under Marquis de St. Simon—Previous to their Arrival such positions had been taken by our Army as to prevent the ennemy's retreating towards Carolina.

In consequence of Your Excellency's orders I had the honour to oppen a correspondance with the French Generals, and Measures have been taken for a jonction of our troops.

Lord Cornwallis is still on York River and is fortifying himself in a strong position—

With the Highest Respect I have the Honor to be
My dear General
Your Excellency's Most obedient humble Servant
Lafayette.

[134]

My dear General   Holt's Forge 1st September 1781

From the bottom of my heart I congratulate you upon the arrival of the French Fleet—Some rumours had been spread and spy accounts sent out—but no certainty untill the Admiral's dispatches came to hand—Inclosed I send you his letter and that of Mis de St. Simon both of whom I request you will have translated by Tilmangh or Gouvion alone as there are parts of them personal which I do not choose to show to others—Thanks to you, my dear General, I am in a very charming situation and find myself at the Head of a Beautiful body of troops—but am not so hasty as Count de Grasse and think that having so sure a game to play, it would be madness by the risk of an attak to give any thing to chance.

It appears Count de Grasse is in a great hurry to return—he makes it a point to put upon my expressions such constructions as may favor his plan—They have been pleased to adopt my ideas as to the sending of vessels into James River and forming a jonction at James town—I wish they may also force the passage at York because then His Lordship has no possibility to escape.

The delay of Count de Grasse's arrival, the Movement of the Grand Army, and the alarm there was at York have forced me for greater security to send a part of the troops to the South Side of James River—to morrow and the day after will be employed in making dispositions for covering a landing—which will be done with Continentals discombered of baggage; and the 5th agreable to the Count's desire a jonction will be made of our troops—I shall then propose to the French General the taking of a safe position within ten or twelve miles of York—such a one as cannot be forced without a much greater loss than we could suffer—and unless matters are very different from what I think they are, my opinion is that we ought to be contented with preventing the ennemy's forages, and fatiguing them by alarming their piquets with Militia without committing our Regulars—Whatever readiness Marquis de St. Simon has been pleased to express to C^{lel} Gimat respecting his being under me, I shall do nothing without paying that deference which is due to age, talents, and experience—but would rather incline to the cautious line of conduct I have of late adopted—Gal Portail must be now with Count de Grasse—he knows your intentions and of course will be consulted in our movements.

Lord Cornwallis has still one way to escape—He may land at West Point and cross James River some miles below Point of Fork—but I thought this post was the most important as the other rout is big with obstacles—However to prevent even a *possibility* I would wish some ships were above York—

The Governor was with me when the letters came—He jumped upon a horse and posted of to his Council—I gave him a Memorandum demanding provisions of every kind for the Fleet and for the Combined Army—We may depend upon a quantity of cattle—but flour ought to be sent from Maryland and Pennsylvania—C^{her} D'Annemours the French Consul is here and will take a method to have his countrymen supplied without starving us—Before he left me the Governor sent people to collect horses for the officers and Vegetables for the men—both articles to be got immediately—C^{lel} White has impressed two hundred horses—but cannot equip 50—I have ordered him to send 100 here that the French Huzzards may be mounted.

Gal Portaïl is of opinion 6000 militia are wanting—I have asked for them—but do not depend upon more than 4000 rank and file—Maryland may furnish 1000 and that I would think to be sufficient—I fear the Croud on account of provisions.

From C^lel Gimat's private letter I find that the Army and Navy are in High Spirits and panting for action—they have been particularly kind to me—my little influence will be employed in preaching patience as our affairs cannot be spoiled unless we do spoil them ourselves.

Your letter of the 22d is just come to hand—it is impossible immediately to answer the part of it that respects Horses and Waggons—but I can give very little hopes—since I am in Virginia it has been impossible to have the Army provided—most of our waggons are extorted from inhabitants—the demand of Count de St Simon will be very large—your best, I was going to say your only chance will be in Maryland—However I will immediately urge the matter with the Governor—I wish the Quarter Master General would come—Major Clayburne is sick and when he was well did very little—we are also in absolute want of the Heads in the Commissary departement—the State Commissary cannot answer the purpose—whatever craft may be found I will send but there is very few and the few boats there is are employed in transporting provisions—the State of Maryland have been collecting horses—Some may also be impressed in Virginia—Should we succeed against Mylord our Cavalry will be perfectly mounted and equipped for a Campaign in Carolina.

Aprehending that Your Excellency might wish to have an official letter on the arrival of the Fleet I have inclosed one.*

Upon a particular inquiry of the country and our circumstances I hope you will find we have taken the best precautions to lessen His Lordship's chances to escape—He has a few left but so very precarious that I hardly believe he will make the attempt—If he does he must give up Ships, Artillery, Baggage part of the Horses all the Negroes—He must be certain to loose the third of his Army and run the greatest risk to loose the whole without gaining that glory which he may derive from a brillant defense.

Adieu, my dear General, the agreable situation I am in is owing to your friendship and is for that reason the dearer to

Your respectful servant and friend

Lafayette.

*See letter no. 133 above.

[135]

Williamsburg Sepr. 8th 81*

My dear General

I had the honor to write you lately giving an account of every thing that came within my knowledge. I was every hour expecting I might be more particular but if you new how slow things go on in this Country, that still I have done the best in my power, I have written and received twenty letters a day from Government and every department whatever. The Governor does what he can the wheels of his Government are so very rusty that no Governor whatever will be able to set them fiercely agoing. Time will prove that Jefferson has been too severely charged. The French Troops my Dear General has landed with immasing celerity they have been already wanting flour meat and salt not however so much as to have been one day without. I have been night and day so much the Quarter Master Collector and Beef driver I have drove myself into a violent headake and feaver which will go off with three hours sleep the want of which has occasioned it. This my Dear General will apologise to you for not writing with my own hand. The French Army is composed of the most excellent Regiments, they have with them a Corps of Hussards which may be of immediate use—The General and all the Officers have cheerfully lived in the same way as our poorly provided american detachment. I think a letter from you on the subject will have a very good effect, last night by leaving our own baggage and accepting of our Officers horses we have been able to move to a position near Williamsburg. It is covered along the front with ravines. The right flank is covered by a Mill Pond on the road to James Town, the left by Queens Creek small rivolets and marshes. We have Militia still in front of our right and left and a good lookout on the river. Our provisions may come to the Cappital Landing. Williamsburg and its strong buildings are in our front—I have upon the lines General Mughlenburg with one thousand Men four hundred of whom are Virginia Regulars and one hundred Dragoons in borrowing Whites unequipped horses we may add one hundred Hussards—There is a line of armed Ships along James River, and a small reserve of Militia which may increase every

---

*Not autographed but signed by Lafayette. The handwriting is that of James McHenry.

day there are in Gloscester County eight hundred Militia driving off Stock—I had recommended with proper delicacy to Count De Grass to send some Naval force up York River, the French armed vessels in Pamunkey are come down to West Point, no movements of Count De Grass has as yet taken place except some ships being below York. Your Excellencys letters to him has been duly forwarded, we are under infinite obligations to the officers and men for their zeal.

I entered into so particular accounts my dear General to show you that propriety and not the desire to advance has dictated our measures we will try if not dangerous upon a large scale to form a good idea of the works, but unless I am greatly decieved their will be madness in attacking them now with our force. Marquis St Simon Count De Grass and General Du Portail agree with me in opinion, but should Lord Cornwallis come out against such a position as we have, every body thinks that he cannot but repent of it, and should he beat us he must soon prepair for another battle—

Now my dear General I am going to speak to you of the fortifications at York—Lord Cornwallis is working day and night and will soon work himself into a respectable situation, he has taken on shore the greatest part of his Sailors. He is picking up what ever provisions he can get, I am told he has ordered the inhabitants in the vicinity of the Town to come in, and should think they may do him as much harm as good. Our present position will render him cautious and I think it a great point, no news as yet in this camp of Monsieur Count de Barrass's Fleet.

I will now answer you that part of your letter respecting provisions for the troops now under in your immediate command—

As I have already wrote to Your Excellency there are some Flour some Wheat Indian Corn and Mills in this Country—I went to Richmond the moment I reciev'd your first letter and afterwards sent Mr McHenry both crying out for magazines and pointing proper places; promises were made, and the liberty of navigation was the only objection, now they are over. I do not know in the name of God what prevents them coming, their is no Continental Commissary of purchases and the State one has little sence, and no activity, I would recommend my Dear General to have great dependance on the Mayriland Flour and that of Pensylvania, the State

Quarter Master keeps writing letters and says he has no means—Government says he has them, but he fell sick a long time ago and we cannot get him from the Mountains—

As to Beaves with the least activity their is enough in the Country and if necessary we must push milittary means which in other instances I have an utter aversion, they have salt a plenty but we cannot get it—The sooner the Heads of the Departments come here the better it will be, a letter from Your Excellency to Government will have a good effect, to be forwarded to the different County Lieutenants, as Government has less attention paid them than even myself and the influence of your request will be immense, as to Waggons my Dear Genl the People are so much attached to them and it is so easy for them to hide them that you cannot concieve what immence trouble I have been at for transporting our little Army to this place, but the superiority on James River could alone help us on, as to Horses my Dear General Major Call is at Richmond almost without saddles and Dragoons. He had orders from General Greene which I have inspected, but have stopped him in Richmond—there is one hundred horses at Portroyal pressed for Col. Lees Legion that may be here immediately upon your arrival, Mayriland speaks of four hundred horses they are impressing, this State promissed 60 Waggons and I have ordered every one Clayborne had.

Notwithstanding what is said of our present wants yet I have good reason for believing that there will be found a sufficiency of supplies in this State and Mayriland for our Armies.

With respect to a proper place for the debarkation of your troops it is the opinion of the Marquis St Simon, and myne, that it must be in James River but we have not had an opportunity yet of fixing on the best spot—it appears however that it must be at or near Williamsburg or James Town.

With the most affectionate regard and esteem
    I am, dr General,
        Your most Obt Humble Serv-
          Lafayette.

[136]

Camp Williamsburg September 8 [1781]*

My dear General

Your letter of the 2d 7ber is just come to hand. Mine of yesterday† mentionned that the ships in York River had gone down. Inclosed is the account I receive of an engagement off the Capes. What disposition has been made for the internal protection of the Bay I do not know. James River is still guarded but we have not as yet received any letter from Count de Grasse relative to his last movements. I hasten to communicate them as your Excellency will probably think it is safer to keep the troops at the Head of Elk untill Comte de Grasse returns. Indeed unless the greatest part of your force is brought here a small addition can do but little more than we do effect. Lord Cornwallis will in a little time render himself very respectable. I ardently wish your whole army may be soon brought down to operate

We will make it our business to reconnoitre the ennemy's works and give you on your arrival the best description of it that is in our power. I expect the Governor this evening and will again urge the necessity of providing what you have recommended

By a deserter from York I hear that two British frigats followed the French fleet and returned after they had seen them out of the Capes. A spy says that two schooners supposed to be French have been seen coming up York River. But we have nothing so certain as to insure your voyage—tho' it is probable Comte de Grasse will soon return—

I beg leave to request, my dear General, in your answer to Marquis de St. Simon you will express your admiration at the celerity of their landing and your sense of their chearfulness in submitting to the difficulties of the first moments. Indeed I would be happy something might also be said to Congress on the subject

Your approbation of my conduct emboldens me to request that as General Lincoln will of course take command of the American part of your Army, the division I will have under him may be com-

*Library of Congress, Washington papers. There is a contemporary copy in the letterbook in the Hubbard Collection.
†We have been unable to find any letter of September 7, 1781. The reference may be to no. 135 above. (Proper names are identified in the "Index" below.)

posed of the troops which have gone through the fatigues and dangers of the Virginia Campaign. This will be the greatest reward of the services I may have rendered, as I confess I have the strongest attachement to those troops

With the highest respect I have the honor to be
My dear General
Your most obed^t h^{ble} Ser^t
Lafayette

[137]

Williamsburg 10th September 1781*

My dear General

Gouvion is just arrived. He says you may be on your way. We hasten to send to the Commanding Naval Officer in the Bay. Hitherto I had no way to write to you by water—But Count de Grasse being at sea we request the officer he has left to have every precaution taken for the safety of navigation. It is probable they are taken, but I would be too uneasy had I not added this measure to those that have been probably adopted

I wrote several letters to you. The surprising speedy landing of the French troops under Marquis de St. Simon—our jonction at Williamsburg—the unremitted ardor of the ennemy in fortifying at York—the sailing of Count de Grasse in pursuit of 16 sails of the line of the British Fleet—were the most principal objects. I added we were short of flour, might provide cattle enough. I took the liberty to advise James River as the best to land in—for the particular spot refered to a more particular examination the result of which we shall send to morrow

Excuse the haste I am in—but the idea of your being in a cutter leaves only the time to add that I am most respectfully
Yours
Lafayette

---

*Library of Congress, Washington papers. There is a contemporary copy in the letterbook in the Hubbard Collection.

[138]

Camp before York September 30th 1781*

My dear General

You have so often been pleased to ask I would give my opinion upon any subject that may occur, that I will this day take the liberty to mention a few articles.

I am far from laughing at the idea of the ennemy's making a retreat—it is not very probable—but it is not impossible. Indeed they have no other way to escape—and since we cannot get ships above York I would be still more afraïd of a retreat by West Point than any thing else. The French Huzzards remaining here our dragoons and some infantry might be stationned some where near Westpoint rather on the north side

I see the service is much done by details, and to use your permission would take the liberty to observe that when the siege is once begun it might be more agreable to the officers and men to serve as much as possible by whole bataïllons

C[lel] Scamel is taken. His absence I had accounted for by his being officer of the day. I am very sorry we loose a valuable officer, but, tho' C[lel] Scamel's being officer of the day has been a reason for his going in front, I think it would be well to prevent the officers under the rank of generals or field officers reconnoitring for the safety of their commands from advancing so near the ennemy's lines

There is a great disproportion between Huntington's and Hamilton's bataïllons. Now that Scamel is taken we might have them made equal, and put the eldest of the two lieutenant colonels upon the right of the brigade

I have these past days wished for an opportunity to speak with Your Excellency on Count de Grasse's demand relative to Mr de Barras's Fleet. This business being soon done, we may think of Charlestown, at least of the harbour, or of Savahna. I have long and seriously thought upon that matter—but would not be in hurry to mention it untill we know how long this will last. However it might be possible to give Count de Grasse an early hint of it in case you agree with him upon the winterly departure of the whole fleet for the West Indias.

*Library of Congress, Washington papers. There is a contemporary copy in the letterbook in the Hubbard Collection.

One of my reasons to wish troops (tho' not in great number) to be sent to Glocester County by way of Westpoint is that for the first days it will embarass any movement of the ennemy up the river or up the country on either side—and when it is in Glocester County it may be thought advantageous by a respectable regular force to prevent the ennemy's increasing their works there and giving us the trouble of a second operation and in the same time it will keep from York a part of the British forces

With the highest respect and most sincere affection I have the honor to be dear G^{al}

Your most obedient h^{ble} servant
Lafayette

[139]

Camp before York September 30th 1781*

My dear General

The letter that accompagnies this being relative to matters of public utility, I shall write also this confidential one where none but my private interests are concerned.

Owing to your partiality and friendship for me, I have during the Campaign acted the Most Agreable part—I commanded the Army in Virginia, I was opposed to Lord Cornwallis, and the troops you entrusted to me had the greatest share in the fatiguing movements that will end in the ruin of the ennemy in this quarter

You was pleased to tell me, my dear General, that you took Gal Lincoln with you because you could not help it—I knew it had been the case, and I am too much used to the most delicate marks of your attachement not to be certain that had it been possible to take either Gal Howe or G^{al} McDougall you would not have liked to have me superseded in the Command of the American troops.

You remember, my dear General, that since I returned from France I never had any body betwen you and me—But now from being the Commander of the Army against Cornwallis I became one of Gal Lincoln's officers who as of course the General leads the troops has nothing almost to say even in the Light Division.

Don't think, my dear General, that I am any way disastisfied—I will chearfully serve any how where ever I am in General Wash-

*Unpublished.

ington's Army—But as the command of the Right Wing in this siege is of the Highest importance to me—as it cannot have any similar effect upon Gal Lincoln's reputation and Military prospects in Europe and the future course of his life, I am sure you will be so very kind to me as to adopt any plan consistent with propriety that may bring on an event so hightly interesting to me that it can bear no comparaison.

Should some dragoons and infantry be thrown into Glocester County, or about West Point, could not Gal Lincoln have the general command of the North side of York River—it is a separate one—it will consist of of upwards of 3000 men, exclusive of what will be added in regulars Militia or dragoons—no body can object to this arrangement, and you will greatly forward the interests of one who thinks himself intitled to the Name of your best friend.

When I propose it, my dear General, it is because I know your Heart is disposed to favor any arrangement that may be to my advantage—because the service you would render to me is immense—and because it cannot hurt any body's pretensions or feelings.

I request, my dear General, this may be a secret betwen us, and at all events I will be persuaded you have done the best you could for your friend

Lafayette.

[140]

Camp before York 16th Octbr. 1781*

My dear General

Your Excellency having personally seen our dispositions, I shall only give an account of what passed in the execution

Colonel Gimat's batallion led the van, and was followed by that of Colonel Hamilton's, who commanded the whole advanced corps, at the same time a party of eighty men, under Col. Laurens, turned the redoubt. I beg leave to refer your Excellency to the report I have received from Col. Hamilton, whose well known talents and gallantry, were on this occasion most conspicuous and serviceable. Our obligations to him, to Col. Gimat, to Col. Laurens, and to each

*The original (written by McHenry and corrected and signed by Lafayette) is in the Library of Congress, Washington papers. There is a contemporary copy in the letterbook in the Hubbard Collection.

and all the officers and men are above expression. Not one gun was fired; and the ardor of the troops did not give time for the sappers to derange the abattis; and, owing to the conduct of the commanders, and bravery of the men, the redoubt was stormed with an uncommon rapidity.

Colonel Barbers batallion which was the first in the supporting column being detached to the aid of the advance arrived at the moment they were getting over the works, and executed their orders with the utmost alacrity. The colonel was slightly wounded. The rest of the column under Gen Mullemberg and Hazen advanced with admirable firmness and discipline. Col. Vose's batallion displayed to the left, a part of the division succesively dressing by him, whilst a kind of second line was forming columns in the rear. It adds greatly to the character of the troops, that under the fire of the ennemy, they displayed and took their ranks with perfect silence and order.

Give me leave particularly to mention Major Barber, division inspector, who distinguished himself, and received a wound by a cannon ball

In making the arrangements for the support of the works we had reduced, I was happy to find Gen. Wayne, and the Pennsylvanians so situated as to have given us in case of need the most effectual support.

I have the honor to be with the most perfect respect your Excellency's

Most ob st

Lafayette

[141]

[October 23, 1781]*

Monsieur le Comte de Grasse seroit heureux de pouvoir faire l'expedition de Charlestown dont il sent tous les avantages; mais les ordres de sa cour, les projets ulterieurs, et les engagements avec les

*Library of Congress, Washington papers. This document together with a contemporary translation is given in [E. S. Kite (ed.)], *Correspondence of General Washington and Comte de Grasse, 1781* (Washington, 1931), pp. 121-23, under the assumption that it is a communication of De Grasse to Washington. It is, however, in Lafayette's handwriting and is apparently his report of his conversation with De Grasse (cf. Gottschalk, *Lafayette and the close of the American Revolution*, pp. 332-33). It was written in French apparently for submission to De Grasse.

espagnols rendent impossible de passer ici le tems necessaire à cette operation; son desir de servir les etats unis est tel qu'il desire entrer dans des arrangements pour une cooperation pendant la campagne prochaine autant que les projets de la cour ne s'y opposeront pas

L'expedition de Wilmington etant moins longue, Monsieur le Comte de Grasse se chargeroit d'y conduire le detachement de deux mille Americains; quant à la maniere d'operer elle se decidera d'après les renseignements particuliers que nous allons prendre

Il faudroit avoir sur le champ des pilotes et des personnes connoissant bien le païs avec qui Monsieur le Comte de Grasse desire causer le plutôt possible pour donner sa parole definitivement Les troupes americaines seront fournies de provisions; l'armée navale ne pouvant pas donner les siennes

Monsieur le Comte de Grasse nous permet de nous servir des bâtiments dans la riviere d'York. Le Loyalist—la Queen Charlotte le Cormoran ont été vendus à l'etat de Virginie—mais Monsieur le Comte de Grasse ne croit pas pouvoir embarquer les troupes americaines à bord de ses vaisseaux. Alors comment nous y prendrons nous pour avoir des matelots qui puissent les maneuvrer. Mr le Cte de Grasse a 15 matelots americains; il y a quelques petits bâtiments armés; si après avoir vu les personnes qui connoissent la côte Monsieur le Comte de Grasse croit pouvoir nous embarquer à bord des vaisseaux de l'armée et nous debarquer sans danger alors il nous deviendra inutile de prendre des bâtiments de transport; si les fregattes peuvent entrer quelquepart à portée, alors on mettra nos troupes dans les fregattes

Le jour de partance le premier Novembre et s'il est possible plûtot

[142]

November 29th 1781*

My dear General

Inclosed you will find some numbers† a copy of which I have kept and which contain some names that may probably occur in our correspondance. I need not telling you, my dear General, that

*Library of Congress, Washington papers. There is a contemporary copy in the letterbook in the Hubbard Collection.
†I.e. a cipher in numerals.

I will be happy in giving your every intelligence in my power, and reminding you of the most affectionate friend you can ever have

The goodness you had to take upon yourself the communicating to the Virginia Army the approbation of Congress appears much better to me than my writing to the scattered parts of the body I had the honor to command. Give me leave, my dear General, to recall to your memory the peculiar situation of the troops who being already in Virginia were deprived of the month pay given to the others. Should it be possible to do some thing for them it would give them great satisfaction

I will have the honor to write to you from Boston, my dear General, and would be very sorry to think this is my last letter. Accept however once more the homage of the respect and of the affection that render me for ever

Your most obedient servant and tender friend
Lafayette

I beg you will present my respects to Mrs. Washington and my compliments to George and the family. Will you be so kind, my dear General, as to remember me to Mr. and Mrs. Moriss

[143]

Alliance off Boston December 21st 1781

My dear General

I am sorry to think we are not yet gone, and there still remain some doubts of our going to morrow—This delay I lament not so much on private accounts as I do it on the account of our next Campaign in the planning of which your opinion as I will deliver it must be of great use to the Common Cause—As to the departement of Foreign affairs I will be happy to justify the confidence of Congress by giving my opinion to the best of my power whenever it is asked for—But the affair of finances will I fear be a difficult point for the American Minister—In which however I will be happy to help him with my utmost exertions—The moment I arrive in France, I will minutely write to you how things stand and give you the best accounts in my power.

I have received every mark of affection in Boston, and am much attached to this town to which I have so many obligations—But on public considerations I have been impatient to leave it and go on board the frigat where I receive all possible civilities but where I had rather be under sails than at anchor.

There is nothing new in this part of the World—for Mr. Temple is not a new thing—but as your curiosity may be raised upon this subject, I will tell you my opinion of the Gentleman.

Before I heard his friends my suspicions were great—after I heard them they were still greater—but I paid Mr. Temple, or rather I returned a visit, and when I came out I had to Mr. Temple this obligation that not the shadow of a doubt remained in his favor—His political character is this—A personal picque made him an opposition man—The only one service he has rendered to America has been the service of a spy—that is the best part of his character—What follows so clearly marks him as an English man in his affections as well as his principles—He is so much said by his very friends to be a man who is in want of monney, and cannot support himself unless he receives monney—which they give as an excuse for his remaining in England, and which, unless Mr. Moriss pays him, is an excuse, I think, for sending him off. It is so well known that when he came with Berkenout, the doctor was the better man of the two, that I can not conceive there still remains any doubt with any body.

But Mr. Temple is pleased to remove them—he tells me the moment he came to London he waited on Lord North and had with him a Conference of three hours upon the State of American affairs —that when he was late here he made it a point to inquire how far the prejudices of the people were removed—and so on—He tells every body that his view is to be employed on the one or the other side, and particularly to be initiated in the American Commission for peace, that Mr. Temple clearly proves these two things—1st that he is in the interests of Britain—2dly that he has not sense enough to hurt any cause but the cause in which he is engaged.

But for Mr. Baudowin's sake whom I greatly regard I wish he was not so prejudiced in favor of his Son in Law—From hence comes that his friends think themselves obliged out of compliment to tolerate Mr. Temple—He is now in the hands of the Attorney General—but as he will be tried for his life, great endeavours will be made to save him—and indeed he is not worth making so much ado—the thing I was wishing for is to have him considered as an English man, and for the discouragement of more sensible spies, sent about other business.

23d

I beg your pardon, my dear General, to give you so much trouble in reading my scribles—But we are going to sail, and my last adieu I must dedicate to my Beloved General—Adieu, my dear General, I know your heart so well that I am sure no distance can alter your attachement to me—With the same candor, I assure you that my love, my respect, my gratitude for you are above expressions, that on the moment of leaving you I more than ever feel the strength of those friendly ties that for ever bind me to you, and that I anticipate the pleasure, the most wished for pleasure to be again with you, and by my zeal and services to gratify the feelings of my respect and affection. Adieu, my dear General,

Your respectfull and tender friend
Lafayette.

Will you please to present my compliments and respects to Mrs. Washington and to remember me to Gal Knox & Gal Lincoln.

✣ 1782 ✣

[144]

L'orient January 18th 1782

My dear General

I thank my stars there is a good opportunity to let you know that after an happy voyage of 23 days I am safely arrived in L'orient, and that my family and friends are in a very good health, which circumstances, my dear General, I am sure will afford you some satisfaction. We are arrived last night, and are setting out this morning in great speed for Versailles and Paris, so that I have but the time to scrible a line, and beg leave to request Your Excellency will please to let my friends know of my safe arrival. However happy I am to be in France, and to enjoy the sight of my friends, I anticipate the pleasure to find myself again in a few months on the American Shore, and to feel that unspeakable satisfaction I ever experienced when after an absence I could once more arrive at head quarters.

As I am just arrived, I cannot be very particular in my intelligences. From what I pick up on the shore I find that Lord Cornwallis's down fall had a glorious effect and was properly felt in France, England, and indeed throughout Europe. The birth of a Dolphin has given a general satisfaction to the French nation, and from attachement to the Queen I have been made particularly happy by this event. The taking of Statia* is a clever affair, and I never read of a prettier *coup de main*. The Dutch will no doubt be greatly pleased with the conduct of the French. Old count de Maurepas is dead. Charlus is Adjudant General of the Gendarmerie of France which [h]is father commands. It appears that the Convoy from Brest

*Probably Saint-Eustatius is meant. (Proper names are identified in the "Index" below.)

to the East and West Indias has met with an accident. 23 Vessels it is said are taken. I am not much acquainted with particulars—but from a bad event we may derive some good if it is an inducement to do what we have been talking about.

Be so kind, my dear General to present my best respects to Mrs. Washington and my compliments to the family and George and to my friends of the Army. On my arrival I found a letter from Madame de Lafayette for America where in she desires her most affectionate compliments to you.

Adieu, my dear General, we are ready to go and yet when I think you are so many thousand miles off I cannot leave writing to you. Viscount de Noailles, Gal Portail, Gouvion, and all the detachement of your Army now at L'orient join in presenting their respects to you, and I, my dear General, I need only adding that I am for ever

Your grateful and respectfull friend
Lafayette.

Count du Charlus being Major General of the Gendarmerie I am told the Prince de Broglio, a son to the General will take his place in your Army.

By an American gentleman I am told that Mr. Deane after endeavouring to apolozige for Arnold's conduct and speaking as well as Arnold acted, is gone to the Austrian Flanders, so that there is no doubt of his being a traitor.

[145]

My dear General Versailles January 30th 1782

Having landed some days ago at L'orient I had the pleasure to inform you of my safe arrival, and hope the letter will have a prosperous passage. You easely imagine, my dear general, that no time was lost in posting off to Paris, where I found my family and friends in perfect health. My daughter* and your George† are grown up so much that I find myself great deal older than I aprehended. The short stay I have hitherto made cannot have fully apprised me of all circumstances. There is nothing very important lately happened, for

*Anastasie-Louise-Pauline.
†I.e. Washington's godson, George Washington Lafayette.

I trust, before this reaches you, you will have heard of the unlucky turn of the weather that forced the out ward bound convoys to put up again in the harbour of Brest. Measures had been taken to be before hand with the ennemy in every quarter of the world. It is true Rodney, it is said, has also been obliged to return. Lord Cornwallis has been taken in a merchant vessel, and ransomed by a French privateer. We heard nothing of Arnold. Should he be brought in to some harbour I shall make it my business to obtain his being delivered as an American deserter. It is said Lord George Germaine is going to quit his post.

As I told you my opinion of the ministers, and also the degree of friendship that subsists betwen me and each of them, I will only add that I am hitherto much satisfied with their zeal and good intentions for America—but find it very difficult, next to impossibility to get monney. On my arrival Mr Franklin told me nothing could be expected. However I had some conversations on the subject. I hope, *betwen us,* some thing may be obtained, but would not have Mr Moriss to be sanguine. What may be done C^{her} de la Luzerne will of course announce, but Congress will be mistaken if they build upon expectations of monney from this quarter. However I will exert myself for the best, to promote that and every other wiew which may be interesting to America. As to grand operations or more minute circumstances of supplies, tho' I have had conversations on the subject with the King and his Ministers, I cannot as yet write you any thing particular and will endeavour to do it by the first good opportunity.

It is generally thought in this quarter, that the exertions of America are not equal to her abilities. Nothing can operate so much for further assistance as pointed assurances of a numerous, well cloathed and well fed army for the war. Congress ought to be very careful of that matter—for you may depend upon it, England are determined to play a desperate game and to try at least an other campaign. Will it be a defensive one in America, and offensive elsewhere, or the reverse of that, I cannot as yet ascertain. But I think the evacuation of Newyork and Charlestown, is as far from their ideas for next campaign, as the very evacuation of London—and to go out of it, they must be driven.

The reception I have met with from the nation at large, from the King and from my friends, will, I am sure be pleasing to you and has surpassed my utmost ambition. The King spoke of you to me in terms of so high a confidence, regard, and admiration, and affection; that I cannot forbear mentionning it. I have been the other day invited at the Marechal's de Richelieu, with all the Marechals of France, where your health was drunk with great veneration, and I was requested to present you with the homages of that body. All the young men of this Court are soliciting a permission to go to America. I must tell you that the news about Cardinal de Bernis, was only a rumour propagated in the provinces, and it appears the King means to be his own first Minister.

Madame de Lafayette requests I will present her respectfull and affectionate compliments to you and to Mrs Washington. Vicount de Noailles begs leave to offer his best respects. Be so kind to present mine to Mrs Washington, and my compliments to the family, to George, to my friends in the Army. Adieu, my dear General, however happy in my situation here, I could not have a moment's rest had I not a certainty that nothing is doing in America, that my services could not for the present be of any use to you, and that the Light Compagnies have joined their respective regiments. It is alwaïs pleasing for my heart to repeat the homage of the respect and attachement that make me for ever

Your most affectionate friend
Lafayette

The next time I write to Your Excellency it will be in cyphers and more particular.

[146]

My dear General   Antony March the 30th 1782

The sailing of the Alliance has been so unexpected that Mr. Franklin and myself have not been able to send the dispatches we intended to forward by that opportunity. There is now a French cutter that is pretty suddenly sent of to America—I expected to write by a frigat which is to sail in a short time, but cannot let this opportunity slip a way, before I have the pleasure to remember me to you, and let you hear of my wellfare.

The taking of Mahon has taken place sooner than was generally expected. Gal Murray and Gal Draper are about quarrelling, as generally happens after a misfortune betwen British commanders. The siege of Gibraltar is going on—the capture of S*t* Kitts has been the better felt in England as upon a letter from Sir Samüel Hood the sanguine part of the nation had conceived hopes to preserve this island. Many provinces in Holland are about aknowledging American Independance. There is a great confusion among the Parliamentary Part of the British Nation. Some are of opinion this is a *finesse* of Lord North, who wishes to throw upon Parliament the blame of having given up their Colonies—it has been long said he would retire—but he has hitherto kept his place, and the Opposition Members do not well agree together. However we have just got intelligence that a change of ministers was going to take place.

I have wrote to Mr. Lewingston about 42 [negociations]* of 40 [peace], about 12 [F. money] and about 22 [Spain] and have requested he would communicate my letter to Your Excellency. We must not hope for 13 [Spanish money] nor notwithstanding their compliments for 14 [Dutch money].

As to the ideas you gave me in writing, I have represented them in the strongest light imaginable. I had with 60 [King of France] a long conversation about it. I had many with 61 [F*h* ministers]. They have plans about 26 [West Indies]—they also are stopped by 22 [Spain] and without 10 [Spanish ships]—I am affraid 63 [Brit*h* Fleet] there will somewhat exceed 28 [F*h* ships], or at least be upon a parr—11 [Dutch ships] are not to be retaned—to get 10 [Sp*h* ships] in 19 [America] is the great affair. Without it 71 [maritime superiority] is very difficult, the more so, as they are not stranger to some ideas about 65 [Great Britain] which however appears to me far from being settled. Tho' nothing is fixed upon the afore mentionned points, I am inclined to believe in 47 [Ch*s*Town] more than in 46 [N. York]. For my part I much prefer the former—but am affraid 22 [Spain] will offer obstacles, they alwais are for 26 [W. Indies]. Had I only to manage 61 [F*h* Ministers] it would be a much easier work. I think we may hope for operating in 51 [Septemb*r*].

Many people are of opinion the ennemy mean to evacuate Newyork and Charlestown—for my part I am not to sanguine, and

---
*The words inserted here in brackets have been written above the line in the original in another hand. They are deciphers of the numerals that precede them. By "Lewingston" Lafayette means Robert R. Livingston. (Proper names are identified in the "Index" below.)

245

think it would be a great mistake for us to calculate upon this supposition either in France or in America.

Under the present circumstances, my dear General, those of foreseen 42 [negociations], or at least possible, and the unfixed situation of those I have just now mentioned I think it consistent with your instructions, and perhaps useful to America that I should remain some time in Europe, that I may avail myself of circumstances and opportunities. I hope, my dear General, you will approuve of my conduct. May I flatter myself that an expectation of being useful, having some what detained my departure, I will nevertheless be considered as a candidate for the command of the Light Infantry —a command which is the utmost of my ambition, which will not displease that Corps—and as on the moment I cease to be useful, the moment a determination is taken, I hope sailing for America, I flatter myself the Infantry will not be drawn out before I can present myself among the candidates.

There will be a decision before 44 [May] and one 28 [F^h ships] may carry it immediately for 26 [W. Indies] and an other do same for 19 [America]—I will have no time lost.

In the present situation of affairs, we must, I think, prepare vigourously, and I hope to fulfill your wishes, at least so far as respects 47 [Ch^s Town]

I so perfectly know the sentiments of Congress, and those of the Nation that I am sure not only their desicions upon political points, but also the expression of them will add a new lustre to the idea they have given of their liberality and noble spirit. I am sure, my dear General, that every thing considered, you will find I am much in the right to wait a few weeks, and see what turn affairs are taking. To serve our noble cause is the utmost of my ambition, and I will embrace every measure that may be productive of that end.

I will also add, my dear General, that every thing I write in this letter being the result of the confidence that has been placed in me, I must write for you alone, and this is as confidential as the most secret parts of our correspondance.

Since I left America, I had one letter from you by the Hermione. I am very happy to hear that a spirit of œconomy and arrangement is diffused throughout every departement, and for many reasons I hope we may have a numerous army for the operations of the campaign. I have been for a few days at this country seat with Marquis de Castries who during the Holy days comes to take some respite of ministerial cares. We are united by an intimate friendship, and am happy to find that since he is at the head of the Navy we have had a serie of successes. Had it not been for the storm that Mr de Guichen met with on his leaving Brest, we should not, independant of the Spaniards, have lost an instant of maritime superiority in the West Indias.

Now, my dear General, I will speack to you of my private concerns. Independant of my situation at Court, and among my societies, the marks of affection I every day receive from the people at large, render me as happy as I can possibly be—such influence as I may have will be truly precious to me whenever it can do some little good to our adorable cause. I am perfectly satisfied with the dispositions of this governement. Both nations will for ever be attached to each other—and I see both are so much the object of British envy and treachery that it will ciment among them an eternal amity and alliance.

M^{de} de Lafayette requests I will present to you her most affectionate and respectfull compliments and also to Mrs. Washington whom she most fervently prays to make after the war a voyage to France, and spend some time in our family where we would be so very happy to receive you. Be pleased, my dear General, to remember me most affectionately to the family, and to present my best respects to Mrs. Washington. My compliments wait upon George—I had a letter from him and wish I had received one from my friend Tilmangh—Be so kind my dear General, to pay my most affectionate compliments to Gal Green Gal Knox, and all my friends in the army. I am so hurried this time, that I cannot write to them. When Tilmangh writes to McHenry and Hamilton I beg he will remember me to them. Adieu, my dear General, most respectfully and affectionately, I have the honor to be,

Your tender and for ever your
best friend
Lafayette

Vicount de Noailles, Count de Charlus, Duke de Lauzun and all the officers of your Army request their best respects to be presented to Your Excellency. The officers are about returning to join their respective Corps.

[147]

Antony March the 31st [1782]*

We have certain intelligence, my dear General, that Lord North is out of place. He has himself announced that event in Parliament, and said a new Minister should be named in the course of two or three days. It is generally believed Marquis de Rockingam will replace him. Charles Fox is likely to get into Administration, and there will not be better principles to be found in the new Ministry than in the former—Can those people think that by covering the trap with new leaves they may better take in the people of America?

Having felt the pulse of France, they will do the same with America. I am glad of it, because it will give Congress an opportunity to appear to advantage.

Adieu, my dear General, let me once more tell you that with the highest respect, with all the tenderness and warmth of a heart devoted to you I have the honor to be

Your most obedient servant and for ever affectionate friend
Lafayette.

[148]

Paris April the 12th 1782

My dear general

However sensible I am that our cause may be better served by my presence here than it could possibly be at this period by my returning to America, I cannot refrain from a painfull sentiment at the sight of many French officers who are going to join their colours in America. I shall, thank God, follow them before any thing passes that may have any danger or any importance. But I am so far from the Army, so far from Head Quarters, so far from American intelligences, that however happy I am rendered here, I cannot help ten times a day wishing myself on the other side of the Atlantic.

This letter, my dear general, is intrusted to Count de Segur, the eldest son of the marquis de Segur Minister of State and of the War Department which in France has a great importance. Count

*Unpublished.

de Segur was soon going to have a regiment, but he prefers serving in America, and under your orders. He is one of the most amiable, sensible, and good natured men I ever saw. He is my very intimate friend. I recommend him to you, my dear general, and through you to every body in America particularly in the Army.

A few recruits are going out with this convoy, and will be protected by a frigat. They are destined to fill up the regiments, and prove nothing either for or against any operation in the campaign. Mr Franklin has not been able to procure vessels to take in some stores he has got at Brest. I have requested Marquis de Castries to let us have what he could spare. It will for this time amount to nothing or very little. But he promised me we should have thousand tons in the next convoy. And upon the whole I like it better, as the convoy will sail under a better protection and two months before *49* [July].*

Inclosed I send you, my dear general, the copy of a letter lately writen by a French cutter. I have little to add on one article, but that my expectations are encreasing about *47* [Chs Town]. But *22* [Spain] will insist upon *26* [West Indies]. We expect intelligences about what they mean at last to do in every quarter with *10* [Spanish Ships]. Upon which I will conclude with *60* [King of F] and *61* [Fh Ministers]. I do not forget *12* [Fh Money]. The moment I know better, one of *28* [Fh Ships] will let you have a full account.

The new Ministry have not as yet done any thing of importance. As Holland was about aknowledging independance, England has endeavoured to take a way their attention from it and has proposed peace to them under the mediation of Russia. Nothing as yet is finally settled. I hope we may then get the better of British cabals; I have requested Mr Lewingston to communicate a few words I have writen in cyphers upon poltical subjects.

Admiral Barrington with twelve ships of the line is to go out and his destination has been kept very secret. Some people imagine he is going to take a way the troops from Newyork and Charlestown, which it is not much in their power to reinforce. It is said Lord North was rather glad of an opportunity to leave the helm at so critical a period, and would not have his name affixed to a disadvantageous peace.

*See note on p. 245 above. (Proper names are identified in the "Index" below.)

Mr Laurens is in England upon his parole. I intend writing this day to him by a private opportunity, and will advise him, if possible, to get a permission to go out of Great Britain. I wish he was in France where; if exchanged, he might confer with the other Commissioners upon the affair of peace.

I beg, my dear General, you will present my best respects to Mrs Washington. Mde de Lafayette, your son George, and my daughter join in the most affectionate compliments to you and to her. Remember me, my dear General, most tenderly to the family, and the gentlemen of the Army. Most respectfully I have the honor to be
Your Excellency's most obedient servant and affectionate friend
Lafayette.

[149]

Paris April the 12th 1782*

My dear General,
Permit me to present to your Excellency Prince de Broglie, the eldest son of the Maréchal who is going to serve in the French Army under your orders. I know you admire his father's virtues and abilities. From his great regard for you Marechal de Broglie has insisted to have his son transfered to a regiment that was in North America. Prince de Broglie's personal merit will no doubt also entitle him to your Excellency's notice and affection which I particularly request in his favor.

With the warmest attachment and highest respect I have the honor to be, my dear General,
Your affectionate friend
Lafayette

[150]

St. Germain June the 25th 1782†

My dear General
How it is possible for me to be here at this period you will hardly be able to conceive, and I confess I am myself more and more surprise at the strange delays. Both duty and inclination lead

*Copy in Harvard College Library, Sparks Mss LXXXVIII, Part I. Unpublished.
†Unpublished.

me to America, and tho' it is not probable you are active in the field, yet the possibility of it is to me a torment. But from the moment I engaged in our noble cause, I made it my sole point to sacrifice every thing to its better success. The hope to fix a plan of Campaign has long kept me here, when Count de Grasse's defeat has ruined the schemes of Ministry and my own expectations. I would then have immediately sailed, when negotiations have kept me here, and the American Ministers have declared they wanted my presence in this part of the world. I am myself sensible of it, and know, in case of a treaty, I may better serve our cause, by the situation I am in, with governement, and my knowledge of America, than I could do in any other capacity during an inactive campaign. I therefore have thought, considering your principles and your sentiments, that you will approuve my submitting to remain a fortnight longer in this place, and unless things become more forward than they now promise to be, I hope by the 20th of next month to set sails for America, and to proceed towards head quarters.

The political situation of affairs, and the intelligences we got have been by me communicated to Mr. Lewingston whom I have requested to impart my long letter to your Excellency, and therefore will not trouble you with repetitions.

A few days ago, upon motives which he will account for to the Congress, Mr. Franklin thought proper to grant Lord Cornwallis a conditional exchange—With this I had nothing to do, and much less yet with the exchange of the sailors that had been detained in England. The only business I have meddled with is that of Lord Cornwallis's aides de camp. They represented that Gal Lincoln's aids had been exchanged along with him, that orders had been sent by Lord Shelburne, in consequence of which the British Commander in chief must by this time have proposed their exchange to you for officers of the same rank at your choice, that there was hardly any doubt but what the business was now effect—Under those circumstances, at a time of negotiations for peace, and with the advice of Doctor Franklin I consented to give the inclosed *conditional* discharge†, but did not think it consistent with my duty to go further—I am obliged to Mylord Cornwallis, and wish to treat him well and his aids. But as I know the ideas of Congress and your delicacy upon

†See note on p. 252 below.

the subject, tho' I thought something ought to be done in the present circumstances, I made it a point to act with caution, and I hope Your Excellency will not think I went farther than I ought to have done. *82**[Count de Grasse] has so foolishly taken a way *71* [maritime superiority] that I am at a loss—I hoped *47* [Charles town] would follow *25* [Jamaica] and perhaps *9* [N. Yk. harbᵒ] and *46* [N. York] would have been also tempted—They will send *28†* to *26‡*—The difficulty is to bring *10* [Spanish ships] to *19* [America], and for that we must have had some advantage in *26* [West Indies], and a French Commander in Chief—As I do not think *42* [negociations] will be so forward as some people expect I will be very careful to improve every opportunity to bring on what I think to be useful on the subjets I have just mentioned.§

[151]

Paris June the 29th [1782]¶

Mr. Grenville says, my dear General, that the enabling Bill has past both Houses. How it will be worded, I do not know. We also expect some answer to a few lines Count de Vergennes has given to Mr. Grenville—But I am affraid those people are not sincere.

I had no letter from you this age, my dear General, and as I hope you have wrote some times I guess many of my letters have shared the same fate. I envy the pleasure the gentlemen of the French Army will have on their landing upon the American shore, and feel the more tired of these political concerns, as I am truly vexed not to join the Army and to remain in a city, three thousand miles from you, in the midst of a campaign—I do not believe it will be

*See the note on p. 245 above. (Proper names are identified in the "Index" below.)
†French Ships.
‡West Indies.
§The letter ends here without the usual complimentary close, because, as Washington's endorsement shows it was enclosed with no. 151 below. A copy of the conditional release of Lord Cornwallis which Lafayette had made for Washington (see Gottschalk, *Lafayette and the close of the American Revolution*, pp. 365-66) was enclosed with this letter. The following note in Lafayette's hand is appended to it:
   Such is about the purpose of the piece I have wrote for these gentlemen—it was done with the doctor's advice, and at the bottom of it he expressed his approbation of the measure.
¶Unpublished.

an active one, and yet being at such a distance, I feel an insupportable degree of uneasiness.

I request, my dear General, you will present my best compliments to my friends in the Army. I am truly ashamed to let them be in the field, and to keep at such a distance from them. They will think I am much altered from what they have known me to be, unless you are pleased, my dear General, to let them know that your political people have kept me here for motives of public utility, and that never could I make a greater sacrifice to my zeal for America than when I delay so much my return to the Army where I heartly wish I could be immediately transported.

M^{de} de Lafayette is well, and I hope in the course of some months your God son will have a brother. She requests her best and most affectionate compliments to be presented to you, and my little family, and I do assure you I had much rather be one of them than to love General Washington.

Be pleased, my dear General, to present my most affectionate respects to Mrs. Washington. My best compliments wait upon the family, and I do assure you I had much rather be one of them than be here speaking of the peace of 48, the peace of 63 [British Fleet]*, the bazis and conditions of a treaty, and be busy to distinguish betwen truth and falsehood in a line where cheating is considered as a very clever improvement.

Adieu, my dear General, I hope you will approuve my conduct and in every thing I do I first consider what your opinion would be had I an opportunity to consult it. I anticipate the happiness to be again with you, my dear General, and I hope I need not assuring you that nothing can exceed the sentiments of respect and tenderness I have the honor to be with
                Your most h^{ble} serv and for
                    ever your most devoted affectionate friend
                            Lafayette.

---

*Apparently Washington or a secretary assumed that the figures 48 and 63 were ciphers and could find no decipher for 48. But it is possible, and the context would seem to require, that 48 stands for the date 1748 and 63 for 1763.

AMENDED [152]

My dear General,   Paris September the 1st 1782*

The bearer of my letter, Chevalier de Lambert, a French gentlemen, will do himself the honor to wait upon you, and I beg leave most earnestly to recommend him to your Excellency's kind patronage.—You know, my dear General, I have ever been averse to the introduction of foreigners in our army, and since I am in France I have been deaf to every application of that sort. In the present instance, however, Chev^{er} de Lambert is recommended to me by one to whom I am devoted by every ties of respect and friendship, and yet I could not have brought myself to grant the Comtesse de Tessé's request had I not been made certain that Chev^{er} de Lambert intends to remain in America. So that he may be considered as a countryman, and wholly devotes himself to the service of the United States. I do not wish him to enter into a foreign Corps such as Armand's Legion, but would request his being placed into some of the lines or one of the regiments of Dragoons. I have written to Gal Lincoln on the subject and would be heartly obliged to your Excellency to have him employed by some of the States in their Continental lines as it has been the case with Mr. Marcellin of C^{lel} Stuard's regiment. God grant, my dear General, I may be with you before you get this letter! But at all events permit me once more to present you with the heartly assurance of my respect, gratitude and friendship. Happy in your sentiments for me, as well as those which for ever devote me to you, I shall, to the last moment of my life, glory in the name of your best friend, and nothing can exceed the high regard, the warm affection I have the honor to be with,

My dear General,
Your obedient servant and
devoted friend
Lafayette

[153]

My dear General   Paris October the 14th 1782

Since the time of C^{lel} Gimat's arrival not a line from you has come to my hands, which misfortune I have much lamented, and I do assure you, my dear general, that when I have not the happiness

*Copy in Harvard College Library, Sparks Mss LXXVIII, Part I. Unpublished.

254

to be with you, it is necessary for me to receive some of your letters.

This will be delivered by Gal du Portail and C^lel Gouvion who are returning to America. I wish I could do the same, but you must by this time know that I am kept in this country by the request of American Plenipotentiaries and with a view to be serviceable to our cause which with me shall ever be the first object. Public intelligences will be given to you by General du Portail. Those of a more secret nature I have communicate to the Secretary of Foreign Affairs* whom I have requested to send the letter to Your Excellency. You will be able to form your own opinion upon the situation of affairs, but tho' the forwardness of affairs do not permit me (consistent with the motives I have explained to you) to depart for the present from this country, yet it is my private opinion that a success is necessary before the general treaty can come to a conclusion.

I have requested C^lel Gouvion to tell you, what it is better not to write, about my plans in case of *40* [peace]†, and in case it gives way to ideas in *26* [W. Indies]. The last I consider as the only way to help your views, and as we must if the short road will not do, take the longer to arrive to the same end, I hope Your Excellency will approuve of the measure. In the former case, my former letters have informed you what I had thought I had better to do which, I hope, will also meet your approbation.

M^de de Lafayette begs her most respectfull and affectionate sentiments to be presented to you and to Mrs Washington. She has born during seven month an infant who lately has come to the world at this early period. She proved to be a daughter, and, however delicate, will I hope, be well brought up. I took the liberty to call her by the name of *Virginia.*

Had not Count de Grasse been so unfortunate‡, my voyage would not have been so unsuccessfull. Now I want to find out means, either in peace or war, to retrieve a part of those advantages which I hoped my presence at this court might have produced. M. de Vaudreuil will be of some aid to the trade. Perhaps may he be able to do some thing against Penobscot. But unless he had entered the harbour of Newyork, which I see has not been done, nothing can be performed by him upon an important scale.

*Robert R. Livingston.
†See note on p. 245 above.
‡De Grasse was defeated in the Battle of the Saints (April 12, 1782).

My next letter, my dear general, will better inform you with respect to myself. Should George have a mind, in both cases, to see the country, I would be extremely happy of it, and will be as careful of him as of my own son.

I beg, my dear General, you will present my best respects to Mrs Washington, and affectionate compliments to the family. I hope, my dear General, that my conduct, actuated as it is by principles of public and American utility will have that approbation of yours which I prefer to that of the rest of the world. Adieu, my dear General, let me hear from you, and be assured that you can never be so tenderly loved, so highly respected as by

Your obt svt and friend
Lafayette.

[154]

Paris October 24 1782

My dear General

My last letter has informed you that in case peace is not made, and our plans do not immediately take place at this Court, I would think it consistent with my zeal for our cause, and my obedience to your intentions to take a round about way to serve our military purposes. Under those circumstances, I have accepted to go this winter with Count d'Estaing, but tho' I am to reenter into the French line as a Marechal de Camp from the date of Lord Cornwallis's surrender, I will however keep my American uniform, and the out side as well as the inside of an American soldier. I will conduct matters, and take commands as an officer borrowed from the United States, as it were occasionally, and will watch for the happy moment when I may join our beloved colours.

My seeing 26 [W. Indies]* will I hope bring about and insure the thing we want, or any other you may wish. In seeing 26 [W. Indies] I will have with me 71 [maritime superiority]. A vessel will go to America in a fort night. What I write to you has been given to me under the greatest secrecy, and untill I am at liberty to mention it, I beg it may be for you *alone*. When matters are better settled, I will be more particular; in the mean while you may prepare your orders to me. As there will be private communications, and

*See note on p. 245 above. (Proper names are identified in the "Index" below.)

they might be sent by two ways, I was thinking officers could be dispatched. George wanted to make a voyage—McHenry had the same desire—You know that with me George will be well taken care of. I give those hints before hand. Your Excellency will fully hear from me by the next vessel. I hope 46 [New York] may take place about 45 [June]. What I am doing was the only way.

In a month time we must know if England is willing to make peace, and if it not made shortly after the meeting of Parliament, it is certain that an other campaign becomes necessary. I do not intend to set out before that time.

C^lel Gouvion is not, I suppose, immediately wanting, and I have presumed to think Your Excellency will not be displeased at my keeping him with me.

My best and most affectionate respects wait upon Mrs Washington, and my tenderest compliments upon the family and my other friends. M^de de Lafayette joins with me in presenting you and Mrs Washington with assurances of her love and respect. You know my heart, my dear general, and I need not telling you how respectfully how affectionately I have the honor to be

Your most obed^t h^ble servant
and devoted friend
Lafayette

[155]

Brest December the 4th 1782

Most secret intelligences

My dear general

My former letters have acquainted you that, however talkative were politicians about peace, an expedition was going to take place the command of which is given to Count d'Estaing. I have also added that upon being requested to go, I have willingly accepted of it, as I thought it the means, the only means in the world to bring about what you have directed me to obtain. C^lel Gouvion must be with you, and I refer you, my dear general, to the letter I wrote by him, as well as to some notes I write to him as I have a full cypher with that gentleman. 26 [W. Indies]* is the first object. 22 [Spain] in the way. We have got here 9 ships of the line to set out with the

*See note on p. 245 above.

257

first fair wind. Your Excellency knows that Count d'Estaing is gone to Spain. We shall have *11* [maritime superiority]—Please to prepare propositions and notions about *46* [N Yk], *47* [Ch^sT], *3* [Penobscot], *2* [New F^dL^d]. One *28* [F^h Ship] is to be sent to *19* [Am.], and then by your orders to *26* [W. Inds.]—I shall write the next opportunity.

Inclosed, my dear General, I have the honor to send you the copy of a letter to Congress. I hope you will be able to tell them you are satisfied with my conduct. Indeed, my dear general, it is necessary to my happiness you will think so. When you are absent, I endeavour to do the thing which you seem likely to have advised had you been present. I love you too much to be one minute easy unless I think you approuve of my conduct.

Peace is much talked of. I think, *betwen* us, much of the difficulty must lay with the Spaniards. And yet I do not think the ennemy are very sincere. They have been heaping chicanes and finesses upon the affair of limits for America, and so on. It is my opinion that, in the bottom of their hearts, they are determined, if they can, to try what turn next campaign will give to their affairs and God grant we may make it a vigorous one, particularly about *46* [New York].

I have arrived here but yesterday morning. I have much of public business upon my hands. So that in requesting my best respects to be presented to Mrs Washington, and my compliments to the family, George and my friends in the Army I will only add the expression of the most tender and gratefull respect I have the honor to be with, my dear General

Your ob^t serv and aff^{ate} friend
Lafayette

⚜ 1783 ⚜

[156]
Cadix, February the 5th 1783

My dear General

Were you but such a man as Julius Cæsar or the King of Prussia, I should almost be sorry for you at the end of the great tragedy where you are acting such a part. But with my dear General I rejoice at the blessings of a peace where our noble ends have been secured. Remember our Valley Forge times, and from a recollection of past dangers and labours, we still will be more pleased at our present comfortable situation—What a sense of pride and satisfaction I feel when I think of the times that have determined my engaging in the American cause! As for you, my dear General, who truly can say you have done all this, what must your virtuous and good heart feel on the happy instant where the Revolution you have made is now firmly established—I cannot but envy the happiness of my grand children when they will be about celebrating and worshipping your name. To have had one of their ancestors among your soldiers, to know he had the good fortune to be the friend of your heart, will be the eternal honour in which they shall glory—and to the eldest of them, as long as my posterity will last, I shall delegate the favour you have been pleased to confer upon my son George.

At the prospect of a peace, I had prepared to go to America—you know me too well, my dear General, not to be sensible of the pleasure I anticipated in the hope to embrace you, and to be reunited with my fellow soldiers. Never did any thing please me so much as the delightfull prospect I had before me—But on a sudden I have been obliged to differ my darling plan, and as I have at last been blessed with a letter of yours, I know you approuve of my lengthtening my furlough upon political accounts—the enclosed copy of a letter to Congress, and my official letter to Mr. Lewingston which I request him to communicate to you, will fully inform you of the reasons that urge me to post off to Madrid*—From there, it will be better for me to go to Paris and in the month of June, I will embark for America. Happy, ten times happy will I be in embracing my dear General, my father, my best friend whom I love with an affection and a respect which I too well feel, not to know it is impossible for me to express it.

In my letters to Congress, you will also see that, independant of the plans I had been permitted to propose to you, in the execution of which we were to have an immense Naval and Land force, it had been at last obtained I should enter Canada. I had my hopes to embrace you at Mont Real, or at least to be met there by a detachment from the Army. The necessity of a division was the ground upon which we had obtained the King of Spain's consent. But now those schemes are over, and we must rejoice at the happiness of those you have rescued from the hands of British tyranny.

Now, my dear General, that you are going to enjoy some ease and quiet, permit me to propose a plan to you which might become greatly beneficial to the Black Part of Mankind. Let us unite in purchasing a small estate where we may try the experiment to free the Negroes, and use them only as tenants—such an exemple as yours might render it a general practice, and if we succeed in America, I will chearfully devote a part of my time to render the method fascionable in the West Indies. If it be a wild scheme, I had rather be mad that way, than to be thought wise on the other tack.

I am so anxious to hear from you, my dear General, and to let you hear from me that I have sent my own servant with a vessel upon whom I have prevailed to set him a shore on the Maryland Coast. Before I leave France, I hope I will receive your answers, and I will be directed where to find you on my arrival. Upon that intelligence I depend to regulate my course, and if you are at home I shall steer for the Bay of Chesepeake.

*William Carmichael, American chargé d'affaires at Madrid, was unable to win recognition from the Spanish court, and Lafayette hoped to be helpful in that regard. See Gottschalk, *Lafayette and the close of the American Revolution*, pp. 397, 401 and 406.

Independant of my public letter to M Lewingston, there is a private one which he will also communicate. Amongs the many favors I have received, I would take it as a most flattering circumstance in my life to be sent to England with the ratification of the American treaty—you know it is but an honorary commission, that would require the attendance of a few weeks, and if any sedentary Minister is sent, I would have the pleasure of introducing him—This, my dear General, is entirely confidential.

Your influence, my dear General, cannot be better employed than in inducing the people of America to strenghten their fœderal Union—it is a work in which it behoves you to be concerned—I look upon it as a necessary measure—Depend upon it, my dear General, that European politics will be apt to create divisions among the States. Now is the time when the powers of Congress must be fixed, the boundaries determined, and Articles of Confederation revised—It is a work in which every well wisher to America must desire to be concerned—It is the finishing stroke that is wanting to the perfection to the Temple of Liberty.

As to the Army, my dear General, what will be its fate? I hope their country will be gratefull—Should the reverse be the case, I would indeed feel very unhappy. Will part of the Army be kept together? If not, I hope we won't forfeit our noble titles of officers and soldiers in the American Army, so that in case of danger we may be called upon from every quarter, and reunite in the defence of a country which the Army has so effectually, so heroically served —I long to know what measures will be taken—Indeed, my dear General, I depend upon your goodness for a very minuted letter, not only on public accounts, but also because I want to be acquainted with every one of your personal concerns.

Adieu, adieu, my dear General, had the Spaniards got common sense I could have dispensed with that cursed trip to Madrid. But, I am called upon, by a sense of my duty to America—I must go, and the differ* the happy voyage. My best, most affectionate respects wait upon Mrs. Washington. Now we are going to quarell, for I must urge your returning with me to France. Her accompagning you there, is the best way I know off to compromise the matter, and so she will make M^{de} de Lafayette and me perfectly happy.

*Probably Lafayette meant *thus defer*.

I request Your Excellency will please to present my compliments to Tilmangh, George, and all the family—Remember me to all my friends in the Army—I am so hurried in sending the vessel a way that I will write to them by other opportunities. They know my love to them, and I have a grateful sense of their friendship. Be so kind my dear General, to remember me to your much respected mother. Her happiness I heartily partake. Adieu, once more, my dear General, with every sentiment of love and respect I am for ever,

Your most devoted and affectionate friend
Lafayette

[157]

Bordeaux March the second 1783.*

My dear General

On the 5 Ult I had the honor to write you a letter, and as Count d'Estaing was pleased to let me have a vessel to carry it, I am not without my hopes to have given you the tidings of a general peace—I also have informed you that upon my going to sail for America, I had received a letter from Mr Carmichael entreating my immediate assistance at Madrid. I therefore gave up my darling plan, and went to the Spanish Court—There I met with repugances and prejudices. I was by turns pressing and haughty, I took care to engage them, and yet not to engage America, and I acted in the most private capacity—After a week's stay and exertions, it came out that Carmichael was received as Chargé d'affaires from the United States and that some hints were given up, some others debated, and a letter made up by me wherein I collect the best constructions I could put upon what they said, and make them take in writing some engagements—As to the United States, I had nothing to say in their names. I send to Congress an Account of what has past, and from obvious motives, in doing the public good, I take care not to interfere with Mr Jay's personal concerns. But, betwen us, I think my journey has not been amiss—I was happy in finding in Madrid my friend Carmichael the first American I ever knew.

Now, my dear General, I am going to Paris, and will stay two months with my family. About that time I expect an answer to my letters by the Triumph, and you know what my wishes are—In case

*Unpublished.

Congress has no command for me, I shall embark, and at all events I will embrace my dear General before the summer is at an end.

It is reported here that Lord Shelburne has resigned and has been replaced by Lord North, but I have no certainty—An American [vessel?] has already displayed our flag before the City of London. On my arrival at Paris, my dear General, I will write to you—For the present I am on my way and just snatch the moment to give Congress and you an account of my conduct. I hope it will met with your approbation, for your approbation, next to your friendship, is necessary to me. I long for the moment when your long wandering soldier will join you again. I hope you think I am right in my delays which were of a public utility.

My best most affectionate respects wait on Mrs. Washington. Remember me most friendly to Tilmangh, George, all the family, and all my friends. Adieu, my dear General, they urge me to finish this letter, and I have only time to tell you once more how respectfully and tenderly I shall ever be

Your most devoted and most affectionate friend
Lafayette

[158]

My dear General   Paris May the 18th 1783*

As there is no knowing when this letter may reach you, I shall content myself with the introduction of Mr. de Venkersky† a Polander whom I often have met in several societies. He is a sensible man, of good family, and, I think, some what deranged in his monney concerns. This is all I know of him, but upon his earnest application, could not deny him the happiness to be presented to General Washington. There is with him a young French gentlemen, named Mr de Fontenille, whose family I am a little acquainted with.

Be pleased, my dear General, to present my best respects to Mrs Washington, and I need not telling you how respectfully how affectionetly I have the honor to be   Your devoted friend
Lafayette

---

*Unpublished. We have been unable to find Lafayette's letter of April 19, 1783, mentioned in Washington's letter to Lafayette, October 12, 1783, Fitzpatrick, *Writings of Washington*, XXVII, 186.

†Washington calls this gentleman Count Wengiersky: *ibid.*, pp. 181 and 186. (Proper names are identified in the "Index" below.)

Paris June the 10th 1783*

My dear General,

Having received no answer to my letter by the Triumph, I may I think, flatter myself before long to hear from you, and I confess I am waiting with great impatience. It is an age my dear General, since I had a line from you, and I have been so happily used to our intimate communications that is very hard to me, not to know any thing of your ideas, your concerns, and your sentiments on every occasion. God grant I may soon have that long wished for letter. Upon its contents, my motions will be determined, and unless my presence here is ordered by Congress, I hope I may soon be reunited to my dear General. Having fully explained myself in my letter by the Triumph, I have thought it useless to repeat my ideas in the subsequent ones, and these lines are only intended to present Doctor Bancroft† who is going by way of England to Philadelphia. I have long known him, first of all in England and afterwards in France where he ever appeared to me a sensible and a warm friend to our cause. Agreable to that party spirit, which to my great concern has ever divided our ministers or envoys in Europe, Doctor Bancroft has been praised by some and criticised by others. But I owe him the justice to say that his public opinions, and his conduct have always appeared to me such as becomes a citizen of the United States.

Your God son, my dear General, is now under inoculation that piece of intelligence, tho' it is not very important is the only one I will give, for this letter will be long on its way and I intend taking speedier opportunities. We are going to have a change in the Ministry and I fancy M^{quis} de Castries will soon resign. The destruction of the Ottoman Empire seems to have been determined upon by Russia and the Emperor. L'Orient has been made a free port for the American trade and I think is very advantageous. When I am writing to you my dear General, I don't know well how to stop, but when I reflect this letter will be so long on the road, I must content myself with presenting my most affectionate respects to Mrs. Washington, my tender compliments to my friends, and to repeat you

---

*Copy in Harvard College Library, Sparks Mss LXXXVIII, Part I. Unpublished.

†On Lafayette's misjudgment of Bancroft, see Gottschalk, *Lafayette and the close of the American Revolution*, p. 19.

my dear General, that every sentiment of filial love, respect and gratitude make me for ever

Your devoted friend
Lafayette

Mme de Lafayette and our little family present their respects to you and Mrs. Washington

[160]

Paris June the 12th 1783*

My dear General

Give me leave to present to you Mr de Beaune a French officer whom respectable persons have so much recommended that I could not deny him this letter of introduction. He is well spoken of, and wishes to improve himself so as to become proper for a consulship in America.

We are anxiously waiting for letters from the Continent and independant of public concerns, letters from my dear General become quite necessary to

his most affectionate, filial, and
respectfull friend,
Lafayette

My best respects wait upon Mrs Washington, and to her and to you my wife and children beg to be respectfully remembered.

[161]

Chavaniac in the Province of Auvergne
July the 22d 1783

My dear General

Your letter of the 10th of May is the last one that came into my hands for which I beg leave to offer you my best thanks, and in case former answers do not arrive, I must again tell you how happy you made your friend by your letters inclosing the proceedings of the Army. In every instance, my dear General, I have the satisfaction to love and to admire you. The conduct you had on that occasion was highly praised throughout all Europe, and your returning to a private station is called the finishing stroke to an unparalleled char-

*Unpublished.

acter. Never did a man exist who so honourably stood in the opinions of mankind, and your name, if possible, will become still greater in posterity. Every thing that is great, and every thing that is good were not hitherto united in one man. Never did one man live whom the soldier, State's man, patriot, and philosopher could equally admire, and never was a Revolution brought about that in its motives, its conduct, and its consequences could so well immortalize its glorious Chief. I am proud of you, my dear General, your glory makes me feel as if it was my own, and while the world is gaping at you, I am pleased to think, and to tell, the qualities of your heart do render you still more valuable than any thing you have done.

Since my last, my dear General, I have received letters from Congress, wherein I am directed to attend to a particular business respecting the payement of debts to Great Britain. I have immediately applied to Count de Vergennes, and will endeavour if not too late, to succeed in that important affair. I have also writen to our American Ministers, and upon that point have sollicited their confidence. Had they spoken to me at the time of the separate preliminaries, the matter would have been arranged to mutual satisfactions—It often happens people do not understand each other, and should they be brought to right again, they hardly could be able to find out a cause of complaint—It some times is the case every where, and some in the Commission have strong prejudices. But it would be improper for me to give more than private hints. My heart is so oppen to you, my dear General, that from you it is impossible for me to conceal any thought.

Nothing new in Europe, but what relates to the Russians and Turks—The first have invaded the Krimée, preparations are making upon the Black Sea, and Russian ships are coming round to the Meditarrean. The expulsion of the Turks from Europe has ever been with Russia a favorite scheme—It appears very improbable to me, that we may compromise matters, in which case, an attempt to that revolution would only be differed. What part the Emperor will take, is as yet very uncertain, nor it is known what Prussia will do about it. England is to be sure, determined to stay neutral, and has not much to do with Levant trade. As to France, she does not wish to quarrel with any body. Her desire is to prevent a Russian war, and it appears she will not do more, but what is absolutely necessary. Such, my dear General, is my private opinion of political affairs in Europe.

It had been said M^{al} de Castries would resign, but now for certain he remains in the Ministry. There have been new disturbances in the British Cabinet. The definitive treaty is not yet at an end. Its termination, the affair recommended to me, the arrival of the Triumph, and our political situation will determine the happy time when I set sails for America—In the course of a fort night, my dear General, I hope to be able to write you very fully. But hearing of an opportunity could not let it pass unnoticed. God grant, I may, instead of writing be enabled to come myself. Adieu, my dear General, Mde de Lafayette joins with me in presenting our best respects to Mrs. Washington. She loves you with all her heart. My affectionate compliments wait upon the family, George, and all our friends. Adieu, Adieu, my dear General, do often remember your adopted son, who with every sentiment of the highest respect and warmest affection has the honour to be

Your ob^t h^{ble} servant and most affectionate friend
Lafayette

[162]

My dear General   Nancy September the 8th 1783*

Your wished for and most heartly wellcome favours have not this long while reached me, and I most warmly request you, my dear General, not to forget writing to a friend who loves you with a filial and unbounded affection. This letter is going by the September packet, and hereafter there will be one sailing every month, by which, while in Europe, I shall most exactly adress my dear and respected General. Along with my dispatches, you will receive the definitive treaty. Since I have returned from Spain (which affair by the bye has been too much neglected) I was not much consulted upon politics by the Commissionners—What I know of the subject is, that after many earnest, and long deluded hopes to get much from England in definitive and commercial arrangements, the last answer has been that the preliminary articles were sufficient to make up a definitive treaty.

Inclosed, my dear General, you will find a copy of my letter

*Unpublished.

to Congress whereby you may judge both of the political situation of affairs, and of the mercantile American concerns that for the present detain me in Europe. As to the first, my private opinion is that a war betwen Russians and Turks is unavoidable—that the Emperor will take a part in it, and that much depends upon the King's of Prussia determination to become either an opponent or partaker to the division of the Ottoman European provinces. As to France, the revolution cannot but greatly hurt her trade, but if she can help it she will not middle with those wars. England is much embarassed in her finances, but tho' she may loose a little, will rejoice at every event which affects France with a greater loss. Such at least, is my private opinion in this affair.

As to the American trade, it has been represented that my presence here might serve the United States, and to me, that consideration shall ever be a determining one. I hope my dear General will approuve my conduct, which approbation, I confess, in every instance will ever prove necessary to my happiness and self satisfaction. But I grieve to be so long from you, such a distance, such an interval of time cannot agree with the tender feelings of a heart who had taken the happy habit to live in your family, among my American friends, who, in any part of the world, never felt himself so much at home, as when he was at Head Quarters. Untill I return to America, my dear General, untill I see you and our fellow supporters of our noble cause, my mind cannot be properly easy, and every mention, every rememberance of America makes me sigh for the moment when I may enjoy the sight of our free and independant shores.

Many months ago, my dear General, I did myself the honour to write you on the subject of the bust the Assembly of Virginia have voted. Not knowing if my thanks ever reached them, but knowing you have mentionned them my uncertainty, I don't think I can do any thing further on the subject, as it would not become me to send to the Assembly House (and to keep for me a copy of) the bust which they have been pleased to adorn with honourable inscriptions—so that I imagine some Minister here will be charged with the direction of that monument of their satisfaction, which, I confess, fills my heart with a pleasing sense of pride and gratitude.

From my letters to Congress you will see I am asking for their orders. While in Europe, I think I may serve them in the way of information and advice—the more so, if they confine themselves to the sending of Consuls. I may also on other accounts prove useful, but I must anew receive direct orders from them to that purpose. Never shall I more glory, and better enjoy myself than in the title of an essential servant to the United States.

By the next packet, my dear General, I will tell you what commercial arrangements have taken place, and also what are my own motions. But should I receive the least hint, or see myself that, by the situation of affairs, every good man's influence is wanting upon the spot, then, my dear General, no public affair (for my own are out of the question) no season of the year, no impediment in the world can prevent my flying to a beloved country whose happiness, glory, and liberty, are dearer to me than my own life.

Your circular letter, my dear General, as well as your modest retirement have had the universal applause of Europe, and my heart has been a partaker in the glory of my dear General from whom every thing that is great and good so naturally flows that it gives a good grace to his heroic actions. Should you think of coming to Europe, of seeing a country where your name is adored, I need not tell you what unexpressible happiness I would feel in receiving you under my roof, in making my house yours, as yours has been and for ever I hope will be mine, and I flatter myself I would know it timely enough not to embark myself in any journey, or voyage to America, that might prevent the happiness I would derive from your friendly, and thousand times wellcome visit.

Mde de Lafayette and my three children are well and all the family join in their respectfull and affectionate compliments to you and Mrs. Washington whom I beg you will present with my most tender respects. Tell her she ought to pay us a visit along with you, and to come in compagny with her grand children. My affectionate compliments wait upon George, all the family, and all our friends— Please to remember me to Mr. and Mrs. Lund Washington and to the young lady.*

It is said in England your retirement is owing to ambitious wiews, and that you intend soon to appear again upon the stage.

---

*Apparently Eleanor Calvert Custis, widow of Mrs. Washington's son, John Parke Custis.

Adieu, my dear general, my heart is so well known to you that I need not telling you how tenderly how respectfully I shall ever be untill my last breath, my dear General

Your most obedient humble servant and most obliged affectionate friend
Lafayette

Our ideas respecting the Fœderal Union and the Army so much coincide with each other, that nothing needs being said betwen us upon those important matters.

[163]

Paris November the 11th 1783

My dear General

However scarce are American letters, yet as the eyes of the world are fixed upon you, I now and then hear what becomes of my dear General. Your visit to Congress, your stay with the Army untill the treaty arrives, your having been voted a statue, are events which are known to every one, and felt by me, so that what to Europe is an information, to me proves to be a cause for the most tender emotions. But now, my dear General, that you are enjoying the sweets of retirement, I hope your absent friend will be some what benefited by it, and your letters cannot but be more numerous than it was possible to have them in your busy times. The convenience of those packets is peculiarly precious to me, and I earnestly beg you will every time enable me to bless the opportunity.

The gazette I have to present, my dear General, is not very interesting—Ottoman disputes appear for a while to be at an end—Russia will keep what she has got—The Emperor stands ready, but will not move for the present—As to the Turks, lucky they are not to be attacked, for their armies cut a bad figure—The King of Prussia is quarrelling with Dantzick that he may have an opportunity to take hold of that city—Spain has made a ridiculous bombardement of Alger, for which every body, and the Algerians too have laughed at her—France is exerting herself to preserve good harmony in the east ward, and for the present Count de Vergennes seems to have well succeeded—As to England, she is much engaged in disputes with Ireland, and very jealous of the Irish Volonteer Assossiation.

M. d'Ormesson the French financier is out of place, and in lieu of him a M. de Calonne has been named—The queen was lately pregnant, but has had a miscarriage—such are the present news at the Court of France—

My last letter from America is dated August the 20th—The place of residence for Congress has not been yet fixed upon—I hope, my dear General, your letter to the States will have a good effect—The more I think of it, the more I examine European Notions, the better am I convinced that American glory, consequence, wealth, and liberty depend upon a tight well framed Fœderal Union—At the same time, it is to be hoped our virtous Army will not meet with ungratefull proceedings—Every honest breast, unless greatly misled, must be shocked at the idea. I am very impatient to hear what has been done—In the mean while, I am collecting the opinions of every American merchant within my reach, and my exertions are bent upon representing what may be most advantageous in mercantile regulations—for tho' one cannot hope for a compleat success, yet it pleases one to think that some good measures may be influenced by a proper representation—This Governement are well disposed to America, and it is far from being the case with the Ministers of Great Britain.

Mr Jay, Mr Adams, and Mr Laurens are in England—Many English gentlemen have been flocking to Paris, some of them eminent characters—and by some I have been told that it was reported in England I would be sent with the definitive ratification—a rumour for which I cannot account.

I am waiting for letters from you, for orders from Congress—It is also the case with the Commissionners—Untill dispatches arrive, we cannot know our fate—but nothing in the world can prevent my going in a little time—As you know what has been writen to me, you can better judge what I will do—but it is at least certain I shall in a few months embrace my dear General, spend with him the spring and summer, and most earnestly entreat him to let me accompagny him to France where his presence will excite the most enthusiastic and affectionate transports—Don't be angry with me, Madam, for you must come too, take along the young girls, and then all will be perfectly right.

Oh that I were at Mount Vernon, by the side of my dear General, reminding him of his past labours, and their glorious happy conclusion! It melts my heart, only to think of it—I feel uneasy—and what I want I know to be a voyage to the free, the beloved shores of our America—Mde de Lafayette, my three children are presented to you with the most tender homage to yourself and Mrs. Washington—Your George is in perfect health.

My best respects, my most tender compliments wait upon Mrs. Washington—Be so kind, my dear General, to remember me to the inhabitants of Mount Vernon—to George to the family of Hdqrs—to all my friends—Adieu, adieu, my dear general, it is not without emotion that I present you with the affectionate respects of yr obt hble serv

Lafayette.

[164]

My dear General   Paris November the 29th 1783*

This letter will be delivered by M. de Sailly who is going over to America, and intends establishing forges of which he is a Master—Upon his application for a letter to you, I the more willingly have granted it, as there may be proper materials about Mount Vernon, and I know Your Excellency will be disposed to encourage M. de Sailly's plans for the improvement of the mines in Virginia.

With the most tender sentiments of that affection and respect which for ever devote me to my dear General I have the honour to be
Your Excellency's
Most obedient servant and most loving friend

Lafayette

My best respects wait upon Mrs. Washington.

AMENDED   [165]

Sir   Paris Dec. the 25th 1783.†

On the receipt of Your Excellency's letter, I took measures to fulfill the intentions of the Society in which I have the honor to be a Member.

*Unpublished. (Proper names are identified in the "Index" below.)
†This is not in Lafayette's handwriting. It is endorsed by Washington: "Extract of a letter from the Marq. de la Fayette to G. Washington 25th Dec. 1784 [sic]." Enclosed with this letter was a translation of a report on the Cincinnati which is endorsed in Washington's hand: "Translation taken from the Paris Gazette which was sent by the Marq de la Fayette 23d Decr 1783." The passage is quoted in full from the *Gazette de France* in E. E. Hume (ed.), *General Washington's correspondence concerning the Society of the Cincinnati* (Baltimore, 1941), pp. 34-35.

As our institution was differently interpreted I wrote a letter to Count de Vergennes of which the inclosed is a copy, and the account I gave was printed in a Court Gazette which I have also the honor to send—At a Kings Council, this day was a week, it has been decided that Count de Rochambeau, his Generals, and Colonels, and also the Admirals should be permitted to wear the order, and a very proper letter upon the subject has been written by Marechal de Segur to M. de Rochambeau.

As to our American officers, I shall examine into the claims of every one when the point is clear, deliver or refuse the order, and in doubtfull cases take the advise of a Board of American Officers Members in the Society.

No foreign Badge but the golden fleece is permitted to French men in this Service. From the distinction shown to our Society and the testimony it bears of having acted a part in this war, our Badge is highly wished and warmly contended for by all those who hope they have some claim to it. The Nation have been very much pleased with the attention our Society has paid to the Alliance, and have found their is something very interesting in that Brotherly Association.

*Major Lenfant is employed in the execution of your orders—A good number of Eagles will be made in twelve days, when I intend to call for the few American officers now here, and together to wait upon the Generals and Admirals of the French Army with the marks of the order.

---

*The passage which follows is not given in the version of this letter contained in Hume, *Washington's correspondence concerning the Cincinnati*, pp. 37-38. Instead, the following (apparently concluding) paragraphs are given:

    Objections are made as in the case of every novelty. The hereditary part of the Institution has its comments, but the general voice is in favor of our Brotherly Society, and General Washington's name as President adds a weight to the Association.

    With the highest and most affectionate respect, I have the honor to be, my dear general,

                  Your obedient humble servant,

                                        La Fayette

❧ 1784 ❧

[166]

Paris January the 10th 1784*

My dear General

The departure of the Washington has been so sudden that I could not get in time on board the particular letter which you ought to have received—so that my correspondance has been confined to an official Cincinnati letter, and a bill of plated wares, which was not by any means my intention—Inclosed I send you a duplicate of the letter respecting our Association—Major L'enfant tells me a tolerable number of Eagles will be made on Thursday, when after having called together the American officers now here, and examined their claims to the marks of the institution, we shall in a body, and with the American regiments wait upon Count de Rochambeau, and the Admirals of the French troops, and present them with the Badges they are to wear—You will receive many applications on that subject, and I need not telling you old Rochambeau wants to be as conspicuous as he can in that, as you know he does in every other affair—but as nothing can be decided before the month of May I will timely write, and I hope I will myself tell you my opinions in the several instances that will be submitted to you—In case the Badge is multiplied, it will loose its price in Europe—and yet, there are some instances who are entitled to regard.

By our last accounts from America, my dear General, we hear that Newyork is evacuated, and that our Army, our virtous and brave army, now are disbanded—Its dissolution, however expected and proper it is, has not been heard of by me without a sigh—How

*Unpublished.

happy I have been at the Head quarters of that Army! How affectionately received in every tent I had a mind to visit! My most fortunate days have been spent with that Army—and now that it is no more, my heart shall ever reverence and cherish its memory—God grant our brother officers may be treated as they deserve! Will not the country remember what evils that army have guarded her against, what blessings they have insured to them? I am told there is a peace establishement of 800 men—and my dear General now is at Mount Vernon where he enjoys those titles every heart gives him, as the Saviour of his Country, the Benefactor of Mankind, the Protecting Angel of Liberty, the pride of America, and the admiration of the two hemispheres—and among all those enjoyements I know he will most tenderly feel the pleasure of embracing his best his bosom friend, his adopted son, who early in the spring will be blessed with a direct course to the beloved landing that leads to the house at Mount Vernon.

There are no great news in France, but it is not the case in England whose people seem as it were distracted—Pitt's party have for the moment got in place, but the majority in the Commons are so much against them that it is impossible for them to remain in the Ministry—It is probable we will in a few days see Mr. Fox and Lord North restored to their former power, when they will undo every thing the others have done—Mrs. Jay, Adams, and Laurens are either at London or Bath, Mr. Barklay is in England, and our old friend Doctor Franklin is confined to his house by the gravel—Under those circumstances I thought it my duty not to neglect the affairs of America—but as I have no instructions, nor any public authority, I can only advise and influence such preparatory measures, as I thing may be agreable to the United States—Some time ago I presented a memorial, which, together with some letters from the Ministers I have on the 26th of last month enclosed to Mr. Moriss—In consequence of those, and of several conferences I had with the Ministers, they have determined to put a final hand to the affair of L'Orient, which I had long ago taken upon myself to begin, and which wanted a definitive conclusion—By a letter of this day to Mr. Moriss I send him some further parts of a correspondance with the Ministry, wherein it is officially announced that Dunkirk, L'Orient, Bayonne, and Marseilles are the four free ports given to the trade of America—This evening I return to Versailles, where there is to be a conference betwen the foreign affairs, naval, and finances Ministers and myself—As I am little acquainted with those matters, I consult upon them with Wadsworth—In all this America neither promises nor asks for any thing, so that she cannot be committed—and her ministers being either sick or abroad, do not, *betwen us*, so much as to mention an earnest word of the Mercantile interest of America in France. European affairs are about the same as when I wrote you last—there is no probability of an impending war—at least for next year—The Emperor is in Italy as a traveller—Unless I am honoured with some particular commands from Congress, I intend embarking for America early in the spring, and I hope to arrive in time for the grand Cincinnati meeting—M^{de} de Lafayette, your son George, and my daughters join in the most respectfull compliments to you, and Mrs. Washington—I give her joy upon your peacefull retirement into private life—I beg, my dear General, you will remember me to George, Mead, Mr. and Mrs. Lund Washington, to all your friends and relations—Adieu, my dear General,

Your most respectfull and affec friend
Lafayette

AMENDED [167]

Sir,   Paris, March 9, 1784*

Your Excellency has been acquainted with my first measures respecting our Society. To my letter of Xber [December] the 25th I beg leave particularly to refer and entrust this with Major L'Enfant who is returning to America.

Having in a body waited upon Count de Rochambeau we delivered him and his officers the marks of the Association. A resolve of theirs for a voluntary subscription will arrive in time to be debated in the Grand Assembly.

Many claims have been raised by French officers, which is not my business to present. But I beg leave to observe that some of them, like in Chevalier de Lameth's case, are entitled to consideration. Count de Rochambeau, I am told, is writing on the subject.

Former dispatches have apologized for the part we have taken respecting Count d'Estaing's officers; the neglect we know was not

*Hume, *Washington's correspondence concerning the Cincinnati*, pp. 107-8.

intended, and, as also in M. de Vaudreuil's case it would have produce a bad effect. The Captains in the navy, ranking as Colonels, have set up a claim to the Association. Some of them, Lapeyrouse, la Touche, Tilly, acted as Commodores. It might be observed that American trade will have to do with naval officers.

As a Board of officers met at my house, the claims of several gentlemen were introduced. Our opinions are submitted to the Assembly, and with them I inclose a list of members who have signed and paid, or to whom on account of their dispositions the instructions are as yet to be sent (etc). Count du Plessis convinced us that he had not resigned.

Our brotherly association has met with general applause—not a dissenting voice to be heard, but in the point of heredity, that creates a debate wherein most of the Americans take the other part. Who can question but what we do not in any account wish to injure those sacred republican principles for which we have fought, bled, and conquered, and what sacrifice has not been made by us, in support of those principles? Which I am sure we are ready to repeat upon every occasion.

It had been my fond hope that I could have arrived in time for the beginning of May. But American claims, an account of which I gave to Congress, detain me for a few weeks. And now when I think this letter will be read among the representatives from all the lines of the Army, my heart is glowing with all the most unbounded sentiments of affection and gratitude. How pleasing it is for me to recollect our common toils, dangers, turns of fortune, our so glorious successes, and that lively attachment which united us with each other under our beloved General. Never can my heart forget the return of affection I have particularly obtained, the numberless obligations I am under my dear brother officers, and the happy hours, the happiest in my life, which I have pass [sic] in their company. Before the month of June is over, I shall, thank God, be again with them, and am impatient for the instant when I may be blessed with a sight of the American shore.

With the highest respect and unbounded affection, I have the honor to be, Sir, Your Excellency's

Most obedient humble servant,
La Fayette

[168]

Paris March the 9th 1784*

Private

My dear General
 Mr. du Bouchet formerly a major in our service having presented me with his claims to our Assossiation, I found myself obliged to tell him that his pretentions were groundless—So far was he convinced of it, that he did not think it proper to apply to our Committee, but has determined upon going himself to America—I candidly represented him that there was a good share of madness in his plan, and that a refusal will set him in a very disagreeable situation—I hoped he was converted when on a sudden I hear he now takes up again his resolution—and after I have done my best to discourage him I cannot refuse him this introductory letter to you, least it might be thought the silence of the Committee is owing to particular motives—Indeed, Mr. du Bouchet's zeal is great, and we cannot but be sensible of his wishes to become a member of the Society—He is as eager a Cincinnatus as he has been a rifleman in the Northern Army.
 With the highest respect and tenderest affection I have the honour to be
My dear General
Your obedient humble servant
Lafayette

AMENDED   [169]

Paris March the 9th 1784

My dear General
 Altho' I write you an other private letter, I must confidentially let you know my opinion upon matters relative to the Society.
 The Captains in the Navy have been much mortified to be left out in the Institutions—they rank as Colonels, they have rendered great services, and it is expected here they will be admitted into the Society—Some of them came with Count D'Estaing, among whom are Suffrein, D'Albert de Rion, and such other great characters—

*Unpublished.

The remainder went under Ternay, Destouches, and Grasse—a few have been sent to carry great news such as the Treaty, or have actually Commanded in Chief, such as La Peyrouse, La Touche—I know they are many, but how can a partial distinction be made—and as they will have much to do with American vessels, in preventing contraband trade, I suppose, or in receiving American Ships into French Harbours, I think it will be impolitic not to put them in a good humour—In the opinion I give, I oppose my own interest, for the less members there will be in the Society, the more it is valued—But I see a substantial public motive to be determined upon, and as the *Capitaines de Vaisseaux* are dispersed throughout the harbours, they will not so much crowd as land officers, because they very seldom come to the Capital—M. *D'Albert de Rion*, La Touche, La Peyrouse, Tilly cannot but have it, and I think it should be general.

As to the land officers many claims have been raised—some of them, I think, deserve consideration—M. de L'estrade, M. de Menonville, such, in a word, as particular reasons may be assigned for, ought to be included—*Above all the Chevalier de Lameth* who has been so cruelly wounded in the Redoubt, who was an aid de Camp, and two months after was a Colonel—I think we must avoid giving grounds of complaint—Inclosed is a letter respecting Count Edward Dillon who was going to Savahana when wounded in the engagement at sea, and was then a Colonel—You will also find a note from M^r de St. Simon respecting his brother—Menonville was his Adjudant General, and in that office they have the honours of Brigadier paid to them when Majors in the tranchees.

Mr de Corny has applied to me, and I could not give him the badge. I promised him I would mention his wishes, and send you his petition—His claims are set up in the capacity of an American officer. Inclosed you will find a petition from Mr de la Neuville and Mr de Vienne, the latter of whom has not the shadow of a title, and if such were admitted, the pretensions would be numberless, and come from very disagreable persons.

Mr du Bouchet who, you know, is not a wit, has taken it in his head to go to America—Had I refused a letter, it would have killed him, and out of pity I gave a private one to you, wherein I observe that he is mad.

In the Resolutions of our Committee, you will find a mention made of Gal Conway which I am going to explain—I don't say that I have merit—but I say I have its consequences—wiz, ennemies—My popularity is great throughout the kingdom and in this city—But amongs the great folks I have a large party against me, because they are jealous of my reputation—In a word, the pitt to one man is for me, and in the boxes there is a division—A plot was lad to draw me into a snare, and Madame Conway was made a tool of to give me and yourself the air of an implacable revenge against that man who is considered here as having been abandonned and ruined by me in America—*Secret meetings were held on the occasion of which I have been advised—I have attended to my letters which I know will be printed—and to avoid the odium of having stifled Connway's claims, I have not discouraged a representation being made in his favor—The man is not worth troubling our heads about him—but as he will become a pretence to a sect who have not hitherto found any against me, it may be better either to give him the badge, or if refused to do it with that secrecy and delicacy which will not subject me to the reproach of having proposed him, in order that he may be humiliated—That whole family is a nest of rogues—du Bouchet excepted who is honest, but a fool.

The French Officers have offered monney—I had rather it was not accepted—but at such a distance I cannot judge what is the best to be done—The formation of a Committee in Europe is very necessary—but it must, for reasons obvious, be quite separated from any society the French Officers may form as it is calculated only for American purposes, and ought to consist but of American officers for the time being in Europe.

After proper allowances have been made both for the Navy officers, and particular cases, I will beg leave to represent that the Members ought not to be too much multiplied—If a greater facility takes place, the institution will sink in proportion that it is bestowed upon too many people, and our officers must be upon their guards not to give the badge without proper motives.

I have been requested to present you with a new model and

---

*The passage which follows up to the end of the paragraph is among those not given in the version of this letter reproduced by Hume (*inter alios*) in *Washington's correspondence concerning the Cincinnati*, pp. 110-11. Instead Hume's version reads: "It might be well to grant him the decoration."

ribbond—and from the persons that gave it could not refuse sending it to America. I need not saying this letter is confidential.

With the highest respect and tenderest affection I have the honour to be

My dear General

Your obedient humble Servant,
Lafayette*

[170]

Paris March the 9th 1784

My dear General

Had I not so perfect a confidence in your friendship, I would very much fear to tire you with my scribbling of this day—but cannot leave my penn before I have again mentionned my tender respectfull affection to my dear General. I want to tell you that Mde de Lafayete and my three children are well, and that all of us in the family heartly join to present their dutiful affectionate compliments to Mrs. Washington and yourself. Tell her that I hope soon to thank her for a dish of tea at Mount Vernon. Yes, my dear General, before the month of June is over you will see a vessel coming up Pottowmack, and out of that vessel will your friend jump with a panting heart and all the feelings of perfect happiness.

I intended to have gone sooner, but a few commercial matters still keep me here—for since no body middles with them, I have undertaken in my private capacity to do what is possible for one who has neither title, or instruction. It is at least a comfort that in my private capacity I cannot commit Congress, and that I never speak but of what I know. Four ports having been declared free, I send Mr. Moriss a letter respecting the duties to be paid there—and I hope Congres will also publish that all duties have been removed from the exportation of brandies

*The note which follows comes after the letter of December 21, 1784, in the Hubbard Collection. It does not appear, however, to belong there. It seems more properly to go with the letters dated March 9, 1784, and particularly with this one. It has not been published heretofore.

I had forgot to mention that Major Lomagne is on every respect entitled to become a member of the Assossiation—But reports having been spread respecting the manner in which he left Armand's Legion I have suspended admitting of him untill he is cleared by the informations you may think proper to take—He says Gal Armand is his personal ennemy.

Duplessis has a little surprised our simplicity—I wish he may have been himself mistaken—But he is gone out of Europe.

Most of the Americans here are indecently violent against our Assossiation. Wadsworth must be excepted, and Doctor Franklin said little—but Jay, Adams, and all the others warmly blame the Army. You easely guess I am not remiss in opposing them. And however if it is found that the heredity endangers the true principles of democraty, I am as ready as any man to renounce it. You will be my compass, my dear General, because at this distance I cannot judge. In case upon better consideration, you find that heredity will injure our democratic constitutions, I join with you by proxy in voting against it. But I so much rely on your judgement that if you think heredity is a proper scheme I will be convinced that your patriotism has considered the matter in the best point of view. *To you alone*, I would say so much, and I abide by your opinion in the matter. Let the foregoing be confidential, but I am sure your disinterested virtue will weigh all possible, future consequences of hereditary distinctions.

There are no news in this moment that are worth relating. What respects balons*, Mr L'Enfent will tell. The present English disputes are some what ridiculous—they must end in a dissolution of Parliament or an union between Pitt and Fox. Adieu, my dear General, accept with your usual goodness the affectionate tribute of a heart so entirely devoted to you that no words can ever express the respect, the love, and all the sentiments with which you know it is glowing for you, and that make me untill my last breath

Your obedient humble ser and affectionate friend

Lafayette

My compliments waït upon George and all the family at Mount Vernon. Be so kind my dear General as to remember me to all our friends. I am very sorry the hurry I was in to serve you occasioned my sending so soon the plated wares. Adieu, my dear General.

[171]

My dear General   Paris April the 9th 1784†

Among the numberless applications I have had for our Society, there is one which, in duty to my feelings, I cannot decline to present. On my first voyage to America, Mms. de Mauroy, Lesser, Valfort, and du Boismartin were with me, and altho' those meritorious

---
*I.e. balloons, upon which several French scientists were experimenting in 1782-83.
†Unpublished. (Proper names are identified in the "Index" below.)

officers had an engagement with Mr. Deane, Congress did not think it in their power to employ them—My instructions being positive, I have answered them, that it was not within my limits to present them with the badge of the Assossiation—But upon their request for a representation of their case, I found it the more impossible for me to neglect it, as independant of their great merit, zeal, and sacrifices, they were my first companions in the voyage, and went over with me in a manner that lays me under particular obligations to them—Give me leave therefore, my dear General, to present you with this sollicitation of mine, which they will forward to Yr Excellency—With the highest respect and most tender affection I have the honour to be

     My dear General
      Your obedient humble servant
       Lafayette.

[172]

Paris May the 14th 1784

My dear General

To my great satisfaction, my departure is fixed upon the tenth of next month, when I intend leaving Paris, and immediately embarking for America—My course will be straight to Pottowmack, and I do most feelingly anticipate the pleasure of our meeting at Mount Vernon—There is nothing new in France, but that the affair of the free ports is quite settled, and that nothing yet has been done respecting the intended regulations for commerce betwen America and the West Indias—Governement are very friendly to the interest of the United States, but labour under many difficulties, the strongest of all is the complaints of flour merchants, manufacturers, and raisers in the country round Bordeaux—There has been a pretention set up a Vienna by the Empress of Russia, for a preeminence of her Ambassador over ours, which is foolish and groundless, and from which she must certainly desist—Some Portuguese disputes respecting a settlement in Africa have been decided to the satisfaction of France—Mr. Pitt's party will be the stronger in the new Parliament —but Charles Fox comes in as a member for Wesminster, and will head an Opposition—The situation of Ireland is critical, the lord Lieutenant's conduct has been foolish, and some resolutions of the people are very spirited—A German doctor called *Mesmer* having made the greatest discovery upon *Magnetism Animal*, he has instructed scholars, among whom your humble servant is called one of the most enthusiastic—I know as much as any conjuror ever did, which remind's me of our old friend's at Fiskills enterwiew with the devil that made us laugh so much at his house, and before I go, I will get leave to let you into the secret of Mesmer, which you may depend upon, is a grand philosophical discovery.

Mr. Jay is gone this morning to Dover where he intends embarking for America—He has taken care of a family picture, including M^{de} de Lafayette, our children, and myself which I beg leave to present to my dear General, as the likenesses of those who are most affectionately devoted to him.

The whole family join with me in the most respectfull compliments to you and Mrs. Washington—Be so kind, my dear General, to remember me to the other inhabitants of Mount Vernon, and to all friends that you may happen to see—Adieu, my dear General, be pleased with your usual kindness, to receive the tender wishes of one who more than any man existing may boast of being, Your Excellency's

                    Most affectionate, respectfull friend
                          and humble servant
                                Lafayette

AMENDED   [173]

                           Philadelphia, Tuesday evening
                           August [10] 1784*

My dear General,

I have already had the pleasure to acquaint you with my arrival in America, and am endeavouring to reach Mount Vernon as soon as possible. My first plan was only to stay here two days, but the affectionate reception I have met with in this city and the returning some compliments to the Assembly render necessary to stay one day longer. On Friday I will be at the Head of Elk. The next day at Baltimore and by Sunday or Monday I hope at last to be blessed with a sight of my dear General. There is no rest for me untill I go to Mount Vernon. I long for the pleasure to embrace you my dear General and the happiness of being once more with you will be so great that no words can ever express it. Adieu my dear General, in

*Copy in Harvard College Library, Sparks Mss LXXXVIII, Part I.

a few days I'll be at Mount Vernon, and I do already feel delighted with so charming a prospect. My best respects wait upon Mrs. Washington, and not long after you receive this, I will tell you myself how respectfully and affectionately I have the honour to be my dear General

       Your most obedient humble servant
          Lafayette

In case your affairs call you to the Springs, I beg leave to go there after you or to accompany you in your journey.

[174]

My dear General   Newyork September the 14th 1784*

This letter will be delivered by Mr. Duché, whose principles, character, and misfortunes entitle him to Your Excellency's patronage—He has a great share in C^her de Chattelux's esteem, and is most particularly recommended by my friend Mr de Malesherbes, who had an opportunity to know him when a lawyer in the city of Paris —This gentleman came with a good sum of monney which he intended to settle with in America—But the greatest part, having been lost in a shipwrek he still more stands in need of advice and patronage —Both of those, my dear General, I earnestly request in his favour, and am happy to assure you that he ever has been a friend to the Rights of Mankind, and that his situation deserves particular notice.

With the most affectionate respect I have the honour to be
  My dear General
       Your obedient humble servant
         and devoted friend
           Lafayette

[175]

My dear General   Albany October the 8th 1784

Every where I have met with delays—but so agreable were they in their nature that I cannot complain of them—It is not quite the case with the Indian Treaty—Altho' the hope to be useful has kept me there longer than I had expected—My presence at the oppening of it had been desired—Many circumstances kept it off—At last it began, and my influence with the Indians was found greater than

*Unpublished.

I myself could expect—I was therefore desired to Speak—to Hearken to Answers—I took the liberty to caution the Commissioners upon such points as you had mentionned me—and did not leave the ground untill they thought they had no farther occasion for me—But as the business is just begining, I cannot give you any farther intelligence, but that great deal of intrigue is carried on by some tory indians of Brant party, and that the Whigg and Tory distinctions are kept up among those tribes to an amasing degree of private animosities.

This day, my dear General, I am going towards Hartfort, Boston, and Newport where the French Ships now are—and (as, if I went by land, I would be so much kept of by my friends as to be very late on our appointed meeting,) I intend submitting myself to the little inconvenience of going by water from Rhode Island to Williamsburg where I hope to be about the 26th and where I will be happy to receive the orders of my dear General.

Waiting upon the Assembly in Richmond, and visiting Frederisburg on my way to Mount Vernon would be my plan—but expect your orders to know where I am to meet you—It is possible you had rather not go to Richmond—In a word, my dear General, as your paternal goodness to me cannot stand upon any kind of ceremony, give me your orders—tell me what I had best to do—and I shall be as you well know happy to obey them.

One thing, my dear General, I very much wish you might grant me—As the time of my stay in Virginia will depend upon your advice respecting French letters which I am to receive there, as it will be then a last visit for this American trip of mine—I will be happy my dear General, if without inconvenience to yourself you may come with me so far, at least, as Philadelphia where your friends depend upon me to have an opportunity to see you.

Could you pay the Virginia visits with me, could I meet you some where, or Frederisburg I suppose, where in that case I would go before I visit Richmond, it would be to me a most heartfelt happiness.

I beg your pardon, my beloved General, but I want to see you, and no heart can better feel the pleasure to be with you than the filial heart of

        Your respectfull and affectionate friend
        Lafayette

The Chevalier* begs leave to be most respectfully presented to you —We unite in respects to Mrs. Washington and compliments to Mr. Washington and children—if you hear from George, I beg you will let me know it.

[176]

Boston October† the 22d 1784

My dear General

On my arrival at Boston I have been so kindly received that no words can express my lively, affectionate gratitude—To those enjoyements I have added the heartfelt pleasure to contemplate the effect, a sudden appearance of your picture, had upon a people whose love to you is as great at least as in any part of the world—Circumstanced as I am here, I could not with any propriety set out so soon as I expected—I am sorry our meeting again is differed—but when you are absent, I endeavour to guess what you would have advised me to do—and then to do it—I am sure you would advise my staying here some time longer—I therefore will not go untill the first or second of next month—and then I embark from Boston in the Nimph frigat to go to York—Mr de Grandchain who commands her begs to be most respectfully remembered to you, and as he expects reaching York about the 8th or tenth, he will in compagny with me wait upon you wherever you may be found—The bearer I send to Mount Vernon in order I may receive your commands at the moment I arrive—So late in the season, I think you will advise my going immediately to Richmond—I hope you will let me know where we are to meet—and I also hope, my dear General, you will not deny my affectionate pressing request to induce your visiting with me our friends in Philadelphia—The C^{her}'s respects and mine wait upon Mrs. Washington and wish to be remembered to all the family—Adieu, my dear General, with the most affectionate and devoted sentiments of filial love and respect

I have the honour to be

Yours
Lafayette

*Chevalier de Caraman. (Proper names are identified in the "Index" below.)
†Lafayette wrote *August* but another hand corrected it to *October*. October is right.

[177]

New York 17th Dec^{bre} 1784*

I shou'd think myself much obliged to Your Excellency if through your Means some of the following seeds might be procured from Kentucké for the use of the King's Garden—viz.
  The seeds of the *Coffe Tree* which resembles the Black oak
    Do. of the *Pappa Tree*
    Do. of the *Cucumber Tree*
    Do. *Black berry Tree*
    Do. *Wild Cherry Tree*
    Do. *Buck-eye Tree*
    Do. *of Wild Rye, Buffalo Grass—Shawanese Salad—Wild Lettuce—Crown Imperial Cardinal Flower—the Tulip-bearing Laurel Tree*—& the Seeds of every thing else curious which that Famed Country produces—
It wou'd be necessary Your Excellency wou'd order the whole to be carefully sent to the care of the director of the French Pacquets at New York, that it might be transmitted to Paris.—
  God bless you, my dear General, I am requested by Mr. St. John to sign this, and do it with the greater pleasure as these seeds and trees will be very wellcome in France

Lafayette

[178]

On board the Nimph Newyork Harbour
December the 21st 1784

My dear General
  I have received your affectionate letter of the 8th inst, and from the known sentiments of my heart to you, you will easely guess what my feelings have been in perusing the tender expressions of your friendship—No, my beloved General, our late parting was not by any means a last interwiew. My whole soul revolts at the idea—and could I harbour it an instant, indeed my dear General, it would make miserable. I well see you never will go to France—The unexpressible pleasure of embracing you in my own house, of well com-

*The last sentence only is in Lafayette's handwriting. Unpublished.

288

ing you in a family where your name is adored, I do not much expect to experience—But to you, I shall return, and in the walls of Mount Vernon we shall yet often speack of old times. My firm plan is to visit now and then my friends on this side of the Atlantick, and the most beloved of all friends I ever had, or ever will have any where, is too strong an inducement for me to return to him, not to think that, when ever it is possible, I will renew my so pleasing visits to Mount Vernon.

Since I have left you, my dear General, we have past through Philadelphia to Trenton, where I was happy to find a numerous and well choosen Congress—Their testimonies of kindness to me, and my answer to them you will see in the newspapers—As to my services abroad, it has been (on motion respecting what I told you) universally decided that public confidence in me was a matter of course—a doubt of which ought not be expressed—But as I know the sense of the Congress, and as M. Jay has accepted and Mr. Jefferson will be minister in France, my situation in that respect will be very agreable.

Orders have been sent to Canada to reinforce the posts, put the Lake vessels in commission, and repel force by force—But I think that if once Congress have the trade to regulate, mercantile interdictions will set those people to rights—Altho' party spirit has a little subsided in Newyork, yet that city is not by any means settled—How far from Boston!

Altho' your nephew* is not arrived, I still hope for the pleasure to see him in Paris—

Gal Greene was in Hartfort when the letter reached him, from where he came to Newyork, and I had the pleasure to spend some days with him—Inclosed I send you a small cypher—Should any public political business require a fuller one, I will write to you under a complete cypher I have had long ago with Mr Jay's present departement.

M. Cary printer of the Volonteer Journal has been obliged to fly for his life and now lives at Mr. Sutter's Hatter Front Street in Philadelphia where he is going to set up a paper—A letter from you becoming a subscriber, and telling him I have mentionned it to you, will the more oblige me as I have promised him to recommend him

*Bushrod Washington.

to my friends—He now is *an American* and we have nothing to do with his quarrel with the Duke of Rutland—which disputes by the bye seem to subside and vanish into nothing—The French packet is not yet arrived.

C^her de Caraman and Captain Grandchain beg leave to offer their respects to you, Mrs. Washington, and all the family—My most affectionate tender respects wait upon Mrs. Washington—I beg she will give a kiss for me to the little girls*, my friend Tub†— and I beg Mrs. Stuart, the doctor‡, Mr. Lund Washington, and all our friends to receive my best compliments—I hope Mr. Harrison will be soon appointed, and I wish his cousin may know it.

Adieu, adieu, my dear General, it is with unexpressible pain that I feel I am going to be severed from you by the Atlantick— every thing that admiration, respect, gratitude, friendship, and filial love can inspire, is combined in my affectionate heart to devote me most tenderly to you—In your friendship I find a delight which words cannot express—Adieu, my dear General, it is not without emotion that I write this word—Altho' I know I shall soon visit you again—Be attentive to your health—Let me hear from you every month—Adieu, adieu.

L.f.

---

*Apparently Elizabeth, Martha and Eleanor, the daughters of John Parke Custis..
†Probably George Washington Parke Custis.
‡Dr. David Stuart, second husband of Eleanor Calvert Custis.

❧ 1785 ❧

[179]

Versailles February the 9th 1785

My dear General

After a pretty tedious passage of thirty days we have safely arrived at Brest, from whence I came to Paris through Rennes, where the States of Brittany were assembled, and where their kindness to me made it necessary for me stop one day—My family, wife, children, and friends I found in perfect health—The politics of Europe are not in a tranquil condition, and from their situation a dreadfull war may break out. What I could collect I have writen to Mr. Jay, and inclose a copy of my letter*—Prince de Condé, and Marechal de Broglio are spoken of to command the two armies—Where I would serve, I had not yet time to arrange—but it will not be with my dear General, and every thing is so short of that happiness, that nothing, when compared to it, can possibly please me—However, notwistanding all preparations, I still am of opinion matters will be compromised and, at least for this year, I hope no war will be necessary—The propriety of my not arriving later than now is very obvoius—Irish disputes are but little spocken off, but may revive

*Charles Theodore, elector of Bavaria, being without direct heirs, had been persuaded by Joseph II, Holy Roman emperor and archduke of Austria, to agree to an exchange of Bavaria for the Austrian Netherlands. At the same time the Emperor Joseph had quarreled with the Dutch Netherlands, insisting on his natural right to navigate the Scheldt River despite treaties to the contrary. Prussia opposed Austria on both issues, and Joseph counted on the support of Tsarina Catherine of Russia in return for aid to Russia against the Turks. France, though allied to Austria, tried to maintain peace by compromise. Lafayette's letter to Jay, February 8, 1785, is in W. A. Weaver (ed.), *Diplomatic correspondence of the United States*, etc. (7 vols.; Washington, 1837), I, 419-20.

with their Congress and their Rewiews—England will take no part in the war, at least in the begining—I have obeyed your orders, my dear General, and besides those you told me, I have presented your compliments to every acquaintance of yours—In a few days I hope for a letter from you—Now, my dear General, that I have once more got used to the happiness of being with, or at least near you, a punctual correspondance, at least, is more than ever necessary to my heart—Should a packet come without a letter from you, I would indeed feel very unhappy—This letter will be but short, not so much on account of my late arrival than because I did not think the third Tuesday was on the 15th—For the same reason my little girl will be deprived of the honour of answering her sweet correspondant* untill next packet—Those two letters have almost turned her head—M^{de} de Lafayette requests her most affectionate compliments to you, and Mrs. Washington. The Chevalier joins with me in assurances of respect to her, to Your Excellency, and we beg to be remembered to the young ones, and Mrs Stuart—My Compliments to the doctor and Mr. Lund W.—Give me leave once more to recommend two things to you—riding now and then—and getting a secretary—Adieu, adieu, my dear General, every sentiment that love, gratitude, regard can inspire, every filial, friendly feelings, shall for ever combine to put me at the head of all those who ever loved a father and friend as

Your affectionate and
humble servant
Lafayette

[180]

Paris March the 19th 1785†

My dear General

Your letter December the 23d has safely come to hand, and nothing short of the Pottowmack plan could have accounted with me for your leaving Mount Vernon—I am glad to hear you are likely to succeed, as it seems to me a matter of great moment—and the part you have taken in the business cannot fail, still more particularly to interest me in its success—I thank you, my dear General, for your in-

---

*Washington, who had received a letter from Lafayette's daughter Anastasie and had replied. See Fitzpatrick, *Writings of Washington*, XXVII, 497-98.
†Unpublished.

formation respecting the act of Maryland*—it is an honour equally flattering to my pride, and pleasing to my heart.

European politics are not yet settled—but there is much reason to hope this will end without bloodshed—Inclosed you will find a declaration from the King of France to the Emperor respecting the Dutch War—Count de Maillebois is gone to Holland where they are raising troops, and where parties run very high—A plan of the emperor for the exchange of Baviera, of which I spocke to you in my last, has been opposed by the Duke of Deux ponts nephew and heir to the elector—So that upon the whole I don't think we shall have a war—In case the Dutch make some sacrifices, they will be small—The intervention of France has saved them—and Count de Vergennes deserves great credit.

Great Britain continues to be very backward in treating with America—Our friend John Temple is appointed British Consul to the United States—notwistanding the ill will and narrow policy of England they run a way with all the commerce of America—That total interruption of trade gives a new force to the clamours of the French merchants against the late admission of foreigners in the West Indies, and makes it impossible to obtain the addition of flour and sugars—at least in the present period—I am very busy about introducing the whale oils in France, and notwistanding every obstacle, hope at least partially to succeed—

On my arrival, I have repeated what I had writen respecting the Mississipy—wiz—the idea, either to get New Orleans or to advise the Spaniards to make it a free port—The former is impossible—as to the second I had no positive answer—but I am sure my opinion was not thrown a way—I have requested a conference with the Duke de La Vauguion who is going to Spain as an Ambassador—It will be very difficult to get that point, and altho' I would not advise America to deviate from firmness, I think they must act with moderation in this affair.

Inclosed is the extract from a book of Mr. Necker† which I thought might give agreable information—I send it in French, because you will find translators enough—That book is very good one,

---
*By a bill introduced in November 1784 and enacted in January 1785, the General Assembly of Maryland made Lafayette and "his heirs male for ever" citizens of that state.
†*De l'administration des finances de France.*

but has raised both a jealousy against, and an adoration for the author which runs into an excess—He is however one of the ablest men in Europe, and certainly one of the first financiers.

The Irish affairs seem to subside—In the course of the summer, I will, I think, visit the Prussian and Austrian Armies, provided there is no war—my ideas about 29* are not very unlikely to succeed—102 [Protestants]† in this kingdom are my present object—and I am not without hopes, with respect to a part of what a rational man might expect *at this period.*

My little family have been writing to yours by Mr. Williams an American gentleman—They join with Mde de Lafayette and me in most affectionate respects to Mrs. Washington and you—Remember me to all our friends—Adieu, Adieu, my beloved general, think often of your absent, tender friend—never could any being in creation love you more, respect you more than I do—Be so kind as to let me hear from you by every packet—adieu, my dear general,

Your respectfull and affectionate friend
Lafayette

Chevalier de Caraman presents his best respects to Mrs. Washington and to you—I kiss Squire Tub, and the young ladies.

[181]

St. Germain Near Paris April the 16th 1785‡

My dear General

To my great disappointement I had no letter from you by this packet—it is however the only regular way to get intelligences, and mercantile opportunities are not by far so much to be depended on. I warmly beg, my dear General, you will not let me be uneasy for want of a line from you. The distance is already so great in itself, and so much greater for the feelings of the tenderest friendship, that the only means ought to be scrupulously observed that tend to alleviate the cruel separation—Since my last letter, there is very little news—warlike preparations have not been given up—but the negoti-

*Undeciphered, but in the letter of May 11, 1785 (p. 296 below), 29 is deciphered "parliament." Lafayette means the Parlement of Paris, the leading court of the realm. (Proper names are identified in the "Index" below.)
†See note on p. 245 above, and p. 296 below.
‡Unpublished.

ations are come to this point which leaves no probability of a war—The proposition to exchange Baviera for the Austrian Low Countries, with the title of Kingdom of Austrasia, has not been accepted—A new object for disputes might be the election of a King of the Romans, which you know is the title which marks the successor to the Empire—The Emperor's interest will be in favour of his Nephew the Young Arch Duke Francis of Tuscany—England and Ireland are negotiating with each other, and will be puzzled to agree, unless the volonteering flame once spent out ceases to support their country—The British Governement seems in no hurry to make a Treaty of Commerce—Much less so, if possible, to give up the posts—I have had a Conference with the Duke de La Vauguion who is gone to Madrid respecting the Mississipy—But the Spaniards are still obstinate, and you will have full time to oppen your navigation, which I consider as the first political, mercantile, and national plan which can now employ the United States—There are great complaints of the merchants against the Arrèt du Conseil in favour of the West India trade*—altho' flour and sugars are excepted—but the Ministry will stick by it, and more cannot be got for the present—Every thing in Europe more and more convinces me of the necessity there is for the States to give Congress powers to regulate trade.

By Mr. Ridout's vessel my children have sent to yours at Mount Vernon a few trifles which are very indifferent but may amuse them two or three days. English dogs are so much in fashion here that the King who likes to ride fast has no French hounds which, says he, are very slow—At last I have discovered a tolerable good breed of them which young M. Adams will take with him in the next packet—A jack ass has been sent to you from Cadix—I expect one from the isle of Maltha and will forward it.

In the course of the summer I will visit the Prussian and Austrian troops—I will have the pleasure to speack much of you—but had rather speack with you—and instead of those German troops, I wish I could once more give you a dinner with my light infantry friends.

Adieu, my dear General, be so kind as to present my most tender respects to Mrs. Washington—Mention me to the young

*An *arrêt* of August 30, 1784, opened certain ports in the French West Indies to trade in certain enumerated articles.

ones—Mrs. Stuard, the Doctor, M. Lund W., Miss Basset if she is with you—I am uneasy about George—My respects wait upon your respected Mother and all the family—Remember me to our friends—M^{de} de La Fayette begs you and Mrs. Washington to accept her most affectionate compliments—Adieu, my dear General, think often of your bosom friend, your adoptive son, who loves you so tenderly, and who is with every sentiment of respect, gratitude, and affection

Your devoted friend
Lafayette.

The queen and her second son are in perfect health.

[182]

Paris May the 11th 1785

My dear General,

This is not the only letter you will get from me by this packet, but as the opportunity is safe, I will trust young M. Adams with some matters which I would not like to be ventured in the post offices of France.

102 [Protestants]* in 12 [France] are under intolerable 80 [despotism]—Altho' oppen persecution does not now exist, yet it depends upon the whim of 25 [king], 28 [queen], 29 [parliament] or any of 32 [ministry]. Marriages are not legal among them. Their wills have no force by law, their children are to be bastards, their parsons to be hanged. I have put it into my head to be a 1400 [leader] in that affair, and to have their situation changed. With that wiew I am going, under other pretences to visit their chief places of abode with a consent of 42 [Castries] and an other. I will afterwards endeavour to gain 39 [Vergennes] and 29 [parliament] with the Keeper of the Seals who acts as Chancellor†. It is a work of time, and of some danger to me, because none of them would give me a scrap of paper, or countenance whatsoever. But I run my chance. 42 [Castries] could only receive the secret from me, because it is not in his departement. Don't answer me about it, only that you have my ciphered letter by M. Adams. But when in the course of the fall or

---

*See note on pp. 245 and 294 above. (Proper names are identified in the "Index" below.)

†Miroménil.

winter you will hear of some thing that way, I wanted you to know I had an hand in it.

100 [Ireland] are spent out, and nothing for 73's [liberty] sake to do that way. I was in hopes Holland would offer some thing that way, but I am affraid not. I don't think 46's [Calonne] political life may last long unless he leaves 1600 [finances] for some other branch.

Before I arrived a letter had gone demanding Long champs. Since which the Ministry were satisfied with that business and a letter went ordering to let it drop. I hope there will be no war in America—but if it was ever the case, either to 840 [South Spain], to 590 [Mississippy] or to the frontier posts and Canada, I depend upon you, my dear General to be offered a command, which in one case my situation as a French man may render personally a little ticklish for me, but for which, in all cases my situation as such, as well as my Roman Catholick creed or supposed to be so at least if any thing, and the confidence you, and the public are pleased to honour me with, may render me a proper choice to propose. But I earnestly hope it will not be the case that you make war, particularly with Spain. Altho' a visit to Mexico and New Orleans I would prefer to any thing I know of. Don't answer to me about it otherwise than in general terms.

Adieu, my dear General, my best respects wait on Mrs. Washington. Remember me to the family.

Your filial and devoted friend
Lafayette

When you arrange your papers, my dear General, I beg you will send me my letters to you, which I will send back a fortnight after I have received them. I had no copies kept of them. And wish to preserve some.*

---

*The envelope is marked in Lafayette's hand: "Forwarded by M. Adams and particularly recommended. Lafayette."

[183]

Paris May the 11th 1785*

My dear General

This letter will be delivered by M. le Comte Doradour of a very good family in Auvergne to whom I am related and who is going to look for a settlement in America—His fortune has been partly deranged by a law suit, and what remains of it he intends to fix in some of the United States—I beg leave to request your good advices and your patronage on his behalf, and have the honour to be

Most respectfully and affectionately, my dear General

Your obedient humble
Servant
Lafayette.

[184]

Paris May the 13th 1785.†

My dear General

My correspondance with you will this time be in two volumes and young Mr. Adams, John Adams's son, has taken care of a letter which I hope he will safely forward—Your kind favour February the 15th only came in the last packet,—I need not telling you, my dear General, how happy I was to hear from you, and how happy you will make me by an exact correspondance and an attention to send the letters in time for the sailing of the packets which now will arrive in France at the Havre a place very near Paris at the mouth of the Seine river—I am very glad to hear your Pottowmack business has succeeded—it is highly important, and I feel doubly happy by reflecting this good is owing to the part you have taken in the affair —The compliment the State of Virginia‡ have paid you is no doubt perplexing—I feel for you, and with you, my dear General, on the occasion—Your reluctance to receive such a present is the more pleasing to me, as I want it to be said in your history—General Wash-

*Unpublished.
†Unpublished.
‡Washington's letter of February 15, 1785 (Fitzpatrick, *Writings of Washington*, XXVIII, 71-74) informed Lafayette of the formation of the Potomac Navigation Company and the James River Navigation Company. A number of shares in both companies was voted to Washington and his heirs forever as a reward for his services.

ington got every thing for his Country—and would not receive any other reward—But on the other hand, you certainly wish to avoid every step which could appear a slight, a want of proper respect, or of gratitude for the compliment which a nation pays to an individual —You better know what to do than I can tell—but if it can be gently turned towards some public popular establishement, you may perhaps avoid a deviation from your plan, and the appearance of slight or ostentation—I will look out for subscribers when the matter comes to be a little better known—And will have an eye upon your recommendation respecting the Engeneer.

There is not much news for the present in this Country—Dutch affairs seem to be in a good train of pacification—but if we believe the rumours that were spread yesterday, Baviera would be invaded, or rather, with the consent of the Elector, taken possession of by the imperial troops—It is true that Elector is a complete fool, and his Ministry are bought by the Emperor—but I cannot think the report is true—altho' that Baviera, or the Ottoman Empire are now more probable grounds of a future war than the Provinces of Holland—Duke de Choiseuil died a few days ago—some think he was not without hopes, and worked pretty hard to reenter the Ministry.

French Hounds are not now very easely got because the King makes use of English dogs as being more swift than those of Normandy—I however have got seven from a Normand Gentleman called *Monsieur le Comte D'oilliamson*. The handsomest bitch among them was a favourite with his Lady who makes a present of her to you—as he was very active in procuring the best blooded dogs, I beg leave to propose your writing a line to him, containing a thankfull notice of the Comtesse, who seems to take much pride in being mentionned to you.

M^{quis} de St Simon has once writen a letter to you the answer to which did not arrive—I think a copy, or an antidated letter would do the business, and the whole will be attributed to Naval Accidents.

Mr Adams has taken with him some proposals for a contract about whale oils which I think to be very advantageous to the commerce of America, and will produce an envoice of about 800,000 French Livres. I have been very busy in bringing it on, and it is the consolation I had for failing in my endeavours to obtain a general exemption of duties upon those oils—You have been very right not to purchase the Spanish jack ass—the best ones come from the Isle of Maltha—Admiral Suffrein who goes there has promised he would within these six months send me the handsomest in the island with a female and the whole will not amount to more than fifty guineas.

My wife, children, and myself are in perfect health, and all join with me in most affectionate respects to you, to Mrs. Washington and we send our love to the young ones—I was very happy to hear George arrived at Charlestown in a better state of health—Remember me to him, to all your family, to my friends about you, or any of them you happen to meet—Adieu, my dear General, I grieve to think we are now separated by this immense ocean—But my heart is with you in every moment, my dear General, and I am happy when I can once more mention to you the sentiments of respect, gratitude, unbounded affection which for ever render me, my beloved General,

Your most devoted friend
Lafayette

[185]

Paris July the 9th 1785

My dear General

This letter will be delivered by the celebrated M. Houdon who is going for your statue to America. Nothing but the love of glory and his respect for you could induce him to cross the seas, as his business here far exceeds his leisure, and his numerous and qualified friends make him very happy at home. Those circumstances I mention as a farther recommendation to your attentions. As I am writing by the same opportunity I will only add a tribute of the tender love, and grateful respect I have the honour to be with

My dear general
Yours
Lafayette

[186]

Sarguemines on the French frontier July 14th 1785

My dear General

Before I leave the borders of France, I wish once more to remind you of your absent friend, and to let you hear that I am well and just beginning my German travels. I have been lately visiting some French towns where I spoke great deal about American trade, and fully answered the wiews I had the honour to communicate in a former letter. Now I am on my way to *the Deux Ponts* where resides our friend the future elector of Baviera*, to *Cassel* where I will see again the Hessian regiments, to *Berlin* where I am told Lord Cornwallis is also going. From there I will wait on the King of Prussia on his grand maneuvres in *Silesia*, visit *Saxony*, see the *Austrian camps in Bohemia,* pay my respects to the Emperor at *Vienna*, return to *Berlin* where grand maneuvrers are to take place at the end of September. And after I have on my way examined all the fields of battle, I will return through *Holland* and be again in Paris by the middle of October.

This letter, my dear General, goes with our old friend Doctor Franklin who, I hope, will be received with that respect he so much deserves. It will be forwarded by his grand son† a very deserving young man who wishes being introduced by me to you, and whom I beg leave to recommend to you attentions. He has been much employed in public service, got nothing by it, and as the doctor loves him better than any thing in the world, I think he ought to have the satisfaction to see him noticed by Congress. You will oblige me to let them know that I spoke to you my mind about it.

You remember an idea which I imparted to you three years ago. I am going to try it in the French colony of Cayenne, but will write more fully on the subject in my other letters. Nothing new now in the political world. War is far at a distance. Adieu, my beloved General, My most affectionate respects wait on Mrs. Washington. Remember me to the young ones, to my aide George, to M. Lund, all our friends, and particularly to Mrs. Stuart. You know my heart, my dear General, and I need not adding the assurances of the filial love, respect, and gratitude I have the honour to be with

Your devoted friend
Lafayette

Gouvion is going with me and has the honour to present his respects to you.

*Lafayette perhaps refers to Count Christian of Deux Ponts, who fought at Yorktown under Rochambeau, but the heir presumptive to the Bavarian throne was Charles, Duke of Deux Ponts.
†William Temple Franklin.

[187]

Vienna September the 3d 1785

My dear General

This letter has been requested of me as an introduction for M. André Michaux whom for many reasons I am very happy to present. In the first place I know you will be glad to know a man whose genius has raised him among the scientifick people, and who, as a botanist, has at his own expense travelled through countries very little known. He now is sent by the King to America, in order to know the trees, the seeds, and every kind of natural production whose growth may be either curious, or useful, and for them the King will set up a nursery at a country seat of his which he is very fond of. I am the more pleased with the plan as it oppens a new channel of intercourse and mutual farming good offices betwen the two nations. I beg, my dear General, you will patronize this gentleman, and I much want it to be said in France that he has been satisfied with his reception in America.

I have been visiting the Prussian army, and now am in the Austrian Capital. I had but an hour ago a long conversation with the Emperor about the United States and American trade, in which I took care properly to answer his questions. Where ever I go I enjoy the unspeackable pleasure to hear my beloved General spoken of with that respect he so well deserves.

Adieu, my dear General, my best respects wait on Mrs. Washington, remember me to the young ones. Most respectfully and affectionately

Yours

Lafayette

🎗 1786 🎗

[188]

Paris February the 6th 1786

My dear General

Your letters September the 1st and November the 8th have safely come to hand for which I offer you thanks the warmer and more affectionate as nothing, while we are separated, can so much rejoice your friend's heart as the unspeakable blessing to hear from his beloved General—A long time has elapsed since which my letters have been unfrequent, uninstesting, and uncertain in point of conveyance—My summer has been devoted to Princes, Soldiers and Post Horses—and while I have been rambling through Cassel, Brunswick, Berlin, Breslaw, Vienna, Prague, Dresden, Potsdam again and Berlin, no opportunity offered that I could trust, nor even any that I could hear of—Since I am returned home, no packet has sailed, and this day for the first time, I can safely write by a packet boat, and put my letters into Mr. Barret's hands, a Boston Gentleman who is on his return to America.

Altho' my former letters have given you an account of my journey, I must repeat to you, my dear General, that at Cassel I saw our Hessian friends, old Knip* among them, I told them they were very fine fellows. They returned thanks and compliments—Ancient foes ever meet with pleasure, which, however, I should think must be greater on the side that fought a successfull cause—At Brunswick I got acquainted with the Duke, formerly the renowned Hereditary Prince, who is now arrived at the height of military knowledge, and of the confidence of the Prussian Army, in which, altho' a sovereign,

*Knyphausen. (Proper names are identified in the "Index" below.)

he acts as a General—No officer at Berlin seemed to me so worthy of attention as General Möllendorf whose name you no doubt have heard—To Potsdam I went to make my bow to the King, and notwisdanding what I had heard of him, could not help being struck by that dress and appearance of an old, broken, dirty Corporal, covered all over with Spanish snuff, with his head almost leaning on one shoulder, and fingers quite distorted by the gout. But what surprised me much more is the fire and some times the softness of the most beautifull eyes I ever saw, which give as charming an expression to his phisiognomy as he can take a rough and threatening one at the head of his troops—I went to Silesia where he rewiewed an Army of 31 bataillons, and 75 squadrons, making in all thirty thousand men, seven thousand five hundred of whom were on horse back—For eight days I made dinners of three hours with him, when the conversation was pretty much confined at first to the Duke of York the King and myself, and then to two or three more—which gave me the opportunity to hear him throughout, and to admire the vivacity of his wit, the endearing charms of his adress and politness, so far that I did conceive people could forget what a tyrannic, hard hearted, and selfish man he is—Lord Cornwallis being there, he took care to invite him at table to a seat by me, having the British King's son on the other side, and to make thousand questions on American affairs—Among others I remember he asked the Duke of York if it was true you intended taking an house in London. From Silesia I hastened to Vienna where I only stayed a few days, had a very long Conference with the Emperor, saw the Generals Laudon and Lasey, and my uncle the Ambassador* with Prince Kaunitz, and after those objects were fulfilled, I posted off through Prague and Dresden, to Potsdam, where the troops were to make sham fights and every kind of warlike maneuvres—Had I stayed in Prussia, I might have gone often to the old King's who has been most peculiarly kind to me—but the very day I arrived at Potsdam, he fell sick and was near dying—The Maneuvres went on however—and there I had new opportunities to know the Hereditary Prince of Prussia†, who is a good officer, an honest man, a man of plain good sense, but does not come up to the abilities of his two uncles—this second uncle

*Marquis de Noailles.
†The future Frederick William II.

Prince Henry I have kept for the last, because it is by far the best acquaintance I have made—I don't examine who is the greater General his brother or he, a question that divides the Military world—but to abilities of the first rate, both as a soldier and a politician—to a perfect litterary knowledge, and all the endowements of the mind—he joins an honest heart, philantropic feelings, and rational ideas on the Rights of Mankind—I have spent a fortnight with him in his country seat and we keep up an epistolary correspondance—As the King was still confined and could not bear being seen in that situation, I determined neither to ask for leave of a visit, nor to wait untill he was up, and our adieus having taken place by letters, I returned home through Magdebourg where the Duke of Brunswick commanded maneuvres similar to those of Potsdam.

It is with the highest satisfaction that I saw the Prussian Army—nothing can be compared to the beauty of the troops, the discipline that is diffused throughout, the simplicity of their motions, the uniformity of their regiments—It is a plain regular machine that has been set these forty years, and undergoes no alteration but what can make it simpler and lighter—Every supposition in war, and every motion deriving from it, has been from a constant use so much inculcated into their heads, that it became almost a mechanic for them—Were the ressources of France, the alertness of her men, the intelligence of her officers, and National Ambition and moral delicacy applied to such a constant system, we could be as superior to the Prussians as our Army is now inferior to theirs—and that is saying great deal—I have also seen the Austrians—but not together—Their general system of œconomy is more to be admired than the maneuvres of their troops—their machine is not plain—our regiments are better than theirs—and what advantage they might have in a line over us, we can surpass with a little use—Indeed, I think there is more instruction of detail in some of our best regiments than those of the Prussians—but their line maneuvres infinitely better than ours—The Austrian Army is much more numerous than either, and costs much less than the French.

On my journey I have examined several fields of battle, and the whole tour has been very useful to my military instruction—it has been also made very agreable by the good reception, and the flattering testimonies I have met from those crowns, staffs, and other great personages—There was at those camps a croud of English officers—among whom Lord Cornwallis, C^lels England, Abercrombie, Musgrave—On our side were Colonel Smith, Gal Portail, and Gouvion—and often did Smith and myself make this observation that, had we been unfortunate in the contest, we would have cut there a poor figure.

Where ever I went, my dear General, I had the pleasure to hear your name pronounced with that respect and enthusiasm which altho' it is a matter of course, and I am so used to it, never fails to make my heart glow with unspeackable happiness—with your eulogium began every conversation on American affairs—And to be your friend, your disciple, and your adoptive son was, as it ever has been, and will be for ever, the pride of my heart, and the most pleasing of my thoughts—I wish the other sentiments I have had occasion to discover with respect to America were equally satisfactory with those that are personal to you—I need not saying that the spirit, the firmness with which the Revolution was carried has excited universal admiration—that every one who cares any thing about the Rights of Mankind is an enthusiast for the principles on which the Constitutions are built—But I have often had the mortification to hear that the want of powers in Congress, of Union between the States, of energy in their governement should make the Confederation very insignificant—The fact is that those people, generally speacking, know very little of the advantages of democratical governements, of the ressources to be found in a free nation, and the parties which are essentially deriving from the Constitution—but they cannot help being more forcibly struck with all the blemishes which we have so often lamented together—It is conveyed to them through every newspaper, and great pains are taken by the British Ambassadors to confirm the reports which they themselves have raised—Numberless of these notions I have set to rights—the King of Prussia, the Emperor, the great men in both countries I found either ill informed, or informed by people who had led them the wrong path—By their conduct in the Revolution, the Citizens of America have commanded the respect of the world—but it grieves me to think they will in a measure loose it, unless they strengthen the Confederation, give Congress powers to regulate the trade, pay off their debt or at least the interest of it, establish a well regulated militia, in a word compleat all these measures which you have recommended to them—I give very frankly my opinion to Congress on this subject, and will write on the same tune to all my friends on that side of the Atlantik.

There are, I am told, some better hopes of a commercial treaty with Great Britain—their rancour is boundless—but I flatter myself their mercantile interest will get the better—I long for the surrender of the Posts, and wish the plenipotentiaries had given themselves time to make France guarantee for the treaty—This blunder of theirs has occasioned great michief—My endeavours are to convince France it is their interest to obtain a measure that gives them a large share in the Indian trade—But in case matters were brought to decided measures against Great Britain, upon you, my dear General, I depend to know it in time, and to indulge my wishes to render farther services to the United States.

Houdon is arrived in Paris—but has not yet brought your bust which he expects by water from London—I wait impatiently for it, and am very sanguine in my hopes of its likeness with you—On hearing of the King of Spain's compliment, I had suspended my negotiation for asses—what now happens is to me a farther proof that kings are good for nothing but to spoil the sport, even when they mean right*—Let your Royal business go on as it may, I have requested Admiral Suffrein to get for me a jack ass and two females, and before the summer is over they will be rolling on the banks of the Pottowmack, and I wish to God I may do the same—Your letter to M. Doillamson has been forwarded, with your compliments to the lady—I have also spoken to Marquis de St. Simon, but wish you may write to him, because he has his share of vanity, and will be glad if you pay affectionate compliments to him, and show a regard for M. de Menonville his Adjudant General, disclaiming the right to make Cincinnati, and leaving it with your best wishes with the Society in Europe—Captain Littlepage delivered to me some letters for Holland which I have sent—His quarrell with M. Jay seems to me very indecent, and I can't conceive that Jay, for so small a debt, could condescend to enter the lists with a young man.

It has been a great satisfaction to me, my dear General, to hear

*Charles III had promised to send Washington two asses, but they had not yet arrived when Washington wrote Lafayette on September 1, 1785; see Fitzpatrick, *Writings of Washington*, XXVIII, 244.

of my friend George's matrimonial happiness—as I write to him on the subject I will not trouble you with my compliments to the young couple*. I give you joy on the success of your Pottowmack plans—There is no doubt but what a good engeneer may be found in this country to conduct the work—France in this point exceeds England—and will have, I think, every advantage but that of the language which is something, altho' it may be replaced by the help of interpreters—An application from M. Jefferson and myself to the Ministry, and more particularly an intimation that you set a value by that measure, will insure to us the choice of a good engeneer—They are different from the military ones, and are called *ingenieurs des ponts et chaussées;* I think five hundred guineas a year while the business lasts, and an assurance not to loose his rank in France will be sufficient to provide you with the gentleman you want.

I cannot finish this long letter, my dear General, without telling you a word of European politicks—the system of France is quite pacific—the Nation feels a partiality for Prussia—Austrian interest, betwen us, is much supported by the Queen—Count de Vergennes is not inclined this way, but acts with caution—From that it results that we will patch up as much as we can—that the ambitious wiews of the Emperor will not be so decidedly opposed as we might do it—The plans of Prussia will be cramped by us—but should matters come to an extremity, and the Emperor set out on a wild scheme against Prussia, we will then be forced to a war against him, as the opinion of the people, and that of the Ministry, most of them at least, is opposed to Imperial encroachements. With respect to England, we are rivalizing each other, but pretty friendly for the present, and pay great regard to our respective Nations—A treaty of Commerce is upon the carpet, and I think our politicks on the Continent draw pretty much the same way, that of avoiding a war, which however England wishes to engage us in, provided she is dispensed with taking a part in it—Our Alliance with Holland has made them very angry, and I think it very advantageous to us. We are very busy about making a harbour at Cherbourg which is a wonderfull undertaking, as it is made with piles of stones thrown in the high sea, and will succeed very well—Our Financeer† and Baron de Breteuil are in

---
*George Augustine Washington and Frances Bassett.
†Calonne. (Proper names will be identified in the "Index" below.)

a oppen dispute, and I don't think the former will last long—but I need not teazing you with the intrigues of Versailles—I thank you most tenderly, my dear General, for the caution you give me, which I will improve, and find that satisfaction in my prudence to think it is dictated by you—I hope, betwen us, that in the course of next winter the affair of the Protestants will take a good turn—an other secret I intrust to you, my dear General, is that I have purchased for hundred and twenty five thousand French livres a plantation in the Colony of Cayenne and am going to free my Negroes in order to make that experiment which you know is my hobby horse.

Great Britain is a little embarrassed in her Irish concerns—some say their affairs in India are not well—Notwisdstanding these reports, India is to them an immense, amazing source of wealth and power—it seems they are moderating their bitter expressions, their injurious publications against America, and from what M. Adams writes, I hope they will, altho' it is slowly, come into more rational measures with respect to the United States.

The King of Prussia is about leaving the stage and cannot last long—The last accounts from Potsdam are very bad—It will make but little odds in politicks if his nephew, as he will no doubt be obliged to do, follows the advices of Prince Henry—The first idea of the Emperor will certainly be to do some thing—but I don't believe this will produce a war, altho' there is no knowing it with a man of his temper.

While on my tour, I need not saying that I have said in conversation with the two Monarchs and every body all what I thought could tend to the advantage of America—In this country I am endeavouring to oppen as many Channels as I can for American trade—There are for about 25 millions French livres worth of Articles that the United States might furnish to France—Those remittances I want to have encouraged by every possible favour—Upon my applications a Committee has been named which I am to attend to morrow—The last part of my business will not be an easy matter—for it tends to no less than the destruction of the tobacco farm*, the

---

*The right to sell tobacco was granted by royal monopoly to tax-farmers known as farmers-general. See Gottschalk, "Lafayette as a Commercial Agent," *American Historical Review*, XXXVI, (1931), 561-70, and F. L. Nussbaum, "The Revolutionary Vergennes and Lafayette versus the Farmers General," *Journal of Modern History*, III (1931), 599-613.

greatest barrier against American trade—but I don't hope my speeches can produce such an effect—M. Barret who takes care of this letter, is going to Boston with a six years contract for whale oil of four hundred thousand French livres a year.

Words cannot sufficiently express to you how much I am pleased with Mr. Jefferson's public conduct—He unites every ability that can recommend him with the Ministers, and at the time possesses accomplishements of the mind and the heart which cannot but give him many friends. Humphreys is now in England—Langbourne is arrived in Paris these two weecks—but the same queer fellow you know him to be, and you will hardly believe that I could not as yet prevail on him to come and see me.

It is with the utmost regret, my dear General, that I heard the losses Mrs. Washington had the unfortunate occasion to lament—I hape she knows my heart well enough to be certain it has most affectionately simpathised with hers—I beg her to accept the homage of my tender respects—M^{de} de Lafayette and the little family beg to be respectfully remembered to her, as well as to you, my beloved General—my best compliments wait on all the inhabitants of Mount Vernon, on all our friends you happen to meet, old Harrison when you write to him, my friend Tub, and the young ladies—My best respects to Mrs. Stuart, to the Doctor, to Mr. Lund and most affectionately I beg to be remembered to your own family, particularly to your respected mother. I beg leave to send under cover to you a few trifles to be presented to Tub and his sisters.

Adieu, my dear General, you know how affectionately and respectfully I have the honour to be

Your devoted and filial friend
Lafayette

[189]

Paris February the 10th [1786]*

The inclosed, my dear General, is a vocabulary which the Empress of Russia has requested me to have filled up with Indian names, as she has ordered an universal dictionnary to be made of all languages.

*The Hubbard Collection contains only a copy of this letter with an endorsement in Washington's hand. The original is in the Library of Congress, Washington papers, and the above text is based upon it.

It would greatly oblige her to collect the words she sends translated into the several idioms of the nations on the banks of the Oyho [Ohio]. Presley Nevill and Morgan at Fort Pitt, Gal Mullemberg in Fayette's County and our other friends could undertake it for us, and be very attentive to accuracy. I beg your pardon, my dear General, for the trouble I give you, but have been so particularly applied to, that I cannot dispense with paying great attention to the business.

This goes with so long an epistle of mine that I shall only present you here with my best love and wishes and am my dear General

Your respectfull & tenderest friend
Lafayette

[190]

Paris May the 24th 1786

My dear General

While I have to lament the distance which separates us, it is an additional, and an heart felt mortification for me, to hear so seldom from my beloved and respected friend, and among the many reasons I have to wish for a greater intercourse betwen my two countries, I don't forget the hope that more frequent opportunities will increase the number of your wellcome letters. This is going by the packet, and will be either forwarded or delivered by M. du Plessis, a brigadier in the French service and Count d'Estaing's intimate friend who intends settling in the State of Georgia. In case it is his good fortune to come to Mount Vernon, I beg leave to present him to you and Mrs. Washington. I have recommended him to Gal Greene and I think that so far as respects the contract with the French Navy they may be useful to each other.

By a letter I have just received from Prince Henry, I find the health of his brother is declining very fast, the new King of Prussia will then receive some proposals from the Emperor, respecting Baviera which will be rejected. The Empress of Russia is more anxious for the attak of the Ottoman Empire than her Imperial friend. They are to meet, it is said, by the next spring in Krimée. The Patriotic Party prevails in Holland, but are not so united together as were to be wished. I have no great opinion of the pretended commercial treaty between France and Great Britain*.

*The Eden Treaty, which was to be signed on September 26, 1786.

This last country is more rancourous than ever toward America. They are far from adopting proper regulations of Commerce, and still less think of giving up the Forts. There are only two ways to obtain them—Sword in hand with a wiew to extend farther and then ready I am. The other to shut up every port against English Commerce untill they have complied with the treaty. I don't think America has much to fear in a war with England, and in case she waits for a general one to set her claims forward she will not have that opportunity probably for some years.

In my last letter I have spoken to you of a committee in which I am a member, and of course an advocate for American Commerce. The next packet will, I hope, furnish you with some popular resolutions. Great deal of time has been employed in examining the affair of tobacco. I did vigourously attak the Farm Generale, and warmly expostulated for its destruction, but they can't be cut down, and must fall by the slower method of Mines. In the mean while Mr Moriss's bargain has engrossed the whole consumption of France at such a price that no America merchant can find the like any where. The Ministry to palliate the evil have obliged the farmers general to purchase annually from twelve to fifteen thousand hogs heads of American tobacco, besides Mr Moriss's envoices, on the same conditions which he has obtained. By those means Morriss's contract will not be broken, but the monopoly is in a measure avoided, and it has been resolved not to make any more bargain of that kind.

In a few days, my dear General, I will go to the new harbour of Cherbourg and from thence, with the Minister of the Navy, to Brest and Rochefort. I will also visit my country seat in Auvergne, perhaps make a tour through Holland, and certainly spend the month of September in Alzace with the French troops that are under the inspection of my father in law the Duke d'Ayen. I will also examine the grounds of the last campaign of Marechal de Turenne.

The Queen is pregnant and will be laying in about the month of July. Count de Charlus, now called Duke de Castries, is commandant in second of the gendarmerie which is commanded by his father.

Adieu, my dearest and most respected General, present my respects and those of Mde de Lafayette and family to Mrs. Washington and accept of them yourself with that warm and paternal friendship with which I have the happiness to be honoured by you, remember me to your respected mother, to all your relations and our friends, and think often of your adoptive son who has the honour to be most respectfully and affectionately

Your devoted friend
Lafayette

My best compliments to George.

[191]

Paris October the 8th [1786]*

My dear General

This will be presented by M^r le Coulteux a relation to the respectable house of French merchants By that name who is going to settle in America. I beg you to honour him with your patronage and advices.

Not knowing when this will reach you I only add my respects most affectionate to Mrs. Washington. Remember me to George, to the young ones, to all friends.

A treaty of Commerce is signed betwen France and England who are to treat each other like the most favoured *European* Nation, which will not interfere with the wiews of the United States.

With those sentiments of Respect and love which my dear General knows to be so deeply rooted in my filial heart I have the honour to be

Your most affectionate friend
Lafayette

[192]

Paris October the 26th 1786

My dear General

To one who so tenderly loves you, who so happily enjoyed the times we have past together, and who never, on any part of the globe, even in his own house, could feel himself so perfectly at home, as in your family, it must be confessed that an irregular lengthty correspondance is far insufficient. I beseech you in the name of our friendship, of that paternal concern of yours for my happiness, not to miss any opportunity to let me hear from my dear General.

*Unpublished.

I have been travelling through some garrison towns in order to preserve the habit of seeing troops and their tactics. Now am mostly at Fontainebleau where the Court is residing for a few weecks. The inclosed letter from the Minister to Mr. Jefferson* will, I hope, prove agreable to the United States. Our Committee will go on this winter, and I will endeavour to propose such measures as may be thought advantageous. Mr. Jefferson is a most able and respected representative, and such a man as makes me happy to be his aid de camp. Congree have made a choice very favourable to their affairs.

The treaty of Commerce betwen France and England is made but not yet ratified. They are to treat each other like the most favoured *European* nation, so that America is safe. News papers will acquaint you with the Dutch quarreles. It is strange to see so many people, so angry, on so small a spot, without bloodshed, but parties are at the same time supported in their claims, and cramped in their motions by the neighbooring powers. France sides with the Patriots. The new King of Prussia interests himself in behalf of the Stat Holder his brother in law, and so does England under hand. But the Republicans are so strong and the State Holder is such a block head, that it will turn out to the advantage of the former†. No present appearance of a war in Germany, the Russians and Turks are quarrelling, but will not so soon make a war. The Empress is going to Krimée, where it is said she will meet the Emperor. She had given me polite hints that I should go to Petersburg. I have answered with a demand of a permission to go to Krimée which has been granted, so that (if the affair of the Forts‡, which I think must be taken does not more agreably employ me) I will set out the last days of February for Krimée, and return by Constantinople and the Archipelago. I will refer to the hints given in a former letter about those Forts which, if timely advertised, would carry me quite a different, and much more pleasing course.

I have been so much affected, my dear General, and so deeply

---

*This is probably the letter of Calonne to Jefferson of October 22, 1786, summarizing the favors already granted to Americans. See Nussbaum, *loc. cit.*, p. 604.

†The stadholder, William V of Orange, and his wife, Wilhelmina, the sister of Frederick William II of Prussia, were so frankly disliked by the Patriot or Republican party of the Netherlands that the next year Frederick William sent an army to protect them.

‡The eight posts on the frontier of the United States in dispute between the United States and England.

mourning for the heavy loss which the United States, and ourselves particularly have had to support, while our great and good friend Gal Green has be snatched from a country to which he was an honour, that I feel a comfort in condoling with one who knew so well his value, and will of course so much have lamented the loss.

There is betwen Mr. Jefferson and Mr. Adams a diversity of opinion respecting the Algerines. Adams thinks a peace should be purchased from them, Mr. Jefferson finds it as cheap and more honourable to cruize against them. I incline to the later opinion, and think it possible to form an alliance between the United States, Naples, Rome, Venice, Portugal and some other powers, each giving a sum of monney not very large, whereby a common armement may distress the Algerines into any terms. Congress ought to give Mr. Jefferson and Adams ample powers to stipulate in their names for such a confederacy.

You will be pleased to hear that I have great hopes to see the affairs of the protestants in this kingdom put on a better footing, not such by far at it ought to be, but much mended from the absurd, and cruel laws of Lewis the fourteenth.

I hope your jack ass, with two females, and a few pheasants and red partridges have arrived safe.

Adieu, my dear General, my best and tenderest respects wait on Mrs. Washington. Remember me to the one who was formerly Master Tub, and now must be a big boy, and also to the young ladies. Be pleased to pay my affectionate compliments to George and his lady, to Doctor and Mrs. Stuart, Doctor Craig, Doctor Griffith, your brothers*, Mrs. Lewis, to your venerable Mother, to all our friends, and often think of your most devoted friend, your adoptive son who with all the affection and respect which you know are so deeply rooted in his heart has the honour to be

My dear general,
Yours
Lafayette

A new instance of the goodness of the State of Virginia has been given me, by the placing of my bust at the Hôtel de Ville of this City. The situation of the other bust will be the more pleasing to me as

---

*John Augustine and Charles Washington. (Proper names are identified in the "Index" below.)

while it places me within the Capitol of the State, I will be eternally by the side of, and paying an ever lasting homage to the Statue of my beloved General.

I have received the hams, and am much obliged to that kind attention of Mrs. Washington. The first was introduced three days ago at a dinner composed of Americans, where our friend Chattelux had been invited. They arrived in the best order. Mde. de Lafayette and the little family beg their respects to Mrs. Washington and yourself.

1787

[193]

My dear General   Paris January the 13th 1787

It is I hope easier for you to conceive than for me to express the painful sensations I feel, when the long waited for opportunity of hearing from you, happens at last to arrive without one line of yours —the regularity of packets is now reestablished, and they will return to the Havre the nearest part of Paris—this will be entrusted to Colonel Franks, who is coming from a successfull negociation at Morocco when Mr. Barcklay and himself behaved very well—I wish our affairs had taken the same turn at Algiers, and think the best way to crush those rascals* should be a confederation betwen the powers at war with them each giving a certain sum, which would be employed by one man, or Council of men, in the fitting out, and constantly keeping in cruize a Naval Squadron adapted to the purpose —The affairs of Holland are not settled—the State Holder is Stuborn —Some patriots carry their wiews very far—Prussia wants to keep up the splendor, if not the power of a brother in law—and France, who of all things is averse to war, wants to conciliate, and throws cold water on them all—it seems that the King of Prussia has not obtained the wisdom of his uncle along with his throne—They say he will go into frivolities—What Great Britain and the United States will do respecting the Forts I do not know, but know very well what I wish America to do, and what part I would like to act in the business—The Empress of Russia is going to Krimée, and had been pleased to invite me there—But I have been suddenly detained by an event which for a long time had not taken place in France—The King has convocated

*The Barbary pirates.

for the end of this month, an Assembly of Notables, composed of principal men in each order of the Kingdom, not holding offices at Court—It will consist of hundred and forty Members, Archbishops, Bishops, Nobles, Presidents of several parliaments, Mayors of towns —Your only acquaintances in the Assembly are Count d'Estaing, Duke de Laval, and your humble Servant, who are three among the six and thirty of the order of Noblesse. The King's letter announces an examination of the finances to be adjusted, of the means to alleviate the taxes of the people, and of many abuses to be redressed— You easely conceive that there is at bottom a desire to make monney some how or other, in order to put the receipt on a level with the expenses, which in this country is become enormous on account of the sums squandered on courtiers and superfluites—But there was no way more patriotic, more candid, more noble to effect those purposes—the King and M. de Calonne his Minister deserve great credit for that—and I hope a tribute of gratitude and good will shall reward this popular measure—My earnest wish, and fond hope is that our meeting will produce popular assemblées in the provinces, the destruction of many schlakles of the trade, and a change in the fate of the Protestants, events which I will promote by my friends as well as my feeble endeavours with all my heart—I had been on the first lists—On the last one I was not, but before I could enquire which was the motive of exclusion, the matter had been set to rights—I will give you an account of the Assembly, not only because what concerns me cannot be stranger to my dear General, but also because every thing is interesting which influences the happiness of 26 millions of people.

You have heard of a certain Beniousky who wanted to have a legion in our Army and who has since gone to Madagascar on an expedition in which some Baltimore Merchants, whom I had warned against it, were interested—Beniousky has pillaged the French settlement at Madagascar—a few men were sent to attak him from the Isle of France, and he was killed—I am going to Versailles, and will request the Minister to send home what citizens of America may happen to be there, as I understand there is one among the prisoners with the badge of the Cincinnati—Beniousky's whole forces were under forty white men.

I have already wrote to you that the Hams are arrived in the best order, and paid my best thanks to Mrs. Washington—But I repeat it in this letter as, from the scarcity of yours, I hope many are lost in the way—This present has been most agreable in the family, and it is difficult to express how wellcomed is a Mount Vernon produce at such a distance.

There is an Italico American of your acquaintance Mr. Mazzeï who seems to me a man very well fitted to be a chargé des affaires in Italy—à propos of chargé des affaires, Mr. Dumas complains that great deal of monney is due to him by Congress, and I think it ought to be paid as soon as possible—as to Mr. Mazzey I have told you, and I think writen my opinion of him, and it seems to me that Congress would make a good choice.

The late disturbances in the Eastern States* have given me great deal of concern and uneasiness—Not that I doubt of the disposition of the people to put things to rights when the evil is demonstrated to them—But in the mean while they hurt their consequence in Europe to a degree which is very distressing, and what glory they have gained by the Revolution, they are in danger of loosing by little and little, at least for a period of time most afflicting to their friends—I hope Congress will not take such a part in the business as would destroy the growing ideas of fœderal measures.

Adieu, my dear General, my most affectionate respects waït on Mrs. Washington, remember me to the Young Family, to George and his Lady, to Mrs. Stuart, Dr. Stuart, Doctor Craig, Col. Humphreys, Harrison, Fitzjerald all our friends whom you happen to meet—Remember me most respectfully to your mother, and the rest of the family—M^{de} de Lafayette, George your God Son, my daughters, beg their most respects to you and Mrs. Washington. God bless you, my beloved General, think often of your absent and most devoted friend, who with all the sentiments of unbounded gratitude, profound veneration, and filial love has the honour to be for ever, my dear General

Your most affectionate and I know your most beloved friend

Lafayette

Should some thing turn out that may make it proper for American soldiers to join their standards—there is one, Colonel Smith who will be very fond to go with me, and I with him.

*Shays rebellion.

[194]

Paris February the 7th 1787

My dear General

The last letter I had from you is dated November the 19th, and announces the safe arrival of the asses who I hope will be less frigid than those of his Catholick Majesty*. Whatever be their intrinsic value, I have found it encreased in a Maryland paper to a degree which does not indeed do justice to the Maltheze Merchants—and as the estimate of the three animals is truly extravagant, I must tell you, altho' it is not very usual for people who make a present to give the receiver a peep into the bill, that the trium Asinanat's cost in Maltha does not much exceed fifty guineas, and yet the jack ass is the best that could be found on the island.

I have given you an account of the Assembly of Notables, wicked people say *not able* which would have already begun had not three of the Ministers, the Count de Vergennes, M. de Calonne, and the keeper of the seals fallen sick very importunately. I am sanguine in the hope that this Assembly will be productive of good consequences. I flatter myself we may get a kind of House of Representatives in each province, not to fix, it is true, but to divide the taxes, and an abolition of several duties on the commercial intercourse within the Kingdom. It is not probable that the affair of the Protestants will come before the house—as the reclamations of the Clergy and a bigoted party might hurt the business,—but we shall, I hope, have it done before long one way or other, and nothing hinders the King deciding at once on that important affair, provided he does not mind too much the opponent party whose only means are to intrigue or complain, and since we have the inconveniences of power, let us in this instance have the benefits of it. The easier so, as the greater part of the Clergy, if unconsulted, will not throw obstacles in the way, and the people at large wish for a more liberal system.

My journey to Krimée will not of course take place, and nothing can be determined upon while the length of our session is not known. I will acquaint you with every thing that is worth crossing the Atlantic. This letter is carried by Col Franks who has particularly well behaved in his mission to Marocco and by Mr. Banister who is going home. This young man is very clever. France has just

*Charles III of Spain.

made a treaty of commerce with Russia which does honour to Count de Segur. The health of Count de Vergennes is rather in an alarming situation. Nothing settled as yet in Holland. The new King of Prussia seems averse to the idea of imitating his predecessor, and does not, as you easely guess, shine the more for it.

We are told that the disturbances in New England are subsiding. God grant it! The people of America ought to be made sensible that any misconduct lowers them the more in the opinions of Europe as they have been so highly and so deservedly admired, and they are most seriously interested in preserving their happiness at home, and their consequence abroad.

Adieu, my most beloved General, be pleased to present my best respects to Mrs. Washington, Mrs. Stuart, your respected mother, all your family. Remember me to George, the young ones, and all friends. Let your affectionate recollection, and fatherly blessing often attend your absent, your dearest, and most devoted friend, and let your heart judge what I so warmly feel, and cannot sufficiently express, that with every sentiment of affection, respect, and gratitude I am my great and good General till the last throb of my heart

Your loving friend
and affet servt
Lafayette

M^{de} de Lafayette and the
young family beg their best
respects to you and Mrs. Washington

[195]

Versailles May the 1st 1787*

My dear General

This letter will be forwarded by Mr. le Mis. de Lotbinieres a French gentleman who had a considerable property in Canada, and now finds himself within the limits of the State of Newyork—He has claims which, the unconstitutional part being set aside, appear to me well grounded—and altho' I told him you had nothing to do in the business, I was requested by himself, and by intimate friends of mine to give him this recommandation.

*Unpublished.

As I write by the same opportunity and my letter will reach Mount Vernon before this, I shall only add the affectionate and filial respect
of
Your devoted and grateful friend
and humble servant
Lafayette

[196]

My dear General   Paris May the 5th 1787

Altho' I cannot omit an opportunity of writing to you, my letter will not be so long and minuted as I would like to make it, because of the constant hurry of business occasioned by the Assembly. Every day, Sunday excepted, is taken up with general meetings, committees, and smaller boards. It is a pretty extraordinary sight at Versailles, the more so as great deal of patriotism and firmness has been displayed.

From the time of this King's arrival to the throne, the expences of the treasury have been encreased of about two hundred French millions a year. But it went at such a rate under M. de Calonne, that having got a monstrous deficiency, and knowing not how to fill it up, he persuaded the King to assemble notable persons of each order, to please them with a plan of assemblies in each province which was much desired, and to get their approbation for new taxes, with which, he durst not by himself saddle the Nation.

The Assembly was very properly choosen both for honesty, abilities and personal consequence. But M. de Calonne's much depended on his own powers of speaking and intriguing as well as on the King's blind confidence in him and all his plans. We were not the representatives of the Nation but have been supported by their partiality to us.

Calonne's plan of a provincial assembly has been amended by us. His plan of a tax in kind was rejected. It has been the case with several other projects. Some others were altered for the better, and sometimes new ones substituted, and we declared that, altho' we had no right to impede, it was our right not to advise unless we thought the measures were proper, and that we could not think of new taxes unless we knew the returns of expenditure and the plans of œconomy.

The more we entered into the business, the less possible it was for the Ministry to do without us. To the Assembly the public looked up, and had the Assembly been dismissed, the credit was gone. As we were going to separate for the Easter days, I made a motion to inquire into bargains by which, under pretence of exchanges, millions had been lavished upon princes and favourites. The Bishop of Langres seconded my motion. It was thought proper to intimidate us, and the King's brother* told in His Majesty's name that such motions ought to be signed. Upon which I signed the inclosed.

M. de Calonne went up to the King, to ask I should be confined to the Bastille. An oratory battle was announced betwen us for the next meeting and I was getting the proofs of what I had advanced, when Calonne was overthrown from his post, and so our dispute ended, except that the King and family and the great men about Court, some friends excepted, don't forgive me for the liberties I have taken, and the success it had among the other classes of the people.

M. de Calonne's successor was M. de Fourqueux an old man who lasted but a fortnight. And now we have got the Arch Bishop of Toulouse at the head of affairs. A man of the most upright honesty and shining abilities. M. de Villedeuil, a clever man, will act under him, and we may consider the Arch Bishop as a prime minister.

We are going to have good houses of representatives in each province, not to vote the taxes but to divide them. We have got the King to make reductions and improvements to the amount of forty millions of livres a year. We are proposing the means to insure a better, and more public method of administration. But will be obliged in the end to make loans and lay taxes. The assembly have acted with firmness and patriotism. The walls of Versailles had never heard so many good things, and our meeting, particularly in the alarming situation of affairs, when the kingdom was driving a way like phaeton's cart, will have proved very beneficial.

I have been much hurt to hear that the unpaid interest of the American debt was considered as a very uncertain revenue. I said every thing that was proper on the subject, but could not prevent that being considered as a fact which hither to has proved but too true. Full justice has been done to the security of the capital. But the ponctuality of the interest has been animadverted upon.

M. de Calonne's letter has met with some difficulties from the

*Comte d'Artois. (Proper names will be identified in the "Index" below.)

farmers which are going to be settled, so that the merchants need not be uneasy. The cloud that was gathering on the Turks and Russians is for the moment clearing up.

My health has been deranged during the assembly, so far as to endanger a little my breast, but a good regimen, and a little patience, without interrupting public business, have got me in a very fair way. Inclosed is a copy of my signed motion which I find in a newspaper. I would have translated it, but you will very easely have it done. When the opinions of the several committees will be printed, I shall send them to America.

My most affectionate respects and those of M^de de Lafayette and family wait on Mrs Washington and you my dear General. Remember me to the whole family and all friends. Most respectfully and tenderly I have the honour to be, my beloved general

Your most devoted and grateful friend
Lafayette

M. de St. John de Crevecoeur the French consul at Newyork has requested my recommendation for some informations he wishes to have. I assured him you would have no objections. Tarleton has printed a journal of the campaigns he has made, wherein he treats Lord Cornwallis very severely.

[197]

My dear General   Paris August the 3d 1787

I have received your first favour from Philadelphia with the greater satisfaction, as it promises me the pleasure to hear again from you before long—a pleasure, my beloved General, which your friend's filial heart wants to anticipate, and enjoys most affectionately. I have not been surprised to hear of your attendance at the Convention, and would indeed have wondered at a denial. On the success of this meeting the very existence of the United States may depend. And you well know that your name will add a great weight to its proceedings. I am sorry to say, but am much more unhappy to observe that the name of America is declining. It gives pleasure to her ennemies. It hurts her interest even with her allies. It furnishes the opponents to liberty with anti-republican arguments. Her dignity is lowering, her credit vanishing, her good intentions questioned by some, her future prosperity doubted. Good God! Will the people of America, so enlightned, so wise, so generous, after they have so gloriously climbed up the rugged hill, now stumble in the easy path? I the more heartly wish well to your meeting as I feel that the happiness of my life would not with[s]tand a disappointement in my fond hopes for the prosperity of our good United States.

I thank you, my dear General, for the fine birds, and excellent beacons you have sent to me. The poor ducks died at the Havre on their arrival. I beg you will send me some again. And beg leave to add a petition for an envoice of mocking birds.

The spirit of liberty is prevailing in this country at a great rate. Liberal ideas are cantering about from one end of the kingdom to the other. Our Assembly of Notables was a fine thing, but for those who imagined it. You know of the personal quarell I had respecting some gifts made to favourites at the expense of the public. It has given me a great number of powerfull and inveterate ennemies, but was very well come to the Nation. I have since that period presented some opinions of mine in very plain terms. I can't say I am on a very favourable footing at Court, if by Court you understand the King, Queen, and King's Brothers, but am very friendly with the present administration. The Arch Bishop of Toulouse is a man equally great by his abilities and uprightness. And the King's Council is better composed than it has ever been.

At the same time the Parliament, warmed by the example of the Notables, makes a great resistance against the new taxes. They will be forced to register the Edicts. But it is well that they have asked for a general assembly of the Nation, and altho' it will not take place now, I anticipate the event, when the assembly of representatives now settling in each province will have taken a proper weight, and felt their own strength. I hope the affair of the Protestants will soon be settled agreable to the motion I had made the day before our dismission.

It is not known wether the Emperor will make terms with the Flemish deputies or risk the sending of an army from his Austrian dominions to that remote part of his empire*. I rather think he will negociate, but would not be surprised if he acted the contrary way. Prussia and Great Britain are supporting the State Holder. France

---

*The Estates of Brabant protested against certain edicts of Joseph II by refusing to pay the ordinary subsidy, and were supported by other estates.

interests herself for the Republican Party. Preparations are making on both sides. But I believe that this too, will take a negociating turn, and be reduced to some skirmishes among the Dutch, unless the King's of Prussia's partiality to his sister* leads him into hasty measures which would involve them all farther than they now expect.

Adieu, my dear and respected General. My best respects wait on Mrs Washington the family and all friends. M^{de} de Lafayette is in Auvergne where I am going to meet her and attend the first session of the Provincial Assembly. With every sentiment of filial love and respect I have the honour to be my dear General

Your respectfull and affectionate friend

Lafayette

[198]

My dear General   Paris October the 9th 1787

I hope the time is drawing near, when I will receive the letter you have announced to me, and while I have the unspeackable satisfaction to hear from my beloved General, I will also gratify my heart felt curiosity to know the proceedings of the Convention. May it have devised proposals, and found in the people a disposition which can insure the happiness, prosperity, and dignity of the United States! I confess that my pride, with respect to America, can bear no mortification, and yet I felt every day that she does not enjoy that consequence which ought to be hers. I hope to God this opportunity may be made use of, so as to give solidity and energy to the Union, without receding however from the principles of democraty, for any thing that is monarchichal, or of the aristocratical kind is big with evils. I am some time affraid least the ill effects of a democratic relaxation be the cause of leaning too much on the other side. But we are to expect that so many enlightened, experienced, and virtuous Senators, will have hit the very point where the people will remain in possession of their natural rights, of that perfect equality among fellow citizens, and yet government, with the powers freely and frequently invested in them, will be able to provide with efficacy and act with vigour. The conduct of Rhode Island is strange indeed.† Has England some personal wiews to answers on that spot?

The affairs of France are still in an unsettled situation. A large

*Wilhelmina, the wife of the stadholder, William V of Orange.
†Rhode Island had refused to send representatives to the Constitutional Convention.

deficiency is to be filled up with taxes, and the Nation are tired to pay what they have not voted. The ideas of liberty have been, since the American Revolution, spreading very fast. The combustible materials have been kindled by the Assembly of Notables. After they had got rid of us, there were the Parliaments to fight with, and altho' they are only courts of Judicature, they have made use of their right of registering, to deny their sanction to any taxes, unconsented by the Nation. Some of them were exiled, some others were not. They made *arrêts* which were broken by the King's Council, and a paper war insued. Count d'Artois, while he came to carry the King's orders, was hissed by the mob. Some ministers have been burnt in effigy. At last the Parliament of Paris very foolishly agreed to an arrangement which was to take back the two proposed taxes, provided they would register an augmentation of the old ones. The provincial Assemblies have held their first meetings. Regulations were given to them by the King. Whereby they were entirely submitted to His Majesty's intendants in each province. We made loud complaints, and the regulations are mending. You see that the king is often obliged to step back, and yet the people at large are unsatisfied. So great is the discontent that the Queen dares not come to Paris for fear of being ill received. And from the proceedings that have taken place these six months past, we shall at least obtain the infusion of this idea into every body's head, wiz—that the King has no right to tax the Nation, and nothing in that way can be stipulated but by an Assembly of the Nation.

The King in France is all mighty. He has all the means to enforce, to punish, and to corrupt. His ministers have the inclination, and think it their duty to preserve despotism. There are swarms of low and effeminate courtiers. The influence of women, and love of pleasure have abated the spirits of the Nation, and the inferior classes are ignorant. But on the other hand the genius of the French is lively, enterprising and inclined to contempt of their rulers. Their minds are getting enlightened by the works of philosophers, and the example of other nations. They are easily actuated by a becoming sense of honour, and altho' they are slaves don't like to confess that it is the case. The inhabitants of the remote provinces are disgusted with the despotism, and the expences of court. So that there is a strange contrast betwen the Turkish power of the King, the regard of the ministry to preserved it untouched, the intrigues and servility of a set of courtiers on the one hand, and on the other the general freedom of thinking, speaking, and writing in spite of the spies, the Bastille, and the library laws, the spirit of criticism, and patriotism in the first class of the Nation, many of them personally servants to the King, mixed with a fear to loose their stations and pensions, the frolicking insolence of the mob in the city ever ready to give way to a detachement of the Guards, and the more serious discontents of the country people, all which ingredients mixed together will by little and little, without great convulsions, bring on an independant representation of the people, are of course a diminution of regal authority. But it is an affair of time, and will be the slower on its way, as the cross interets of powerfull people will put bars in the wheels.

There have been great changes in administration. The Arch Bishop of Toulouse is Prime Minister. He is honest, sensible, and enlightned. I confess he has committed errors since he is in place. Yet do I think him a man of the first rate. He has been twisted of in the two storms of interior and foreign politics. But should a more calm weather come on, I am sure he would be able, and disposed to do great things. Marechals de Castries and Segur have resigned. The former is still much consulted. It is a great loss to the Council. You know I am much connected in friendship with him. The two new ministers are for the war Count de Brienne brother to the Arch Bishop, and Count de la Luzerne, the chevalier's brother for the Navy. He has been sent for Hispaniola where he now commands. I think this one may be usefully disposed towards American concerns. You know that my friend Mr de Malesherbes is again one of the Council. Upon the whole this new administration are composed of very honest men, some of whom very sensible. It is a great thing to have a prime minister who acts the king's part. I wish they had some men among them of military experience. It is much to be feared we shall have a war.

The Ottoman Empire has been long threatened. France supported it against its ennemies, while she advised the Turks against bringing upon themselves a fatal war with the two imperial courts. But through the intrigues of England, the Grand Signor has been driven into hostilities against the Russians, and now the Turkish Empire in Europe must probably fall. It has been a march stolen of us, and it is still doubtfull wether France will support the Turks, unfaithfull, and mad as they are, or occupy some interesting posts in the Mediterrean, on which the English have long had an eye—such as Candia, the Morée, and perhaps Œgipt.

You will also hear, my dear General, of the dismal event that took place in Holland. The indecision of our ministry, the blunders of M. de Verac the French Ambassador, the rascality of a cowardly advanturer, the Rhingrave de Salm, are no doubt much to blame. Verac knew nothing of what was doing, said nothing of what was to be said. Mr de Salm who had infatuated this Court spoke great wonders, and did nothing but to run a way. And the ministers were slow in their preparations, dilatory in recalling their ambassador, and compleatly deceived in their negotiations. But it must be said on the other hand that the Patriotic Party in Holland could never agree in any plan, and were almost as much opposed to each other as they were to the state holder. And the entrance of the King of Prussia's troops was equally contrary to the laws of honour since there was a negotiation on foot, and to those of politics since he throws us into an Austrian alliance very disadvantageous to him. We have been surprised, he mislead, the Dutch ruined, and England is the only one that gained in the bargain.

It is unknown wether Great Britain will be satisfied with keeping a very advantageous treaty of commerce with us, and having regained her influence in Holland or wether she will take this opportunity to revenge for the American war. The later is the British King's wish, and is probable enough. These alliances will then probably be formed. France, the Emperor, Russia, and Spain against England, Prussia, and an army of Hanoverians, Hessians, and Brunswickers helped with the Stateholderian influence in Holland, unless we find means to enter it with an army, and raise up again the Republican Party, which now is pretty difficult. I have been thinking what part America ought to take, and this is my humble opinion. There is no doubt but what the United States will either join France or remain neutral. In the first supposition, they will recover the forts, and Canada will probably be an addition to the Confederacy. But how far is it to be expected that the Southern, and part of the Eastern States will like a war that would deprive them of a portion of their trade, and is America so situated a to support a war without great inconvenience to herself? I would think that a neutrality suits better her interests, but such a neutrality as will actually help her allies, and increase her own wealth. You know that by the treaty the possessions of each other in America are mutually garanteed. France must be induced not to insist upon a litteral compliance with this point, while she enjoys the full advantage of an other article that empowers her to introduce and refit her fleets, and to sell her prizes within the harbours of the United States. France would there by find a shelter, a magazine, a repairing yard where ever she pleases and the United States would have the profit of the sale. At the same time, some letters of marque could be given to American privateers, mixed with French who would bring in under French coulours a part of the West India English produce. In the mean while the American merchants will go on trading with both. And the United States cannot be quarrelled with by England, since on one hand they strickly comply with their treaty, and on the other they cannot prevent the French from purchasing and fitting out vessels where ever they please. I would not have a fear of appearing timid or ungrateful to carry the United States farther than such a friendly, helping neutrality as I have described—which if well managed may enable us to get France to insist on the restoration of the forts in the treaty of peace. But I would be afraïd of a war, on account of the expense.

You know, my dear General, that the letter to M. Jefferson has been attended with embarassements and misunderstandings owing not to any change of disposition in the Ministry, but to the subterraneous chicanes of the farm, which the hurry and crisis of internal business, and the frequent ups and downs of the several ministers prevented administration to set to rights*. The work has been lately finished by my friend Mr Jefferson and myself as well as we could settle it for the present. And considering the intricate difficulties of fiscal laws and exclusive privileges under which this country still labours, I hope you will find that the trade from the United States receives as much favour as it was possible to obtain uptill the present state of things is changed for the better.

*The monopoly of American tobacco trade arranged by a contract between Robert Morris and the Farm was the major issue, and eventually was excluded from the Arrêt du Conseil of December 29, 1787. See Nussbaum, *loc. cit.* and "American tobacco and French politics 1783-1789", *Political Science Quarterly*, XL (1925), 507-14.

I shall now, my dear General, tell you some thing of myself, a part in my Gazettes that I know is not uninteresting to you. After the Assembly of Notables has been ended (where in I had the misfortune to displease their Majesties, royal family, and a set of powerfull men and courtiers, while that conduct of mine, much criticized there, made me very popular among the Nation at large, and was countenanced by the Parliaments who repeated what I had said) I turned my thoughts towards the Provincial Assembly in Auvergne. The presidency was not given to me, and I did not wish for it. That I previously I had declared, because the president being named by the King, is not so free in his motions as a private member. I even wished to be named by the Assembly a member at the county meetings, altho' I could not attend on account of the American commercial business which have called me back and keep me here. The first session of the Assembly was only to compleat its members, because the system of deputation is only to take place in three years time, and the first nomination was made half by the King and the other half by ourselves, who also named one half of the subordinate assemblies, they to compleat themselves by their own choice. I made a tour through the province, where in I was received by all classes of the inhabitants with the most affecting marks of love and confidence. In the mean while there was some thing going on in Holland much to my wishes and advantage, had it not been spoiled by the very men who ought to have supported it. The Dutch had long ago thought of introducing me into their affairs, and it was lately much agitated to put me at the head of the twenty thousand embodied volonteers, in case they did agree to meet, a measure which the interest of the cause, and the opinion of the most sensible among them called for very earnestly—I could also, and would no doubt as soon as affairs grew serious, have been put at the head of the whole military forces in the Republican provinces—While that plan was arranging, much to the satisfaction of the Arch Bishop of Toulouse and Marechal de Castries (for altho' I am not on very good terms with the crowned heads, it does not in the least lessen my influence with the Ministers some of which I am very friendly with, particularly the prime Minister) and while *Ternant* who has acted a noble and important part in the Dutch service did expect the proposal would immediately be made, the Rhingrave de Salm, and his friend the French ambassador did put a stop to the whole transaction by persuading the leaders that such a proposition would not please the Court of France—And as the matter originated with the Dutch, not with the Ministry, who had nothing to do in the business, it was abandonned, or at least procrastinated. And they now say that they have in this as well as in other things been deceived by the absurdity of the French ambassador and the knavery of the Rhingrave.

Amsterdam had a little fight the other day with the Prussians. But they have since capitulated.

Mr de Moustiers sends me word that he is just going. I shall have time and probably a safe opportunity to write before he sails. But as this letter is of a very confidential nature, and is not fit for post offices, particularly in this country, I think it safer to lodge it into that gentleman's hands, and will continue it in a few days. Adieu, my dear General, with filial tenderness and respect I have the honour to be

Your devoted and loving friend   Lafayette

[199]

My dear General   Paris October the 15th 1787*

This letter will be delivered by Mr du Pont the son of a very sensible and honest gentleman, who has been much emploïed in affairs of administration, and is now very zealously engaged in drawing up a report for our commercial affairs. His son goes out for his instruction, and with a wiew to fit himself for future emploïment. I beg leave to recommend him to your patronage and advices, and am happy, my beloved General, in every opportunity to remind you of your tenderest, and I am bold to say, your dearest friend who shall, as long as he lives, glory to be

Your adoptive son and most respectfull
servant
Lafayette

[200]

My dear General   Paris, October the 15th 1787

I have a few days ago written to you by M. de Moustier, the new Minister from this Court. He is a sensible and honest man with whom I think that the people of America will be satisfied. He is very

*Henry E. Huntington Library and Art Gallery, Kane Collection, HM5034. Unpublished.

desirous to be presented to you, and I have invited him in your name to Mount Vernon, as well as M^de de Brehan, a very agreable lady, his sister in law, who goes out with him. Inclosed is, my dear General, the copy of an official letter to Congress wherein I have expressed my sentiments on the present state of affairs. What is become of the happy years, my beloved General, when, before my sentiments were formed, I had time to model them after your judgement! This comfort at least remains for me to endeavour guessing what your opinion will be on every case that occurs. There is nothing new since I wrote my last. Amsterdam has ended her resistence and there are now States Generals, and Provincial States for each of the seven provinces, regularly elected, which are to a man bound to the State Holderian Party. It is one of the vices of their constitution, that the voice of their magistrates, howsoever elected is mistaken for the voice of the Nation. Mr. Jefferson and myself are now employed in commercial affairs for the United States. Mr. de Calonne's letter will be framed into a arrêt of the Council, and additional favours will be so adjusted as to take in every thing that is consistent with this Governement. The disposition of the Ministers is as good as we can wish—and I am happy in the good fortune America had, that such a man as Mr. Jefferson was sent to this country.

Nothing as yet is decided with respect to war—if it breaks out the fault will lie with England. The new Secretary at War has created a Board of eight general officers to carry on the affairs of that departement whereof he is the president. Such a measure is very meritorious, and cannot fail to do him great honour. He is, as you know, the brother of the Archbishop.

Adieu, my dear General, I hope you think often of an adoptive son who loves you with all the powers of his heart, and as long as it has any life, shall ever be

Your most gratefull, affectionate,
and respectfull friend
Lafayette

My best and tenderest respects wait on Mrs. Washington. Remember me most respectfully to your mother and relations, particularly to George—I pay my compliments to all friends. Adieu, my dear General.

⚜ 1788 ⚜

[201]

Paris January the 1st 1787 [1788]

My dear General

I am fortunate in this opportunity to wish you a Happy New Year, and to devote the first moments of this day to the heartfelt pleasure to remind you, my beloved General, of your adoptive son and most affectionate, devoted friend. I beg you will present my best respects to Mrs. Washington. Mde de Lafayette joins in the most tender compliments to you and to her and I hope, my dear General, that you will be so kind as to mention me very affectionately to all the family and friends.

It is needless for me to tell you that I read the new proposed constitution with an unspeackable eagerness and attention. I have admired it, and find it is a bold, large, and solid frame for the Confederation. The electionneering principles with respect to the two Houses of Congress are most happily calculated. I am only affraid of two things—1st the want of a Declaration of Rights 2dly the great powers and possible continuance of the President, who may one day or other become a State Holder. Should my observations be well founded, I still am easy on two accounts. The first that a Bill of Rights may be made if wished for by the people before they accept the Constitution, my other comfort is that you cannot refuse being elected President, and that if you think the public vessel can stir without such powers, you will be able to lessen them, or propose measures respecting the permanence, which cannot fail to insure a greater perfection in the Constitution, and a new crop of glory to yourself. But in the name of America, of mankind at large, and your own fame, I beseech you, my dear General, not to deny your acceptance of the office of President for the first years. You only can settle that political machine, and I foresee it will furnish an admirable chapter in your history.

I am returned from the Provincial Assembly of Auvergne wherein I had the happiness to please the people and the misfortune to displease governement to a very great degree. The Ministry asked for an encrease of revenue. Our Province was among the few who gave nothing, and she expressed herself in a manner which has been taken very much amiss. The internal situation of France is very extraordinary. The dispositions of the people of which I gave you a picture are working themselves into a great degree of fermentation, but not without a mixture of levity and love of ease. The Parliaments are every day passing the boundaries of their Constitution, but are sure to be approuved by the Nation, when, among many unrational things, they have the good policy to call for a General Assembly. Governement see that the power of the crown is declining, and now want to retrieve it by an ill timed and dangerous severity. They have monney enough for this year, so at least they think, for my part, I am heartily wishing for a Constitution, and a Bill of Rights, and wish it may be effected with as much tranquillity and mutual satisfaction as it is possible.

The Emperor has made a foolish attempt on Belgrade, but cannot fail to take it an other time, and at the entrance of the spring the two imperial courts will oppen a vigourous and no doubt successfull campaign against the Turks. These have been led into a war by Great Britain, and should France take a decisive part, it is more probable she will side with Russia. But this Governement will avoid being committed in the affair, and perhaps will not be the better for it. The King of Prussia is now courting France, and proposes, I think, to withdraw his regiments from Holland. But this is a very insufficient, and probably a very useless reparation.

Enclosed, my dear General, are an Arrêt of the Council, and a letter to Mr. Jefferson* both of which after long negotiations we have had the satisfaction to obtain. I expected it might be finished before my journey to Auvergne, but new difficulties have arose and

---

*The arrêt of December 29, 1787 and Calonne's letter of October 22, 1786; see the notes on pp. 314 and 330 above.

Mr. Jefferson and myself have but lately ended the business. I am more and more pleased with Mr. Jefferson. His abilities, his virtues, his temper, every thing of him commands respect and attracts affection. He enjoys universal regard, and does the affairs of America to perfection. It is the happiest choice that could be made.

Adieu, my dear General, with filial love and respect I have the honour to be

Your devoted and affectionate friend
Lafayette

[202]

Paris January the 2^d 1788

My dear General

I have writen to you by way of England, and will only inclose a duplicate of the Arrêt of the Council and letter to Mr Jefferson which I hope may serve the commerce of the United States. I am the more wishing for an encrease of intercourse betwen the two nations as Mr Jefferson and myself have pledged ourselves with the Ministry that it would be the case. And indeed it is equally necessary to keep up the dispositions of France, and change those of Great Britain, who now have all the profits, while they grant no favours. You see, my dear General, that a wide field is now oppened to the speculations of American merchants.

The Emperor is determined on a war against the Turks. How far this winter's negotiations may adjust matters I don't know. But it is probable that the Ottomans will have to fight with the two imperial courts, and cannot fail very dearly to pay for the sport. European politics have much changed since the King of Prussia and Grand Signor gave themselves up to British influence. An alliance with the imperial courts would now better suit France, and she could not be a looser in the bargain. But her first aim will be to avoid a war. The internal situation of this country is rather embarassing for governement, who, also* they have insured the service for the whole year, must still be a little busy in managing a spirit of opposition sometimes unrational in the Parliaments and a spirit of freedom in the people which will occupy the stage untill it is filled by a National

*Apparently *altho' is* meant. (Proper names are identified in the "Index" below.)

Assembly where public affairs will be set to rights. In the mean while the provincial assemblies are doing much good. And I hope that the Constitution of France is improving a great deal. Adieu, my beloved General, my respects to Mrs Washington. Remember me to the family and all friends. Most affectionately, most respectfully, and gratefully

Your devoted and filial friend
Lafayette

[203]

Paris February the 4th 1788

My dear General

Your letters become more and more distant, and I anxiously wish for your speedy appointement to the Presidency, in order that you may have a more exact notice of the opportunities to write to me. This will not tell you much of politics. The two Imperial Courts are preparing for a vigorous campaign against the Turks. Russia intends sending a squadron into the Mediterranean, and altho' it does not much suit either England or France, none, I think, will earnestly expostulate against it. The Turks would fight, as Lord Cornwallis once wrote about me, if they know how. They shall be beaten without doubt, and cannot fail to pay dearly for their new connection with Great Britain. I am told that the King of Prussia also repents for what he has done, but he is too wild to be trusted. He is strenghtening the Germanic Confederacy set on foot by the late King, and England has taken into her pay a good number of German princes. It seems affairs are slowly working towards an alliance betwen the Imperial Courts, France and Spain. It goes on as gently as it possible for politics to move. France is afraïd for her Levant trade. She wants to mend her deranged finances. Governement is not a little embarassed by a spirit of opposition that has of late introduced itself. So that every means to pacify, to mediate, and to lay still will be emploïed by France. Yet is she so powerfull by her ressources, her fertility, her position, and all the advantages she is endowed with, that she must be calculated much above the mark where her rivals now place her. And the moment she gets a National Assembly, she will leave far behind every thing in Europe. England has gone a little too far for her own abilities and intentions. I am told there is a deficiency in the last quarter. She is uneasy at the fermentation kept up in Holland by the horrid conduct of the State Holderians—and at the prospect of the Quadruple Alliance. Yet as our Ministry are known to seak peace with great perseverance, the British Cabinet think themselves enabled to take a higher tone than what they seriously intend.

We are anxiously waiting for the result of the State Conventions. The New Constitution has been much examined and admired by European philosophers. It seems the want of a declaration of rights, of an insurance for the trial by juries, of a necessary rotation of the president, are, with the extensive powers of the executive, the principal points objected to. Mr. Jefferson and myself have agreed that those objections appear'd to us both well grounded, but that none should be started untill nine states had accepted the Confederation. Then amendments, if thought convenient, might be made to take in the dissidents. As to what respects the powers and possible permanency of the president I am easy, nay I am pleased with it as the reducing of it to what is necessary for energy, and taking from it every dangerous seed will be a glorious sheet in the history of my beloved General.

You have received an Arrêt du Conseil and letter to Mr. Jefferson which I hope will prove advantageous to the trade. The former has excited a pretty considerable fermentation among some commercial and financeering people who think we have been too partial to the United States. I have requested the Ministers to call the opponents in a committee, and hope to support every article to their satisfaction. It is better not to mention this circumstance for fear of giving some unnecessary uneasiness to the merchants in America.

The edit giving to the *non catholic subjects of the king* a civil estate has been registered. You remember, my dear General, what I wrote to you three years ago. You easely guess that I was well pleased last Sunday in introducing to a ministerial table the first Protestant clergyman who could appear at Versailles since the Revolution of 1685*.

M^{de} de Lafayette, Anastasia, George your son, and Virginia are all well and beg to be most respectfully presented to you and to M^{rs}

---

*In 1685 Louis XIV revoked the Edict of Nantes, by which Henry IV had guaranteed civil rights to the French Protestants.

Washington to whom I beg you to offer my affectionate respects. Remember me, my dear General, to the family and all friends. Inclosed is a letter from Mis de Bouillé who has been much flattered with the one he received from you. Adieu, my beloved General, for God's sake don't miss any opportunity to write to
  Your most respectfull loving, and filial friend
                                        Lafayette

[204]
                    Paris March the 6th 1788*
My dear General
  Give me leave to present to you Mr Van der Kemp a gentleman whose conduct in the Patriotic cause of Holland entitles him to your attention and patronage. He is recommended to me most particularly by the first characters among the Patriots. I have many opportunities to see the refugees from Holland, many of whom had wished to entrust their military affairs to one who had been educated at General Washington's Head Quarters. They have spoken to me of Mr Van de Kemp their fellow sufferer in such terms as makes me happy to introduce him to you.
  With filial love and respect I have the honour to be
              my dear General
                    Yours
                          Lafayette

[205]
                    Paris March the 18th 1788
My dear General
  I wish I could begin this letter with the aknowledgement of a late favour from you, but none having come to hand I have no other comfort but to attribute it to ill fortune and not to any fault of yours. I am so happy to hear from you, my beloved General, and so uneasy when I do not, that I hope you will never willingly deprive me of a satisfaction so dear to me, yet so short of the happy habits I had taken in America.
  The politics of Europe begin to unfold themselves, in the east ward at least. Russia is preparing for a vigourous campaign, and will
*Unpublished.

soon besiege Oksakow, while an other army is combining itself with an Austrian body of troops. The Grand Army of the Emperor, commanded by himself assembles about Belgrade, which he endeavoured to surprise but did not succeed. The Russians are sending a fleet with five thousand men into the Mediterranean. And the Venitians are also arming a fleet. The Turks have raised numerous flocks of armed men. Their cavalry, which in the first shock, is not despicable, has, it is said, surrounded three thousand of the Austrians and cut of their heads, as is usual among them. They also had a successfull skirmish against the Russians. But there is no doubt of the advantage which such disciplined armies as those of the allied empires will have over a banditti of men who are totally strangers to discipline, military knowledge, and rational calculations. They may succeed with detached corps, and must disperse before the main body of their ennemies. The only difficulties will be the want of provisions, the bareness of the country, and the dangers of the plague. And should the Imperial Courts, not wistanding those embarrassements, go so far as Constantinople, there they will find a bone of contention to know who will possess that metropolis.

The King of Prussia has taken no part as yet. Poland is uneasy, and fears to loose something in the general arrangement. Holland is making a treaty with Prussia and one with England. Nothing in Great Britain has the appearance of a war. France wants peace at any rate. Spain is arming and objects to the entrance of the Russians in the Mediterranean, but will probably yeld to the demands of France. It is not improbable that the two Imperial Courts will, after one campaign, content themselves for the present with a considerable encrease of their possessions. But it could also be foreseen that a war may be kindled through all Europe, and end with the total destruction of the Ottoman Empire in Europe. So that it is not easy to determine which of the two events will take place.

The internal affairs of France are not yet settled. Many considerable reforms have taken place in the expense. But a great deficiency still subsists, and as the Parliaments have declared themselves unfit to assent to taxes, as the Provincial Assemblies are not yet the representatives of the people, I think the King will be obliged to assemble the Nation sooner than is expected by his Ministers. The printed account of the finances is to come out in a few days. I know that governement intend to postpone the States Generals to the latest period consistent with their engagement which is before 1792. But I believe this desireable event will take place next summer twelve month. It is the only way to put things to rights, and to fix unalterable principles in the administration of this country.

I have some reasons to think that governement is preparing an attack on the Parliaments, who altho' they are only a judicial court have shown a spirit of resistence, and refused to register any new tax untill the States Generals have met.

The troops have been divided into armies, and grand divisions. The four generals will be Marshals of France. The grand divisions under lieutenant generals, I have asked to be emploïed with the Duke D'ayen my father in law in the Southern Provinces and am the eldest g^{al} officer under him. The divisions are about ten thousand men. The commands of us major generals are called brigades. Two corps of light infantry will be added to my regiments. We will serve two months.

Adieu, my beloved General, my best respects wait on Mrs. Washington and family. With most tender respect and filial love I have the honour to be
    Your affectionate and devoted friend
            Lafayette

[206]

Paris May the 4th 1788 *

My dear General

I have been requested to present to you M. de Saint Fris a Captain in a French R^{gt} of Dragoons who is going as a traveller through the United States, and of course wishes to pay his respects to General Washington. He has been particularly recommended to me, and as I don't know when this introductory letter will reach you and I am sure it will not arrive before my despatches of a later date.

I shall only present you with the affectionate respects of
    Your filial friend
            Lafayette

*Unpublished.

[207]

My dear General   Paris May the 20th 1788*

I have been requested to introduce to you Mr de Chastel de la Vallée a French gentleman who intends to visit the United States, and will probably settle in one of them. He is particularly recommended to me by the Mquis de Bouillé to whose lady he is related, and I beg, my dear General, you will honour him with your advices in his intended plan.

Not knowing when this can reach you, and having a speedy opportunity to write I shall only present you, my beloved General, with the filial Respect and And [sic] Affection of

Yours most devoted friend
Lafayette

AMENDED   [208]

My dear General   Paris May the 25th 1788

In the midst of our internal troubles, it is a comfort to me that I may rejoice in the happy prospects that oppen before my adoptive country. Accounts from America give me every reason to hope the New Constitution will be adopted. Permit me once more, my beloved General, to insist on your acceptance of the Presidency. The Constitution as it is proposed answers most of the purposes, but, unless I am much mistaken, there are some parts which would not be quite free of some danger had not the United States the good fortune to possess their Guardian Angel, who may feel the advantages and inconveniences of every article, and will not be able, before he retires again, to ascertain to what degree governement must necessarily be energic, what powers might be diverted into a bad use, and to point out the means to attain that perfection, to which the New Constitution is already nearer than any past or present governement.

The affairs of France are come to a crisis, the more difficult to manage as the people in general have no inclination to go to extremities. Liberty or Death is not the motto on this side of the Atlantic. And as all classes are more or less dependant, as the rich love their ease, and the poor are depressed by want and ignorance, the only way is to reason or persuade the Nation into a kind of passive discontent or non obedience which may tire out the levity and undo

*Unpublished.

the plans of governement. The Parliaments, notwistanding the inconveniences attending them, have been necessary champions to stand forth. You will see by the publications, for we have sent over every thing, that the King has assumed pretentions, and the Courts of justice have stated principles which so widely differ that one could hardly believe those assertions are made in the same country and century. Matters could not rest there. Governement have employed the force of arms against unarmed magistrates, and expelled them*. And the people will you say? The people, my dear General, have been so dull that it has made me sick, and phisicians have been obliged to cool my inflamed blood. What has the more wounded up my anger, is a Bed of Justice wherein the King has established a *Court Pleniere*† composed of judges, peers, and courtiers, without one single representative, and there Ministers had the imprudence to say that all taxes and loans should be registered. Thank God, we have got the better, and I begin to hope for a Constitution. The magistrates have refused sitting in the *Cour Pleniere*—The peers, who are thirty eight, a few of whom have sense and courage, will not however obey. Some, like my friend La Rochefoucauld behaved nobly. The other follow at a distance. The Parliaments have unanimously protested and made an appeal to the Nation. Most of the inferior courts reject the new regimen. Discontents breack out every where, and in some provinces are not despicable. The clergy—who happen to have an Assembly are remonstrating. The lawyers refuse to plead. Governement are embarrassed and begin to apoligise. Their commandants have been in some parts pursued with dirt and stones. And the midst of these troubles and anarchy the friends of liberty are daily reinforced, shutt up their ears against negociations, and say they must have a National Assembly or nothing. Such is, my dear General, our bettering situation, and I am for my part very easy when I think that I shall before long be in an Assembly of the Representatives of the French Nation, or at Mount Vernon.

    I am so taken up with those affairs, that I can tell you but little of European politics. My disapprobation of ministerial plans, and

*On May 6, 1788, two members of the Parlement were arrested in the Palais de Justice.

†On May 8, 1788, Louis XVI by the traditional ceremony of a *lit de justice* ordered the Paris Parlement to register a decree abolishing itself and establishing a plenary court in its place.

what little exertions I could make against them have induced me to cease my visits at the Arch Bishop's house, and the more I have been connected with him and the Keeper of the Seals*, the greater indignation I have professed against their infernal plan. I am glad our American Arrêt du Conseïl has taken place before the full tide of these troubles, and am now, through other Ministers, endeavouring to bring about a plan for the total enfranchisement of duties on the whale oil, which would put the American merchants on the same footing with the French, even with respect to bounties, and that without obliging the fisher men to leave their native shore. Should we succeed in that, our next object must be the trade with the West Indies. I am happy in the ambassador we have in this country, and nothing can excell M. Jefferson's abilities, virtues, pleasing temper, and every thing in him that constitutes the great states man, zealous citizen, and amiable friend. He has a young gentleman with him, Mr Short, a Virginian, who is a very able, engaging, and honest man; this letter will be delivered by Mr de Warville, a man of letters, who has writen a pamphlet against Chattelux's journal†, but is however very clever, and wishes very much to be presented to you. He intends to write the History of America, and is of course very desirous to have a peep at your papers which appears to me a deserved condescension as he is very fond of America, writes pretty well, and will set matters in a proper light. He has an officer with him whom I also beg leave to recommend. M. de la Terriere is his name.

But to come to politics, I must tell you that the war betwen the Imperial Powers and the Turks is going on. The emperor has made several attempts, but there is a fatality in that man which makes him ever begin and never finish any thing. The skirmishes have generally been doubtfull. He has taken a town, but was severely brushed in an other assault, and the same day met with a second defeat. Those matters, however trifling, show that the Turks are either very ill attaked, or more lucky than we did expect. The siege of Belgrade will be the grand expedition that way and is not begun. There has been

*Brienne, archbishop of Toulouse, was chief of the Council of Finances (a sort of prime minister) and Lamoignon was now keeper of the seals. They were regarded as responsible for the effort to abolish the Paris Parlement.
†*Examen critique des* Voyages dans l'Amérique Septentrionale de M. le Marquis de Chatellux *dans laquelle on réfute principalement ses opinions sur les Quakers, sur les Nègres, sur le peuple et sur l'homme* par J.-P. Brissot de Warville (London, 1786).

a jonction made by the Austrians and Russians in an other quarter, but they have not much the means to operate. The Grand Army of the Russians are moving towards Ozakow which Prince Potemkin, a former lover, and the bosom friend of the Empress is going to besiege. Paul Jones has entered the Russian service and will command a squadron on the Black Sea. All the powers are negociating for a peace, but at the same time Spain, Sweden, Danemark are arming. Those will be observation fleets, and it is expected that a peace will take place this winter. We must of course wish for decisive actions. Should they be unfavourable to the Christians it may disgust them. And you never can get a concession from the Turks, untill the Prophet has shown his displeasure by suffering them to be flogged. In case both parties maintain their ground, a general war is aprehended for the next year.

I beg, my dear General, you will present my most affectionate respects to Mrs Washington, and to your respected Mother. Remember me to the family, the young ones, your relations, to all friends. M^{de} de Lafayette and children join in the best respects to you and Mrs Washington. My younger daughter Virginia is now under inoculation. Adieu, my beloved General, I don't live one day without grieving for this hard separation which deprives me of the blessed sight of what is dearest to me, and leaves me so few opportunities to tell you, by dear General, with all the love of a devoted heart that I am forever with the most affectionate respect

Your filial, gratefull friend
Lafayette

I had a letter from M. de Moustier who (betwen us) appears to me not well pleased. We must humour him a little, that his representations be favourable. It is said that the Russian Fleet destined to the Mediterranean is counter manded altho' Spain had consented. How far this is certain I don't know. I have just received an official communication of a resolve signed by more than three hundred gentlemen of the order of Noblesse in Britanny *declaring it infamous* to accept a place in the New Administration—to which I very plainly have given my assent. Adieu, my dear general.*

---

*Regarding the extraordinary lapse of time between this letter and the next see the "Preface," p. xx above. We have been unable to find Lafayette's letter of September 5, 1788, mentioned in Washington's letter to Lafayette, January 29, 1789, Fitzpatrick, *Writings of Washington,* XXX, 184.

1790

AMENDED [209]

Paris January the 12th 1790

My dear General

I cannot let the packet sail without a line from your filial friend, who, altho' he depends on Mr Short for your information, wants to express you those affectionate and respectful sentiments that are never so well felt as in uncommon circumstances—How often, my beloved General, have I wanted your wise advices and friendly support! We have come thus far in the Revolution without breaking the ship either on the shoal of aristocraty, or that of faction, and amidst the ever reviving efforts of the mourners and the ambitious we are stirring towards a tolerable conclusion—Now that every thing that was is no more, a new building is erecting, not perfect by far, but sufficient to ensure freedom, and prepare the Nation for a Convention in about ten years, where the defects may be mended—I will not enter in all the details I have already related—Common Sense* is writing a book for you—There you will see a part of my adventures—I hope they will turn to the advantage of my country and mankind in general—Liberty is sprouting about in the other parts of Europe, and I am encouraging it by all the means in my power—Adieu, my beloved General, my best respects waït on Mrs Washington—Remember me to Hamilton, Harrison, Knox, &c. &c. and all our friends—Most respectfully and affectionately

Your most devoted and filial friend
Lafayette

I wish Mr Jay, John Adams, Wadsworth, and Doctor Franklin could witness the difference betwen this France, this Capital, and the once they have seen.

*I.e. Thomas Paine. (Proper names are identified in the "Index" below.)

346

AMENDED [210]

My dear General   Paris March the 17th 1790

It is with the utmost concern that I hear my letters have not come to hand, and while I lament the miscarriage, I hope you do not impute it to any fault on my part—In these times of troubles, it has become more difficult to know, or to reach opportunities, and how this will be carried I leave to the care of Mr Payne who goes to London.

Our revolution is getting on as well as it can with a Nation that has swalled up liberty all at once, and is still liable to mistake licentiousness for freedom—The Assembly have more hatred to the ancient system than experience on the proper organization of a new and constitutional governement—The ministers are lameting the loss of power, and affraïd to use that which they have—and as every thing has been destroïed and not much new building is yet above ground, there is much room for critics and calomnies.

To this may be added that we still are pestered by two parties, the Aristocratic that is panting for a counter revolution, and the factious which aims at the division of the Empire, and destruction of all authority and perhaps of the lifes of the reigning branch, both of which parties are fomenting troubles.

And after I have confessed all that, my dear General, I will tell you with the same candour that we have made an admirable, and almost incredible destruction of all abuses, prejudices, etc. etc. that every thing not directly useful to, or coming from the people has been levelled—that in the topographical, moral, political situation of France we have made more changes in ten month than the most sanguine patriot could have imagined—that our internal troubles and anarchy are much exagerated—and that upon the whole this Revolution, in which nothing will be wanting but energy of governement just as it was in America, will propagate implant liberty and make it flourish throughout the world, while we must waït for a Convention in a few years to mend some defects which are not now perceived by men just escaped from aristocraty and dispostism.

You know that the Assembly have adjourned the Westindia affairs, leaving every thing in the actual state, wiz. *the ports oppened* as we hear they have been to American trade. But it was impossible, circumstanced as we are, to take a definitive resolve on that matter —The ensuing legislature will more easely determine, after they

347

have received the demands of the Colonies who have been invited to make them, particularly on the object of *victualling*.

Give me leave, my dear General, to present you with a picture of the Bastille just as it looked a few days after I had ordered its demolition, with the main kea of that fortress of despotism—It is a tribute which I owe as a son to my adoptive father, as an aid de camp to my General, as a Missionary of Liberty to its Patriarch.

Adieu, my beloved General, my most affectionate respects waït on Mrs. Washington, present me most affectionately to George, to Hamilton, Knox, Harrison, Jay, Humphrey and all friends Most tenderly and respectfully   Your most affectionate and filial friend
Lafayette

AMENDED   [211]

My dear General   Paris August the 23rd 1790

What would have been my feelings, had the news of your illness reached me before I knew my beloved General, my adoptive father was out of danger! I was struck with horror at the idea of the situation you have been in, while I, uninformed, and so distant from you, was anticipating the long waited for pleasure to hear from you, and the still more endearing prospect to visit you, and present you with the tribute of a Revolution, one of your first offsprings. For God's sake, my dear General, take care of your health, don't devote yourself to much to the cabinet, while your habit of life has from your younger years, accustomed you to a constant exercice—Your preservation is the life of your friends, the salvation of your country —it is for you a relligious duty not to neglect any thing that may concern your health. I beg you will let me oftener hear from you. I write when an opportunity offers. And to my great sorrow I hear my letters must have miscarried, or been detained. But as our correspondance can have no other bounds but the opportunities to write, it was not a reason, give me leave to say, for you to miss any that may have offered—and you may easly guess what I am exposed to suffer, what would have been my situation had I known your illness before the news of your recovery had comforted a heart so affectionately devoted to you.

This letter will be delivered by two gentlemen, one of them

an artillery officer, who are going to settle on the banks of famed Scioto. How profitable the scheme may be to them, I do not determine, but as they personally are entitled to regard, and are much recommended to me, I beg you will honour them with your kind reception and good advices.

The proceedings of the National Assembly cannot fail being known to you—we have run or cut down every thing that was—and perhaps was it the only way to get rid of the innumerable obstacles that opposed our Revolution. We afterwards have made an immense emission of resolves, constitutional, legislative, administrative, and of the later great deal too much. Happy it has been for us that I persuaded the Assembly to begin with a Declaration of Rights, as among our decrees, few may be found that are not consonant with the most perfect principles of Natural Rights, so that our errors being on the popular side, and of the speculative turn, monarchial influence, and practice will fit us to meet in a few years a second Convention, while had we gone half way only, or taken an other rule than that of Nature, it would have been impossible to conquer our difficulties, or destroy our prejudices—It is from such a motive that I have been so eager to unroot out not only the reality but even the smallest appearance of aristocraty among us.

Now we are disturbed with revolts among the regiments—And as I am constantly attacked on both sides by the Aristocratic and the Factious party I don't know to which of the two we owe these insurrections. Our safeguard against them lies with the National Guard. There is more than a million of armed citizens—among them patriotism reigns—and my influence with 'em is as great as if I had accepted the chief command—I have lately lost some of my favour with the mob, and displeased the frantic lovers of licentiousness, as I am bent on establishing a legal subordination—But the Nation at large are very thankful to me for it. It is not out the heads of the Aristocrats to make a counter revolution. Nay, they do what they can with all the crowned heads of Europe who hate us like the devil. But I think their plans will be either abandonned or unsuccessfull. I am rather more concerned with a division that rages in the popular party. The Clubs of the Jacobines, and *89** it is called, have divided

*The Club of 1789 was founded in May 1790 and was made up largely of those who advocated the principles eventually incorporated in the Constitution of 1791.

the friends of liberty who accuse each other, Jacobines being taxed with a disorderly extravagance, and *89* with a tincture of ministerialism and ambition. I am endeavouring to bring about a reconciliation. The affair of the 6th of October will be reported in the house next week†. I don't think there will be against Duke D'orleans, and am sure there are not against Mirabeau sufficient charges to impeach them. There is some thing cloudy in the present systems of those two men, altho' they do not seem actually connected—they are both cowards, but the prince most particularly so.

I hope our business will end with the year—at which time this so much blackened Cromwell, this ambitious dictator, your friend, shall most deliciously enjoy the happiness to give up all power, all public cares, and to become a private citizen in a free monarchy, the constitution of which, altho' I could not help it being very defective now, will lay a foundation for the more excellent are to be made in a few years.

The people begin to be a little tired with the Revolution and the Assembly—one part to be ascribed to the French temper, and numberless private losses—the other part owing to the faults of the Assembly, the intrigues and the ambition of most of its leaders. But we have got wind enough to run the ship into harbour.

I depend on my friend Short to give you political intelligences. His abilities, zeal, and the affection and esteem he enjoys put him in a situation to give you the best informations. M. Jefferson and myself know his worth, and can warrant it. He is a most valuable man to do American business here.

My best respects wait on Mrs. Washington. I beg you to present my tenderest compliments to Hamilton, Knox, Jefferson. Be so kind as to show them my letter as well as to Mr. Jay to whom I also beg my affectionate compliments and to all friends.

Adieu, my dear General, M^{de} de Lafayette and family join in affectionate respects to you and Mrs. Washington. Most tenderly and respectfully I have the honour to be my beloved General

Your devoted friend
Lafayette

†A committee of the National Assembly reported that there were insufficient grounds for believing Orleans and Mirabeau responsible for the attack on the royal palace at Versailles on October 5 and 6, 1789; and the National Assembly so moved on October 2, 1790.

❦ 1791 ❦

[212]

Paris January the 25th 1791

My dear General

Give me leave to introduce and recommend to you M. Kellerman, the son of an able and patriot general officer in the French service. It is not under the embroidered regimentals that we find the greater proportions of friends to the Revolution—For which reason I am the better disposed to oblige such as have sided with us.

The National Assembly have, whislt I was engaged in quelling a riotous fight in one of the suburbs where some men had been killed*, voted a bill to prohibit foreign oil, except that imported by the Americans. But to my great concern the Aristocratic Party, helping the mercantile interest on our side of the house, have altered the article, so that the duty has been increased from five to twelve livres. In vain has it been moved to put of the debate untill I could be present. The opponents have carried it. But I hope we may get the Diplomatic Committee to interfere.

Adieu my dear General, my best respects wait on Mrs. Washington. Remember me to all friends. Most affectionately and respectfully

Your filial friend
Lafayette

---

*The disorders at La Chapelle on January 24, 1791, are meant. The debates in the National Assembly are to be found in the *Archives parlementaires*, 1st series, XXII, 470-75.

[213]

Paris March the 7th 1791

My dear General

Whatever expectations I had conceived of a speedy termination to our Revolutionary troubles, I still am tossed about in the ocean of factions and commotions of every kind—For it is my fate to be on each side, with equal animosity attacked, both by the Aristocratic, Slavish*, Parliamentary, Clerical, in a word by all ennemies to my free and levelling doctrine, and on the other side by the orleanoise, factious, Anti Royal, licentious, and pillaging parties of every kind, so that my personal escape from admidst so many hostile bands is rather dubious, altho' our great and good Revolution is, thank Heaven, not only insured in France, but on the point of visiting other parts of the world, provided the restoration of public order is soon obtained in this country, where the good people have been better taught how to overthrow despotism than they can understand how to submit to the law. To you, my beloved General, the Patriarch and Generalissimo of Universal Liberty, I shall render exact accounts of the conduct of your deputy and aid in this great cause.

You will hear that the National Assembly have permitted the cultivation of tobacco throughout the kingdom, as it was already established in the frontier provinces—to which they have been in duced on three accounts, 1stly because they thought a prohibition inconsistent with the principles of the Bill of Rights 2dly because the removal of the excise barriers to the extremities of the Empire made it necessary to have one general rule—3dly because the departements formerly called Alzace and Flanders being greatly contamined by a foreign and aristocratic influence, there was no doubt of the impending attack of the rebel princes Condé and Artois taking place, and being countenanced even by the country farming people, had we cut them of from that branch of cultivation, all of a sudden.

But what is greatly exceptionable is a duty fixed on the introduction of American tobacco, with a premium in favour of the French vessels, and a duty much too high, altho' it was lately lessened on American whale oil. But I beg you, and all citizens of the United States, not to be discouraged by that hasty, and ill combined

*I.e. opposed to the emancipation of slaves. (Proper names are identified in the "Index" below.)

measure, which I hope before long to see rectified in consequence of a report of the Diplomatic Committee, including the whole at once, and for which my friends and myself have kept our arguments. I shall send you the report, the debate, and the resolve. Should we obtain an easy introduction of American tobacco, no cultivation of any importance can take place in France, and it will be the better for both countries.

M. de Ternant has been named Plenipotentiary Minister to the United States. I have warmly wished for it because I know his abilities, his love for liberty, his early, steady, and active attachement to the United States, his veneration and love for you. The more I have known Ternant, the more I have found him a man of great parts, a steady, virtuous, and faith full friend. He has deserved a great share in the confidence of the National Assembly, the patriotic side I mean, the King has a true regard for him, in a word I hope he will on every account answer your purposes, and serve America as zealously in the diplomatic line, as he did when in the army.

Adieu, my beloved General, my best respects wait on Mrs. Washington. Remember me most affectionately to Hamilton, Jefferson, Knox, Jay and all friends. M^{de} de Lafayette and children beg their tender respects being joined to mine for you and the family. Most respectfully and tenderly I am my dear General

Your filial friend
Lafayette

Inclosed is a letter which Ternant has requested I would join to mine

You have made M. Poirey the happiest man in the world for which Mde de Lafayette and myself are very thankfull.

[214]

Paris May the 3^d 1791

My dear General

I wish it was in my power to give you an assurance that our troubles are at an end, and our Constitution totally established. But altho' dark clouds are still before us, we came so far as to foresee the moment when a legislative corps will succeed this Convention, and, unless foreign powers interfere, I hope that within four month your friend will have reassumed the life of a private and quiete citizen.

353

rage of parties, even among the patriots, is gone as far as it short of blood shed. But altho' hatreds are far from sub-..rs don't appear so ill disposed as they formerly were ...s a coalition among the supporters of the popular cause. I ...yself am exposed to the envy and attacks of all parties for this simple reason, that who ever acts or means wrong finds me an insuperable obstacle, and there appears a kind of phœnomenon in my situation, all parties against me, and yet a national popularity which in spite of every effort has been unshakable—A proof of this I had lately when disobeïed by the Guard, and unsupported by the administrative powers who had sent me, unnoticed by the National Assembly who had taken fright, the king I do not mention as he could do but little in the affair, and yet the little he did was against me, given up to all the madnesses of licence, faction and popular rage, I stood alone in defense of the law, and turned the tide up into the Constitutional Channel*. I hope this lesson will serve my country, and help towards establishing the principles of good order. But before I could bring my fellow citizens to a sense of legal subordination I must have conducted them through the fear to loose the man they love. Inclosed is the speech I delivered on the occasion. I send it not for any merits of it, but on account of the great effect it had on the minds of the people, and the discipline of an army of five and forty thousand men, upwards of thirty of whom are volunteers, and who to a man are exposed to all the suggestions of a dozen of parties, and the corruptions of all kinds of pleasures and allurements.

The Committee of Revision is going to distinguish in our immense materials every article that deserves to be constitutional, and as I hope to convene in a tolerable state of union the members of that Committee, as their votes will in the House influence the popular part of the Assembly, I hope that besides the restoration of all Natural Rights, the destruction of all the abuses, we may present to the Nation some very good institutions of governement, and organise it so as to ensure to the people the principal consequences, and enjoïements

---

*On April 18, 1791, Louis XVI and his family attempted to leave Paris in order to observe Easter at St. Cloud. A popular demonstration, supported by some National Guards, prevented them from doing so. Lafayette resigned as commander of the Parisian Guard, and reconsidered only after the Guard and the Municipality had assured him of their support in his effort to preserve the rights of individuals guaranteed by the constitution.

of a free constitution, leaving the remainder to the Legislative Corps to mend into well digested bills, and waïting untill experience has fitted us for a more enlightened, and less agitated National Convention.

In the mean while our principles of Liberty and Equality are invading all Europe, and popular revolutions ripening every where.

Should foreign powers employ this summer with attaks against our Constitution, there will be great bloodshed, but our liberty cannot fail us. We have done every thing for the general class of the country people, and in case the cities were frightened into submission, yet the peasants would swarm round me, and fight to death, rather than give up their rights.

Adieu, my beloved General, my best respects waït on Mrs Washington. Remember me to Hamilton, Jay, Jefferson, Knox, and all friends. Most respectfully and affectionately I am my dear general
Your filial friend
Lafayette

[215]

My dear General   Paris June the 6th 1791

I most heartly thank you for your letter dated March the 19th, the more wellcome to me, as I had long lamented your silence, and was panting for news from you, my dear General, wherein I could be informed of every thing respecting your public and private concerns. I rejoice and glory in the happy situation of American affairs. I bless the restoration of your health, and wish I could congratulate you on your side of the Atlantick. But we are not in that state of tranquillity which may admit of my absence—the refugees* hovering about the fronteers—intrigues in most of the despotic and aristocratic cabinets—our regular army divided into tory officers, and undisciplined soldiers—licentiousness among the people not easily repressed—the Capital that gives the tone to the Empire tossed about by antirevolutionary or factious parties—the Assembly fatigued by hard labour, and very unmanageable—the priests that have taken the oath, and those who have not playing the devil†. However, accord-

*The émigrés, who were trying to secure foreign intervention on their behalf.
†On November 27, 1790, an oath of loyalty to the new constitution was required of priests. This measure divided the clergy into two camps—those who took the oath (constitutional clergy) and those who refused to do so (non-juring clergy).

ing to our popular motto, *ca ira*, it will do—we are introducing as fast as we can relligious liberty. The Assembly has put an end to her existence by a new convocation, has unfitted her own members for immediate reëlection, or places in the executive—and is now reducing the Constitution to a few principal articles, leaving to the Legislative Assemblies to examine and mend the others, and preparing every thing for a convention, as soon as our machine will have had a fair trial. I stand the continual check to all interior factions and plots. By the enclosed speech of mine, and the giving up my commission* I gave a spring to the power of law over licentiousness, and was I equally supported in repressing it, as I would be against aristocratic exertions the people would soon be brought to a proper sense of liberty. As to the surrounding Governements they hate our Revolution, but don't know how to meddle with it, so affraid they are to *catch the plague.* We are going to take measures to discipline the army, both officers and soldiers. They will prepare to encamp and leave the cities. Their generals will have the same power as in time of war. M. de Condé and his party will be summoned to explain themselves, and if they continue cabaling, and enlisting declared traïtors. To M. de Ternant I refer for more particulars.

M. Jefferson and myself had long thought that Ternant was a very proper man to act as French Minister in America. He in a great measure belongs to both countries. He is sensible, honest, well informed, and has a plain and decisive way of doing business which will be very convenient. He has long been an officer under your commands—feeling and acting in an American capacity. He is personally much attached to you, and I had in this Revolution many instances to experience his friendship to me. He might have been a Minister in the Council, but was rather backward on the occasion, and behaved like a prudent, not an ambitious man—so that I take him to be fit to answer your purpose.

He will let you know what has past in the Assembly respecting American affairs. The last transactions are an undoubted proof of their sentiments, and show that their faux pas in the regulation of duties are to be attributed to want of knowledge or sense, not of

---

*See the note on p. 354 above. Lafayette's speech was probably the one delivered to the municipal council of Paris on April 22, 1791, and quoted in *Mémoires du Général Lafayette*, III, 67-69.

friendship. They have considered me as an American, who did only mind American profit, and did not know matters so well as a few mercantile men, most of them on the Aristocratic side of the House who presented foolish calculations—and you know the difficulty to unmake our decrees. But you may depend on this point that brotherly measures to unite the two nations with the ties of most intimate affection, of common principles, and common interest will be most heartily received in France, and on that ground you may work your plan, and send it to France, with a private copy for me. The United States and France must be one people, and so begin the Confederation of all Nations who will assert their own rights.

I have, in the affair of the Black Free Men, voted according to my conscience, not to policy. Should the British take advantage of my honesty, I hope you will influence the Colonies to submit to a decree so conformant to justice*.

M. Short who does the business of the United States with all the zeal and ingenuity of a most patriotic and most sensible man, who is respected and loved in France in a manner equally useful to the public and honourable to himself has written to M. Jefferson respecting New Orleans. France will do every thing in her power to bring Spain to reason. But will have a difficult, and probably unsuccessful task. Upon the whole that navigation we must have, and in case the people of Louïsiana wish to make a fifteenth state, who devil can help it, and who ought, Spaniards excepted, not rejoice at it. Certainly I should'nt be a mourner.

My best respects to Mrs Washington. My complimetns to the family—to my dear aid George and his family. Most respectfully and affectionately my beloved General

Your filial friend
Lafayette

---

*On May 11, 1791, Lafayette supported a proposal to leave the question of emancipation to the initiative of the colonies, on the grounds that Negro proprietors also were colonists. On May 15, a motion somewhat to that effect was passed, though allowing only the children of free-born Negroes admission into colonial assemblies. Lafayette apparently feared England would intrigue to prevent acceptance of the decree.

1792

[216]

Head Quarters Metz
January the 22d 1792

My dear General

This is a very different date* from that which had announced to you my return to the sweets of private life, a situation hitherto not very familiar to me, but which I, after fifteen revolutionary years, I had become quite fit to enjoy—I have given you an account of the quiete, and rural mode of living I had adopted, in the mountains where I was born, having there a good house, and a *late* mannor now unlorded† into a large farm, with an English overseer for my instruction, I felt myself very happy among my neighbours, no more vassals to me, nor any body, and had given to my wife and rising family the only quiete weecks they had for a long time—When the threats, and mad preparations of the Refugees, and still more the countenance they had obtained in the dominions of our neighbours induced the National Assembly and the King to adopt a more vigourous system than had hitherto been the case.

Three Armies were formed—fifty thousand men *each on paper*, the Right and Left ones under Luckner and Rochambeau, that on the Center under me. I had refused every public emploïement that had been offered by the people, and still more had I denied my consent to my being appointed to any Military command—But when I saw our liberties and Constitution were seriously threatened and my services could be usefully emploïed in fighting for our old cause, I could no more resist the wishes of my country men, and as soon as

---
*There seems to have been a lost letter, which apparently was dated from Chavaniac. See *Mémoires du Général Lafayette*, III, 418 n.

†Feudal obligations and aristocratic titles had been abolished by the National Assembly.

the King's express reached my farm I sat out for Paris, from thence for this place, and don't think it uninteresting for you, my dear General, to add that I was every where on the road most affectionately welcomed.

Now the surrounding German Princes have submitted to dismiss every armed corps of Refugees, to forbid every recruiting, collecting, equipping our noble deserters, so that the poor fellows are hunted by our Ambassadors from petty Courts to other petty Courts—to cut short to which a formal application will be made to the Emperor* and Diet of the Empire at Ratisbonne.

Monsieur the King's brother has been constitutionally divested from his right to Regency—So will the younger brother. They as well as Prince Condé and some others are to be tried for their life (in their absence) before a National Court—Indeed measures have been heaped, and rather hurried to throw them out.

But the most important part of our business is to know what part the Great Powers of Europe will act—That everyone of them hates us is obvious, but notwistanding they would crush us to pieces, they are affraid to touch us, least their subjects catch what they call the French evil. We have boldly asked the Emperor for a cathegorick answer by the 10th of February—A Bill has passed with the sanction of the King, declaring it infamy, and high treason to listen to the proposal of any alteration whatsoever, any negociation with respect to the principles and letter of the Constitutional Act.

The Army I command will of course be the first to act. I am to have twenty thousand men to garrison the fronteers from *Montmedy* to *Bitche* and thirty thousand to take the field—I do not hope to come up at first quite to those numbers, but in case I want reinforcements, the National Guards will help me—I will send you an exact return of my Army when it is finally arranged, for I alwaïs consider myself, my Dear General, as one of your lieutenants on a detached command.

The regular regiments are short of their complement—The volonteer Bataïllons do very well, in general, the soldiers and non commissioned officers of the Army are patriots but want discipline—A third part of the officers are good—an other third gone—the re-

*On the death of Joseph II, his brother Leopold II succeeded him as Holy Roman emperor (1790-92).

mainder very ill affected, and will soon I hope go out—They are tolerably well reimplaced—We want general officers most of them being tories—I am going, and am the only one whose popularity can stand it, to establish, in spite of the Clubs and Jacobine clamours, a most severe discipline, and I think the Army afterwards will do pretty well.

M. D'orleans can not recover himself from the muddy swamp into which I have kicked him by the middle of October 1789—and whatever happens to all arround him, he hardly can raise his head above the dirty heap which entangles him on every side.*

Adieu, my beloved General, remember me most respectfully to Mrs. Washington. My best compliments wait on Hamilton, Knox, Jefferson, Jay, Major Washington, Cokran, and all other friends.

With respectful and filial love I am my Dear General
Your affectionate and dutiful friend
Lafayette.

[217]

My dear General,   Paris, March the 15th 1792.†

I have been called from the army to this capital for a conference between the two other generals, the ministers and myself and am about returning to my military post. The coalition between the Continental powers respecting our affairs is certain, and will not be broken by the Emperor's death. But altho warlike preparations are going on, it is very doubtful wether our neighbours will attempt to stiffle‡ so very catching as that of Liberty is.

The danger for us lies with our state of anarchy owing to the ignorance of the people, the number of non proprietors, the jealousy of every governing measure, all which inconveniences are worked up by designing men or aristocrates in disguise but both extremes tend to defeat our ideas of public order. Don't believe however, my dear General, the exagerated accounts you may receive, particularly

---

*Though Orleans was never found guilty of inciting the insurrection of October 5-6, 1789, Lafayette had obliged him to withdraw temporarily from France by taking an anomalous diplomatic post in England.

†Copy in the Harvard College Library, Sparks Mss LXXXVIII, Part II. (Proper names will be identified in the "Index" below.)

‡A second copy in Sparks Mss LXVI adds here in a hand other than the original copyist's the words *a flame*.

from England—That Liberty and Equality will be preserved in France, there is no doubt, in case there was, you well know that I will not if they fall survive them. But you may be assured that we will emerge from this unpleasant situation either by an honourable defense or by internal improvements. How far this Constitution of ours, insures a good government has not been as yet fairly experienced—This only know that it has restored to the people their rights, destroyed almost every abuses—and turned French vassalage and slavery into national dignity and the enjoyment of those faculties which nature has given and Society ought to insure.

Give me leave, my General, to you alone to offer an observation respecting the late choice of the American ambassador. You know I am personally a friend to Gouverneur Moriss and ever as a private man, have been satisfied with him. But the aristocratic, and indeed counter revolutionary principles he has professed, unfitted him to be the representative of the only nation whose politics have a likeness with ours, since they are founded on the plan of a representative democracy. This I may add that surrounded with ennemies as France is, it looks as if America was preparing for a change in this government; not only that kind of alteration which the democrats may wish for and bring about, but the wild attempts of aristocracy, such as the restoration of a noblesse, a house of Lords, and such other political blasphemies, which while we are living can not be restablished in France. I wish we had an elective Senate, a more independent set of judges, and a more energitic administration, but the people must be taught the advantages of a firm government before they reconcile it to their ideas of freedom, and can distinguish it from the arbitrary systems which they have just got over. You see my dear General, I am not an enthusiast of every part of our Constitution, altho I love its principles which are the same as those of the United States, excepting heredity in the president of the execuive, which I think suitable to our circumstances. But I hate every thing like despotism and aristocracy, and I can not help wishing the American and French principles were in the heart and on the lips of the American ambassador to France. This I mention *for you alone*, and only for the case when arrangements suitable to Gouverneur I wish might in future and yet I beg this hint of mine, may never be mentioned to anybody. Give me leave, my dear General, to add the tribute of praise which I owe to Mr. Short, for the sentiments he has professed and the esteem he has acquired in this country. I wish this gentleman was personally known to you.

There have been changes in the ministry. The King has chosen his council amidst the most violent popular party, in the Jacobine Club, a Jesuitic institution, more fit to make deserters from, than convert to our cause—The new ministers however, being unsuspected, have a chance to restore public order and say they will improve it. The Assembly are wild uninformed and too fond of popular applause the King slow and rather backward in his daily conduct, altho now and then he acts fully well. But upon the whole, it will do, and the success of our revolution cannot be questioned.

My command extends on the frontiers from *Givet* to *Bitche*. I have sixty thousand men, a number that is encreasing now, as young men pour in, from every part of the empire to fill up the regiments. This volontary recruiting shows a most patriotic spirit. I am going to encamp thirty thousand men with a detached corps of about five and four thousand in an intrenched camp. The remainder will occupy the fortified places. The armies of Marechals Luckner and Rochambeau are inferior to mine because we have sent many regiments to the South ward, but in case we had a war to undertake, we may gather respectable forces.

Our *Emigrants* are beginning to come in—Their situation abroad is miserable, and in case even we quarell with our neighbours, they will be out of the question—Our paper money has been of late rising very fast—Manufactures of every kind are much employed—The farmer find his taxes alleviated, and will feel the more happy under our Constitution as the Assembly are going to give up their patronage of one set of priests*—You see my dear General, that altho we have many causes to be, as yet unsatisfied, we may hope every thing will bye and bye come to rights. Licentiousness under a mask of patriotism is our greater evil as it threatens property tranquillity and liberty itself. Adieu my dear General. My best respects wait on Mrs Washington. Rember me most affectionately to our friends, and think sometimes of your respectful, loving, and filial friend.

Lafayette

*The Legislative Assembly (1791-92) passed several laws intended to restrict the activity and influence of the non-juring clergy.

1797

[218]

Hambourg October: the 6th 1797.*

My dear General,

I am the happier to be able to inform you, as I am sure you shall be happy to hear that on the 19th September my two friends†, family, and myself left the Olmutz Bastille, and that tomorrow morning we shall be on Danish territory out of the reach of the Coalitionary Powers—in vain would I attempt, my beloved General, to express to you the feelings of my filial heart, when, at the moment of this unexpected restoration to liberty and life, I find myself blessed with the opportunity to let you hear from me—this heart has for twenty years been known to you—words, that, whatever they be, fall so short of my sentiments would not do justice to what I feel— But you will be sensible of the affectionate and delightful emotions with which I am now writing to you, and I know also it is not without some emotion that after five years of a deathlike silence from me, you will read the first lines I am at last enabled to write—With what eagerness and pleasure I would hasten to fly to Mount Vernon, there to pour out all the sentiments of affection, respect, and gratitude which ever bound me and more than ever bind me to you— Your paternal goodness to my, to our Son was not unexpected but has been most heartily felt—your constant solicitude in my behalf I have enjoyed as a welcome consolation in captivity, and dont wonder, my respected General, that those friendly exertions have not

*Copy in the Harvard College Library, Sparks Mss XXIV. Unpublished.
†Céser de La Tour-Maubourg and Bureaux de Pusy had been imprisoned with Lafayette since August 1792 and were released at the same time as he.

been able to operate the difficult work, which in spite of and threatening armies, and repeated demands from the French government, it has been an affair of five months to effect, after the hostilities had ceased—But at last we are out, and I had the satisfaction to see the United States take a part in this last transaction, whereby I am released with my two friends, and that part of my family which was not under your immediate protection in the happy country where George and his excellent friend have experienced so much kindness. Would to God this family might for the first time meet again at Mount Vernon, and be reunited in your friendly and paternal arms. My own health, altho' it is impaired, could, I think, tolerably support a voyage. My daughters are not ill. But Mrs. Lafayette's sufferings in this cruel unhealthy captivity have had such a deplorable effect upon her, that in the opinion of every physician, and every man of sense, it would be an act of madness to let her embark in this advanced season of the year. We shall retire somewhere on the Danish territory, about sixty or seventy English miles from Hambourg, and there in a remote country house quietly wait for the Spring. In the mean while we all are burning with impatience to see George. It is a comfort of which his mother after so many afflictions, and in such a state of health, is in great need—and altho' I depend the more upon my return to America in the Spring as the new measures taken in France seem to remove the probability, and of course to dispense with the duty which in some letters to M^{de} L.f. you have pointed out for me, we all wish that George might return to Europe so as to be with us as soon as possible and before we ourselves can begin a voyage for which his company, in going back with us, would at any rate be an agreeable addition. Such are, my beloved General, the ideas of people who on their emersion from the tomb, want to gather as soon as possible all the happiness that is within their reach, which however cannot be completed until they enjoy the blessing to be with you. I have flattered myself that in the present situation of politics, so painful to me, altho' particulars are yet unknown, it might be not quite unserviceable to offer you a safe express to carry whatever instructions you, or some members of government could perhaps think of sending over. What has been, can be, or is wished to be done I do not know. I am perfectly ignorant of every public, even of my personal concerns. I know only that my heart is just the same as it has ever been. This letter will set out immediately I hope, my dear General, that in a few days I can write more fully. In the mean while I beg and hope you will read in my heart those sentiments so warmly grateful, so affectionately devoted which I want adequate words to express but which have so long animated this heart, and shall animate it as long as it can vibrate. My best and most tender respects to Mrs. Washington. My wife and daughters join in the same sentiments of veneration, love and gratitude to her and to you. Adieu, my beloved and respected General,

     Your filial and grateful
      affectionate friend
       Lafayette

[219]

My dear General, Lemkuhlen December the 27th 1797*

It is a melancholy thought to me that while I could be so happy at Mount Vernon, I am still almost as much separated from you as I have been for five years in the coalitionary prisons. But altho' I lament yet I cannot repent the determination we have been obliged to take, much less on account of my health which has been recovering fast enough, than for the very bad and lingering condition in which my wife was at the time, and will, I am afraid, continue to be for the winter. She is, however, slowly mending in her health, and with great deal of care, tranquility, and patience she shall at last be well again. But any kind of travel, and still more so a boisterous voyage could not but greatly hurt her, and we must wait for the spring to think of leaving the solitary country seat in Holstein, on Danish territory, which we have, in common with my friend Latour Maubourg and his numerous family, hired for six months. Here we live in proper retirement, and here I hope for the inexpressible delight soon to be blessed with a letter from my beloved and respected general.

Naval chances are now so dubious that I cannot depend upon my letters having reached you. Should they have miscarried I am sure your paternal goodness will not think it is my fault. I hope, however, that you have by this time received a letter written from

*Copy in the Harvard College Library, Sparks Mss LXXXIX. Another copy with minor variations is to be found *ibid.*, Sparks MSS XXIV. Unpublished.

Hamburgh immediately after my having been set at liberty, a piece of news which you certainly have heartily welcomed. There I could for the first time, not sufficiently express, it is impossible, but with the most affectionate feelings of a heart overflowing with grateful and filial love mention to you, my dear general, the obligations I have to your friendly and fatherly care of my son George. There also I expressed to you the impatience and very natural wish his mother, sisters, and myself had to embrace him as soon as possible, an impatience for which I knew you would feel with us, so far as not to find it unrational to let him come to us, should he arrive only to reembark immediately with us. I am sure that your sympathising heart will have forwarded this plan, but altho he now probably is nearer to the European shores than to the happy and beloved banks of Potomac I beg leave to inclose old copies of my first letters to him, and to my excellent friend Mr. Frestel both of whom have found in you a kindness which has been in my captivity the greatest consolation we could receive, and shall as long as we live be the happiest remembrance that can warm our grateful hearts.

This letter being as it were sent at random, I shall not expatiate on politics, indeed we are in every respect very far from the busy stage. It is said that the public and secret arrangements made between France and the Austrian court will not meet much opposition at the Radstadt* congress. You are more directly acquainted than you could be from this quarter with the state of the American negociation in Paris. I have heard nothing about it for some time but newspaper reports. I expect to know some thing more by and bye. I need not telling you that this affair has made me very unhappy. God grant it had been and could be in my power to be of material service in adjusting it. The little that my present situation can admit of shall never be wanting. I never thought I should live to see such an event, which has very much damped the pleasure of my return to this world†.

*Following the Peace of Campo Formio between France and Austria (October 17, 1797), a congress of the states of the Holy Roman Empire was convened at Rastatt (December 16) for the settlement of German affairs.

†An American commission arrived in Paris in October 1797 to negotiate disputes arising out of the capture of American vessels by French privateers. Talleyrand, the foreign minister of the French Directory, refused to receive them formally, and there shortly developed the scandal known as the XYZ affair.

My wife and daughters beg their most affectionate respects to be presented to you and to Mrs Washington, to whom I request to be most tenderly and respectfully remembered. My compliments wait on my friend George Washington. How happy I shall be to hear my son's particular and every day repeated accounts about you, every body and every thing that surrounds you. It shall to my enchanted mind recall the liveliest sentiments of my heart, the happiest hours of my life.

Adieu my respected and beloved general, you know the veneration, gratitude and love of

Your filial friend
Lafayette

1798

[220]

Witmold-Holstein
April the 26th, 1798*

My dear general,

This letter will be presented to you by Mr. Forster, whose father the celebrated professor and Captain Cooke's fellow traveller has requested in behalf of his son these recommendatory lines. I am sure his name was to you a sufficient introduction; and in his personal merit there is also a sufficient inducement to wish for his welfare. Yet I should be highly pleased to hope that my recommendation may prove an additional claim to the benevolence of my friends in America, and particularly to your kind dispositions in his favour.

Altho' we are writing to you more at length, my dear general, I cannot let this opportunity pass without telling you that we are still on Danish territory, man, wife, daughters and son, whose gratitude and love to you are deeply engraved in his heart and in the hearts of us all. We are all healthy, my wife excepted. She had been a little better for a few weeks; but the disease, which all the physicians justly attribute to the Austrian Bastille has lately returned with distressing symptoms, and after having waited so long to embark with her, I shall be obliged to go without the female part of my family, and while Georges and myself are preparing to visit you, she must return to France where the hot bath are particularly appropriated to her case.

Our best respects wait on Mrs Washington. Be pleased also to remember to Miss Eleanor those of the family who have the honor

*Copy in the Harvard College Library, Sparks Mss LXXXIX. Unpublished.

of her acquaintance, and the rest of it who so heartily wish for that pleasure. Our compliments to Mr Custis, who, I dare say, hardly remembers to have seen me at Mount Vernon.

Adieu, my beloved general, how happy shall I be when you will fold to your heart

Your respectful and filial friend
Lafayette

[221]

Witmold-Holstein,
May the 20th 1798*

My dear General,

Your letter December the 5th under cover to George has but lately reached our hands, and while such delays make me more and more lament the distance which separates us from you, I cannot be easy about the fate of my part of the correspondence. I beg leave, amidst so many unhappy chances, to hope that omissions will not be laid on my account and that repetitions will be allowed. Indeed, my dear general, the best way I have to answer your affectionate enquiries is to take a short review of my past and present situation.

On our emerging from the captivity in which, out of their superlative hatred to true liberty and legal order the coalesced governments had, as long as they could possibly do it, obstinately detained my friends and me, I became acquainted with the revolutionary events of the 4th September. There were men in the victorious party who had greatly influenced my rescue from the Olmutz Bastille. But in that part of the vanquished one which ought to be distinguished from a few real conspirators, I had friends entitled to my gratitude and esteem, and while it must be acknowledged that a foolish plot was going on, and had in the elegant circles become fashionable, while it is by the best patriots and undeserving victims now freely confessed that in their endeavours to fix the republican system on the liberal basis of liberty and justice, they ought to have better expressed their dissentiment from the plotters, and avoided reducing the executive leaders to a necessity of self defence. Yet in the tyranical measures of the 18th Fructidor† and obvious consequences,

*Copy in the Harvard College Library, Sparks Mss LXXXIX. Unpublished.
†I.e. September 4, 1797, when the legislative councils of France were purged by the Executive Directors. (Proper names are identified in the "Index" below.)

there was a perfect incompatibility with the principles and the sentiments of the man who had embraced the American cause, headed the French revolution of 1789, and opposed the anti-constitutional violences of 1792. I therefore confined myself to acknowledgments of the exertions whereby we had been conquered out of the coalitionary fangs, and to every act becoming a French citizen in foreign countries. But I determined to embark for America with my family as soon as my wife's health could permit it. And now that, after having so long waited for her, I find she cannot for this year bear the voyage, I shall send her to France with her daughters and son in law*, while in the middle of July George and myself set out for the United States, unless my uneasiness for her weak and precarious state of health should force me to expect her before we embark. In the mean while altho' I have very frankly spoken of the fructidorian transactions, and given to the estimable objects of the proscription every mark of respect in my power, I cannot say that I have personally to complain of the actual directors, no further at least than that they wish for my temporary absence, so long, say their friends to mine, as arbitrary measures are reckoned necessary, which by me are in no case allowed, and which I am known in every case to oppose. It is true that once a foolish calumny has, say they, inadvertently, escaped their pen, and they are far from showing themselves friendly to my popularity in France. But upon the whole there is nothing hostile in their manner to speak of or to act by me. My principles and conduct are always by them and their friends in conversation mentioned with regard. My suitable return to France is not even questioned; and while a delay of that return agrees so well with them that they seem jealous of every thing which tends to promote it, I am by their represenatives abroad treated not only as a fellow citizen but as one to whom particular attentions are to be paid. This situation I am very well pleased with. I cannot approve or abet despotic measures of any kind; nor can I recede from the fundamental principles of liberty which in this European revolution I was the first to proclaim.

Now that the directory is afraid of the very jacobins who had supported the fructidorian coup de main, the jacobins are very likely

---

*On May 9, 1798, Anastasie married Charles de La Tour-Maubourg, the brother of Lafayette's fellow-prisoner at Olmütz.

to be in their turn *fructidorited*. When a system more congenial to the pure and liberal ideas of liberty will prevail in the Commonwealth I do not pretend to determine. But I am sure that at such a time it shall be proper for me to revisit France, and to revisit it sooner I cannot by any means wish. You see, my dear general, that no duty at this moment interferes and that every sentiment conspires in the actual plan, and the ardent desire I have to be with you in the month of September when I hope to be able on the 19th to celebrate at Mount Vernon the anniversary of my restoration to liberty and life.

But there is a circumstance which from every public motives and private feelings makes me more unhappy than I can find words to express the anxiety of my mind. I mean the deplorable disputes between the United States and France. I see that instead of subsiding, as I had expected it would be the case, they appear to be worse than ever. Let us hope at least that my heart will not be rent with the dismal news of a declared war between the two nations. But there is already too much of it. How I lament that my present situation puts it out of my power to become the useful instument of an honorable reconcilaition. I have, however, said and written to France the little that now depends on me. And on this only point I never have received significant answers. You know on what grounds, and with what sentiments I have in former times employed myself between two countries to both of which I was bound by the ties of patriotic duty and affection. But in the present circumstances I have nothing to meddle with, but some private endeavors to soften, expostulate, and convert, to complain and to blame, and to those inefficacious solaces of my anxiety I join my incessant and fervent wishes for such a conclusion as may perfectly suit the interest of both countries and their most delicate feelings of national honor. I am sure, my dear general, that your powerful influence will be employed in removing the obstacles that are found on your side of the Atlantic, and that you will, in the name of the universal respect that is so justly paid to you, and of remembrances which recall the happy times of union among the American patriots, that you will, says I, recommend to the leading statesmen in both parties not to let political or personal piques encrease the difficulties, already too great, to fill up the breach and bring about a reconcilation.

To the confidential communication of my personal situation and to the very inadequate expression of my feelings on the deplorable misunderstanding which could not but rend my own heart, I beg leave to add a short notice respecting the whole family. We have spent the winter in Holstein, on Danish territory, in a hired country seat about sixty English miles from Hamburgh. My friend Latour Maubourg and his family hire with us. We had visits from France and other countries. There arrived, as you have in time known it, our son George with his companion*. But after having received the friends who during so long a captivity had been entitled to our gratitude, and could come to this distant place, we have thought it better to inhabit the country seat of our Aunt M'de de Tessé† who has purchased a few years ago a valuable and pleasing estate in Holstein where she resides with my wife's sister. Here my eldest daughter Anastasie was married to Charles Maubourg my friends youngest brother. I am highly pleased with George, whose heart and head will, I hope, render him worthy of the paternal protection you have so affectionately given to him, the sense of which is more warmly felt, more deeply engraved in our hearts than words can express it.

My wife, my daughters, my son in law beg the tender homage of their affection, gratitude and respect to be presented to you, my dear general, and to Mrs Washington. I hope she will with her usual friendship to me accept my most affectionate respects. I beg also you will present them to Miss Eleanor with whom I will be inexpressedly happy to renew my old acquaintance. My compliments await on her brother. Receive you all the fervent wishes, the grateful sentiments, the everlasting attachments that bind every one of us to you. Adieu, my dear and beloved general, you know how happy I am to have so good a right to call myself
Your respectful, filial,
and obliged friend,
Lafayette.

---

*George Washington Lafayette left New York with his tutor, Monsieur Frestel, on October 26, 1797, and reached Lehmkuhlen in February 1798. See Étienne Charavay, *Le Général La Fayette 1757-1834* (Paris, 1898), p. 369.

†The copyist has written Tellé, but Tessé is correct. (Proper names will be identified in the "Index" below.)

AMENDED [222]
Witmold near Plön-Holstein
August the 20th 1798*

My dear General

However uncertain I am of the fate of my letters, I am happy in the opportunities to let you hear from me, and altho' the filial and grateful sentiments which from my youth have animated my heart need not being remembered to you, it is to me, while so unwillingly separated from you a great and necessary consolation to express them. In case you have received some of the accounts of myself and family which I took much care to forward, it will be to day sufficient to acquaint you that my wife who, as I wrote to you, has been very ill this Spring is now so far recovered as to have been able, not without great deal of moral and bodily pain to leave us for her indispensable journey to France—Her two daughters and son in law have accompagnied her. But Anastasia being a little unwell, tho' nothing alarming in it, has made a halt in Holland, with Charles Maubourg, while her Mother and Virginia have proceeded on their way to Paris where they have now have been a few days arrived. Here I am, on an estate belonging to our aunt M^{de} de Tessé, where Georges and myself anxiously expect to know how the dear traveller, in her low state of health, has borne the fatigue. There are also for her measures to be taken respecting what property remains to us, or rather to her in which, amidst the general difficulties of the times, and the ones peculiar to myself, my opinion may be wanted. In a letter from Hamilton, wherein he affectionately speacks of my intended departure for America, he seems to be sensible of inconveniences arising from the present unhappy misunderstanding betwen the two Republics. That advice it is useless now to discuss, as the two private concerns I have mentionned, and the precautions I owe to my wife's enfeebled and agitated frame of body and mind oblige me not to dispose of myself and our son, for a voyage in which she might soon accompagny us, before her letters from France have acquainted us with the state of her health, and the situation of her affairs. How painful these delays are to me, I think superfluous to tell to you, my dear General, who so well know that

*Cornell University Library, Sparks Mss (autograph duplicate mentioned on p. 378 below). Erroneously dated April 20, 1798 in *Mémoires du Général Lafayette*, IV, 431.

affection, duty and propriety point out the beloved shores of America as the natural place of my retirement. But on you I depend to explain as opportunities offer, to my friends, the motives which have from month to month kept me on this Continent. That obligation to your goodness will be the greater, as I cannot know whether the expressions of my respect and gratitude ever have reached the United States.

You are, no doubt, regularly informed of European politics. While it is to be hoped, for the good of mankind, that North and South America shall gradually adopt the principles on which the independance and liberty of the United States are happily founded, it is probably the fate, and I don't deny that it has been the original plan of the French Revolution to go round the old world. That the Coalition of the kings of Europe against our first Constitution, and their foolish contempt of our national military institution could in the events and communications of the war accelerate the emancipation of their subjects was an other early and awowed idea. But as the promoters in Europe of a doctrine truly American of Virtuous Liberty and Legal Equality were of course more averse to its being disfigured and polluted than the old governements to whose secret encouragements the revolutionary excesses are chiefly owing, so were they far from pretending that any imitation of their conduct, or the opportunities given by kingly or aristocratic agressions to help their neighbours in asserting their own rights, could ever give them the least claim on the independance of other nations. But without recurring to circumstances in which the loss of so many dear friends and relations have made me a most unhappy sufferer, and without examining the present ones farther than to know what, amidst the realities or probalities of arbitrary monarchy, military despotism, and jacobine anarchy is now the best chance for genuine liberty, it appears evident not only to me whose natural inclinations and American habits might mislead me, but to many patriots more monarchial than I am, that it ought to be sought for within the system of elective governements. When and how they shall be consolidated on a firm bazis of morality and justice God knows, but that it could easely be done if earnestly intended, I do not doubt.

In the mean while every monarch on this Continent trembles at the irresistible power of France. It has been lately attempted to draw the Swedish, Danish, and Prussian courts into a coalition against her, but in vain. The Kings of Sardinia and Naples wear still their crowns. The Radstat peace is not yet concluded. The last news were favourable. Mr. Pitt who is personally interested to blow the fire, and the Russian Emperor* whose folly has taken an Anti Gallican turn are in hopes that the House of Austria will come in again. But this is rather shy. The uncertainty in this respect cannot last. The spirit of insurrection in Ireland owing to ministerial cruelty and arbitrariness has lately been damped by Lord Cornwallis's more liberal conduct. All eyes are fixed on the Mediterranean†. The idea of possessing Ægipt is not new. I myself, under the ministry of M^{ms} de Vergennes and Castries had collected informations and made proposals, and as the occupation of Candia entered in the plan, Dumas has, on his return from America reconnoitred that island. From the abilities and power of Bonaparte we may conclude that his expedition is carried on the largest scale and that in his consequent operations the fate of Asia is much interested. At Maltha the French, Spanish, and Italian knights refused to fight against their countrymen or allies. Hitherto we don't know that the fleet has been interrupted by Horatio Nelson. It seems to me that the British governement, or admirals, perhaps both may thank themselves for a good deal of mismanagement. Among the friends who can give me minute information is my former aid de camp Louïs Romeuf who after having past the winter with me is now in Bonaparte's staff.

I am sure, my dear general, that your paternal heart has felt for me in the ever to be lamented differences between America and France the making up of which requires much liberality and prudence. Far am I from objecting to the unanimous spirit with which the independance and dignity of the United States are asserted. I love it, I am proud of it, and how could I estrange myself from sentiments and measures in which I have been, for two and twenty years a zealous, and it is my right to say a patriotic partaker? But I hope it may stop just where public honour and interest has bidden it to go. And should party spirit, personal prejudice, discontent, or pride encrease the difficulties it is my comfort to think that your character

*Tsar Paul succeeded Catherine II in 1796.
†Bonaparte's Egyptian expedition set sail from Toulon on May 19, 1798.

and disposition both so exalted shall give you the power as I know you have the inclination to make up this unfortunate quarell betwen two nations whom we have seen so happily united under your command.

My means of information are very imperfect. I never adressed the Directory but once. It was for the return to France (taking care to put myself out of the question) of the officers who having been brought by me out of the fronteers in 1792 ought not to share in my responsability. There I introduced a word on American affairs. I did it in my letters to Talleyrand who has continued very constant and friendly to me. From those quarters nothing on that subject has been answered. But on the 29th Messidor (June the 17th) a letter has been writen to me by a late senator* on whose honesty and personal friendship I may depend, wherein he reminds me that I went first to America not only unlicenced but forbidden, and warmly advises my going over as a volunteer for a reconciliation betwen my native and adoptive countries. Whether the proposal has been known to the actual rulers I cannot say. There he announces a reformation of the laws respecting the neutral vessels. To that letter which came by post I answered in the same way that when I engaged in the American cause, my object was precise and distinct, that in this business I dont see it so clear before me, and that to make use of the deserved confidence of the United States I should first have convinced myself, and then be enabled to convince them that the French governement intends to act with that generosity and good will which I ever thought to be the best policy to employ with the Sister Republic. That hint, and my declarations upon it may be insignificant. Yet I think it ought to be confidentially communicated to you. I have since heard of some measures to restrain the privateers whose depredations I firmly believe have far exceeded the intentions and often escaped the knowledge of Governement. I have been told by men friendly to America, averse to the French executive that in the conduct of American captains at sea there have been real causes of complaint. That I cannot judge, but think it my duty when I hear of things which may be redressed to let them be known to you.

In fact, my dear General, I now for my part, and as far as my

*Probably Dupont de Nemours, who had recently resigned from the Conseil des Anciens.

private intelligence can go, am persuaded that the French Directory are earnest in their actual wish to be at peace with the United States. I know that the aristocratic party whose hatred to America, from the beginning of the European Revolution is inexpressible, and the British governement who since the Declaration of Independence have neither forgiven nor forgotten are now exulting at the prospect of a rupture betwen two countries who have been allied in the cause of liberty, and exerting themselves by any means, on both sides, to precipitate a war. Corruptive intrigues of foreign powers in America I despise, but not so their management of the passions of men—the most honest, and very sensible too, not the less apt some times to be inflammed. But there you are, my dear General, independant of the parties, venerated by all, and in case your informations lead you to expect, as I fondly hope, on the part of the French rulers a proper disposition, you shall no doubt exert your influence to prevent the widening of the breach, and to ensure an honourable and lasting reconciliation.

I beg you, my dear General to present my affectionate repects to Mrs. Washington and Miss Eleanor. Georges with whom at every hour of the day I have the pleasure to speack of Mount Vernon, of its beloved and venerated inhabitants, of the ever dear and most profoundly felt obligations the father and the son are under to him who has become a father to both, requests his dutiful respects to be offered to you, to Mrs. Washington. The gratitude he owes to her shall animate his heart as long as it vibrates. He intended to write by this opportunity to her and to Miss Eleanor. I desired him to send his letters with a copy of this by an other vessel who is to sail in a few days.

Adieu, my respected General, receive with your usual affection the unadequate expressions of the sentiments which bind to you for ever

Your filial friend
Lafayette

P. S. 21st

I just now hear, that Vaublanc's daughter who has married Gal Pinkney's nephew* is going with her mother to America; they intend

---

*Unidentified. The article "Vaublanc" in *Biographie Universelle* (XLIII, 16) says that Vaublanc's only daughter married an engineer named Segond.

to land at a short distance from Mount Vernon. You have no doubt heard of Vaublanc's character. He is an honour to his country and to his friends among whom none is more attached nor under so great obligations to him as I am proud to be. He stood up my advocate in August 1792, and his speech on the occasion is a master piece of eloquence*. He has been exposed to great dangers, has rendered great services, and is justly venerated by all parties. He now is under the proscription of the 18th Fructidor. The wife and daughter of this good and great states man, both personally entitled to much respect and affection wish to be particularly introduced to you. I earnestly beg you, my dear General, Mrs. Washington, and Miss Eleanor to welcome them on the American shore with attentions which from you cannot fail to be precious to them. Yesterday's letters announce that a Continental peace is expected to take place in a very short time. Hamburg's news will be later.

[223]

Witmold Holstein
September the 5th 1798.†

My dear General.

I have had sometime ago the pleasure to write you a letter the duplicate of which shall accompany this. The intelligence has since come to us of your having accepted the command of the armies; but you will not be the less pleased to hear of the dispositions to a fair reconciliation on the part of the French directory which I hope will be reciprocated by the American government. To what I took the liberty to say in my last letter, I must add that my private informations from Paris confirm me in the belief therein expressed. I am also acquainted that besides the direct communications, the Batavian directory have resolved to propose their mediation, and a letter to that purpose was to have been sent to America. Among the motives I have to hope for the restoration of harmony between the two countries, I was glad to hear this very day a gentleman say that the same opinion had been lately expressed in Hamburgh by Governor Morris. Under these promising circumstances I am happy to find

*On August 8, 1792, a motion to impeach Lafayette was debated in the Legislative Assembly and defeated.
†Copy in the Harvard College Library, Sparks Mss LXXXIX. Unpublished. (Proper names will be identified in the "Index" below.)

you are more than ever in a situation to improve them, and in a way becoming the honor and interest of the United States, to make up this unhappy quarrel, the actual termination of which, on proper terms, altho' it may blast the boasting hopes of a foreign government, will leave America increased in her national character and political consequence.

Notwithstanding the intrigues of the British cabinet, the courts of Sweden, Denmark, and Berlin persist in their determination to keep their neutrality and to protect the tranquility of northern Germany. The Neapolitan ladies have more success at Vienna*. The renewal of an Austrian war, and of course the downfall of the throne of Naples are probable. Every account assures that Bonaparte has arrived in Alexandria, and that he has not been interrupted on his voyage. The interior situation of France and the neighboring republics is the same, nor is there any appearance of alteration in the civil measures. Holland, however, is an exception, the jacobines had on the 21st January overset the patriots, these have regained ground, and the new elections are much approved; it is this new government whose interest in the reconciliation will be expressed to you. A private circumstance may lead you to form a judgment on them. When I got out of prison the then Batavian government had intended to invite me there, this idea has been again taken up by those who have lately come in. Nothing on my part is yet determined, altho' my being nearer my family during their stay of a few months in France might forward the business upon which my wife is now employed†. I have had the satisfaction to hear she has well borne the journey. She says her accounts on the public treasure shall be settled in a month, the arrangements relative to landed property will require sometime more. She promises to me in a fortnight long letters by a friend. By the last opportunity, my dear general, I informed you that Mde. de *Vaublanc* and her daughter married to Genl. Pinkney's nephew was to embark for America and intended to land in Virginia. They are ladies of great personal merit. My friend Vaublanc

---

*Caroline, the sister of the late Emperor Leopold II, was the queen of Naples. Her daughter, Maria-Theresa, was married to Leopold's son and successor, Francis II. Thus Queen Caroline was both the aunt and mother-in-law of the Austrian ruler.

†Mme de Lafayette, not being formally considered an *émigrée*, had gone to France to try to regain some of her property and to sound out the government regarding Lafayette's return.

is an honor to his country and to our cause. He acted a most conspicuous part in the legislative assembly of 92, two days before the 10th of August he stood my defender in a most eloquent speech. He was almost miraculously saved to display in the council of cinq-cent the same enlightened, energetic, upright character. He is such a man as does above all please you. Now he is one of the wandering victims of the 18th fructidor; but is not forever lost to his country. Give me leave, my dear general, to recommend the two ladies to your benevolent attentions. The same request I take the liberty to present to Mrs Washington and Miss Eleanor. I know the value they set by the pleasure and honor of your acquaintance; I am sure it will prove very satisfactory to you, and am happy in the opportunity to show to them my gratitude and respect. When you write to Mr. Pinkney or in case you see him will you have the goodness to express to that excellent man the sense I have of the obligations that forever bind me to him. I know that you have been very kind to Doctor Bollman, gratitude to the heroic young Huger may make me appear partial, but his noble character, independence of personal concerns, has made on my heart an impression which no words can express, and to it I know no adequate price but the esteem and friendship of General Washington. Georges who writes by another vessel requests his best and most grateful respects to be presented to you, my beloved general, and to Mrs Washington, the ambition of his life shall ever be to deserve the testimonies of parental goodness with which you have penetrated his heart, he begs also to be respectfully remembered to Miss Eleanor, my affectionate compliments wait upon her. I beg leave to offer a filial tribute of attachment and respect to Mrs Washington. Georges makes me happy in the expressions of her kindness to me. We both pay our compliments to Mr. Custis. Adieu, my dear general, the adoptive father of the whole family, with every sentiment of affection and respect I shall to the last moment of my life be
                                              Your filial friend
                                                    Lafayette

1799

AMENDED   [224]
                              Vianen, 19 avril 1799.*

Mon Cher Général,

M. Murray, que j'ai eu le plaisir de voir, et dont je suis particulièrement heureux d'apprendre la mission de plénipotentiaire en France, vous donne sans doute en détail les nouvelles de la politique européenne. La coalition profite des avantages que lui donne malheureusement la conduite du gouvernement français. Il est sûr qu'au lieu d'avoir acquis à la cause populaire la majorité du peuple dans les nations alliées ou en guerre, comme cela fût arrivé si l'on eût suivi un bon système, les actes de tyrannie et de brigandage, à l'intérieur ou au dehors, ont dégoûté beaucoup de monde soit en France, soit à l'étranger. Le retour aux principes de liberté pourrait seul, et encore avec difficulté, réconcilier les esprits au nouvel ordre de choses. Cependant les institutions populaires et l'égalité légale ont de si grands avantages sur les diverses aristocraties que nous avons renversées, les conseils des rois et des empereurs sont, à l'exception de M. Pitt, si absurdes, les chefs contre-révolutionnaires si fous, et l'armée française si substantielle, si disciplinée et si brave, que je suis convaincu que la lutte qui se renouvelle dans ce moment se terminera encore d'une manière favorable à la France, pourvu cependant qu'elle revienne à ces principes de liberté et de justice sur lesquels la révolution a été fondée. Quelque haine que le gouvernement porte à cette classe d'hommes appelés constitutionnels, il s'est dernièrement si effrayé des anarchistes, que son influence dans les élections a été

---

*Mémoires du Général Lafayette, V, 23-25, where it is unfinished (as below). The original was probably in English.

anti-jacobine*, d'où il est résulté une assez grande proportion de bons représentants, si, avec la méthode connue de *déporter* et *d'annuler*, les conseils français peuvent s'appeler une représentation. Les événements civils et militaires seront probablement, cet été, fort importants............

AMENDED [225]

Mon cher Général, Vianen, 9 mai 1799.†

Votre bonne lettre du 25 décembre 1798 m'est heureusement parvenue; et puisque mon ami Bureaux de Pusy n'a pas encore mis à la voile, il pourra joindre, à quelques lignes d'introduction qu'il doit vous remettre, les tendres remercîments d'un coeur vraiment filial. Non, mon cher général, jamais je n'ai eu la pensée d'attribuer votre silence à quelque négligence. J'aurais soupçonné toutes les pirateries européenes, ou imaginé des obstacles beaucoup moins vraisemblables, avant d'éprouver la crainte de quelque diminution dans cette amitié qui m'est acquise depuis si long-temps, et dont mon coeur m'assure que je suis toujours digne. Je vois que vous aurez reçu plus de lettres de moi que je ne le supposais; je regrette que les expressions trop positives de mes espérances m'aient privé de vos réponses, mais vous m'aurez d'autant plus excusé que vous aurez vu combien, en dépit de toutes les difficultés, je souhaite me retrouver en Amérique.

Cependant, en apprenant les dissensions intérieures qui me paraissent encore plus contre nature qu'à ceux qui ont été témoins de leurs progrès, ces différends survenus entre les États-Unis et le gouvernement français dont je ne puis influencer ni mème connaître d'une manière certaine les dispositions, j'ai quelquefois intérieurement discuté les arguments que renferme votre franche et affectueuse lettre. Un mot d'Hamilton‡ m'avait fait réfléchir sur ce sujet et aux tendres motifs qui me portaient à souhaiter l'arrivée d'une ligne de vous, se joignait le besoin de recevoir les conseils de votre amitié. Mes propres objections avaient été écartées par la résolution de réclamer le droit que je crois avoir acquis de ne pas me mêler dans

---

*In the election of 1798, the Directors had used their influence to encourage "bolts" in the electoral assemblies and then by a law of May 11, 1798, had secured the recognition of those candidates whom they preferred.

†*Mémoires du Général Lafayette*, V. 36-41. The original was probably in English.

‡Hamilton wrote Lafayette on April 28, 1798, to discourage him from coming to America (*ibid.*, IV, 410-11).

les querelles des partis. Dès ma jeunesse, ma tête, mon coeur et mon bras, ont été consacrés à l'indépendance de l'Amérique. J'ai servi en Europe les cause et les amis de la liberté; pénétré de vos leçons, mon cher général, de celles de vos amis, j'ai avec quelque hardiesse, et non sans obtenir l'approbation publique, proclamé, soutenu durant trois ans, sur le grand et orageux théâtre de la révolution française, ces principes pour lesquels vous avez si glorieusement combattu et vous nous avez si heureusement dirigés.—Du moment où je n'ai pu, en restant fidèle à ces mêmes principes de droit naturel et de justice publique, conserver la haute position que la faction triomphante offrait d'élever encore, j'ai laissé à d'autres le soin de moissonner le champ de gloire militaire que j'avais semé. Retenu pendant cinq années dans les griffes impériales ou royales, j'ai expié les services rendus à la libertè et à l'ordre légal. Lorsque je fus délivré ensuite par le gouvernement français, ma fortune dépendait de ma complaisance; les trois cinquièmes de mon bien avaient été employés pour la cause du peuple, et le reste était alors confisqué en son nom; mais je n'ai pu condescendre à approuver l'arbitraire ni à tolérer l'immoralité. Ne devais-je donc pas espérer qu'après avoir embrassé cordialement mes vieux frères d'armes sur le rivage américain, mes heureuses visites à Mount-Vernon, ma retraite dans une ferme, ne seraient pas troublées par les sollicitations des partis?

Votre opinion, mon cher général, est pour moi, comme elle a toujours été, d'un poids immense. Je sais qu'il vous tarde de me presser su votre cœur paternel, et pourtant vous me détournez du voyage qui nous donnerait à tous deux tant de joie. L'avis de M. Martin*, votre digne ami, est, il est vrai, conforme au vôtre. Je dois avouer aussi, comme une faiblesse peut-être, que je ne suis pas sans l'espoir éloigné de pouvoir, tout proscrit que je suis, n'être pas tout à fait inutile pour amener une négociation américaine. En attendant, on me gêne assez sur le choix d'un asile. La reprise de la guerre rend pour moi inconvenant et dangereux d'habiter toute la portion de l'Europe à l'est du Rhin. Il sert peu en France de posséder l'estime et la bienveillance de la nation, et quoique le gouvernement batave s'accorde avec le peuple dans la faveur qu'il me témoigne, ma délica-

---

*Unidentified. Possibly an error for Murray, the American minister to the Hague, who was in fact also trying to discourage Lafayette from going to the United States.

tesse pourrait être engagée à éviter de les commettre avec un puissant allié. Jusqu'à ce moment, je suis parfaitement placé ici sous tous les rapports. Ce n'est pas seulement parce que vous m'avez convaincu, mais par déférence pour votre opinion, que je diffère mon départ jusqu'à l'arrivée de votre réponse, bien persuadé que vous aurez la bonté de remédier aux inconvénients d'un délai mal interprété, peut-être, par quelques amis et le peuple américain. Dans les cas improbable où j'arriverais subitement, soyez certain, mon cher général, que mes motifs seraient assez puissants pour vous convaincre à votre tour de l'urgence de ma détermination. J'ai la confiance qu'alors les différents partis laisseraient un ancien ami à toute son indépendance.

Les explications que vous me donnez sur la politique intérieure m'affligent beaucoup; et d'autant plus, que, connaissant votre haute situation et la droiture de vos jugements, il ne m'est pas permis d'en rien retrancher, comme il est d'usage dans les rapports des partis. Lorsque je vous ai écrit, mon cher général, que les directeurs français désiraient sincèrement se rapprocher des États-Unis, je n'étais influencé par aucune partialité personnelle ni par une confiance exagérée en eux; je jugeais seulement par l'évidence de leur intérêt en qualité de Français, de membres d'un gouvernement ennemi de la Grande-Bretagne, et d'après les renseignements que j'avais recueillis. Encore à présent, je le répète, je crois fermement qu'ils souhaitent une réconciliation appelée par les vœux du pueple. J'espère donc que la bonne intelligence va régner entre les deux républiques.

M. Murray vous tient au courant des nouvelles politiques. Les gens honnêtes de tous les partis doivent être indignés de l'assassinat qui vient d'être commis sur les plénipotentiaires français à Rastadt. Si cette horrible nouvelle, que nous avons apprise hier, se confirme, je regretterai particulièrement l'un d'entre eux, Roberjot, qu'on songeait à nommer directeur, et sur les bonnes intentions duquel je croyais pouvoir compter. George, en arrivant d'amérique, m'avait appris la perte de mon cher aide-de-camp, votre digne neveu. Je suis profondément touché du sentiment affectueux qui l'a porté à donner mon nom à son fils aîné.* Mes vœux les plus tendres suivront toujours

---

*George Augustine Washington died in February 1793. His second (and oldest surviving) son was born in 1791 and named George Fayette Washington.

tout ce qui nous reste de cet excellent homme. Je connaissais déjà les détails que vous me donnez sur la conduite des agents jacobins en Amérique, après le 10 août; j'ai déploré et abhorré toutes ces intrigues. C'est ainsi qu'avec d'immenses sommes d'argent et trop de succès, le gouvernement anglais a agi dans ma patrie nouvellement affranchie. C'est la vieille méthode du machiavélisme. Combien elle répugne à la noble doctrine de la liberté! Qui le sait mieux que vous, mon cher général? et j'ai le droit d'ajouter: qui le sait mieux que moi?

Je suis avec une tendresse filiale, etc. . . . .

APPENDIX I

A. In Letter 165 above, p.273, 1.25, after "order" insert:

Count d'Estaing has represented that Mr de Bougainville Count Dillon, and, I think, two other Colonels were with him auxiliary to our troops, and that Savahan,* tho the attempt was unsuccessfull, has been attended with great fatigues and dangers. The claim I think to be very proper and the Candidates are few, we might act according to the known Sense of the Society. But claims are raising for Captains of ships which seem to me quite an other affair, the Consideration of which, cannot, in my opinion, but be differed untill the Grand Society meeting

Major L'enfant having it from you that M. de Vaudreuil had been left out through mere mistake and should be considered as the other Admirals, I have advised the Major to pay him a visit and will not advise him against delivering to him one of the Marks, which M. de Vaudreuil will not wear untill the official letter is arrived. My reasons for it are that such a mistake could not but hurt his feelings, and that, circumstanced as he is, we ought not to give such an officer a ground of complaints.

in all those matters, I had nothing to do but to hazard an opinion. Major L'enfant knows your orders and the Society's intention. So far as respects the Business entrusted to me, I shall execute it in the best manner I can, and I am glad to see our Society meets with Approbation. Objections are made, as is the case in every novelty. The hereditary part of the institution has its comments. But the general voice is in favour of our Brotherly Society, and General Washington's name as president adds a weight to the Assossiation

With the highest and most affectionate respect I have the honour to be

     My dear General
     Your obedient Humble
     Servant
     Lafayette

---

*At the unsuccessful siege of Savannah in 1779 by a Franco American force Estaing commanded the French fleet.

B. *In Letter 167 above, p.277, 1.19, after "occasion" insert:*

There is an Unanimous Opinion of the officers Here which they Beg Leave to Present, Wiz—that all American Officers in Europe Ought to Resort to a Committee of Which this city is a Natural Center and that the Committee Be instructed to correspond With the Grand Assembly

C. *The more complete English text of Letter 224, pp. 381-82 above follows:*

[Vianen] 19th April [1799]*

Au Gal Washington

Mr. Murray whom I have had the pleasure to see, and whose appointement as a plenipotentiary to france, makes me particularly happy, will no doubt give a full account of european politics. The coalition are improving the opportunities unfortunatly given them by the Bad conduct of the french gov^t & certain it is, that instead of having on the popular side, the majority of each allied people, & of the hostile nations, as it should have been, had good sistem been poursued, the acts of tiranny & pillage within & without, have disgusted many in france, & many abroad, whom nothing but the return of liberty, and that with difficulty, can again reconcile to the new order of things. However there are in popular institution, in legal equality so many advantages over the various aristocraties we had overthrown, the concils of the royal & imperial cabinets, Mr Pitt excepted, are so very absurd, the counter revolutionary chiefs are so mad, & the french army so substantial, well disciplined, & brave, that I am convinced the contest which is now renewed shall again end favorably to france,—provided however she returns to the principles of liberty & justice upon which the revolution was begun for it seems to me there is, not only honestly, but politically no other way to close it.—but however averse gov^t have been to that description of men called *Constitutional*, they have been lately so affraid of the anarchist that their influence in the actual elections has been anti Jacobine, which has produced a pretty good proportion of good representatives—so far as, with the method of *transporting* & *annulling* it may be called a representation. The Civil and military events of this summer will probably be interesting.

*Cornell University Libraries, Rare Book Room, Dean Collection.

D. *The more complex English text of Letter 225, pp.382-85 above follows:*

My dear general,   Vianen 9 Mai 1799*

Your kind and Welcome letter of the 25 december is safely arrived and as my friend Bureau de Puzy has not yet sailed, he will, along with some introductory lines, carry these my affectionate and filial thanks—No, my dear general, it never entered my Head to attribute your Silence to any neglect of yours, and I would have suspected European piracies, or things much more incredible, Rather than any abatement in that friendship I have been so long used to experience, and conscious, as far as heart can go, to deserve— I find a greater proportion of my scribling has reached you than I had thought, and while I regret the Sanguine forwardness that has deprived me of your answers, you will, I know, Readily apologize for it, as it denotes, how ardently, in Spite of difficulties, I long to be in america.

Yet on hearing of the interior divisions which to me appear more unnatural than to those who have witnessed their progress on finding how much in the differences between the united States and france, the later had been to blame, and how far I am not only to influence, but even to ascertain the dispositions of her government, I had some times, within myself, Resolved the arguments contained in your Candid and affectionate letter—a hint from Hamilton had made me think on it—and among the tender motives to wish for a line from you, I had also an expectation of your friendly advices— My own objections, However, have been hitherto removed by the determination I have formed, & the right I may claim, not to embroil my long-earned tranquility with party politics—I have from my youth, head, heart, & hand been devoted to american independence and freedom—I have in Europe Served the Cause & the friends of liberty, and on the extensive & tempestuary Stage of the french revolution, impressed with your lessons, my dear general, and those of our friends, I have with some boldness proclaimed, and not without public approbation for three years Supported the principles for which you have so gloriously fought, and So Succesfully led us—and the moment I could not, consistent with those principles of natural Right and public justice, hold the high

*Collection University Libraries, Rare Book Room, Dean Collection.

Station, which the conquering faction offered to Raise still higher, I left to others to Reap the field of military glory I had Sown—Five years have I in the imperial & royal fangs, which unluckily Seized me, Expiated my Services to liberty & legal order—Now thought I, although I was rescued by the french government, and altho' my fortune (not the three fifths Spent in the cause of the people, but the remainder of the two fifths confiscated in his name) might depend on it, that I could any how condescend to approve arbitrariness, or caress immorality—now could not I expect that after I have heartily embraced on the American Shore my old Brothers & companions, my happy visits at Mount Vernon, my retirement on a Small farm, I am too Utterly ruined to approach the Cities, will not be invaded by party stimulations?

Your opinion however My dear G^{al} has with me, as it ever had, an immence weight—I know you long to fold me to your paternal heart, yet you advise me against your own Satisfaction & mine—you are better informed, & to your judgement I am used to submit—your worthy friend Mr Murray to whom I have confidentially imparted it confesses his opinion coincides with yours, & I must confess, perhaps as a Weackness, that I am not without some distant hopes, that, altho' an objet of proscription, I may become not quite useless to the purpose of an American negociation —I am nevertheless narrowly circumstanced as to the conveniency of an azilum—The renewal of the war, renders the right side of the Rhine, to the Eastern end of Europe, either unsafe, or improper for me—in france, it little avails to enjoy the esteem & benevolence of the nation, and altho' the Batavian gov^t go with the people in their favour to me, it may become a matter of delicacy, which however I dont believe, to avoid comitting them with an imperious ally—Hitherto I am here, on every account perfectly well,—I owe not only to the conviction you have produced in me, but to an advice whatever, coming from you, to differ my intended voyage untill you have answered this letter, & I am Sure you will have the Kindness to obviate the inconveniences which these delays, perhaps by some friends misunderstood might have with respect to them, or the people at large—but in the improbable case where I would suddenly pop upon you, be certain, my dear g^{al} that my motives should be such as to convince you of their urgency, & then I hope individual independence would be left to an harassed old friend by american parties—be pleased therefore, my dear g^al to continue directing your letters to me in Europe, & to inclose them to Mr Pitcairn, the american consul in hambourg. or to Mr Murray in holland as opportunity offers.—

The account you give me of internal politics, pains me great deal, the more so as knowing the Superiority of your Station, & the uprightness of your judgement, I am not allowed these defalcations which in party-matters are generally warranted. permit me to take this opportunity, as I dont remember whether a former account made part of the received letters, to State a fact respecting Doctor Logan—I happened to be in hamburg, with my wife then going to paris, when that gentleman, whom my Son remembered to have Seen at your house, called upon me—he was on his way to france, & having letters of recommendation to some influencing people, he told me, What, he intended, in private conversation. to represent to them respecting the injustice & impolicy of the french gov^t by the united states—it was indeed the very things I had lately written, & you would have expressed—it was at that time difficult for americans to have a french pass, & as the Chargé d'affaires came the same day to take leave of the family, I requested him to give one to the Doctor, Since which I had from him a letter expressing hopes that came also to me from well informed friends, who added the remonstrances of an american called Logan, had had a good effect—that I would think useless to repeat, had I not seen in a paper, that the Doctor had been blamed, & it is incumbent on me to let you know What I have to say in his favour—

While I have written to you My Dear g^al that I thought the french Directory to be Sincerely wishing for a reconciliation with the united states, I was impelled not by any partiality for, neither by an overrated confidence in them, but by the evidence of their interest as french citizens, as members of gov^t as enemies to great Britain, & by every information I could gather, & now, I again Say that I firmly believe they wish for a reconciliation, which I Know to be the warm friendly desire of the nation at large, so that I hope, the two Republics will come to a good understanding.

As to general politics Mr Murray will acquaint you with them—honest Men in all parties cannot but execrate the assassination of the french plenipotentiaries at Radstat, if the horrid news, we have got but yesterday is unhappily confirmed—one of them, Roberjot, who was spoken of for a Director, I particularly regret he was a sensible man, on whose good intentions I could depend—

George had on his return from America acquainted me with the melancholy news that my Dear aid de Camp, your worthy nephew was no more—I heartily feel the affectionate attention he had to call after me his eldest Boy—my tenderest Wishes shall ever attend what remains of that excellent Man.

What you tell me of practices which after the 10th of august were carried within the united states by agents of the Jacobine faction, I had already heard, lamented, & abhorred,—Such were with an immense deal of money, & too much Success poured upon my enfranchissed country by the British gov^t that is the old doctrine of Machiavelisme—how repugnant to the noble doctrine of liberty, who Knows better than you, my dear G^{al}, & I have a right to say, who Knows better than me.

George is still in paris—the late defeats have encreased his disposition, warm enough already, to serve in the army, & my friends agree in that opinion,—not his mother,—Georges has got a good head, & a good heart, nothing will he do but what behoves an honest friend of liberty,—my advise will not go before I weigh the matters & then I think that much confidence may be had in his own judgement.

My wife, my daughters, and son in law, join in presenting their affectionate respects to Mrs Washington & to you my dear g^{al}[.] the former is recovered & sets out for france on monday next with Virginia—our little grand Daughter is well,* will your charming one accept our tender regard?†

With filial love and respect I am my Dear general

       Yours
       Lafayette

 Mr Frestel is now in Paris, & in good health; I need not adding the meeting made Georges, and both indeed very happy.—

*Anastasie de Latour—Maubourg's daughter, Célestine.
†Probably Eleanor ("Nellie") Custis.

APPENDIX II

Corrigenda and Addenda

(In counting lines, begin with the number of the letter, where such appears on the page.)

Letter or Item	Page	Line	
Preface	viii	31	*Delete* short
	xix	13	*Read* town *for* towns
	xxvii	31	*Read* Ronald *for* Roger
29	54	passim	*Read* and *for* & *and* G^{al} *for* Gen
		2	*Read* Lime *for* Line
		4	*Read* Dear General *for* My dear General
		6	*Read* Excellency *for* excellency
		9	*Read* schall *for* shall
		13	*Insert* had *between* have *and* no *and read* objection *for* objections
		20	*Read* do'nt *for* dont
		22	*Read* I'll *for* I
		24	*Read* C^{lel} *for* Col^{nl}
		32	*Read* obedient servant *for* obt svt
		n.	The original in the American Antiquarian Society (Worcester, Mass.) shows that Lafayette signed "Mquis de Lafayette," but "Mquis de" has been crossed out.
33	64	34	*Read* Lafayette *for* La Fayette
38	71	5	*Read* oblig'd *for* obliged
		10	*Delete* that
	72	passim	*Read* General *for* general
		33	*Read* seperation *for* separation
		36	*Insert on a separate line* d^{er} general *below* friend *and above* Lafayette
		37	*At the middle of the page, below* Lafayette *insert* turn the page
50	93	23	*Read* stocks *for* stock
56	105	14	*Read* advice *for* advise
108		passim	*Read* General *for* general
	184	6	*Read* sollicitudes *for* solicitudes
		n.	Corrections have been made in this printing on the basis of the original in the Library of Congress.
	185	4	*Read* afforded *for* offered *and* Board of War *for* board of war
		9	*Read* endeavored *for* endeavord

397

Letter or Item	Page	Line	
		11	*Insert* a comma *between* that *and* desertion *and read* lessened. *for* lessen'd
		14	*Read* a miss *for* amiss
		16	*Read* peculiarity *for* pecularty
		18	*Read* over alls *for* overalls
		19	*Read* over alls *for* overalls
		20	*Read* detachement *for* detachment
		21	*Read* monney *for* money
		22	*Read* payement *for* payment of it *and* year's *for* years
		25	*Insert* as soon as possible *between* have *and* this *and read* monney *for* money *and* Congress *for* congress
		30	*Read* aprehend *for* apprehend *and* my *for* the *and insert* for the *between* nor *and* maps
		32	*Read* Continental *for* continental
		34	*Read* easely *for* easily *and* Annapolis *for* Anapolis
	186	1	*Read* on public accounts was *for* was on public accounts
		2	*Read* Stüben *for* Stuben *and* 10h April *for* 10th of April
		3	*Read* added *for* ad'ed
		5	*Read* aprehend *for* apprehend *and* amount *for* amounts
		6	*Read* Frederisburg *for* Fredericksburg
		8	*Read* lengthtening *for* lengthning
		10	*Read* detirmined *for* detirmin'd
		11	*Read* detachement *for* detachment
		12	*Read* forced *for* force *and* impressed *for* impress'd
		13	*Read* Frederisburg *for* Fredericksburg
		14	*Read* ennemy *for* enemy *and* to morrow *for* tomorrow
		17	*Read* With the highest respect and tender afection I have the honor to be dr gal/Yours/ Lafayette *for* I am my dr genl &c
		18 and n.	The postscript does not appear in the Library of Congress original.
110	188	7	*Read* Peters Burg *for* Petersburg
		16	*Read* servant *for* ervant

398

Letter or Item	Page	Line	
121	204	20	*Read* Pensylvan's *for* Pennsylvan's
131	221–23	passim	*Read* C^{lel} *for* Col° *and* G^{al} *for* General *and* ennemy *for* enemy
	221	10	*Read* Pennsylvanians *for* Pensylvanians
		15	*Read* volonteers *for* volunteers
		19	*Read* delaïed *for* detained
		23	*Delete* the
		24	*Read* bataïllon *for* battalion
		28	*Read* Navy *for* navy *and* reconnoitred *for* reconnoitered
		29	*Read* guns *for* gun
		31	*Read* Gloster *for* Glocester
		33	*Read* a French *for* French
		34	*Read* concerning *for* respecting
		n.	Corrections have been made in this printing on the basis of the original in the Library of Congress.
	222	1	*Read* county *for* country
		3	*Read* Army *for* army
		8	*Read* mentionned *for* mentioned
		14	*Read* tool is *for* tools are
		15	*Read* particulary *for* particularly *and* equipe- *for* equip-
		22	*Read* subsistence *for* subsistance
		24	*Read* departements *for* departments
		24–25	In the original the sentence beginning "Mr. Clayborne" is crossed out. *Read* Mg. *for* M. Genl
		32	*Read* monney *for* money
		34	*Read* monney *for* money
	223	1	*Read* [P.S.] *for* P.S.
152	254	n.	*Read* LXXXVIII *for* LXXVIII
165	272	5	*Read* honour *for* honor
		n.	Corrections have been made in this letter on the basis of the original in the Society of the Cincinnati, Washington, D.C. For an unpublished lengthy addition see Appendix I above, p. 389.
	273	4	*Read* honour *for* honor
		6	*Read* Order *for* order
		7	*Read* writen *for* written

Letter or Item	Page	Line	
		11	*Read* advice *for* advise
		13	*Read* Golden Fleece *for* golden fleece
		19	*Read* some thing *for* something
		20	*Read* ssiation *for* ciation
		21	*Read* L'enfant *for* Lenfant
167	276–77	passim	*Read* Assossiation *for* association
	276	5	*Delete* of
		6	*Read* L'enfant *for* L'Enfant
		10	*Read* volontary *for* voluntary
		12	*Insert* it *between* which *and* is
		17	*Read* neglect, we knew *for* neglect we know
		n.	Corrections have also been made in this letter on the basis of the original in the Society of the Cincinnati. For an unpublished addition see Appendix I above, p. 390.
	277	1	*Read* produced *for* produce
		2	*Read* Navy *for* navy
		3	*Read* other claims *for* a claim *and* La peyrouse *for* Lapeyrouse *and* La Touche *for* la Touche
		4	*Read* may *for* might
		5	*Read* Naval Officers *for* naval officers
		6	*Read* At *for* As *and* Officers *for* officers
		8	*Read* enclose *for* inclose
		9	*Read* Dispersion *for* dispositions *and* institution *for* instructions
		10	*Delete* as *and* etc *and read* C^{lel} *for* Count
		12	*Read* Brotherly *for* brotherly
		13	*Read* on *for* in
		16	*Read* Republican *for* republican
		17	*Read* conquered? and *for* conquered, and
		18	*Read* principles which *for* principles? Which
		19	*Read* occasion? *for* occasion.
		21	*Read* begining *for* beginning *and* concerns *for* claims
		22	*Read* give *for* gave *and* Congres *for* Congress
		27	*Read* attachement *for* attachment
		30	*Read* under to *for* under *and* Brother Officers *for* brother officers
		31	*Read* past *for* pass [*sic*] *and* compagny *for* company

Letter or Item	Page	Line	
167	277	33	*Read* panting *for* impatient
		36	*Read* honour *for* honor
		38	*Read* Lafayette *for* La Fayette
169	280	5	*Read* amongst *for* amongs
173	284	3	*Read* [August 10, 1784] *for* August [10] 1784
		7	*Read* these *for* here
		9	*Read* renders *for* render *and insert* for me *between* necessary *and* to
		12	*Read* get *for* go
		n.	The original of this letter in the collection of David Gage Joyce was offered for sale by Hanzel Galleries, Inc., Chicago, Illinois, on September 23–24, 1973.
	285	3	*Read* shall *for* will
		8	*Read* Spring *for* Springs
		9	*Read* accompagny *for* accompany
208	342	13	*Delete* not *between* will *and* be
	343	14	*Read* impudence *for* imprudence
	345	10	*Read* unfavorable *for* unfavourable
		23	*Read* My *for* by
		35	*Read* General *for* general
		n.	See above "Preface to the Second Printing," pp. *xxx-xxxi*.
209	346	28	*Read* onces *for* once
210	347	12	*Read* organisation *for* organization
211	349	n.	*Read* Jan. *for* May
222	373	19	*Delete* have *between* they *and* now
		n.	The correct reference is to the Cornell University Libraries, Rare Book Room, Sparks Collection. *Read* pp. 377 and 378 *for* p. 378.
	377	4	*Read* begining *for* beginning
224 and 225	381–85		See "Preface to the Second Printing" pp. *xxix*, *xxxii* and the complete English texts in Appendix I above, pp. 390-394.
Index	389	n.	*See also* Supplementary Index *to this printing*
	394	12 col. 1	*Read* 222n. *for* 222
	400	49 col. 2	*Delete* 163
	402	18 col. 1	*Read* 277 *for* 276

401

Letter or Item	Page	Line	
Index	403	46 col. 2	In the entry *Lafayette, Memoirs of* only references to pp. 138n., 158n., 186n., 224n. are to the *Memoirs of*. All other references are to *Mémoires du*. See also Supplementary Index.
	406	40 col. 2	*Read* France *for* Italy
	413	52 col. 2	*Read* xxiv *for* xxv

INDEX

Index

See also "Supplementary Index."

ABBOT, Captain (apparently Stephen Abbot, captain in the Eleventh Massachusetts), 111
Abercromby, Sir Robert (1740-1827), British colonel, 306
A.B.H. (unidentified American spy),128
Aboville,François-Marie, comte d' (1730-1817): as colonel in command of Rochambeau's artillery, 103
"Adamant," British warship, 125, 128
Adams, John (1735-1826): as member of the Continental Congress, 32; as commissioner to France, 75; as minister to the United Provinces, 135; as peace commissioner, 271, 275, 282; as minister to the United Provinces, 298; as minister to Great Britain, 309, 315; as vice-president of the United States, 346
Adams, John Quincy (1767-1848), 295-99
Africa, 283; princes of, 141
Albany (N. Y.), 26, 27, 31-35, 37, 139, 285
Albert de Rions, Charles-Hector, comte d' (1728-1810): as captain of the "Sagittaire" in Estaing's fleet and the "Marseillais" and the "Pluto" in De Grasse's, 278-79
"Alcide," British warship, 124
Alexandria (Egypt), 379
Alexandria (Va.), 172, 187
Algiers, 270, 315, 317
Allen's Creek (Va.), 201
"Alliance," frigate in the American navy, 73, 90, 96, 102, 135, 238, 244
Alliance: Franco-American, xii, 58-59; 77, 118, 183, 247, 273, 329-30, 357, 376; Franco-Spanish, 141; Franco-Dutch, 308; against the Barbary pirates, 315, 317; Franco-Austrian, 329; Quadruple (proposed among France, Spain, Austria and Russia in 1788), 336-38
Alsace (France), 312, 352
"Amazone," French warship which carried Rochambeau's son to France with special requests, 145. *See also* La Pérouse
Ambler's Plantation (near Jamestown, Va.), 204
Amelia County (Va.), 211
"America," warship in Arbuthnot's fleet, damaged in a storm (February, 1781), 151-52
America: Lafayette's attitude toward,viii, xiv, xvii-xix, 4, 55, 59, 75-77, 134, 159, 241, 246, 248, 251, 253, 259, 262, 267-68, 272, 275, 277, 283-84, 309, 324, 326, 329-30, 333-36, 339, 342, 348, 357, 368, 376, 383; Frenchmen in, x, 19, 249-50, 254-55, 265, 272, 276, 278-80, 285, 300, 302, 313, 344, 353, 356, 375, 377-79; French relations with, xii, 40, 57-58, 60, 62, 77, 108, 118, 156, 243, 244, 281, 299, 314 and n., 324, 328, 330, 350, 361, 366 and n., 375-76, 382-83, 385; conditions in, 9, 12, 42, 92, 100-01, 120, 121, 239, 244, 260, 355; maneuvers in, 28, 30, 38, 41, 79-80, 122, 245, 246, 252, 258; communications with, 78, 242, 256, 271, 274, 284, 303; coasts of, 134, 252; Spanish attitude toward, 258, 293; English attitude toward, 293, 297, 309, 312; Lafayette's projected return to, xxi, xxiii, 364, 370, 373, 374, 377, 382-84; ministers (*see* Commissioners; Franklin; Jefferson;

[Names in italics indicate bibliographical data.]

etc.). *See also* Commerce, Franco-American *and* United States.

American: officers, x, 43, n., 51-52, 54, 58, 171-74, 176-77, 181, 200, 202, 206, 233, 235, 261, 273-75, 277; Revolution, xiii, xvii, xxi, xxiv, 14, 55, 74, 238, 246, 256, 259, 266, 306, 319, 327, 347, 370; institutions, 22, 306; attitude toward France, 58-62, 376, 378-79; vessels, 90, 154, 156-57, 161, 168-69, 263; confederation, 261, 270-71, 306, 326, 329; debts to England, 266-67; claims, 277; debt to France, 323; commerce (*see* Commerce). *See also* Continental

Americans, xiv, xxi-xxii, xxiv, 26, 248, 277, 306, 316, 318, 319, 321, 325, 332, 351, 384

Amsterdam (Holland), 332, 333

Anciens, Conseil de (upper house of the French legislature under the Directory), 376 n., 382

André, John (1751-1780), adjutant-general in the British army, xv.

Annapolis (Md.), xix, 156-59, 161, 164-66, 168-70, 172, 185

Annemours, chevalier ——— de, French consul at Richmond, 226

Ansbachers (British mercenaries from Ansbach, Germany), 124, 211, 215

Antony (near Paris, France), 244, 247, 248

Appomattox River (Va.), 194-96, 208, 212

Aquakanac, i.e., Acquacononck (Passaic, N. J.), 126

Arbuthnot, Marriot (1711-1794), vice-admiral in the British navy, 126

Archbishop of Toulouse. *See* Brienne

Archipelago (Turkey), 314

Archives parlementaires, 351 n.

Arendt, baron ——— d', colonel of the German Regiment in the Continental Army, 132

"Ariel," American warship, 132, 136, 144, 145, 151, 159

Armand (i.e., Armand-Charles-Tuffin, marquis de la Rouërie) (1750-1793): as colonel of the Continental Partisan Legion, 6-7, 52-53, 254; as brigadier-general, 281 n.

Arms. *See* Supplies

Army. *See* Austrian; British; Continental; French; *etc*.

Arnold, Benedict (1741-1801): as major-general in the Continental Army, xv, 26, 28-31; as brigadier-general in the British army, 116, 117, 123-25, 145, 148, 152, 155, 159, 160, 162, 165, 166, 170, 175, 179, 186, 192-93, 195, 196-97, 242, 243

Arnold, Margaret Shippen, wife of Benedict Arnold, xv, 125

Arrêts du Conseil, 295 and n., 330 n., 335 and n., 336, 338, 344

Articles of Confederation, 261, 306

Artillery, 18, 32, 35, 87, 101, 103, 108-09, 125, 150, 154, 161, 168-69, 182, 186, 189, 194, 196, 203, 212, 216, 219, 220, 222, 223, 227. *See also* Aboville; Knox; Stevens; *etc*.

Artois, Charles-Philippe, comte d' (later King Charles X of France) (1757-1836): as chairman of the Second Bureau of the Council of Notables, 323 and n., 325, 327; as émigré, 352, 359

Asia, 375

Assembly: of French clergy, 343; National (*see* National Assembly); of Notables (*see* Notables)

Atlantic Ocean, xx, 248, 289, 290, 307, 342, 355, 371

Attorney-General. *See* Payne

Augusta (Ga.), 134

Austria, xxi-xxiii, 291 n., 302, 306, 308, 325, 329, 335-37, 344-45, 366 and n., 375, 379; army of, 294-95, 299, 301, 305, 325, 340

Austrian Netherlands. *See* Belgium

Auvergne (province of France), 265, 298, 312, 326, 331, 335

Ayen, Jean-Paul-François de Noailles, duc d' (1739-1824), Lafayette's father-in-law, lieutenant-general in the French army, 312, 341

Balloons, 282 and n.

Baltimore (Md.), xix, 154, 157, 172, 184-85, 187-88, 214-15, 221, 284, 318

Bancroft, Dr. Edward (1744-1821): as secretary to Franklin, 264 and n.

Banister, Mr. ———, 320

Barbary pirates, 317 n. *See also* Algiers *and* Morocco

Barber, Frances (1751-1783): as lieutenant-colonel in the First New Jersey, 143, 176, 177; in the Light Division, 236

Barber, William, major and inspector of the Light Division, 236

Barcelo, Antonio (1730-1797), lieutenant-general in the Spanish navy, 141

Barclay, Thomas, American consul in Paris, 275; on Moroccan mission, 317
Barras-St.-Laurent, Jacques-Melchior, comte de († ca. 1800), chef d'escadre, successor to Ternay as commander of Rochambeau's convoy, 229, 233
Barren Hill (Pa.), xii
Barret (or Barrett), Mr. ——————, of Boston, Mass., 303, 310
Barrington, Samuel (1729-1800): as rear-admiral in British Channel Fleet, 249
Barron, James, commodore in the Virginia naval forces, 214
Bassett, Frances. See Washington, Mrs. George Augustine
Bastille, xx, 323, 328, 348; Austrian (see Olmütz)
Batavian Republic. See Holland
Bath (England), 275
Battery (in New York City), 128
Baudowin. See Bowdoin
Bavaria, 291 n., 293, 295, 299, 301 and n., 311
Bayonne (France), 275-76
Beaune, M. —————— de, French officer, 265
Bed of justice (*lit de justice*), 343 and n.
Bedel, Timothy (ca. 1740-1787): as colonel of New Hampshire militia, 27, 34
"Bedford," British warship in Arbuthnot's fleet, damaged in a storm (February, 1781), 151-52
Belgium, 242, 291 n., 295, 325
Belgrade (Serbia): as a Turkish possession, 335, 340, 344
Bemis, S. F., xxi n., xxii n., xxiii n.
Beniowski, Maurice-Auguste de (1741-1786), Polish adventurer, "King of Madagascar," 318
Bennington (Vt.), 37
Bergen (N. J.), 124, 128, 199
Bergen Neck (N. J.), 111
Bergen Point (N. J.), 124
Berkenhout, Dr. John (1730?-1791), British secret agent, 239
Berlin (Prussia), xxii, 301, 303, 379
Bernis, François-Joachim de Pierre, cardinal de (1715-1794), 244
Bethlehem (Pa.), 8
Billingsport (N. J.), 40
Bitche (France), 359, 362
Blackley, John, second-lieutenant in the First Canadian Regiment, 35

Black Sea, 266, 345
Black Water River (Va.), 218
Block Island (R. I.), 90
Board of War, xi, xii, 14-15, 20, 26, 27, 36, 37, 153, 174, 176, 178, 180-81, 183, 185
Bohemia, 301
Boismartin. See Duboismartin
Bollmann, Dr. Justus Erich (1769-1821), who tried to free Lafayette from Olmütz, xxiii, 380
Bonaparte, Napoleon (1769-1821), xxiii, xxiv, 375 and n., 379
Borda, Jean Charles (1733-1799), chevalier de (1733-1790), naval major in Estaing's fleet, 66
Bordeaux (France), 262, 283
Boston (Mass.), xii, 27, 30, 32, 66, 70, 74, 90, 103, 141, 310; harbor, xvi, 82, 238; French in, 56-58, 60, 62-63, 65, 90; Lafayette in, 62-63, 68, 71-72, 145, 238-39, 286, 287, 289
Bottom's Creek (Va.), 188
Bouchet, Denis-Jean-Florimond Langlois de Montheville, marquis du (1752-1826): as major on Gates's and later on Rochambeau's staff, 278-80
Bouillé, François-Claude-Amour, marquis de (1739-1800), formerly governor of Martinique, 339, 342
Bourbonnais, Regiment de (French), 90
Bowdoin, James (1727-1790): as president of the Massachusetts constitutional convention, 97, 239
Brabant (province of Belgium), 325 n.
Brandon (Va.), 191, 194
Brandywine (Pa.), ix, 135
Brant, Joseph (1742-1807), Mohawk Indian chief friendly to the English, 286
Bréhan, ——————, marquise de, Moustier's sister-in-law, 333
Brenton's Point (R. I.), 95
Breslau (Germany), 303
Brest (France), 66, 79, 140-41, 174, 241-43, 247, 257, 291, 312
Breteuil, Louis-Auguste le Tonnelier, baron de (1733-1807): as Louis XVI's minister of the king's household, 308-09
Brice, Edmund, one of Lafayette's companions on the "Victoire": as major and aide-de-camp to Lafayette, 7, 31, 66
Brienne, Athanase-Louis-Marie de Loménie, comte de (1730-1794): as minister of war, 328, 333

407

Brienne, Etienne-Charles de Loménie de (1727-1794), archbishop of Toulouse: as Louis XVI's controller-general of finances, 323, 325, 328, 331, 333, 344 and n.
Brissot de Warville, Jean-Pierre (1754-1793): as writer on America, 344 and n.
Bristol (R. I.), 63, 64, 66
Bristol Point (R. I.), 95
Britanny, 291, 345
British, 68, 89, 166, 247, 260, 271, 357. *See also* England
British ambassadors, 306
British army, 15, 63, 72, 80, 95, 105, 119, 143; in New Jersey, 6-7, 25, 46-51, 111-12; in Pennsylvania, 8, 10-13, 38-42, 44-46; in New York, xv, 29, 33, 37, 86, 93, 94, 101, 110-11, 114, 116, 124-30, 140; in Rhode Island, 54, 59, 62, 64, 96, 99, 104, 105; in the South, xv-xvi, 106-07, 118, 121-22; in the Virginia campaign, xvi, 147-236
British Commander-in-Chief. *See* Carleton
British fleet, 55, 57-58, 65-66, 86-89, 95, 99, 108, 110, 112, 126, 128-29, 145, 147, 157, 162, 164-68, 172, 182, 187, 196, 203, 210-13, 218, 221, 223, 231-32, 245, 249, 253 and n., 375. *See also* Channel Fleet *and* Cork Fleet
British ministry, 205, 208, 210, 245, 248-49, 267, 271, 275, 338, 375, 377, 385
British officers, 30, 33, 35, 160, 192, 245
British peace commissioners, 41, 67-68. *See also* Carlisle
British women, 33
Brock's Bridge (Va.), 200
Broglie, Charles-François, comte de (1719-1781), lieutenant-general in the French army, viii
Broglie, Charles-Louis-Victor, prince de (1756-1794), son of Maréchal de Broglie: as colonel-en-second of the Regiment de Saintonge in Rochambeau's army, 242, 250
Broglie, Victor-François, duc and maréchal de (1718-1804), 242, 250, 291
Brookline. *See* Brooklyn
Brooklyn (N. Y.), 85, 86, 88
Browne, Thomas (†1825), Loyalist lieutenant-colonel commanding the King's Rangers, 128
Brunswick (Germany), 303, 329

Brunswick Camp. *See* New Brunswick
Brunswick, Karl Wilhelm Ferdinand, duke of (1735-1806), Prussian field marshal, 303-05
Buisson. *See* Dubuysson
Bull's Ferry (N. J.), 111
"Bumont," British warship (?), 145
Buol-Schauenstein, Johann Rudolf, Graf von (1763-1834): as Austrian envoy to Hamburg, xxiii n.
Bureaux de Pusy, Jean-Xavier (1750-1805): as companion of Lafayette in captivity and exile, 363 and n., 364, 369, 382
Burgoyne, John (1722-1792), lieutenant-general in the British army, 35
Burnet, Dr. William (1730-1791), surgeon-general of the Eastern District of the Continental Army, 124 and n., 128
Butler, Richard (1743-1791), lieutenant-colonel of Morgan's Rifles, 6
Butts Hill (R. I.), 99, 105

Cadiz (Spain), xvii, 138, 141, 259, 295
"Cæsar," warship in Estaing's fleet, 57-58
Cæsar, Julius, xvii, 259
Call, Richard Keith (1757-1792), major in the Third Light Dragoons (Continental), 230
Calonne, Charles-Alexandre de (1734-1802): as controller-general of finances, 270, 297, 308 and n., 309, 314 and n., 318, 320, 322, 323, 333, 335 n.
Camden (S. C.), 192, 198
Campbell, William (1745-1781), brigadier-general in the Virginia militia, 224
Campeche, Bay of (in the Gulf of Mexico), 142
Campo Formio, Peace of, 366 n.
Camus (probably M. de Camus, ensign on the "Eveillé"), 221-22
Canada, 24, 64, 321; projected invasions of, xi-xiii, xv, xvii, 25, 26-29, 31, 36, 87, 107, 260, 329; frontier posts of, 289. *See also* Posts
Canadian prisoners, 35
Canadians: "Congress' Own" (Hazen's Regiment), 20, 27, 37; Livingston's, 35
Candia (i.e., Crete), 329, 375
Cape: Fear (N. C.), 165, 174; Henry (Va.), 222
Capes of Delaware, 178
Capes of Spain, 141

Capes of Virginia, 159, 160, 165; battle of the (March 16, 1781), 164, 167; battle of the (September 6, 1781), 231, 232
Capital Landing (Va.), 228
Caraman, Victor-Louis-Charles de Riquet, chevalier (later comte) de (1762-1839): as Lafayette's companion on the 1784 visit to America, 287 and n., 290, 292, 294
Carey, Mathew (1760-1839), Irish-American publicist, 289-90
Carleton, Sir Guy (1724-1808), successor to Clinton as British commander-in-chief in America, 251
Carlisle, Frederick Howard, Earl of (1748-1825): as president of the British peace commission of 1778, 67-70
Carmichael, William (†1795), as secretary to John Jay in Madrid, 138; as chargé d'affaires, 260 n., 262
Carolina Maria (1752-1814), queen of Naples, 379 and n.
Carolinas. *See* North Carolina *and* South Carolina
Cassel (Germany), 301, 303
Castaing La Grace, Pierre de (1751-1795?), first lieutenant and aide-de-camp to Duportail, 144, 145
Castries, Charles-Eugene-Gabriel de la Croix, marquis and maréchal de (1727-1801): as friend of Lafayette, 15, 127; as minister of the marine and the colonies, xv, 137, 138, 140, 158, 171, 174, 178, 247, 249, 264, 267, 296, 312, 328, 331, 375; as commandant of the Gendarmerie, 312. *See also* Charlus
Catherine II (the Great) (1729-1796): as tsarina of Russia, 283, 291 n., 310-11, 314, 317, 345, 375 n.
Catholicism, 297
Cavalry, American, 198, 209, 214-15, 222; British, 203, 208, 210, 223; Prussian, 304. *See also* Dragoons; Horse; Lauzun; *etc.*
Cayenne (island in French Guiana), 301, 309
Chaffault. *See* Duchaffault
Champlain, Lake, 25, 37
Channel Fleet (British), 141
Charavay, Etienne, 372 n.
Charles III (1716-1788): as king of Spain, 79, 260, 307 and n., 320 and n.
Charles Emanuel IV (1751-1819), king of Sardinia, 375

Charles Theodore (1724-1799), elector of the Palatinate and Bavaria, 291 n., 293, 299
"Charleston," American warship, 166, 167
Charleston (S. C.), 87, 110, 119, 121, 132-34, 145, 147, 173, 191, 214-15, 233, 236, 243, 245-46, 249, 252, 258, 300
Charlottesville (Va.), 199, 202
Charlus, Armand-Charles-Augustin de la Croix, comte de (afterward duc de Castries) (1758-1842), son of the Marquis de Castries; as colonel-en-second of the Regiment de Saintonge in Rochambeau's army, 127, 137 and n., 138, 148, 158; as a general of the French Gendarmerie, 241-42, 247, 312
"Charon," British warship, 164, 211
Chartres. *See* Orléans
Chastel de la Vallée, Monsieur ———— de, French traveler in America, 342
Chastellux, François-Jean, chevalier (later marquis) de (1734-1788): as maréchal de camp under Rochambeau, 95, 127, 135; as man of letters, 285, 316, 344 and n.
Chavaniac, Lafayette's ancestral château in Auvergne, 265, 312, 358 and n.
Cherbourg (France), 308, 312
Cherry Valley (N. Y.), 34
Chesapeake Bay, 85, 87, 146-48, 151-52, 154, 156-57, 159, 161, 164, 166, 169, 179, 182, 185, 210-11, 213, 215, 220, 225, 231-32, 260
Chesterfield County (Va.), 196
Chesterfield Court House (Va.), 186
Chickahominy River (Va.), 194, 219
Choin, André-Michel-Victor, marquis de (1744-1829): as major and aide-de-camp to Estaing, 56
Choiseul, Etienne-François, duc de (1719-1785), chief minister of Louis XV, 299
Choiseul, vicomte de (probably Jean-Baptiste-Armand de Choiseul-Meuse [1735-1815], later governor of Martinique), 187
Choisy, Claude-Gabriel, marquis de (1723-1799?), brigadier-general left by Rochambeau in command of Newport, 205
Chouin. *See* Choin
Christiana Creek (Del.), 170
Cincinnati, Society of the, 272 and n., 273 and n., 276-80, 282-83, 307, 318

Cinq Cents (i.e., The Five Hundred, lower house of the French legislature under the Directory), 380, 382
Ciphers, 135, 138, 237 and n., 245 and n., 249 and n., 252 and n., 253 and n., 255 and n., 256 and n., 257 and n., 258, 289, 296-97
City Point (Va.), 196
City Tavern (Philadelphia), viii
Clayburne (i.e., Richard Claiborne, major and deputy quartermaster general in Virginia), 222, 227, 229-30
Clinton, George (1739-1812): as governor of New York, 26, 33, 34
Clinton, Sir Henry (1738?-1795), commander-in-chief of the British forces in North America, xvi, 41, 64, 93, 97, 99, 102, 109, 114, 120, 123-24, 128, 167
Clostercamp, battle of (1760), 127
Clothier General's Department, 83
Clothing, 8-13, 18-19, 27-32, 35, 38, 82-84, 87, 92-99, 102, 107, 110, 132-35, 141, 144-45, 150, 171-76, 180-81, 185, 188, 199, 206, 209, 220-24, 243
Club of 1789, 349 and n., 350
Coalition (Austria, Prussia, England, etc.) against France, 360, 363, 369-70, 374-75, 381
Cochran, Dr. John (1730-1807): as surgeon-general in the Middle Department of the Continental Army, 72 and n.; greetings to, 360
Colombe. *See* La Colombe
Colonies: British, 245; French, 318, 348, 357 and n.
Commander of Artillery. *See* Aboville
Commerce, 306, 320, 329; Franco-American, xvii, 132, 136, 264, 268, 271, 275-83, 286, 293, 295, 299, 301, 309-10, 314 and n., 324, 330 and n., 331-33, 336, 338, 344, 347, 351-53, 356-57, 376; Anglo-American, xxii, 267, 289, 293, 295, 312, 314, 330; Levant, 266, 337; Spanish-American, 295; Austro-American, 302; Anglo-French, 307, 308, 311, 313, 314, 329; Franco-Russian, 320-21
Commissaries, 48 n., 227, 229
Commissioners (American) in France: (1776-1783), 37, 239, 250-51, 255, 264, 266-68, 271, 276, 307; (1797), 366 and n.; (1799), 381
Committees (French): on American commerce, 309, 312, 314, 338; Diplomatic (of the National Assembly), 351, 353; on revision of the Constitution of 1791, 354-55
Commons, House of, 275
Communication: problems of, 69, 78-79, 83, 89, 90, 94, 95, 102-04, 109, 117, 121-22, 127, 132-34, 137, 142, 149-50, 153, 188, 201, 208, 210, 222; by post, 152, 155, 164, 183-84, 190, 199, 212, 296, 332, 376; by vessel, 244, 249, 256-57, 267, 269, 270-71, 276, 286, 290, 292, 294, 296, 298, 303, 311-12, 317, 345 n. 346-48, 365, 377
Conanicut (R. I.), 93, 95, 99, 103
Condé, Louis-Joseph de Bourbon, prince de (1736-1818), 291, 352, 356, 359
"Confederacy," American vessel, 133, 136
Confederation. *See* American confederation
Conflans, Hubert de Brienne, comte and maréchal de (ca. 1690-1777), 5-6
Congress of the Confederation, 271; Lafayette's relations with, 163, 183, 188, 193, 197, 204, 224, 238, 246, 251, 258, 260, 262-64, 266, 268-69, 271, 276-77, 281, 295, 301, 306-07, 319, 333; and France, 185, 243, 281, 314; and England, 248, 289; and Washington, 270; and French officers, 283; attitude toward Lafayette of, 289; and the Barbary pirates, 315. *See also* Continental Congress *and* Congress of the United States
Congress of the United States, xxii, 334. *See also* Congress of the Confederation *and* Continental Congress
Connecticut, 85-86, 89, 91, 92, 97, 98; Council of, 89, 91, 93
Connecticut Farms (N. J.), 114
Connecticut River, 54, 93
Constantinople (Turkey), 314, 340
Constitution: of France (1791), 349 n., 353, 354 and n., 355 and n., 356, 358-59, 361-62, 370, 374; of the United States, 334-35, 338, 342, 350. *See also* Articles of Confederation
Consuls: French, 265; American, 269
Continent. *See* United States
Continental Army, viii-xii, xiv-xv, 4, 15, 18, 20-23, 60, 63, 68, 74, 77-85, 96, 101, 103-06, 116; 118-19, 128, 131, 133, 135, 242, 244, 247-50, 253, 258, 260, 262, 318,

410

353; in New Jersey, 6-7, 46-52, 87, 108, 111, 114, 119, 121; in Pennsylvania, 8-13, 24, 38-42, 44-46; in New York, 27-28, 32, 37-38, 88, 94, 140; in Rhode Island, 55, 56, 99; in the South, 106, 237; in the Virginia campaign, 144-236; after the war, 261, 265, 270, 271, 274-75, 277, 282

Continental Congress, 135, 139; Lafayette's relations with, viii-xiii, 3-4, 24, 27-28, 33, 73-79, 117, 141, 150, 153, attitude toward Lafayette of, xi, 34-35, 37, 69, 71; and French officers, 5 and n., 18, 20, 52-53, 63; and Washington, 12, 14-15, 30, 32, 43, 132, 141; and England, 67, 137; and France, 80, 137, 142. *See also* Congress of the Confederation *and* Congress of the United States

Convention, Constitutional (1787), 324-25, 326 and n. *See also* Neutrality

"Conway Cabal," x-xii, 32, 36-37.*See also* Conway; Gates; etc.

Conway, Thomas, comte (1733-1800): as brigadier-general in the Continental Army, x-xi, 3; as major-general and inspector-general, xi-xii, 14, 15, 18, 20, 24-26, 30, 37; in the Society of the Cincinnati, 280

Cook, Captain James (1728-1779), British explorer, 368

Cooper's Ferry (N. J.), 25

Cope, ―――――, British officer, 30

Coriel's Ferry. *See* Coryell's Ferry

Cork (Ireland) Fleet, 88, 125, 127, 128

"Cormorant," British warship captured by the French, 237

Cornell University Library, xxvii, 373 n.

Cornwallis, Charles, Earl (1738-1805): as lieutenant-general of the British army in the South, xv-xvi, 107, 138, 152-53, 163, 170, 179, 191-98, 202-08, 210-13, 215-17, 220, 223, 225-27, 229, 231, 234, 256, 324, 337; as American prisoner on parole, 241, 243, 251, 252 n.; in Germany, 301, 304, 306; as lord lieutenant of Ireland, 375

Corny, Louis-Dominique Ethis de (1736-1790): as commissary of war to Rochambeau's army and brevet lieutenant-colonel of Continental cavalry, 279

Coryell's Ferry (over the Delaware River), 25, 26

Coudray. *See* Ducoudray

Coulteux. *See* Le Coulteux

Council: of Massachusetts Bay, 62; of French ministers, 174, 273, 325, 327, 328, 356, 362; of Finances (French), 344 n.; of Anciens (*see* Anciens); of Cinq Cents (*see* Cinq Cents); of Notables (*see* Notables)

Councils of war, 46, 47, 58, 60, 61, 95, 105, 170

Cour plenière, 343 and n.

Courts martial, 21-23

Coventry (Conn.), 54

Craig, i.e., Dr. James Craik (1730-1814), chief physician and surgeon of the Continental Army, 315, 319

Cranberry (N. J.), 48-50

Cranberry Creek (N. J.), 48

Cranestown (Montclair, N. J.), 114

Crèvecœur, Hector St. Jean de (1731-1813): as French consul in New York, 288, 324

Crimea (Russia), 266, 311, 314, 317, 320

Cromwell, Oliver (1599-1658): Lafayette likened to, 350

Custis, Eleanor Calvert (1754-1811), Martha Washington's daughter-in-law: as widow of John Parke Custis, 269 and n., 271; as wife of Dr. Stuart, 290 and n., 292, 296, 301, 310, 315, 319, 321

Custis, Eleanor ("Nellie") Parke (1779-1852), granddaughter of Martha Washington, 271, 290 and n., 292, 294-96, 301, 310, 315, 319, 321, 368-69, 372, 377-78, 380

Custis, Elizabeth ("Eliza") Parke (1776-1832), granddaughter of Martha Washington, 271, 290 and n., 292, 294-96, 301, 310, 315, 319, 321

Custis, George Washington Parke (1781-1857), grandson of Martha Washington, 290 and n., 292, 294-96, 301, 310, 315, 319, 321, 369, 372, 380

Custis, John Parke (1755-1781), son of Martha Washington, 168, 269 n., 290 n.

Custis, Martha Parke (b. 1777), granddaughter of Martha Washington, 271, 290 and n., 292, 294-96, 301, 310, 315, 319, 321

Cuyler, Jacob, deputy commissary general of purchases in the Continental Army, 26

411

DAMAS, Joseph-François-Louis-Joseph-César, comte de (1758-1829: as colonel and aide-de-camp to Rochambeau, 138-39, 217
Danbury (Conn.), 89
Danzig, as semi-autonomous Polish city, 270
Dauphin, i.e. Louis-Joseph-Xaxier-François (1781-1789), first son of Louis XVI, 241
Day, Benjamin, deputy quartermaster general at Williamsburg, Va., 196
Dayton, Elias (1737-1807): as colonel of the Second New Jersey, 144, 147-48
Deane, Silas (1737-89): as American commissioner in Paris, 242, 283
Decker's Ferry (on Staten Island, N. Y.), 124-25
Declaration of Independence, 377
Dekalb, Johann, baron (1721-1780): as major-general in the Continental Army, ix, xi, 3, 32, 37
Delaware: River, 6, 11-12, 25, 40, 44, 122; State of, 45, 170; Bay, 87, 125; Capes of, 178
Democracy, 282, 306, 326, 361, 374, 381
Denmark, 345, 363-65, 368, 372, 375, 379
Desandrouins, Jean-Nicolas, vicomte de 1729-1792), colonel in command of Rochambeau's engineers, 103
Deserters, 27-28, 71, 171, 173, 181-83, 185, 186 and n., 187-88, 208, 223, 231, 243
Destouches, Charles - René - Dominique Sochet, chevalier (1727-1793), brigadier in Ternay's fleet, commander of the "Neptune" and *ad interim* successor to Ternay, 146, 151-52, 162, 173-74, 210, 279
Deux Ponts (or Zweibrücken), 301
Deux Ponts, Charles-Auguste-Christian, duc de (1754-1795), 293, 301 and n.
Deux-Ponts, Christian, comte de Forbach, marquis de (1754-1817): as colonel of the Regiment Royal Deux Ponts in Rochambeau's army, 301 and n.
Dickenson, Philemon (1739-1809): as major-general of New Jersey militia, 50, 51
Dillon, Edouard, comte (1750-1840): as colonel of the Regiment de Dillon under Estaing, 279

Directory (French government in 1795-1799), 364, 366 n., 369 n., 370, 376-78, 382 n., 384
Discipline (military), 8-9, 19 and n., 21-23, 29, 30, 42, 54, 80, 104, 114, 116, 131, 147, 150, 180-81, 186, 188, 214, 236, 340, 359-60, 381
Dismal Swamp (Va.), 165, 212
Dobb's Ferry (N. Y.), 109
Dobbs, Captain William, American pilot, 102, 104
Doctors, 31, 33, 35, 129
Dod's (i.e., Dodd's Tavern [N. J.]), 115
Doillamson. *See* Oilliamson
"Dolphin," American armed sloop, 157
Dolphin. *See* Dauphin
Domices Ferry (N. Y.), 128
Doradour, ————, comte, French immigrant to America, 298
Dover (England), 284
Dragoons: American, 84, 104, 112, 117, 202, 203, 208, 209, 219, 221, 222, 228, 230, 233, 235, 254; British, 201, 203; French 341. *See also* Hussars; King's Dragoons; Queen's Light Dragoons; etc.
Draper, Sir William (171-1787): as lieutenant-general and lieutenant-governor of Minorca, 244
Dresden (Germany), 303, 304
Duboismartin, François-Augustin (1745?-1796?), one of Lafayette's companions on the "Victoire," 282-83
Dubuysson des Hays, Charles-François, chevalier (later vicomte) (1752-1786): as lieutenant-colonel in the Continental Army and aide-de-camp de Dekalb, 139
Duchaffault de Besné, Louis-Charles, comte (1708-1794), lieutenant-general in the French navy, 66, 98, 99
Duché (i.e., D.-J.-A. Ducher, later in the French consular service in the United States), 285
Ducoudray (i.e., Philippe-Charles-Jean-Baptiste Tronson du Coudray), French officer (1738-1777): as major-general in the Continental Army, 18
Duer, William (1747-1799): as member of the Continental Congress, 25, 26
Dumas, Charles Frederic William, diplomatic agent of the United States, 319
Dumas, Guillaume-Mathieu, comte

(1753-1837): as member of a military mission to Turkey, 375
Dundas, Francis (†1824), lieutenant-colonel in Cornwallis' army, 218, 221
Dunkirk (France), 275-76
Duplessis. *See* Mauduit
Duplessis (not to be confused with Mauduit du Plessis), said to be a brigadier in the French army, 311
Dupont de Nemours, Pierre-Samuel (1739-1817), leading Physiocrat, 332, 376 and n.
Dupont, Victor-Marie (1767-1827): as attaché to the French legation in the United States, 332
Duportail, Louis Le Bègue de Presles (1743-1802): as brigadier-general of engineers in the Continental Army, 15, 46, 47, 144, 153, 226, 229, 242, 255; in Germany, 306
Dutch, 241, 245, 291 n., 293, 299, 314, 326, 329, 331-32
Dutch Netherlands. *See* Holland

East Indies, 242
East River (N. Y.), 85, 86
Eastern States. *See* New England
Eden Treaty, 307-08, 311 and n., 313-14, 329
Edenton (N. C.), 141
Edict of Nantes, Revocation of the, 315, 338 and n.
Egypt, 329, 375 and n.
Eightieth Regiment (British), 208, 215
Eleanor. *See* Custis, Eleanor Parke
Elector of Bavaria. *See* Charles Theodore
Elizabethtown (N. J.), 112-14, 125, 129-30
Elk. *See* Head of Elk
Elk River, 154, 157, 161
Ellis, Joseph, colonel of New Jersey militia, 6
Emigrés (French), 352, 355 and n., 356, 358, 359, 362, 379 n.
Emperor. *See* Joseph II, Leopold II, *or* Francis II
Empress of Russia. *See* Catherine
Engineers, commander of (French). *See* Desandrouins
England, 42, 75, 76, 118, 125-26, 129-30, 167, 208, 261, 336; relations with America of, xxii, 241, 243, 245, 249, 257, 266, 269, 271, 312, 314 n., 317, 326, 330, 336, 337; proposed invasions of, 78-80, 245; Americans in, 239, 250-51, 264, 267, 271, 275, 310; in European politics, 266, 268, 275, 292-93, 295, 307-09, 311, 314, 325, 328-29, 333, 335-38, 340, 357 and n., 360 n., 361, 379, 384; engineers of, 308. *See also* British
England, Sir Richard (1750-1812): as British colonel, 306
English: customs, 22; ministry, 39; men, 271; hounds, 295, 299. *See also* British
Englishtown (N. J.), 52
Ennis. *See* Innis
Equality, 326, 355, 361, 374, 381
Estaing, Charles-Hector, comte d' (1729-1794): as vice-admiral in the French navy, xii-xiii, 55-63, 65-68, 79-80; as commander of the combined Franco-Spanish forces, 137-38, 141, 145, 256-58, 262; in the Society of the Cincinnati, 276-78; in French affairs, 311, 318
Estates: General, (France), 325, 327, 335, 337, 341; General (Holland), 333; of Brittany, 291; of Brabant, 325 n.
Europe, xviii, 12, 18, 65, 77, 134, 162, 366, 383; Lafayette detained in, xxiii, 268-69, 364, 374; attitude toward Lafayette of, 4, 28-30, 235; military practices of, 9-10, 20; attitude toward America of, 14, 40, 55, 87, 120-21, 241 246, 265, 269-71, 274, 306, 319, 321, 338; political affairs in, 79, 124, 131, 266-67, 276, 291, 293, 308, 328, 336-37, 339-40, 343-45, 374, 381; Americans in, 264; Society of the Cincinnati in, 280, 281 n., 307; and the French Revolution, 346, 349, 355-56, 359-60, 374, 377. *See also* Austria; England; France; *etc.*
"Eveillé," French warship, 173-74

Falmouth (England), 148
Farm, i.e., Farmers-General, 309 and n., 312, 324, 330 and n.
Fayette County (Pa.), 311
Ferdinand IV (1751-1825): as king of Naples, 375
Feudalism, 358 and n., 361
Ficher. *See* Fischer
Fifty-Fourth Regiment (British), 128
Finances, Director of. *See* Necker
Fischer, Jean-Chrétien (1713-1762), lieutenant-general, commander of the first chasseurs in the French army, 5

413

Fishburne, William (1760-1819): as major and aide-de-camp to Wayne, 143
Fishkill (N. Y.), 41, 78, 80, 127, 284
Fitzgerald, John: as colonel and secretary to Washington, 319
Fitzpatrick, John C., x n., xii n., xiv n., xvi n., xviii n., xix n., xxi n., xxii n., xxiii n., xxiv n., 5 n., 21 n., 43 n., 263 n., 292 n., 298 n., 307 n., 345 n.
Flag Staff (on Staten Island, N. Y.), 124
Flanders, French, 352; Austrian (*see* Belgium)
Flatbush (on Long Island, N. Y.), 129
Fleet, Combined (Franco-Spanish), xvii, 141, 257, 260. See also French fleet *and* Spanish fleet
Flemington (N. J.), 24
Fleury, François-Louis Teissèdre, vicomte de (1749-1796?), lieutenant-colonel in the Continental Army (until 1779) and then major in the Regiment de Saintonge in Rochambeau's army, 139
Florida, 134
Flushing (on Long Island, N. Y.), 128
Fontainebleau (France), 314
Fontenille, M. ——— de, companion of Count Wengiersky, 263
Food. See Provisions
Forman, David (1745-1797): as brigadier-general of New Jersey militia, 48-50, 52
Forster, Mr. ———, younger son of J. R. Forster, 368
Forster, Johann Reinhold (1729-1798), famous geographer and traveler, 368
Fort: Lee (N. J.), 108, 111, 119; Mifflin (Pa.), 135; Pitt (Pittsburg, Pa.), 311; Schuyler (N. Y.), 30, 32, 34, 37; Washington (N. Y.), 39, 108, 119-20, 128, 130. See also Posts
Forty-Second Regiment (British). See Highlanders
Forty-Third Regiment (British), 215
Four Miles Creek (Va.), 209
Fourqueux, Michel Bouvard de, *ad interim* successor of Calonne, 323
Fox, Charles James (1749-1806): as leader of the Opposition in Parliament, 248, 275, 282-83
France: aristocracy of, vii-viii, x, xxiv, 127, 271, 317-18, 328, 331, 345-47, 349, 351-52, 357, 358 n., 360-61, 374, 377, 381; Americans in, ix, 37, 73, 241, 250, 264, 277, 289, 357; American attitude toward, x, xxiii, 58-60, 139; attitude toward Lafayette of, xi, 76, 80, 234, 244, 247, 280; American relations with, xii-xiii, xxi-xxii, xxiv, 4, 15, 16, 20, 22, 24, 29, 32, 57, 65, 68, 72, 78-79, 82-83, 108, 119, 135-37, 139, 141, 144, 183-84, 238, 241, 246, 271, 276, 288, 293, 296, 298, 302, 307, 309, 330, 336, 366 and n., 371, 373, 375-76, 381-82; Lafayette in xii-xiv, xvii-xviii, xix-xx, 241, 254 (*see also* Chavaniac; Paris; Versailles; *etc.*); religious problems in, xvii, 294, 296-97, 315, 318, 320, 338, 356; economic problems in, xvii, 318, 320, 322-23, 337, 342; political conditions in, xviii, xxi, 327-28, 337, 340-41, 343, 364, 379; invitations to, xviii, 261, 271, 288; revolution in, xx-xxi, xxiv, 326-27, 335, 342-43, 346-52, 356, 361-62, 370, 374, 381, 383; in European affairs, xxiii, 266, 268, 270, 275, 283, 291 and n., 293, 299, 308, 314, 317, 320-21, 325, 328-29, 335, 337, 340, 366 and n., 375; military plans of, 5, 76, 78, 98, 132; relations with England of, 67-68, 71, 79, 87, 248, 311, 314, 360 n., 384; imports from, 84, 93, 312; harbors of, 132, 135, 260, 279, 283; laws of, 185, 296, 354; American loans from, 245; borders of, 300; engineers of, 308; Lafayette's exile from, 368, 370-73, 376, 379 and n.; king of (*see* Louis XVI). *See also* French *and* Commerce, Franco-American
Francis II (1768-1835): as archduke of Tuscany, 295; as Holy Roman emperor, xxii-xxiii
Francisco. See Rendon
Franklin, Benjamin (1706-1790): as United States minister to France, ix, xiv, 75, 78, 139-40, 144-45, 174, 238, 243-44, 249, 251, 252 n., 275, 282, 301; in retirement, 346
Franklin, William Temple (1760-1823), Benjamin Franklin's grandson, 301 and n.
Franks, Lieutenant-Colonel David Solebury: in Morocco, 317, 320
Frederick II (the Great) (1712-1786), king of Prussia, xvii, 132, 259, 268, 270, 301, 304-06, 309, 311, 317, 321, 337
Frederick William II (1744-1797), king

414

of Prussia, xxii, 304 and n., 309, 311, 314 and n., 317, 321, 326, 329, 335-37, 340
Fredericksburg (Va.), 168, 186, 188, 190, 207, 212, 215, 286
Freedom. *See* Liberty *and* Independence
Free ports, 264, 275, 281, 283, 293
French army, xii, xiv, 305, 314, 341; under Estaing, xiii, 55, 62; under Rochambeau, xiv-xvi, 82, 85, 87, 88, 91, 93-96, 100-03, 120, 122, 127, 131, 133, 140, 156, 159, 169, 183-84, 188, 190, 199, 210, 220, 248, 250, 252; under Choisy, 205; under St. Simon, 227, 228, 231, 232; under Ayen, 312; in the French Revolution, 349, 355-56, 358-60, 362, 381
French clergy, 320, 343, 352, 355 and n., 362 and n.
French court, 15, 78, 118, 132, 184-85, 236-37, 244, 247, 255-56, 271, 273, 314, 318, 323, 325, 329, 332
French fleet: under Estaing, xii, 55-63, 67, 69, 132; at Ushant, 65-66; under Ternay, 85-90, 94-102, 122; under Guichen, 98, 241-43, 247; as convoys, 132, 249; under Destouches, 147-48, 158-64, 166, 173, 181-82, 190, 213; under Tilly, 151, 154; under La Touche-Tréville, 173-74; under De Grasse, xvi, 220-21, 225, 227-29, 231-33, 237, 245-46, 252 and n., under Barras, 229, 233; under Vaudreuil, 255. *See also* Fleet, Combined
French Generals. *See* Rochambeau *and* Ternay. *See also* Estaing; Grasse; St.-Simon; *etc.*
French hospital, 59, 62
French hounds, 295, 299
French ministry, 22, 66, 75-77, 98, 118, 141, 243, 245, 251, 264, 267, 275-76, 297, 299, 308, 310, 312, 323, 327-33, 335-36, 338, 340, 343-44, 347
French navy, 311. *See also* French fleet
French officers, 257, 265, 273, 276-77, 280, 305, 311, 344, 349, 351, 359, 376; in the American army, x, xii, 18-19, 29-30, 32, 36, 53, 59, 62, 68, 71-72, 139, 187, 248, 254, 274, 356; naval, 55, 56, 58, 67, 229, 278; in Rochambeau's army, 100, 103, 127, 252; in St. Simon's army, 228; in the Society of the Cincinnati, 273. *See also* Conway; Dekalb; Ducoudray; *etc.*

French Revolution. *See* France, revolution in
Frestel, Félix, George Washington Lafayette's tutor, xxii, 366, 372 and n.
Fructidor, coup d'état of (September 4, 1797), 369 and n., 370-71, 378, 380

GALVAN, WILLIAM (†1782), French officer, major in the Continental Army 174, 177, 181, 189, 209, 213
Gansevoort, Peter (1749-1812): as colonel commandant of Fort Schuyler, 37
Gardiner's Bay (in Long Island Sound), 152, 162
Gates, Horatio (1729-1806): as major-general in the Continental Army, 3, 14; as member of the Board of War, 24, 27, 30, 32, 33, 35; as commander of the Southern army, 106, 135
Gazette de France, 272 n.
George. *See* Washington, George Augustine
Georgetown (S. C.), 173-74
Georgia, 20, 134, 311
Germain, i.e., George Sackville, Viscount, better known as Lord George Germain (1716-1785): as British secretary of state for the colonies, 243
Germans. *See* Ansbachers; Hessians; *etc.*
Germantown (Pa.), ix
Germany: Lafayette in, 300-02, 379 (*see also* Hamburg; Holstein; *etc.*); war in, 314, 316; princes of 337, 359. *See also* Austria; Prussia; *etc.*
Gibbs, Caleb (†1818), commander of Washington's bodyguard: as captain in the Continental Army, 25 and n.; as major, 115, 116
Gibraltar, 79, 245
Gimat, Jean-Joseph Sourbader, chevalier de (1743 or 1747-1792?): as aide-de-camp to Lafayette with rank of major, 6; as lieutenant-colonel in the Light Infantry, 111, 174, 177, 194, 222, 226-27, 235; in France, 254
Gist, Mordecai (1742-1792), brigadier-general in the Continental Army, 158
Givet (France), 362
Glocester. *See* Gloucester
Glory, xi, xiii, xvi, 3, 16, 17, 25, 26, 28, 29, 58, 114, 116, 120, 138, 157, 161, 190, 227, 259, 266, 269, 271, 300, 319, 334, 355, 383

415

Gloucester (N. J.), battle of, ix, 6-7
Gloucester (Va.), 215, 217-18, 221, 223
Gloucester County (Va.), 209, 215, 219, 229, 234, 235
Gloucester Road (in New Jersey), 6
Gloucester, William Henry, Duke of (1743-1805), nephew of George III of England, viii
Glouster. *See* Gloucester
Glover, John (1732-1797): as brigadier-general in the Continental Army, 54
Golden Fleece, Order of the, 273
Goode's Bridge (Va.), 208, 212
Goodell (apparently an error for McDougall), 30
Gotchius (probably Major John Mauritius Goetschius of the New Jersey militia), 111
Gottschalk, Louis, viii n., xi n., xvi n., 33 n., 46 n., 236 n., 252 n., 260 n., 264 n., 309 n.
Gouvion, Jean-Baptiste, chevalier de (1747-1792): as lieutenant-colonel of engineers in the Continental Army, 34, 126, 130, 139, 148, 151-52, 154-55, 166, 178, 183, 199, 217, 225, 232; as brevet colonel, 242, 255, 257; in Germany, 301, 306
Governor: of Havana (see Navarro); of Maryland (*see* Lee); of Virginia (*see* Jefferson *or* Nelson)
Grand Army (Washington's), 37, 41, 100, 103, 155, 172, 175-76, 187, 206, 213, 226
Grandchain, i.e., Guillaume - Jacques - Constant Liberge de Granchain de Sémerville, comte de (1744-1805), naval lieutenant who represented the French fleet in the negotiations of the Yorktown capitulation: as captain of the "Nymphe," 287, 290
Grasse - Tilly, François - Joseph - Paul, comte de (1723-88), lieutenant-general in the French navy, xvi, 219 and n., 221-22, 225-26, 229, 231-33, 236 and n., 237, 255 and n., 279
Graves, Thomas (1725?-1802): as British rear-admiral, 85-87, 89-90, 145
Great Bridge (Va.), 223
Great Britain. *See* England
Great Lakes, 289
Great Timber Creek (N. J.), 6
Greaves. *See* Graves

Greene, Christopher (†1781), colonel of the First Rhode Island, 99
Greene, Nathanael (1742-1786): as major-general in the Continental Army, 6-7; as quartermaster general, 38, 46, 55, 58, 61, 78, 89; as commander of the Southern army, xv-xvi, 122, 134-36, 155, 157, 159, 163, 166, 169-71, 173-75, 179-80, 186, 188-89, 191-93, 195, 198-99, 203-04, 209, 214, 217, 221, 230, 247, 251-52; after the war, 289, 311; death of, 315
Greene, William (1731-1809): as governor of Rhode Island, 97, 103
Gregory, Isaac, brigadier-general of North Carolina militia, 160, 212, 216, 218
Grenville, Thomas (1755-1846): as British peace commissioner in Paris, 252
Griffith, Dr. David (†1789), formerly surgeon and chaplain of the Third Virginia, 315
Guards (British regiment), 196, 207-08, 210
Guichen, Luc-Urbain de Bouëxic, comte de (1712-1790), lieutenant-general in the French navy, 98, 102 and n., 120, 134, 141, 247
Guilford Courthouse, battle of (March 15, 1781), 163

Hackensack (N. J.), 126
Haddonfield (N. J.), 6-7
Hagen, Dr. ———, 113, 116
Hague, The, 383 n.
Halifax, (N. C.), 191, 194-96
Halifax (N. S.), 64, 87, 102
Hamburg (Germany), xxiii, 363-64, 366, 372, 378
Hamilton, Alexander (1757-1804): as lieutenant-colonel and aide-de-camp to Washington, 48-49, 51, 54, 93, 131; as possible envoy to France, 137, 139, 140; quarrel with Washington of, 184 and n.; as lieutenant-colonel in the Light Division, 233, 235, 247; as secretary of the treasury, 246, 348, 350, 353, 355, 360; in private life, 373, 382 and n.
Hamilton, Elizabeth Schuyler, wife of Alexander Hamilton, 146, 148-49, 156, 158, 160, 163, 167, 171
Hamilton, John (†1817), Loyalist lieutenant-colonel commanding the North Carolina Volunteers, 196

Hampton (Va.), 157, 159, 162 n., 163, 165, 196
Hampton Roads (Va.), 164, 166, 210-13
Hancock, John (1737-1793): as major-general of Massachusetts militia, 62-63
Hand, Edward (1744-1802): as brigadier-general in the Continental Army, 131
Hanoverians, 329
Harlem (N. Y.), 119
Harrison, Benjamin (1726-1791), formerly governor of Virginia: as candidate for speaker of the Virginia House of Delegates, 290; Lafayette's greetings to, 310
Harrison's cousin: possibly Richard Harrison (1750-1841), American consul at Cadiz, 290
Harrison, Robert Hanson (1745-1790): as lieutenant-colonel and secretary to Washington, 159; as chief justice of the Maryland General Court, 319, 346, 348
Hartford (Conn.), xv, 89, 90, 117, 122, 183, 286, 289
Harvard College Library, xxiv n., xxvi, xxvii, 54 n., 138 n., 186 n., 202 n., 250 n., 254 n., 264 n., 284 n., 360 n., 363 n., 365 n., 368 n., 369 n., 378 n.
Havana (Cuba), 135, 142; governor of (*see* Navarro)
Havre, Le, 78, 298, 317, 325
Hawker, James, captain in 1780 of the British frigate "Iris," 147
Hay, Udney (†1806), lieutenant-colonel and assistant deputy quartermaster general in the Continental Army, 26
Hazen, Moses (1733-1803): as colonel of the Second Canadian Regiment in the Continental Army, 20, 26-27, 37; as brigadier-general, 236
Head of Elk (Elkton, Md.), 150-54, 156, 161, 163, 168-69, 171-72, 175-76, 180, 200, 224, 231, 284
Heath, William (1737-1814), major-general in the Continental Army: as commander of the Eastern Division, 62; as commander in Rhode Island, 88, 93-97, 99, 100, 104-05; as commander at West Point, 127
Hell Gate (N. Y.), 87
Hend........ (apparently Henderson, ———, who seems to have been an American spy), 128

Henry IV (1553-1610), king of France, 338 n.
Henry (i.e., Friedrich - Heinrich - Ludwig), Prince (1726-1802), brother of Frederick II of Prussia, xxii, 304-05, 309, 311
Henry, Patrick (1736-1799), as possible envoy to France, 137
"Hermione," French frigate, 145, 173, 246
Hessians, 6, 108, 124, 128, 196, 301, 303, 329
Hice town. *See* Hightstown
Highlanders (Forty-Second Regiment), (British), 124, 128
Hightstown (N. J.), 49 and n.
Hillsborough (N. C.), 122-23
Hispaniola (Haiti), 328
Historical Society of Pennsylvania, xxvii, 187 n.
Hite (probably Joseph Haight, lieutenant-colonel of New Jersey militia), 6
Holker, John (1745-1822): as French consul-general in the United States, 66
Holland, xxiii, 166-67, 223, 245, 249, 291 n., 293, 297, 299, 301, 307-08, 311-12, 314 and n., 317, 321, 329, 331, 335, 338-40, 373, 378-79, 383-84
Holstein, xxiii, 365, 368-69, 372-73, 378
Holt's Forge (Va.), 225
Holy Roman Empire, 291 n., 295, 308, 359 and n., 366 n.
Hood, Samuel, Viscount (1724-1816): as rear-admiral in the British navy, 245
Hood's (Va.), 190
Hook. *See* Sandy Hook
"Hope," British warship, 168
Hopewell (N. J.), 46
Horses: officer's, 7, 226, 228; Lafayette's, 61; post, 69, 303; American, 87, 168-69, 191, 197, 210, 212-13, 219, 221, 226, 228, 230; French, 89, 109-10; British, 111, 130, 196, 198, 207-08, 213, 215, 227; impressment of, 186, 188-89, 195, 209, 227. *See also* Cavalry; Dragoons; *etc.*
Hospitals, 32-34, 59, 145, 222, 224
Hôtel de Ville (city hall of Paris), 315
Houdon, Jean - Antoine (1741 - 1825), sculptor, 300, 307
Howe, Robert (1732-1785), major-general in the Continental Army, 93, 234
Howe, Sir William (later Viscount) (1729-1814): as general in command of the British army in America, 9, 154
Howland's Ferry (R. I.), 99

417

Hubbard Collection, xvi, xxiv, and n., xxvi, xxvii, 43 n., 138 n., 144 n., 146 n., 147 n., 149 n., 150 n., 153 n., 154 n., 156 n., 159 n., 161 n., 164 n., 165 n., 167 n., 168 n., 172 n., 175 n., 176 n., 178 n., 179 n., 180 n., 184 n., 187 n., 188 n., 191 n., 192 n., 193 n., 196 n., 197 n., 199 n., 200 n., 201 n., 203 n., 204 n., 205 n., 207 n., 210 n., 211 n., 213 n., 214 n., 215 n., 216 n., 218 n., 221 n., 231 n., 232 n., 233 n., 235 n., 237 n., 281 n., 310 n.

Huger, Francis Kinloch (1773-1855), who tried to free Lafayette from Olmütz, 380

Humanitarianism, 75, 260, 334, 346, 357, 374

Hume, E. E., 272 n., 273 n., 276 n., 280 n.

Humphreys, David (1752-1818), formerly lieutenant-colonel and aide-de-camp to Washington: as secretary to the American commission for negotiating treaties of commerce, 310, 319; as diplomatic agent, 348

Hunter's Works, forge and armament factory at Falmouth, Va., 190

Huntington, Ebenezer (1754-1834): as lieutenant-colonel in the Light Division, 233

Huntington, Samuel (1732-1796), president of the Continental Congress, 165

Huntington Library, xxvii, 332 n.

Hussars, French (under St. Simon), 226, 228, 233

Imperial Courts. *See* Austria *and* Russia

Independence: of the United States, 14, 20, 37, 75, 77-79, 245, 249, 260, 269, 271, 374-75, 383; of Ireland, 75

India, xi, 307, 309

Indians (American), 32-34, 36-37, 285-86, 310-11

Innis, James, lieutenant-colonel in the Fifteenth Virginia, 190, 218

Inoculation, 264, 345

"Intrepid," British warship, 124

Ireland, 75, 270, 283, 295, 297, 375

"Iris," British warship, 145-48

Irish, 16, 24, 291, 294, 309; Volunteer Association, 270

Isle de France (French colony), 318

Italy, 276, 319

Ivy (Va.), 223

Jackson, Henry (†1809), colonel of Jackson's Additional Continental Regiment, 49, 51

Jacobins xxi, 349-50, 360, 362, 370-71, 374, 379, 382, 385

Jamaica (British West Indies), 252

Jamaica (on Long Island, N. Y.), 124, 129

James River (Va.), 182, 189, 191-94, 201, 209, 212, 219, 225-26, 230-32; Navigation Company, 298 and n., 299

Jamestown (Va.), 196, 219, 225, 228, 230

Jay, John (1745-1829): as minister plenipotentiary to Spain, 135, 262; as peace commissioner, 271, 275, 282; as secretary of foreign affairs, 284, 289, 291 and n., 307, 346, 348; as chief justice of the Supreme Court, 350, 353, 355, 360; as negotiator of Jay's Treaty, xxii

Jefferson, Thomas (1743-1826): as governor of Virginia, 157, 164, 169, 201, 228; as minister to France, 289, 308, 310, 314 and n., 315, 330, 333, 335-36, 338, 344; as secretary of state, xxi, 350, 353, 355-57, 360

Jeffery's Hook (on Manhattan Island, N. Y.), 130

Jerseys. *See* New Jersey

Johnstone, George (1730-1787): as member of the Carlisle peace commission (1778), 67

Johnstown, (N. Y.), 32

Jones, Allen (1739-1807), brigadier-general of North Carolina militia, 194

Jones, John Paul (1747-1792): as American naval captain, 88, 90, 125, 132, 135, 144-45; in Russian navy, 345

Joseph II (1741-1790), archduke of Austria and Holy Roman emperor, 264, 266, 268, 270, 276, 291 n., 293, 295, 299, 301-02, 304, 306, 308-09, 311, 314, 325 and n., 329, 335-36, 340, 344, 359 n.

Kakiate (N. Y.), 113

Kalb. *See* Dekalb

Kaunitz-Rietburg, Wenzel Anton, Prince von (1711-1794), Austrian chancellor, 304

Kedze (?) Ferry (R. I.), 99

Kellermann, François-Christophe, later duc de Valmy (1735-1820): as maréchal de camp (major-general), 351

Kellermann, François-Etienne, later duc de Valmy (1770-1835): as son of General Kellerman, 351
Kemp's Landing (Va.), 212, 223
Kentucky, 288
Keppel, Augustus, Viscount (1725-86): as admiral and commander-in-chief of the British Grand Fleet, 65-66
King of Prussia. *See* Frederick II *or* Frederick William II
Kings Bridge (N. Y.), 39, 128
King's Dragoons (French regiment), 76, 79
Kings Ferry (N. Y.), 91, 121, 127
King's Garden (Jardin Royal des Plantes in Paris), 288
King's Mountain (N. C.), battle of (October 7, 1780), 224
Kite, Elizabeth S., 236 n.
Knollenberg, Bernhard, xi n.
Knox, Henry (1750-1806): as brigadier-general in command of artillery in the Continental Army, 18, 46, 115, 240, 247; as secretary of war, 346, 348, 350, 353, 355, 360
Knyphausen, Baron Wilhelm von (1717-1800), lieutenant-general of the Hessians in the British army, 124, 141, 167, 303 and n.
Kononikut. *See* Conanicut
Krimée. *See* Crimea

La Chapelle (near Paris), 351
La Colombe, Louis-Saint-Ange Morel, chevalier de (1755-1800?): as captain and aide-de-camp to Lafayette, 72, 76
Lacy, Franz Moriz, Count (1725-1801), Austrian field marshal, 304
Lafayette, Anastasie-Louise-Pauline (b. 1777), Lafayette's daughter, xxiii, 242 and n., 284, 292 and n., 295, 358, 363-66, 368, 370 and n., 372-73; greetings to Washington's family from, xviii-xix, 250, 265, 269, 272, 276, 281, 284, 294, 300, 310, 312, 316, 319, 321, 324, 338-39, 345, 350, 353, 367
Lafayette, George Washington (1779-1849), Lafayette's son and Washington's godson, xiv, xxii, xxiii, and n., xxiv, 77, 242 and n., 253, 259, 264, 284, 295, 358, 363-64, 366, 368-70, 372 and n., 373, 377, 380, 384; greetings to Washington's family from, xviii-xix, 250, 265, 269, 272, 276, 281, 284, 294, 300, 310, 312, 316, 319, 321, 324, 338-39, 345, 350, 353, 367
Lafayette, Marie-Adrienne-Françoise de Noailles de (1759-1807), Lafayette's wife, xxi-xxiv, 77, 81, 242, 244, 247, 253, 255, 257, 261, 267, 284, 292, 296, 326, 334, 358, 363-66, 368, 370, 372-73, 379 and n.; greetings to the Washingtons from, xviii-xix, 250, 265, 269, 272, 276, 281, 284, 294, 300, 310, 312, 316, 319, 321, 324, 338-39, 345, 350, 353, 367
Lafayette, Marie-Antoinette-Virginie de (1782-1849), Lafayette's younger daughter, xxiii, 253, 284, 295, 345, 358, 363-66, 368, 370, 372-73; greetings to Washington's family from, xviii-xix, 255, 265, 269, 272, 276, 281, 284, 294, 300, 310, 312, 316, 319, 321, 324, 338-39, 345, 350, 353, 367
Lafayette, Marie - Paul - Joseph - Roch-Yves-Gilbert du Motier, marquis de (1757-1834): first stay in America (1777-1779), vii-xiii, 3-74; return to France (1779-1780), xiii-xiv, 74-81; second stay in America (1780-1781), xiv-xvii, 82-240; as American diplomatic agent in France (1782), xvii, 241-58; in Spain (1782-1783), xvii, 259-62; in post-war affairs in France (1783-1784), xvii-xviii, 262-84; third stay in America (1784), xix-xx, 284-90; in France again (1785), 291-300; trip to Germany (1785), 300-06; as leader of the French reform movement (1785-1789), xx, 306-45; as commander of the Parisian National Guard (1789-1791), xx-xxi, 346-57; as commander of the French Army of the Center (1792), xxi, 358-62; as prisoner in Prussia and Austria (1792-1797), xxi-xxiii; as exile from France (1797-1799), xxiii-xxiv, 363-85
Lafayette College Library, xxv, xxvii, 214 n.
Lafayette, *Memoirs of*, xiii n., xxvi, 138 n., 158 n., 186 n., 213 n., 216 n., 224 n., 356 n., 358 n., 373 n., 381 n., 382 n.
Lagrange-Bléneau, château of, inhabited by Lafayette after 1799, xxiv-xxv
La Luzerne, Anne-César, chevalier (later marquis) de (1741-1791): as French minister to the United States, xiv, 75,

76, 78, 102, 114-15, 117-18, 122, 132-34, 136-37, 145, 151, 174, 183-84, 188 and n., 243, 328

La Luzerne, César-Henri, comte de (1737-1799): as minister of the marine, 328

Lambert, ———, chevalier de, 254

Lameth, Charles-Malo-François, chevalier (later comte) de (1757-1832): as captain and aide-major-général des logis to Rochambeau, 276, 279

Lamoignon, Chrétien-François de (1735-1789): as keeper of the seals, 344 and n.

Lancaster (Pa.), 8-10, 13, 20

La Neuville, Louis-Pierre Penot Lombard, chevalier de (1744-18—): as colonel in the Continental Army, 64, 279. *See also* Noirmont

Langborn, William, ensign of the Sixth Virginia, aide-de-camp to Lafayette, 204; in England, 310

Langres, i.e., César-Guillaume de la Luzerne (1738-1821), bishop of, 323

"Languedoc," Estaing's flagship, 55, 57

La Pérouse, Jean-François de Galaup, comte de (1741-1788): as captain of the French warship "Amazone," 174, 277, 279

Larochefoucauld-Liancourt, François-Alexandre-Frédéric, duc de (1747-1827): as peer of France, 343

Lasey. *See* Lacy

La Terrière, Monsieur ——— de, French officer, companion of Brissot, 344

La Touche, Louis-René-Madeleine Levassor, vicomte de (later comte de La Touche-Tréville) (1745-1804): as naval lieutenant commanding the "Hermoine," 173-74, 277, 279

La Touche-Tréville, comte de (uncle of the Vicomte de La Touche): as chef d'escadre in the French navy, 145, 173

Latour-Maubourg. *See* Maubourg

Laudon, Freiherr Gideon Ernst von (1716-1790), Austrian field marshal, 304

Laumagne, ———, vicomte de, major in Armand's Partisan Corps, 281 n.

Laumoy, Jean-Baptiste-Joseph, chevalier de (1750-1832): as colonel of engineers in Continental Army, 6

Laurel Hill (on Manhattan Island, N. Y.), 119

Laurens, Henry (1724-1792): as member of the Continental Congress, 4; as president of the Continental Congress, xiii, 28; as English prisoner, 137, 250; as peace commissioner, 271, 275

Laurens, John (1754-1782), lieutenant-colonel and aide-de-camp to Washington, 137, 139-42; in the Light Division, 235

Lauzun, Armand-Louis de Gontaut, duc de (later duc de Biron) (1747-1793): as commander of Lauzun's Legion in Rochambeau's army, 102, 109-10, 122, 127, 149, 198, 247

Lauzun's Legion, 109-10, 120-21, 149, 182, 198, 222

Laval, Anne-Alexandre-Marie-Sulpice-Joseph de Montmorency, marquis (later duc) de (1747-1817): as mestre de camp and commander of the Regiment de Bourbonnais in Rochambeau's army, 127; in French affairs, 318

Lavaud (possibly Etienne Laveaux, afterward governor of St. Domingo), 187

La Vauguyon, Paul-François de Quélin de Stuer de Caussade, duc de (1756-1828): as French ambassador to Spain, 293, 295

Law, 23

Lawrence. *See* Laurens

Lawson, Robert (†1805), brigadier-general in Virginia militia, 195, 202

Lebanon (Conn.), 97

Le Coulteux, Monsieur ———, related to Le Coulteux and Co., French merchants and bankers, 313

"Ledrout," French Indiaman, 145

Lee, Arthur (1740-1792): as United States commissioner to France, 75

Lee, Charles (1731-1782): as major-general in the Continental Army, xii, 46, 50, 52

Lee, Henry ("Light Horse Harry") (1756-1818): as major in command of Lee's Legion of Continental cavalry, 111-14, 116-17; as lieutenant-colonel, 230

Lee, Richard Henry (1732-1794): as member of the Continental Congress, 4

Lee, Thomas Sims (1745-1819): as governor of Maryland, 154, 157, 159, 169, 172, 214

Legislative Assembly of France (1791-

1792), 355-56, 358, 362 and n., 378, 380
Lemkuhlen, i.e., Lehmkuhlen, a village near Plön in Holstein, 365, 372 and n.
L'Enfant, Pierre - Charles (1754-1825), brevet-major of engineers in the Continental Army: in Paris, 273-74, 276, 282
Lenox, Mr. ————, a British deputy commissary of prisoners, 130
Leopold II (1747-1792), archduke of Austria and Holy Roman emperor, 359 and n., 360, 379 n.
Leslie, Alexander (ca., 1740-1794), major-general in the British army, 120, 125, 132, 196, 210, 211, 215
Lesser, Jean Thevet de (1737-1832?), one of Lafayette's companions on the "Victoire," 282-83
L'Estrade, Claude-Amable-Vincent de Roqueplan, baron de (1729-1819), lieutenant-colonel of the Regiment de Gatinais in Estaing's and St. Simon's forces, 279
Levant, 266, 337
Levies, New. *See* Recruits
Lewingston. *See* Livingston
Lewis, Elizabeth Washington (1733-1797), Washington's sister, 315
Liberty, xviii, xxi, xxii, 261, 275, 297, 324-25, 327, 336, 342-43, 346, 348, 350, 352-53, 355-56, 358, 360-61, 369-71, 374, 377, 381, 383, 385. *See also* Independence
Liberty Pole (N. J.), 111, 347
Library of Congress, xxvii, 8 n., 10 n., 38 n., 44 n., 46 n., 85 n., 105 n., 120 n., 144 n., 146 n., 147 n., 149 n., 150 n., 153 n., 154 n., 156 n., 159 n., 161 n., 164 n., 165 n., 167 n., 168 n., 172 n., 175 n., 176 n., 178 n., 179 n., 180 n., 183 n., 184 n., 187 n., 188 n., 191 n., 192 n., 193 n., 196 n., 197 n., 199 n., 200 n., 201 n., 203 n., 205 n., 207 n., 210 n., 211 n., 213 n., 214 n., 215 n., 216 n., 218 n., 231 n., 232 n., 233 n., 235 n., 236 n., 237 n., 310 n.
Light Cavalry (American), 110
Light Infantry: American, xv, 45, 84, 105, 108-11, 116, 118, 122, 126, 171, 179, 186 n., 202, 206, 209, 212-14, 219, 221, 242, 246, 295; British, 196, 207-08, 210-11, 215, 223; French, 341; camp, 105, 108-10, 112, 115, 117-18, 120, 123-24, 126-29; Division, xv, 233-35, 238

Lincoln, Benjamin (1733-1810): as major-general in the Continental Army, xvi, 26, 137, 187, 231, 234, 235, 251; as secretary of war, 240, 254
Lindsey (apparently Lieutenant William Lindsay [†1838] of the First Continental Dragoons) at the battle of Gloucester (N. J.), 6
Liquor, 48, 281
Littlepage, Lewis (1762-1802), American adventurer: as captain in the Royal Allemand Regiment (French), 307
Little Timber Creek (N. J.), 6
Livingston, James (1747-1832), colonel of the First Canadian Regiment, 35
Livingston, Robert R. (1746-1813): as American secretary of foreign affairs, 245 and n., 249, 251, 255 and n., 260-61
Loan, French, 323
Loans, American: of France, 75, 174, 185, 243, 245, 249; of Spain, 138, 245; to Lafayette, 185; of Holland, 245
Lomagne. *See* Laumagne
Lombard, Louis-André-Joseph, chevalier de, captain of the "Provence" in Ternay's fleet, 174
"London," British warship, 164
London (England), 110, 239, 243, 263, 275, 304, 307, 347
Longchamps, Charles-Julien, who, having assaulted Marbois, was not extradited, despite the demands of the French government, because he had claims to American citizenship, 297
Long Island (N. Y.), 40, 88, 93, 119, 123-25, 128-30, 206
Long Island Sound, 86, 102
Lorient (France), 132, 136, 241-42, 264, 275-76
Lotbinière, Michael - Eustace - Gaspard, marquis de (1723-1799), French-Canadian nobleman, 321
Louis XIV (1638-1715): as king of France, 315, 338 n.
Louis XVI (1754-1793): as king of France, xxi, 57, 58, 69, 76, 79, 80, 82, 243-45, 249, 293, 295-96, 299, 302, 317-18, 320, 322-23, 325, 327-28, 331, 340, 343 and n., 353, 354 and n., 358-59, 362
Louis-Charles (1785-1795), second son of Marie-Antoinette ("Louis XVII"), 296
Louisiana, 357
Lowell's Point (Va.), 213

421

"Loyalist," British warship captured by the French, 237
Luckner, Nicholas, baron and maréchal de (1722-1794), 358, 362
Lund. *See* Washington, Lund
Luzerne. *See* La Luzerne
Lyme (Conn.), 54
Lynnhaven (Va.), 164, 167

McDougall, Alexander (1732-1786): as major-general in the Continental Army, 234. *See also* Goodell
McHenry, James (1753-1816): as major and aide-de-camp to Lafayette, 154, 219, 228 n., 229, 235 n., 247, 257
McLane, Allen (1746-1829): as major in the Continental Army, 163-64
McPherson, William (1751-1813): as major and aide-de-camp to Lafayette, 162, 169, 179-80, 211, 214
Madagascar, 318
Madeira (Portugal), 125
Madrid (Spain), 260 and n., 261-62, 295
Magdeburg (Germany), 305
Mahon. *See* Port Mahon
Maillebois, Yves-Marie Desmarets, comte de (1715-91), lieutenant-general in the French army, 293
Malbern Hill. *See* Malvern Hill
Malesherbes, Chrétien-Guillaume de Lamoignon de (1721-1794): as president of the Cour des Aides, 285; as minister, 328
Malta, 295, 300, 320, 375
Malvern Hill (Va.), 205, 207, 209-14
Marbois, François de Barbé de (1745-1837): as secretary to the Chevalier de La Luzerne and French consul-general in the United States, xiv. *See also* Longchamps
Marcellin, Antoine-Claude de: as lieutenant in the Second Pennsylvania, 254
Maria-Theresa (†1807), wife of Emperor Francis II, 379 and n.
Marie Antoinette (1755-1793), queen of France, 67, 241, 270-71, 296, 308, 312, 325, 327, 331
Marine Committee, 71
"Marseillais," vessel in Estaing's fleet, 57
Marseilles (France), 275
Marshall, James Markham (1764-1848), on special mission on behalf of Lafayette, xxii

Martin, M. ————, 383 and n.
Martin, Nicholas, captain of the "Nesbitt," 158
Maryland, 154, 159, 168, 179, 214, 221-22, 226-27, 229-30, 260, 293 and n., 320; Continental troops of, 169, 216-17, 219, 221, 224; governor of (*see* Lee, Thomas Sims)
Massachusetts, 91, 103
Mattapony River (Va.), 221
Matthews, David, Loyalist mayor of New York City (1780), 124
Maubourg, Charles de La Tour de, married Lafayette's daughter Anastasie (1798), 370 and n., 372-73
Maubourg, Marie-Charles-César-Fay Latour, comte de (1758-1831), Lafayette's companion in captivity and exile, 363 and n., 364-65, 369, 370 n., 372
Mauduit du Plessis, Thomas-Antoine, chevalier de (1753-1791): as captain of artillery in the Continental Army, 6-7; as lieutenant-colonel, 18, 30; as aide-major of artillery in Rochambeau's army, 139; in the Society of the Cincinnati, 277, 281 n.
Maurepas, Jean-Frédéric-Phélypeaux, comte de (1701-1781), chief minister of Louis XVI, 241
Mauricinia. *See* Morrisania
Mauroy, Charles-Louis, vicomte de (1734-1813), one of Lafayette's companions on the "Victoire," 282-83
Maxwell, William (1733-1796): as brigadier-general in the Continental Army, 23, 49, 51
Mayor of New York City. *See* Matthews
Mazzei, Philip (1730-1816), Italian physician, agent in Italy for Virginia, vii and n., 319
Mead (probably Richard Kidder Meade [1746-1805], lieutenant-colonel and aide-de-camp to Washington), 276
Measam, George, major and commissary of clothing in the Continental Army, 26 and n.
Medicine, 9, 45, 96, 150, 217, 222. *See also* Doctors; Hospitals; *etc.*
Mediterranean Sea, 266, 329, 337, 340, 345, 375
Menonville, Louis-Antoine Thibaut de (b. 1738), major in the Regiment de

Touraine and adjutant-general to St. Simon, 279, 307
Mercer, John Francis (1759-1821): as lieutenant-colonel of Virginia militia, 209
Mercereau (probably Joshua Mersereau [1730-1804], American spy on Staten Island), 116, 123 and n., 127 and n.
Mesmer, Dr. Friedrich Anton (1733-1815), propounder of Mesmerism, xvii, 283-84
Metz (France), 358, 359
Mexico, 297
Michaux, André M. (1746-1802), botanist, 302
Mifflin, Thomas (1744-1800), major-general in the Continental Army: as member of the Board of War, 24; as member of the Continental Congress, 135, 140
Militia: United States, 8, 10-13, 27, 34, 39, 40, 46, 83, 85, 101, 106, 119, 122, 207, 306; Rhode Island, 55, 63, 93-96, 99, 103-05, 134, 205; New Jersey, 6-7, 41, 45, 49, 52, 143, 207; Virginia, 151, 159-62, 166, 182, 186 n., 189-91, 194-98, 200-02, 204, 209, 211-12, 218-19, 221, 223, 226-29, 235; Maryland, 154, 159, 221, 227; Loyalist, 119, 125-26, 140
Minister plenipotentiary (French). See La Luzerne or Moustier
Mirabeau, Honoré-Gabriel de Riquetti, comte de (1749-1791), French revolutionary leader, 350 and n.
Miroménil, Armand-Thomas Hue de (1723-1796), Louis XVI's keeper of the seals, 296 and n., 320
Mississippi River, 293, 295, 297, 357
Mitchell, Nathaniel (1753-1814): as brigade-major and inspector to Muhlenberg, 195
Molens. See Mullens
Möllendorf, Wichard Joachim Heinrich von (1724-1816): as Prussian general, 304
Money, xxii, 27-32, 93, 107, 123, 125, 129, 137, 141, 171-72, 183, 185, 193, 220, 222, 238-39, 271, 280, 299, 309, 315, 318, 322-23, 335. See Loans and France, economic problems in
"Monk," British warship, 168
Monmouth Court House (N. J.), xii, 50, 51

Montagu, Anne - Paule - Dominique de Noailles, marquise de (1766-1839), Adrienne de Lafayette's sister, 372
Montaigu (probably Captain James Montagu, of the British navy), 147
Montmédy (France), 359
Montreal (Canada), 260
Morea, the, 329
Morgan, Daniel (1736-1802): as colonel of Virginia Riflemen, 46, 50, 61; as brigadier-general, 122, 208
Morgan, George (1743-1810), Indian agent and colonel in the Continental Army, 311
Morgan's (Daniel) Corps of Virginia Riflemen, 6-7, 19, 52
Morgan Library, xxvii, 3 n., 192 n.
Moriss. See Morris
Morocco, 317, 320
Morris, Gouverneur (1752-1816): as a member of the Continental Congress, x n.; as United States minister to France, 361; in Germany, 378
Morris, Lewis, Jr., lieutenant-colonel and aide-de-camp to Greene, 169, 174, 221, 223
Morris, Mary White (1749-1827), wife of Robert Morris, 238
Morris, Robert (1734-1806): as American superintendent of finance, 222, 238-39, 243, 275, 281; as merchant, 312, 330 n.
Morrisania (N. Y.), 86-88
Morristown (N. J.), 114-15, 121, 143-44, 146-47, 149-50, 171, 173, 176
Motier, family name of the Lafayettes, xxiii
Mouchy, Philippe de Noailles, duc and maréchal de (1715-1794), Adrienne de Lafayette's uncle, 5
Mount Vernon (Va.), home of George Washington, xix-xx, xxiii, 168, 271-72, 275, 281-87, 289, 292, 295, 310-11, 319, 322, 333, 343, 363-65, 369, 371, 377-78, 383
Moustier, Eléanor-François-Elie, marquis de (1751-1817): as French minister to the United States, 332, 345
Moylan, Stephen (1737-1811): as colonel of the Fourth Continental Dragoons, 198
Muhlenberg, John Peter Gabriel (1746-1807): as brigadier-general in the Con-

tinental Army, 162, 194, 212-13, 228, 236; as brevet major-general, 311
Muir, Francis, captain in the Continental Army, 195
Mullens, Thomas (1736-1791), aide-de-camp to General Conway, 14 and n., 22, 24
Murnan, Jean-Bernard-Bourg Gauthier de (1748-1797): as major of engineers in the Continental Army, 149
Murray, James (1719?-1794): as lieutenant-general and governor of Minorca, 244
Murray, William Vans (1762-1803): as United States minister at the Hague, 381, 383 n., 384
Musgrave, Sir Thomas (1738-1812), British colonel, 306
Mutiny, 143, 151

NANCY (France), 267
Nantz, i.e., Nantes (France), 65-66. See also Edict of Nantes
Naples, kingdom of, 315, 375, 379 and n; king of (see Ferdinand IV)
Narrows (in New York Harbor), 128-29
Nash, Abner (ca. 1740-1786): as governor of North Carolina, 194
Nation: French, xiii, xxii, xxiv, 59, 79, 118, 241, 243, 247, 273, 305, 308, 322, 325, 327-28, 331, 335, 340, 342-43, 346-47, 349, 354, 371, 383; American, xiii, xxiv, 246-47, 299, 371; English, 245, 308; Dutch, 333
National Assembly of France (1789-1791), 336-37, 343, 347, 349, 350 and n., 351 and n., 352-56, 358 n.
National Guard: of France, 349, 359; of Paris, 354 and n.
Navarro García de Villadares, Diego José (1708-1784): as governor of Cuba, 142
Navy Board, 74, 151, 159
Necker, Jacques (1732-1804): as director-general of finances in France, 75, 137; as writer, 293 and n., 294
Negroes, xvii, 187, 209, 213, 224, 227, 260, 301, 309, 352 and n., 357 and n.
Nelson, Horatio, Lord (1758-1805): as British rear-admiral, 375
Nelson, Thomas, Jr. (1738-1789): as commander-in-chief of the Virginia militia, 193-94; as governor of Virginia, 202, 217-19, 222, 224, 226-28, 231

"Nesbitt," Maryland privateer, 157-58
Neutrality, Convention of (i.e., Armed Neutrality of 1780), 135
Neville, John (1731-1803), colonel of the Fourth Virginia: as father of Presley Neville, 73
Neville, Presley (1756-1818), aide-de-camp to Lafayette: as major in the Continental Army, 21: as brevet lieutenant-colonel, 73, 74, 76, 137; at Fort Pitt, 311
Newark (N. J.), 114, 130
New Bridge (N. J.), 111-12, 120
New Brunswick (N. J.), 52
Newcastle (Del.), 175
Newcastle (Va.), 224
New England, xii, 171, 182, 189 n., 206 n., 207, 319, 321, 329
Newfoundland, 258
New Heaven, i.e., New Haven (Conn.), 96
New Jersey, 11-12, 25, 40, 41, 44, 50, 114, 116, 120, 123, 167, 182, 199, 205; Continental troops of, 83, 144, 171, 176, 182, 189 n., 207. See also Gloucester; Newark; etc.
New Kent Mountain (Va.), 216
New London (Conn.), 54, 86, 89, 106
New Orleans (La.), 293, 297, 357
Newport (R. I.), xii, 56, 57, 59, 64, 67, 89, 91, 93, 95-97, 99, 100, 103-04, 110, 138-39, 159, 286
Newtown (Conn.), 89
Newtown (on Long Island, N. Y.), 129
New Windsor (N. Y.), 139, 153
New York City: xxi, xxiii, 112, 125, 137, 146, 324, 372; proposed attacks upon, xv, 28, 34, 37-39, 42, 85-88, 91, 94, 99, 101, 105-09, 112-13, 119, 133, 171-73, 178, 182 and n., 184, 190, 199, 202, 205-06, 216, 245, 252, 257-58; Lafayette in, xix, 285, 288-89; British in, 33, 66, 118, 120, 124, 127-29, 142, 145, 147-48, 151-53, 166, 203, 207-11, 215, 217, 224; expected evacuation of, 60, 64, 243, 249, 274; British reinforcements from, 167, 175, 196
New York Harbor, xx, 57, 85-88, 99, 173, 252, 255, 288
New York State, 26, 39, 44, 321
Nicholson, James (ca. 1736-1804): as commodore of the Continental Navy, 154, 156-59, 161, 168-69

"Nimph." *See* "Nymphe"
Noailles Cavalry, Regiment of the, 5
Noailles, Emmanuel-Marie-Louis, marquis de (1743-1822), Adrienne de Lafayette's uncle: as French ambassador in Vienna, 304
Noailles, Louis-Marie, vicomte de (1756-1804), Lafayette's brother-in-law: as mestre de camp en second of the Regiment de Soissonnais in Rochambeau's army, 127, 135, 138-39, 242, 244, 247
Noirmont, René-Hippolyte Penot Lombard de (1750-1792), brevet major (later lieutenant-colonel) in the Continental Army: as brother of the Chevalier de La Neuville, 64
Nolan, J. Bennett, xix
Norfolk (Va.), 213
Normandy, 299
North, i.e., Frederick, Earl of Guilford, better known as Lord North (1733-1792): as British prime minister, 245, 248-49, 263; as leader of the Opposition, 275
North America, 374
North Anna River (Va.), 199
North Carolina, xv, 57, 106-07, 134, 141, 161, 183, 188, 191, 194, 198-99, 208-09, 212, 216-17, 219, 224-25, 227
North River, 32, 44, 74, 83, 85, 87, 93, 106, 119, 121, 125, 173, 183
Northern: Department, 15, 26, 27, 30, 32; Army, 29, 278; regiments, 171; states, 197
Notables, Assembly of (1787), 317-18, 320, 322-25, 327, 331
Nussbaum, F. L., 309 n., 314 n., 330 n.
"Nymphe," French frigate, xix, 287-88

Ochakov, siege of (1788), 340, 345
Odell, William, Loyalist major in the British army, organizer of the Loyal American Rangers, 128
Ogden, Aaron (1756-1839): as captain in the First New Jersey, 123
Ogden, Matthias (1754-1791): as colonel of the First New Jersey, 115-17
Ognon River. *See* Onion River
O'Hara, Charles (1730-1802): as British brigadier-general, 196, 215
Ohio River, 311
Oilliamson, Marie-Gabriel-Eléanor, comte d', Norman nobleman, 299, 307

Oksakow. *See* Ochakov
Old Point Comfort (Va.), 211
Olmütz (Austria), castle at, where Lafayette was imprisoned, xxii-xxiv, 363, 368-69, 370 n., 379, 383
Olney, Mr. (apparently George Olney, auditor in the Quartermaster Department in New London, Conn.), 93, 96, 97
Olney, Stephen (†1832), captain in the First Rhode Island, 216
Oneida Indians, 33-34
Onion River (Vt.), also known as Winooski River, 34
Onoyeda. *See* Oneida
Orange County (Va.), 203
Orléans, Louis-Philippe-Joseph, duc d' (1747-1793): as Duc de Chartres, 66; implicated in revolutionary disorders, 350 and n., 352, 360 and n.
Ormesson, Henri-François de Paule Le Fèvre d' (1751-1807); as controller-general of finances, 270
Osburn, Mr. ——— (of Virginia), 189
Ottoman Empire, 264, 266, 268, 270, 299, 311, 328, 336
Ouessant. *See* Ushant
Oyster Bay (N. Y.), 87-88
Ozakow. *See* Ochakov

Paine, Thomas (1737-1809), English liberal, xxi; as author of *Common Sense*, 346 and n.; as friend of the French Revolution, 347
Palais de Justice (Paris), 343 n.
Pamunky River (Va.), 194, 215, 229
Paramus (N. J.), 130, 139
Paris (France), xiv, xviii, 76, 241-42, 250, 260, 262-63, 271, 272 and n., 280, 285, 288-89, 291, 294 n., 298, 301, 310, 315, 317, 327, 346, 354 n., 355, 359, 366 and n., 373, 378; letters from, 252, 254, 256, 263-65, 270, 272, 274, 276, 278, 281-83, 292, 296, 298, 300, 303, 310-11, 313, 317, 320, 322, 324, 326, 332, 334, 336-37, 339, 341-42, 346-48, 351-53, 355, 360; Municipality of, 354 n., 356 and n.
Parker, Josiah (1751-1810), colonel of Virginia militia, 209, 212, 216
Parlements, 296, 318, 327, 335-36, 341, 343, 352; of Paris, 294 and n., 325, 327, 331, 343 and n., 344 n.

425

Parliament (British), 245, 248, 252, 257, 282
Parr, James, major in the Sixth Pennsylvania, 111
Parsons, Samuel Holden (1737-1789): as brigadier-general in the Continental Army, 89-92, 104
Passaic River (N. J.), 112
Paterson, John (1744-1808): as brigadier-general in the Continental Army, 46
Patriotic parties: of Holland, 311, 314 and n., 317, 326, 329, 331, 339, 379; of France, 351, 353-54, 369
Patriotism: for France, 16, 80, 320, 328, 347, 349, 351, 359, 362, 374; for the United States, 26, 43, 80, 282, 371, 375
Patterson. *See* Paterson
Paul I (1754-1801), tsar of Russia, 375 and n.
Paulus (or Powles) Hook (Jersey City, N. J.), 128-29
Payne, Robert Treat (1731-1814): as attorney-general of Massachusetts, 239. *See also* Paine
Peace, British commissioners of, 41-42, 67-68; proposals of, 76, 77, 79, 122, 130, 208, 245-46, 249, 378; negotiations of, xvii, xxiii, 251-53, 255-59, 262, 266, 345; with Barbary pirates, 315; efforts to preserve, 291 n.
Peekskill (N. Y.), 88
Pennsylvania, 39, 86, 226, 229; Assembly of, 135, 140-41, 284; Continental troops of, 24, 49, 83, 121, 126, 141, 143-44, 151, 155, 175, 182-83, 186 n., 189 and n., 195-99, 202, 204, 206, 208, 212, 217, 219, 221, 236 (*see also* Wayne)
Penobscot (Me.), 255, 258
Pensacola (Fla.), 123, 142
Petersburg (Va.), 188, 191, 193-96. *See also* St. Petersburg
Philadelphia (Pa), xxiii, 10, 11, 38-42, 44, 57, 71, 73, 82, 117, 122, 136, 146-47, 173, 175, 177-79, 182-83, 209, 264; Lafayette in, viii, 69, 131, 133, 139, 141-42, 144-45, 150-51, 155, 284, 286-87, 289; supplies from, 85, 153, 161, 170, 176, 222, 224; Constitutional Convention in, 324
Philip's House (N. Y.), 109
Phillips, William (1731-1781), major-general in the British Army in America, 130, 170, 180-81, 186, 188-94

Pickering, Timothy (1745-1829): as colonel in the Continental Army and member of the Board of War, 20; as quartermaster general, 115, 144, 148, 152, 227
Pillaging, 45
Pilots: American, 58, 102-03, 237; British, 213
Pinckney, Charles Cotesworth (1746-1825): as major-general in the United States Army, 377, 379-80
Pinckney, ———, nephew of General Pinckney, 377, 379
Pitt, William (1759-1806): as prime minister of England, 275, 282, 375, 381
Plön (Holstein), 373
Point Comfort (Va.), 190
Point of Fork (Va.), 201, 203, 226
Poirey, Joseph-Léonard (b. 1748), military secretary to Lafayette in America, captain in the Parisian National Guard: brevetted captain in the United States Army, 353
Poland, 22, 263, 340
Pompton (N. J.), 144, 146
Pontgibaud, Charles-Albert, comte de Moré de (1758-1837): as major and aide-de-camp to Lafayette, 110 and n., 111
Poor, Enoch (1736-1780), brigadier-general in the Continental Army, 46
Portail. *See* Duportail
Port Mahon (Minorca), 244
Portraits: of Washington, 63, 287; of Lafayette's family, 284
Port Royal (Va.), 230
Portsmouth (N. H.), 65
Portsmouth (Va.), 152, 155, 157, 160, 162, 164, 168, 181-82, 186, 191, 194-95, 197, 203, 205, 207-13, 215-18, 221-24
Portugal, 135, 138, 283, 315
Posts (on Canadian boundary), 289, 295, 307, 312, 314 and n., 317, 329-30
Potemkin, Grigory Aleksandrovich, Prince (1739-91): as Russian field marshal, 345
Potomac River, xviii, xix, 172, 190, 210, 212, 281, 283, 307, 366; Navigation Company, 292, 298 and n., 299 308
Potsdam (Germany), 303-05, 309
Prague (Bohemia), 303-04
Preakness (N. J.), 82, 85, 94
President of Congress. *See* Huntington, Samuel

426

Princeton (N. J.), 150
Prisoners, 210; exchange of, 33, 37, 193, 251, 252 n.; keeping of, 155
Protestants (French), xvii, 294, 296, 309, 315, 318, 320, 325, 338 and n.
Provence, Louis-Stanislas-Xavier, comte de (1755-1824), older of Louis XVI's two brothers (later Louis XVIII), 325, 359
Providence (R. I.), 41, 53-55, 90, 96, 97, 102
Provinces, United. See Holland
Provincial Assemblies: of France, 318, 320, 322-23, 325, 327, 337, 340; of Auvergne, 326, 331, 335; of Holland, 333
Provisions: American, 10-13, 24, 31, 35, 38, 42, 45, 48, 51, 53, 54, 85-87, 103, 105-06, 110, 119, 125, 132, 147, 150, 154, 219, 222, 227, 229-32, 237, 243; French, 55, 58, 62-63, 91, 94, 117, 151, 226, 228, 237, 348; English, 108, 128, 130, 160, 179, 187, 229; Russian, 340
Prussia, xxi, xxii, 266, 291, 304, 306, 308, 317, 325, 329, 375; army of, 294-95, 301-05, 314 n., 329, 332; king of (*see* Frederick II)
Pulaski, Count Casimir (1748-1779): as brigadier-general in the Continental Army and chief of dragoons, 22
Putnam, Israel (1718-90): as major-general in the Continental Army, 30

QUADRUPLE ALLIANCE. See Alliance
Quartermaster in Virginia. See Clayburne
Quartermaster's Department, 20, 27, 38, 113-15, 148, 154, 227-30. See also Greene and Pickering
Quebec (Canada) 25, 64
"Queen Charlotte," British tender captured by the French, 237
Queen's Creek (Va.), 228
Queen's Light Dragoons (British), 3
Queen's Rangers (British), 112, 128, 208, 210-11, 215

"RABAUK." See "Roebuck"
"Raleigh," British warship, 125
Rappahannock River (Va.), 199
Rastatt (Germany), Congress of (1797-1799), 366 and n., 375, 384
Ratisbon (Germany), Diet of, 359

Rawdon (i.e., Francis Rawdon-Hastings), Lord (1754-1826): as adjutant-general in the British army, 208, 214
Reading (Pa.), 8
Recruits, 8, 13, 89-91, 106, 135, 141, 182, 191, 201-02, 208, 216, 219, 221, 224, 249
Redbank (N. J.), 135
Reed (possibly James Randolph Reid, major in Hazen's Canadian Regiment), 177
Reidezel. See Riedesel
Rendon, Francesco, Spanish agent in Philadelphia, 142
Rennes (France), 291
Republicanism, 277, 324, 369
Republican party. See Patriotic parties
Rhine River, 383
Rhode Island, 29, 39, 55, 59-61, 63-64, 66, 89, 93, 95, 102, 106, 123, 125, 135, 173, 286, 326; French forces in, xii, xiv-xv, 86, 88, 90, 93, 94, 96, 98-100, 103, 110, 117, 122, 134, 146, 149, 151, 199, 208; Washington's journey to, 149, 153, 158, 172; battle of (August 29, 1778), 61-63; Continental troops of, 182
Richelieu, Louis-François-Armand du Plessis, duc and maréchal de (1696-1788), 244
Richmond (on Staten Island, N. Y.), 113, 116, 124
Richmond (Va.), xix, 179, 186, 188-94, 196-98, 201, 203, 205, 219, 223, 229-30, 286-87
Ridout, Thomas, owner of the "Peggy," 295
Riedesel, Friedrich Adolph, Freiherr von (1738-1800), general commanding a Brunswick contingent under Burgoyne, 139
Rights of Man, 285, 305-06, 334-35, 338, 349, 354, 383; Declaration of the (1789), 349, 352
Ringo's Tavern (N. J.), 25-26
Rivington, James (1724-1802), Loyalist publisher of New York, 129
Roanoke River (Va.), 196, 212
Roberjot, Claude (1752-1799), French diplomat assassinated on his return from the Congress of Rastatt, 384
Robertson, Colonel (probably James Robertson, colonel of the Sixteenth Regiment [British]), 145
Robertson, James (1720?-1788), Loyalist

427

governor of New York and major-general in the British army, 124

Robertson's (General James) Corps, 128

Robertson's (Colonel James?) Regiment of New Levies, 124, 128, 145

Robin's Tavern (N. J.), 50

Rochambeau, Jean-Baptiste-Donatien de Vimeur, comte de (1725-1807): as lieutenant-general commanding the French expeditionary force in the United States, xiv-xvi, 88, 93-104, 110, 117, 121-22, 133-36, 145, 148, 152, 156, 188, 301 n.; in the Society of the Cincinnati, 273-74, 276; in the French Revolution, 358, 362

Rochefontaine, Etienne-Nicolas-Marie Béchet, chevalier de (1755-1814): as captain of engineers in the Continental Army, 176

Rochefort (France), 74, 312

Rockingham, Charles Watson Wentworth, Marquess of (1730-1782): as British prime minister, 248

Rodney, George Brydges, Baron (1719-1792), British admiral, 124-26, 128-29, 243

"Roebuck," British warship, 125

Rome, i.e., the Papacy, 315

Romeuf, Captain Louis, aide-de-camp of Lafayette (1792), 375

Ross, John (1726-1800), Philadelphia merchant: as an American agent in France, 83, 132, 135

Rowland's Ferry (R. I.), 95

"Rowley." See "Raleigh"

Ruffin, William, Virginia planter, 223

Ruffin's Ferry (Va.), 222-23

Russia, 249, 264, 266, 268, 270, 283, 291 n., 314, 321, 324, 328-29, 335-37, 339-40, 344-45, 375

Rutland, Charles Manners, Duke of (1754-1787): as lord lieutenant of Ireland, 290

SAFFORD, SAMUEL, lieutenant-colonel of Warner's Additional Continental Regiment, 37

Sailly, S——— de, French immigrant to America, 272

St. Augustine (Fla.), 18, 132, 133, 137, 142

St. Clair, Arthur (1735-1818), major-general in the Continental Army, 143, 151, 205, 207

St. Cloud (near Paris), 354 n.

St. Domingo, 134, 138

Ste. Même. See St. Maisme

St. Eustatius (Dutch West India island), 241 and n.

St. Fris, Monsieur ——— de, captain of dragoons in the French army, 341

St. Germain (near Paris, France), 250, 294

St. Jean d'Angély (France), 74, 78

St. John. See Crèvecœur

St. Kitts (in British West Indies), 245

St. Lawrence River, 102

St. Maisme, Jean-Baptiste-Louis-Philippe de Félix d'Olières, comte de (b. 1751), colonel of the Regiment de Soissonnais in Rochambeau's army, 148

St. Petersburg (Russia), 314

St. Sauveur, chevalier de, French naval lieutenant killed in a Boston streetfight (1778), 65

St. Simon, Claude de Rouvroy, baron de (1752-1811): as captain in the Regiment de Touraine under his brother, the Marquis de St. Simon, 279

St. Simon-Montbléru, Claude-Anne de Rouvroy, marquis de (1743-1819): as maréchal de camp in the French army, 225-32, 279, 299

St. Victor, François-Anselme, captain in the Regiment de Soissonnais in Rochambeau's army, 148

Sakonnet Passage (R. I.), 95

Salm, Rhingrave de (i.e., Fréderic, prince de Salm-Kyrbourg [1746-1794]): as maréchal de camp in the French army, 329, 331-32

"Sandwich," British warship, 124, 128

Sandy Hook (N. J.), 85, 86

Sandy Point (Va.), 209

Sardinia, king of. See Charles Emanuel IV

Sarguemines, i.e., Sarreguemines (France), 300

Sartine, Antoine-Jean-Raymond-Gualbert-Gabriel, comte d'Alby de (1729-1801): as minister of the marine, 137-38, 145

Savannah (Ga.), 134, 214, 233, 279

Saxony, 301

Saybrook (Conn.), 54

Scammel, Alexander (†1781), colonel of the First New Hampshire, 233

Scheldt River, 291 n.
Schenectady (N. Y.), 32, 37
Schullchill. *See* Schuylkill
Schuyler, Philip John (1733-1804): as major-general in the Continental Army, 26, 32, 33, 36
Schuyler's Ferry (N. J.), 126
Schuylkill River (Pa.), 8, 10-12, 40
Scioto River (Ohio), 349
Sconectedy. *See* Schenectady
Scott, Charles (1733-1813): as brigadier-general in the Continental Army, 46, 48, 49, 51
Seas, superiority on the, 63, 86-87, 98-99, 101-02, 105-07, 123, 133, 137, 141, 155, 163, 171-72, 181-82, 191, 195, 197, 208, 211-12, 224, 245, 247, 252, 256, 258
Second Division (of Rochambeau's army), 90, 97-100, 102-03, 120, 173, 178, 184
Segond, Madame ——————— de, daughter of the Comte de Vaublanc, 377 and n., 378-80
Ségur, Louis-Philippe, comte de (1753-1830): as colonel-en-second in the Regiment de Soissonnais in Rochambeau's army, 248-49; as French ambassador to Russia, 321
Ségur, Philippe-Henri, marquis and maréchal de (1724-1801): as minister of war, 248, 273, 328
Seine River, 298
Sekonnet. *See* Sakonnet
"Sénégal," frigate in Estaing's fleet, 58
"Serapis," British frigate captured by Americans, 132, 135
Seventy-First Regiment (British), 196
Seventy-Sixth Regiment (British), 215
Shaw, Captain Daniel, American pilot, 102, 104
Shays' Rebellion, 319 and n., 321
Shelbon. *See* Shelburne
Shelburne (N. Y.), 37
Shelburne, i.e., William Petty, Marquess of Lansdowne, better known as Lord Shelburne (1737-1805): as secretary of state for the home department, 251; as prime minister, 263
Sheldon, Elisha, colonel of the Second Continental Dragoons, 198
Short, William (1759-1849): as secretary to Jefferson in Paris, 344; as chargé d'affaires in Paris, 346, 350, 357, 362

Shrewsbury (England), 128
Silesia (Germany), 301, 304
Simcoe, John (1752-1806), Loyalist lieutenant-colonel who raised and commanded the Queen's Rangers, 112, 128, 201, 213
Skinburry (probably Skenesborough, now Whitehall, N. Y.), 34
Skinner, Cortlandt (1728-1799), brigadier-general of the New Jersey Volunteers (Loyalist), 130
Smallwood, William (1732-1792), major-general in the Continental Army, 169
Smith (Francis?), British brigadier-general, 127, 130
Smith, William Stephens (1755-1816): as lieutenant-colonel in the Continental Army, inspector and adjutant in Lafayette's Light Infantry, 126, 129-31, 144, 175, 177; in Germany, 306; as secretary of legation in London, 319
Soan's Bridge (over the Chickahominy River in Virginia), 222
Sophie-Hélène-Béatrix (1786-1787), fourth child of Marie Antoinette, 312
Sound. *See* Long Island Sound
South (of the United States), xv, 121-22, 125, 129, 132-33, 135, 138-39, 150, 154, 160, 170-72, 179-80, 182-83, 186 n., 188, 190, 202, 205, 208. *See also* Southern
South America, 374
South Carolina, 57, 106-07, 134, 141, 179, 183, 188, 191, 199, 208-09, 217, 219, 224, 227
Southern: Department, 15; states, 105-07, 134, 141, 166-67, 178, 182, 329; army, 106, 118, 136, 162, 169-71, 175, 177, 180, 199, 214, 217; members of Congress, 138
Spain, 75, 79, 98, 132, 134, 138, 141, 245, 249, 252, 257-58, 267, 270, 293, 297, 329, 337, 340, 345, 357; king of (*see* Charles III). *See also* Spanish
Spanish: military plans, xv, 132-34, 140, 237; fleet, 66, 98, 123, 132-34, 137, 142, 245, 247, 249, 252 (*see also* Fleet, Combined); generals, 132-33, 136; government, 135, 258, 260 n., 261-62, 293, 295; jackasses, 295, 300
Sparks, Jared, xxv n., xxvi, 54 n., 202 n., 221 n.

Sparks Mss. See *Harvard College Library*
Spies, 22, 66, 112, 114, 123-25, 128-30, 145-47, 162, 166-67, 169, 179, 189, 211, 213, 223, 225, 231, 239-40, 328
Spiting devil. See Spuyten Duyvil
Springs (i.e., Burning Springs, W. Va., belonging to Washington), 285
Spuyten Duyvil (N. Y.), 130
Stadholder, party favoring, 333, 338. See also William V
Staël, Anne-Louise-Germaine Necker, baronne de (1766-1817), vii and n., viii
Stark, John (1728-1822): as brigadier-general in the Continental Army, 27, 34, 37
Staten Island (N. Y.), 86, 112-13, 118, 123-25, 127-30, 206
States. See Estates General *or* United States
Statia. See St. Eustatius
Statues, 268, 270, 300, 307, 315-16
Staunton River (Va.), 201
Stephen, Adam (†1791): dismissed as major-general in Continental Army, 5
Stephens. See Stevens
Steuben, Friedrich Wilhelm August Heinrich Ferdinand, Baron von (1730-1794): as major-general in the Continental Army, xvi, 40 n., 46, 47, 151, 153-55, 157, 159-62, 169, 186, 191, 198, 201, 202 and n., 205, 207
Stevens, Ebenezer (†1823): as major of artillery in the Continental Army, 35; as lieutenant-colonel, 157, 161
Stewart, John, lieutenant-colonel in the First Maryland, 169
Stewart, Walter, colonel of the Second Pennsylvania, 254
Stirling, William Alexander, Lord (1726-1783): as major-general in the Continental Army, 15, 25, 26, 46
Stony Point (N. Y.), battle of (June 1, 1779), 81
Stores. See Supplies
Stratford (Conn.), 53
Stuard. See Stewart, Walter
Stuart, Dr. David (1753-1815), second husband of Eleanor Calvert Custis, 290 and n., 292, 296, 310, 315, 319
Stuart, Lt. Col. See Stewart, John
Stuart, Mrs. See Custis, Eleanor Calvert
Suffolk (Va.), 162, 164, 209, 212

Suffrans (i.e., Suffern, N. J.), 115
Suffren - Saint - Tropez, Pierre - André, bailli de (1729-1788): as captain of the "Fantasque" in Estaing's fleet, 278; as vice-admiral, 300, 307
Sullivan, John (1740-1795): as major-general in the Continental Army, 53-56, 58, 59, 61-63, 66-69
Sumner, Jethro (1753-1785), brigadier-general in the Continental Army, 194, 198
Sumter, Thomas (1734-1832), brigadier-general of South Carolina State Troops, 135, 142
Supplies, 10-13, 32, 37, 38, 42, 87, 89-92, 97-103, 114, 125, 135, 141, 162, 169, 176, 181, 183, 189, 191, 195, 198, 201-02, 208, 219-21, 224, 230; English, 108, 203; from France, 243, 249
Susquehanna Ferry (Md.), 174, 176, 178-80, 183, 185
Susquehanna River, 39, 174, 176, 180, 185
Sutter, Mr. ———, hatter, of Front Street, Philadelphia, 289
Sweden, 345, 375, 379

Talleyrand-Perigord, Charles-Maurice de (1754-1838): as writer, vii and n., as French minister of foreign affairs, 366 n., 376
Tamage (perhaps Benjamin Tallmadge, major in the Continental Light Dragoons), 129
Tappan (N. Y.), 198
Tarleton, Sir Banastre (1754-1833): as lieutenant-colonel of British cavalry, 141-42, 194, 206-08, 211, 213; as writer, 324
Tarleton's Legion, 196, 206
Tax Reform in France, 318, 320, 322-23, 325, 327, 335, 340-41, 343, 362. See also Farm
Temple, John (1732-1798), Bowdoin's Loyalist son-in-law, 239-40, 293
Ternant, Jean-Baptiste, chevalier de (1751-1816), brevet colonel of Continental cavalry: as colonel in the Dutch service, 331-32; as French minister to the United States, 353, 356
Ternay, Charles-Henri d'Arsac, chevalier de (1722-1780), chef d'escadre commanding the fleet which convoyed Rochambeau's army, 83, 88,

90, 93-95, 98-104, 134-36, 173, 279
"Terrible," British warship, 124, 128
Tessé, Adrienne-Catherine de Noailles, comtesse de (1741-1814), Adrienne de Lafayette's aunt, 254, 372 and n., 373
Thirty-Third Regiment (British), 196
Throop, Benjamin (†1822), major in the Fifth Connecticut, 75-77
Thugut, Franz Maria, Baron (1734-1818), Austrian chancellor, xxiii and n.
Ticonderoga, Fort (N. Y.), 32
Tilghman, Tench (1744-1786), lieutenant-colonel in the Continental Army: as Washington's secretary, 25 and n., 225, 247, 262-63
Tilly, Arnaud Le Gardeur de (1733-1812): as captain of the "Eveillé" in Rochambeau's convoy, 151-52, 277, 279
Tilmangh. See Tilghman
Tinicum Island (in the Delaware River), 40
Tiverton (R. I.), 61, 104
Tories, 14, 33, 34, 37, 104, 128, 196, 286
Totowa (N. J.), 112, 114, 116-17
Toulon (France), 375 n.
Toulouse, Archbishop of. See Brienne
Tousard, Anne-Louis, chevalier de (1749-1817): as captain of artillery in the Continental Army, 63-64
Tower, Charlemagne, 165 n., 201 n., 202 n., 213 n.
Tower of London, 137
Transportation, problems of, 69, 87, 90-91, 93, 97-98, 101, 105-07, 113, 115-16, 125, 147, 150, 154, 156, 168-70, 173, 180-81, 186, 188-89, 191, 212, 220, 227, 230, 237, 288
Treaty of: Aix-la-Chapelle (1748), 253 and n.; Franco-American Alliance (1778), 330; Paris (1763), 253 and n.; Paris (1783), 261, 267, 270, 279, 312, 330. See also Alliance and Coalition
Trenton (N. J.), 147, 150, 153, 173, 289
Trescott, Lemuel, major in the Ninth Massachusetts, 213
Tréville. See La Touche-Tréville
"Triomphe," French vessel that brought the news of the peace preliminaries to America, xvii, 260, 262, 264, 267
"Triumph," British warship, 125. See also "Triomphe"
Troop. See Throop or Troup
Troup, Robert (†1832), lieutenant-colonel in the Continental Army and aide-de-camp to Gates, 29 and n.
"Trumbull," American warship, 151
Trumbull, Jonathan (1710-1785): as governor of Connecticut, 89, 91-93, 97, 99, 104
Tryon County (N. Y.), 34
Tub. See Custis, George Washington Parke
Tuileries Palace (Paris), xxi
Tupper, Benjamin (1738-1792): as colonel of the Tenth Massachusetts, 200-01
Turenne, Henri de la Tour d'Auvergne, vicomte and maréchal de (1611-1675), 312
Turkey Point (Md.), 158
Turks, 291 n., 314, 324, 328-29, 335-37, 340, 344-45. See also Ottoman Empire
Twenty-Second Regiment (British), 126
Twenty-Third Regiment (British), 196
Tynicum Island. See Tinicum Island
Tyver town. See Tiverton

Union. See American confederation
United States of America, xiii-xiv, xxi-xxiv, 57, 80, 85-87, 97-100, 110, 122, 237, 254-56, 262-64, 268-71, 275, 283, 293-95, 298, 302, 306-09, 313-19, 324-26, 329-30, 333, 336-38, 341-42, 352-53, 357, 361, 364, 370-79, 382-85. See also America
Ushant, battle of (July 27, 1778), 65-66

Valfort, Louis Silvestre de (1727-1804?), one of Lafayette's companions on the "Victoire," 282-83
Valley Forge (Pa.), xii, xvii, 13, 16, 42-44, 259
Van der Kemp, Francis Adrian (1752-1829), Dutch patriot, 339
Van Shaick. See Wanschoys
Varnum, James Mitchell (1748-1789): as brigadier-general in the Continental Army, 7, 53, 54, 104
Vauban, Jacques-Anne-Joseph Le Prestre, comte de (1754-1816): as mestre de camp and aide-de-camp to Rochambeau, 136
Vaublanc, Mme ——— de, wife of the Comte de Vaublanc, 377-80
Vaublanc, Vincent-Marie-Viénot, comte de (1756-1845), 377 and n., 378 and n., 379-80
Vaudreuil, Louis-Philippe de Rigaud,

marquis de (1724-1802): as chef d'escadre in command of the French fleet of the Antilles, 255; in the Society of the Cincinnati, 277

Vaux, Noël de Jourda, comte de (1705-1788), lieutenant-general in the French army, 78

Venice, Republic of, 315, 340

Venkersky. *See* Wengiersky

Verac, Charles-Olivier de St. George, marquis de (1743-1828): as French ambassador to Holland, 329, 331-32

Vergennes, Charles Gravier, comte de (1717-1787), French minister of foreign affairs, xv, 145, 171, 174, 252, 266, 270, 273, 293, 296, 308, 318, 320-21, 375

Versailles (France), 67, 71, 78, 118, 136, 241-42, 276, 291, 309, 318, 321-23, 338, 350 n.

Vianen (near Utrecht, Holland), 381-82

"Victoire," the vessel which brought Lafayette to America in 1777, 5

Vienna (Austria), 283, 301-04, 379

Vienne, Louis-Pierre, marquis de (1746-1825?): as brevet colonel in the Continental Army, 279

Villedeuil, Laurent de, 323

Vioménil, Antoine-Charles du Houx, baron de (1728-1792): as maréchal de camp and second in command in Rochambeau's army, 156-57, 166, 169

Virginia: campaign xv-xvi, 155, 164, 166, 170, 186 n., 188-94, 197-99, 201, 205, 207-11, 217, 220, 222, 232, 234, 238; Continental troops of, 5, 24, 43, 204, 208, 212-13, 217, 219, 221, 224, 228; British in, 106, 112, 193, 202-04, 207, 210; coast of, 147, 151; government of, 153, 202, 217, 219, 226, 228-30, 237, 268, 298; attitude toward Lafayette of, 268, 315-16; settlers in, 272, 379; Lafayette's visit to (1784), 286; governor of (*see* Jefferson *or* Nelson)

Virginia Gazette, 142

Volunteer's Journal, Carey's publication in Ireland, 289

Vose, Joseph (†1816): as colonel of the First Massachusetts, 175, 177, 181, 190, 200; in the Light Division, 236

Vrigny, Louis Cloquet de (1733-1793?), one of Lafayette's companions on the "Victoire" (later lieutenant-colonel in the Continental Army), 5-6

WADSWORTH, JEREMIAH (1743-1804): as colonel in the Continental Army and commissary general of purchases, 91, 93, 97; in France, 276, 282; as member of Congress, 346

Wanschoys (possibly Goose Van Shaick [1736-1789], colonel of the First New York), 37

Wanyer's (?) Horse, 126

Warren (R. I.), 63, 65-67

Warville. *See* Brissot de Warville

"Washington," American warship, 274

Washington, Bushrod (1762-1829), nephew of George Washington, xxiv n., 209, 289 and n.

Washington, Charles (1738-99), brother of George Washington, 202-03, 315 and n.

Washington, Elizabeth Foot (Mrs. Lund), 269, 276

Washington, Frances Bassett (Mrs. George A.) (†1796), 296, 315, 319

Washington, George (1732-1799): as commander-in-chief of the Continental Army, vii-xvii, 3-272; as a private citizen, xvii-xx, 272-324; as president of the Constitutional Convention, 324-32; as private citizen again, 332-45; as president of the United States, xx-xxiv, 346-62; as private citizen again, 363-72; as commander-in-chief of the United States Armies, xxiv, 373-85; death of, xxiv

Washington, George Augustine (†1793), nephew of George Washington: as ensign and secretary to Washington, 135; as lieutenant and aide-de-camp to Lafayette, xvi, 203-04, 209, 219 and n., 221 and n.; in George Washington's "family," 238, 242, 244, 247, 256-58, 263, 267, 269, 272, 276, 282, 301, 312-13, 315, 319, 321, 333, 348; bad health of, 296, 300; family of, 308 and n., 357; as major, 360, 367; death of, 384 and n., 385

Washington, George Fayette (b. 1791), son of George Augustine Washington, 384 and n.

Washington, John Augustine (1736-1787), brother of George Washington, 315 and n.

Washington, Lund (1737-1796), third cousin of George Washington and manager of Mount Vernon, 172, 187, 269, 276, 290, 292, 296, 301, 310

Washington, Martha Dandridge Custis (1732-1802), wife of George Washington, 72, 77, 132, 261, 269 n., 271, 290, 292, 311; Lafayette's greetings to, 25, 28, 31, 67, 74, 77, 81, 131, 135, 138-42, 146, 148-49, 156, 158, 160, 163, 167, 171, 174, 177, 188, 190, 192, 199, 238, 240, 242, 244, 247, 253, 256-58, 261, 263-64, 267, 285, 287, 290, 292, 295-97, 301-02, 315, 326, 333-34, 337, 341, 346, 348, 355, 357, 360, 362, 365, 368, 377-78, 380; Lafayette's family's greetings to, xix, 250, 255, 265, 267, 269, 272, 276, 281, 284, 292, 294, 296, 300, 310, 312, 316, 319, 321, 324, 334, 338-39, 345, 350, 353, 365, 367-68, 372, 377

Washington, Mary Ball (1708-1789), George Washington's mother, 168, 262, 296, 313, 315, 319, 321, 333, 345

Watch Hill Point (R. I.), 99

Watering Place (on Staten Island, N. Y.), 112-13, 116, 124-25

Wayne, Anthony (1745-1796): as brigadier-general of the Pennsylvania Line, 24, 46, 49, 51, 143, 155, 191, 195, 197-98, 208, 212, 217, 219, 222-23, 236

Weaver, W. A., 291 n.

Weedon, George (ca. 1730-1790): as brigadier-general in the Continental Army, 212

Wengiersky, Count, Polish gentleman traveling in the United States, 263 and n.

Westchester County (N. Y.), 100, 102

West Indies, xvi-xvii, 64, 79, 87, 102, 126, 128, 133, 136-37, 145, 187, 193, 206, 233, 242, 245-47, 249, 252 and n., 255-58, 260, 283, 293, 295 and n., 330, 344, 347

Westminster (England), 283

Westover (Va.), 196, 219, 222-23

West Point (N. Y.), xv, 89, 91, 106, 119, 121, 126-27, 152, 176

West Point (Va.), 226, 229, 233-35

Whigs, 14, 286

White, Anthony Walton (1750-1803): as colonel of Continental cavalry, 221, 226, 228

Whitestone (on Long Island, N. Y.), 87, 124, 129

Wihecomoco (i.e., Wicomico) River (Md.), 154

Wilhelmina, i.e., Frederick Sophie Wilhelmina (1747-1820), wife of William V of Orange, 314 n., 326 and n.

William V of Orange (1748-1806), stadholder of the United Provinces, 314 and n., 317, 325, 326 n., 329, 333

Williams, Jonathan (1750-1815), Franklin's grandnephew and secretary, 294

Williamsburg (Va.), 161, 164-65, 167, 169, 190, 193-94, 196, 203, 209, 218, 228, 230-32, 286

Williamson, General Andrew (Loyalist), 214

Wilmington (Del.), 8-10, 170, 196

Wilmington (N. C.), 130, 166, 173, 179, 194, 212, 237

Wilton (Va.), 192-93

Winter quarters, 8-10, 120-24, 129

Wistown Bay. *See* Whitestone

Wittmoldt (in Holstein), 368-69, 373, 378

Woodford, William (1734-1780), brigadier-general in the Continental Army, 5, 43, 46, 129, 137

Woodruff, Mr. ———, American spy, 128

Xyz affair, 366 n.

Yellow House (near Pompton, N. J.), 144

York (Pa.), 14, 24, 198

York, i.e., Yorktown, Va.), xvi, 159, 162 and n., 185, 215, 217-18, 221, 223, 225-26, 229, 231-35, 279, 287, 301 n.

York, Frederick Augustus, Duke of (1763-1827), second son of King George III, 304

York Island (i.e., Manhattan Island, N. Y.), 88, 108, 119, 124, 130, 206

York River (Va.), 182, 215, 218, 221, 223, 225, 229, 231, 235, 237

Yorktown, *See* York

SUPPLEMENTARY INDEX

SUPPLEMENTARY INDEX

America, xxxiii, 391
American Antiquarian Society, xxix, 397
American Independence, War of, xxxi

Batavian Republic, 392
Bougainville, Louis-Antoine de (1729-1811), circumnavigator, a commander in Estaing's fleet, 389

Chavaniac, Château de, xxix, xxxiii
Chicago, University of, Libraries, xxxiii
Cincinnati, Society of, xxix, xxxi, 389, 399, 400
Constitutional (French party), 390
Cornell University Libraries, xxix, xxxiii, 401
Custis, Eleanor ("Nellie") Parke, 394 and n.

Dean, Arthur H. and Mary Marden, Collection, xxix, xxxiii
Dillon, Edouard, 389
Directory, xxxii, 393

Estaing, Charles-Hector, comte d', 389
Europe, xxxiii, 390, 391, 392

Fabius, Emmanuel, xxix
Fitzpatrick, John C., xxxi n., xxxii n., xxxiii n.
France, xxxii, 390, 391, 393
Franco-American relations, xxxi, xxxii
Frestel, Félix, 394

Gottschalk and Maddox, xxx n.
Great Britain, 393, 394

Hamburg (Germany), xxxii, 393
Hamilton, Alexander, 391
Hanzel Galleries, xxix, 401
Harvard College Library, xxxii n.

Jackson, Andrew (1767-1845), president, xxxii
Jacobins, 390, 394

Lafayette, Adrienne de Noailles de, xxxiii, 393, 394
Lafayette, Anastasie de. See Maubourg.
Lafayette, General, xxix, xxx, xxxi, xxxii, xxxiii, 397, 401

Lafayette, George Washington, 394
Lafayette, Virginie de, 394
Lafayette College Library, xxxiii
Lafayette family, xxxi
Lafayette, Mémoires du général, xxix, xxx n., xxxi, xxxii, 402
Lafayette Papers Project (Cornell), xxxiii
Lagrange-Blénau, Château de, xxxiii
L'Enfant, Pierre-Charles, 389, 400
Library of Congress, xxix, 397, 398, 399
Logan, Dr. George (1753-1821), prominent Quaker, political figure, and agriculturist, xxxii, 392

Maubourg, Anastasie de La Tour de, 394
Maubourg, Celestine de La Tour de (b. 1799), Lafayette's granddaughter, 394
Maubourg, Charles de La Tour de, 394
Mount Vernon, 392
Murray, William Vans, xxxii, 390, 392, 393

Paris, 393, 394
Pitcairn, Joseph, American diplomat, 393
Pitt, William, 390

"Quasi war" (1797-1801), xxxi, xxxii

Rastatt, 394
Rhine River, 392
Roberjot, Claude, 394

Savannah (Ga.), 389
Sparks, Jared, xxxi, xxxii
Sparks Collection (Cornell), 401

United States of America, xxxii, 391, 393

Vaudreuil, Louis-Philippe de Rigaud, marquis de, 389
Vianen (Holland), 390, 391

Washington, Bushrod, xxxiii
Washington, George, xxix, xxx, xxxi, xxxii, xxxiii, 389
Washington, George Augustine, 394
Washington, Martha, 394
Washington family, xxxi